89.19

MW00965047

THE CIVIL WAR

THE CIVIL WAR

Paul A. Cimbala

The Greenwood Press "Daily Life through History" Series

American Soldiers' Lives
David S. Heidler and Jeanne T. Heidler, Series Editors

GREENWOOD PRESS
Westport, Connecticut • London

Library of Congress Cataloging-in-Publication Data

Cimbala, Paul A. (Paul Alan), 1951–
    The Civil War / Paul A. Cimbala.
        p. cm. — (The Greenwood Press "Daily life through history"
series, ISSN 1080–4749. American soldiers' lives)
    Includes bibliographical references and index.
    ISBN 978–0–313–33182–4 (alk. paper)
    1. United States. Army—Military life—History—19th century.
2. Confederate States of America. Army—Military life.   3. United States—
History—Civil War, 1861–1865—Psychological aspects.   4. United
States—History—Civil War, 1861–1865—Social aspects.   5. Soldiers—
United States—Social conditions—19th century.   6. Soldiers—
Confederate States of America—Social conditions.   7. Motivation
(Psychology)—United States—History—19th century.   I. Title.
    E607.C56   2008
    973.7'1—dc22   2008001139

British Library Cataloguing in Publication Data is available.

Library of Congress Catalog Card Number: 2008001139
ISBN: 978–0–313–33182–4
ISSN: 1080–4749

First published in 2008

Greenwood Press, 88 Post Road West, Westport, CT 06881
An imprint of Greenwood Publishing Group, Inc.
www.greenwood.com

Printed in the United States of America

The paper used in this book complies with the
Permanent Paper Standard issued by the National
Information Standards Organization (Z39.48–1984).

10 9 8 7 6 5 4 3 2 1

MAY 21 2009

In memory of Peter Cimbala, 1909–1966

CONTENTS

SERIES FOREWORD

More than once during the military campaigns undertaken by American armies, leaders in both civilian and martial roles have been prompted to ask in admiration, "Where do such people come from?" The question, of course, was both rhetorical and in earnest: the one because they knew that such people hailed from the coasts and the heartland, from small hamlets and sprawling cities, from expansive prairies and breezy lakeshores. They were as varied as the land they represented, as complex as the diversity of their faiths and ethnic identities, all nonetheless defined by the overarching identity of "American," made more emphatic by their transformation into "American soldiers."

They knew and we know where they came from. On the other hand, the question for anyone who knows the tedium, indignity, discomfort, and peril of military service in wartime is more aptly framed, "Why did they come at all?"

In the volumes of this series, accomplished scholars of the American military answer that question, and more. By depicting the daily routines of soldiers at war, they reveal the gritty heroism of those who conquered the drudgery of routine and courageously faced the terrors of combat. With impeccable research and a deep understanding of the people who move through these grandly conceived stories—for war, as Tolstoy has shown us, is the most grandly conceived and complex story of all—these books take us to the heart of great armies engaged in enormous undertakings. Bad food, disease, haphazardly treated wounds, and chronic longing for loved ones form part of these stories, for those are the universal afflictions of soldiers. Punctuating long stretches of loneliness and monotony were interludes of horrific violence that scarred every soldier, even those who escaped physical injury. And insidious wounds could fester because of ugly customs and ingrained prejudices: for too long a span, soldiers who happened to be minorities suffered galling injustices at the hands of those they served, often giving for cause and comrades what Lincoln called "the last full measure of devotion," despite unfair indignities and undeserved ignominy. And sadly, it is true that protracted or unpopular wars could send veterans returning to a country indifferent about their sacrifices, sometimes hostile to the cause for which they fought, and begrudging even marginal compensation to their spouses and orphans. But quiet courage, wry humor, tangible camaraderie, and implacable pride are parts of these stories as well, ably conveyed by these gifted writers who have managed to turn the pages that follow into vivid snapshots of accomplishment, sacrifice, and triumph.

Until recently the American soldier has usually been a citizen called to duty in times of extraordinary crisis. The volunteer army of this latest generation, though, has created a remarkable hybrid in the current American soldier, a professional who nevertheless upholds the traditions of American citizens who happen to be in uniform to do a tough job. It is a noble tradition that ennobles all who have honored it. And more often than not, they who have served have managed small miracles of fortitude and resolve.

Walter Lord's *Incredible Victory* recounts the story of Mike Brazier, the rear-seat man on a torpedo plane from the carrier *Yorktown* in the battle of Midway. He and pilot Wilhelm Esders were among that stoic cadre of fliers who attacked Japanese carriers, knowing that their fuel was insufficient for the distance to and from their targets. Having made their run under heavy enemy fire, Esders finally had to ditch the spent and damaged plane miles short of the *Yorktown* in the rolling Pacific. He then discovered that Brazier had been shot to pieces. Despite his grave wounds, Brazier had managed to change the coils in the radio to help guide the plane back toward the *Yorktown*. In the life raft as he died, Mike Brazier never complained. He talked of his family and how hard it had been to leave them, but he did not complain. Instead he apologized that he could not be of more help.

In the great, roiling cauldron of the Second World War, here was the archetype of the American soldier: uncomplaining while dying far from home in the middle of nowhere, worried at the last that he had not done his part.

Where do such people come from?

We invite you to read on, and find out.

David S. Heidler and Jeanne T. Heidler
Series Editors

PREFACE

The American Civil War was an extraordinary event. It was a military, political, social, and constitutional milestone that shaped that nation's understanding of unity and freedom, if imperfectly, into the next century. No American war—not the Revolutionary War, not the Great War, not the Second World War, not Vietnam—was so essential to defining what America was and should become. Despite a general acceptance of the Civil War's—or the War between the States'—significance, there remains much about it that causes heated debate, ranging from the relative virtues of various generals and to the comparative rectitude of their causes. Historians, battlefield reenactors, politicians, and cultural partisans continue to argue about why the war came, why it turned out the way that it did, and what its outcome actually meant. Most interested individuals, however, do not question the extraordinary sacrifices of the men who fought it.

Just a look at the casualty figures suggests that the war was an incredible event. Four years of hard fighting, grueling marches, and rugged camp life took their toll. Some 620,000 men and boys lost their lives either on the battlefield or from battle wounds and in prisoner of war stockades or in their own camps and hospitals. Add to the death toll the men who endured chronic illnesses, awkward gaits, abscessing amputations, and terrible disfigurement, and the total casualty figure approaches 1.1 million. That figure would no doubt be even higher if the men who appeared whole, but suffered psychological damage, could be included. Surely there were scoundrels, skulkers, and criminals among the dead, wounded, and surviving soldiers. Most Civil War soldiers, however, deserve respect because they put aside their civilian lives and left behind loved ones to answer the call of patriotic duty or, perhaps, simply to be a part of a great adventure. Regardless, even the bored youths who wanted action in their lives deserve respect because, despite the hardships, for whatever their reasons, they stayed on in the ranks to do a difficult job. They were not always eager combatants, but the most heroic of them swallowed hard, offered a prayer, overcame their fear, and charged into the enemy's guns.

The Civil War, part of the American Soldiers' Lives series, is my attempt to understand why these men made the sacrifices that they did. The book's first chapter provides an overview of the war, from secession of Southern states and the firing on Fort Sumter in 1861, to the final battles and capture of Confederate president Jefferson Davis in spring 1865. By exploring how and why Northern and Southern men rallied to their flags (chapters 2 and 3), trained to be soldiers (chapter 4), lived in camp (chapter 5), marched to the fight (chapter 6), endured combat (chapter 7), and dealt with the aftermath of battle (chapter 8), we can appreciate how such a grand drama of national scope touched the lives of individuals, especially when we pay attention to what those participants had to say about their experiences. Importantly, their stories did not end with the final surrender of Confederate forces. Thus we also need to pay attention to their transition to peace, discussed in chapter 9, and how they created the memories that they nurtured into their old age, as shown in the epilogue. The book concludes with an extensive bibliography of topically arranged books and Web sites, both primary and secondary sources.

Civil War soldiers left behind a mountain of letters, diaries, and memoirs to assist scholars in the task of understanding their wartime lives. Readers today are indeed fortunate because publishers, and especially a long list of university presses, have seen fit to devote so much of their resources to printing the writings of Civil War soldiers. The main source of information for this volume is the published letters, diaries, and memoirs of the men who fought the war. This volume's bibliography only hints at the firsthand accounts available to an individual who wishes to become familiar with the men who fought at Bull Run, Pea Ridge, Gettysburg, Atlanta, and Petersburg. In this book, I have tried whenever possible to allow these extraordinary individuals to tell their own stories in their own words.

Anyone wishing to understand the lives of Civil War soldiers, however, must also listen to the scholars who have spent years delving into these documents and trying to draw larger conclusions from so many particulars. This present effort relied heavily on such work, as the bibliography indicates, but there are some scholars who deserve special mention, if only to alert readers unfamiliar with their work to the rich scholarship on the Civil War soldier that they have produced. Years ago, I planned to attend Emory University to study with Bell I. Wiley, the man who forced Civil War historians to pay attention to the common soldier. While I was too late to become one of his students—he had retired the year before I entered into the history doctoral program—he kindly discussed slavery and the Civil War with me, read my master's thesis, and made me feel that what I had to say mattered. No one can begin to consider the Civil War soldier without starting with Wiley. And scholars who have followed in his path have continued to expand our knowledge of the soldier. Even more important, they asked questions of the sources that had escaped Wiley. Joseph T. Glatthaar, James I. Robertson Jr., James M. McPherson, Earl J. Hess, Carol Reardon, Reid Mitchell, Larry Daniel, and J. Tracy Power, among others, have all dealt with the soldiers' experiences and have enriched the Civil War bibliography with their insightful work. This study would have been an impossible task without their efforts and those of the long list of scholars noted in the bibliography.

In addition to publications that deal specifically with the soldiers' experiences, I have relied extensively on battle and campaign histories. Stephen W. Sears, Gordon C. Rhea, Peter Cozzens, George Rable, and other scholars have taken what many scholars once considered an old-fashioned subject and turned it into an exciting, engaging, and innovative field of study. Most recent battle histories as well as a new breed of company, regimental, and army histories are much more expansive in their treatment of the men who fought the war than the works of an earlier generation of scholars. Unit and campaign historians, for example, usually discuss the social aspects of the men's lives as well as their connections to the home front. In the process, they greatly enrich our understanding of the soldiers beyond the battlefield, without ignoring the most critical aspect of war: the battle itself.

ACKNOWLEDGMENTS

Along with my debt to Civil War scholars in general, I am particularly beholden to the efforts, encouragement, and examples of individuals who helped move this book to completion. Anne Thompson and Heather Staines kept their faith in the project even as the author lagged behind deadlines. David Heidler and Jeanne Heidler, two extraordinary historians and patient people, set aside their own work to listen to the concerns of the author, encourage his progress, and finally, read the book in manuscript form. This volume is but one in their worthy series on the lives of soldiers during America's wars, but it probably required more of their attention than the others. John David Smith and Randall M. Miller, my constant scholarly exemplars, continued to set the standards to which I needed to rise. Dan T. Carter, the man with whom I ended up studying at Emory, turned out to be an extraordinary mentor to whom I continue to owe much. As always, Elly and Peter kept me focused on what is really important even as they distracted me from the project. Finally, this book is dedicated to the memory of my father, Peter Cimbala, a soldier of another war, who probably would have enjoyed reading about men who were much like him and his army buddies. For more than two years, he put aside his civilian life and traveled beyond his Trenton, New Jersey, neighborhood through Fort Dix to North Africa, Sicily, France, and Germany. Fortunately, unlike so many of his compatriots, he came home.

TIMELINE

1860

November 6	Abraham Lincoln elected president
December 20	South Carolina secedes
December 26	Major Robert Anderson, United States, moves troops from Fort Moultrie to Fort Sumter, Charleston, South Carolina, harbor

1861

January 9	Mississippi secedes
	South Carolina forces at Charleston fire on *Star of the West,* which fails to relieve Fort Sumter
January 10	Florida secedes
January 11	Alabama secedes
January 19	Georgia secedes
January 26	Louisiana secedes
February 1	Texas convention votes to secede (approved by popular vote February 23)
February 4	Seceded states meet in convention at Montgomery, Alabama
February 8	Montgomery convention adopts provisional constitution of the Confederate States of America (CSA)
February 9	Jefferson Davis of Mississippi selected as provisional president of the CSA; Alexander Stephens of Georgia becomes vice president
February 18	Jefferson Davis is inaugurated
March 1	Confederacy takes charge of military situation at Charleston

March 4	Abraham Lincoln is inaugurated
April 12	Confederates fire on Fort Sumter in Charleston, South Carolina, harbor
April 13	Surrender of Fort Sumter
April 14	Formal surrender ceremony at Fort Sumter
April 15	Lincoln declares an insurrection in effect and calls for 75,000 militia to put down the rebellion
April 17	Virginia legislature passes ordinance of secession (approved by popular vote May 23)
April 19	Pro-CSA riots in Baltimore, Maryland
	Lincoln initiates blockade of CSA ports
May 3	Lincoln calls for additional volunteers and increases size of regular army
May 6	Arkansas secedes
	Tennessee legislature passes ordinance of secession (approved by popular vote June 8)
May 20	North Carolina secedes
	Confederate Congress votes to move government to Richmond
May 29	U.S. secretary of war Simon Cameron accepts offer of Dorothea Dix to assist in establishing hospitals for soldiers
July 21	First Battle of Bull Run or Manassas, Virginia
August 10	Battle of Wilson's Creek, Missouri
October 21	Battle of Ball's Bluff, Virginia
November 6	Jefferson Davis is elected president of the Confederacy for a six-year term
November 7	Battle of Port Royal Sound, South Carolina, followed by U.S. occupation of Hilton Head and Port Royal region

1862

February 6	CSA Fort Henry on the Tennessee River falls to U.S. forces
February 8	Battle of Roanoke Island, North Carolina
February 16	CSA Fort Donelson on the Cumberland River surrenders to U.S. forces
February 25	U.S. forces occupy Nashville, Tennessee
March 7–8	Battle of Pea Ridge or Elkhorn Tavern, Arkansas
March 9	USS *Monitor* engages CSS *Virginia* during Battle of Hampton Rhodes, Virginia
March 26–28	Battle of Glorieta, New Mexico Territory
April 5	U.S. forces besiege Yorktown, Virginia
April 6–7	Battle of Shiloh or Pittsburg Landing, Tennessee
April 11	Fort Pulaski, near Savannah, Georgia, surrenders to U.S. forces
April 16	CSA conscription act signed by Davis

April 25	New Orleans, Louisiana, falls to U.S. forces
May 3	CSA forces withdraw from Yorktown
May 5	Battle of Williamsburg, Virginia
May 25	Battle of Winchester, Virginia
May 29–30	CSA forces leave Corinth, Mississippi
May 31–June 1	Battle of Seven Pines or Fair Oaks, Virginia
June 9	Battle of Port Republic, Virginia
June 19	Lincoln approves act prohibiting slavery in territories
June 25	Seven Days Battle begins on Virginia peninsula
June 26	Battle of Mechanicsville, Virginia
June 27	Battle of Gaines' Mill, Virginia
June 29	Battle of Savage's Station, Virginia
June 30	Battle of Fraser's Farm or White Oak Swamp, Virginia
July 1	Battle of Malvern Hill, Virginia
July 14	U.S. government provides for pensions for disabled servicemen and survivors of dead servicemen, a program that will continue to expand after the war ends
August 9	Battle of Cedar Mountain, Virginia
August 28	Battle of Groveton, Virginia
August 29–30	Battle of Second Bull Run or Manassas, Virginia
September 1	Battle of Chantilly, Virginia
September 4	CSA Army of Northern Virginia invades Maryland
September 14	Battle of Crampton's Gap, Maryland, and Battle of South Mountain or Turner's Gap, Maryland
September 15	CSA forces capture Harper's Ferry, Virginia
September 17	Battle of Antietam or Sharpsburg, Maryland
September 19	Battle of Iuka, Mississippi
September 22	Preliminary Emancipation Proclamation issued by Lincoln
October 3–4	Battle of Corinth, Mississippi
October 8	Battle of Perryville, Kentucky
December 7	Battle of Prairie Grove, Arkansas
December 13	Battle of Fredericksburg, Virginia
December 29	Battle of Chickasaw Bayou, Mississippi
December 30	Battle of Murfreesboro or Stones River, Tennessee, begins

1863

January 1	Emancipation Proclamation
January 3	Battle of Murfreesboro or Stone's River, Tennessee, ends
January 31	First South Carolina Colored Volunteers officially mustered into U.S. service, although organization and training began earlier
March 3	U.S. conscription act signed by Lincoln

April 17	U.S. colonel Benjamin H. Grierson begins cavalry raid from La Grange, Tennessee
May 1	Battle of Port Gibson, Mississippi
May 1–4	Battle of Chancellorsville, Virginia
May 2	Grierson's raid ends at Baton Rouge, Louisiana
May 3	Second Battle of Fredericksburg, Virginia
May 4	Battle of Salem Church, Virginia
May 16	Battle of Champion's Hill, Mississippi
May 28	54th Massachusetts, the first northern black regiment, after assembling and training at Readville, Massachusetts, since February, embark for Hilton Head, South Carolina
June 9	Battle of Brandy Station, Virginia
June 15	Second Battle of Winchester, Virginia
June 23	Tullahoma, Tennessee, campaign starts as U.S. forces move from Murfreesboro, Tennessee
July 1–3	Battle of Gettysburg, Pennsylvania
July 4	Vicksburg, Mississippi, surrenders to U.S. forces
July 8	Port Hudson, Louisiana, surrenders to U.S. forces
July 13–16	New York City draft riots
July 18	54th Massachusetts attacks Battery Wagner, Morris Island, South Carolina
August 21	CSA guerillas sack Lawrence, Kansas
September 6–7	CSA forces abandon Battery Wagner and Morris Island, South Carolina
September 9	U.S. forces occupy Chattanooga, Tennessee
September 10	CSA forces evacuate Little Rock, Arkansas
September 19–20	Battle of Chickamauga, Georgia
November 19	Gettysburg Address
November 24	Battle of Lookout Mountain, Tennessee
November 25	Battle of Missionary Ridge, Tennessee
November 26– December 1	Mine Run, Virginia, campaign
December 8	Lincoln issues Proclamation of Amnesty and Reconstruction

1864

February 14	U.S. troops occupy Meridian, Mississippi
February 20	Battle of Olustee, Florida
March 10	Red River, Louisiana, campaign commences
April 8	Battle of Sabine Crossroads, Louisiana
April 12	Fort Pillow, Tennessee, Massacre
May 5–6	Battle of the Wilderness, Virginia
May 7	Atlanta campaign begins

May 8–19	Fighting at Spottsylvania Court House, Virginia
May 11	Battle of Yellow Tavern, Virginia
May 14–15	Battle of Resaca, Georgia
May 15	Battle of New Market, Virginia
May 16	Battle of Drewry's Bluff, Virginia
May 23–26	Battle of the North Anna, Virginia
May 25–June 4	New Hope Church, Georgia, campaign
June 1–3	Battle of Cold Harbor, Virginia
June 10	Battle of Brice's Crossroads, Mississippi
June 11–12	Battle of Trevilian Station, Virginia
June 15–18	U.S. attacks on Petersburg, Virginia, fail, and siege begins
June 27	Battle of Kennesaw Mountain, Georgia
July 9	Battle of Monocacy, Maryland
July 11–12	CSA forces demonstrate in Washington, D.C., suburbs
July 14	Battle of Tupelo, Mississippi
July 20	Battle of Peachtree Creek, Georgia
July 22	Battle of Atlanta, Georgia
July 24	Battle of Kernstown, Virginia
July 28	Battle of Ezra Church, Georgia
July 30	Battle of the Crater, Petersburg, Virginia
	CSA forces capture and burn Chambersburg, Pennsylvania
August 5	Battle of Mobile Bay, Alabama
August 18–21	Battle of the Weldon Railroad or Globe Tavern, Virginia
August 25	Battle of Reams Station, Virginia
August 31–	
September 1	Battle of Jonesboro, Georgia
September 2	U.S. forces occupy Atlanta, Georgia
September 19	Battle of Winchester, Virginia
September 22	Battle of Fisher's Hill, Virginia
September 29–	
October 2	Battle of Peebles' Farm, Virginia
October 19	Battle of Cedar Creek, Virginia
November 8	Lincoln reelected
November 15	U.S. forces begin marching across Georgia from Atlanta to the sea
November 30	Battle of Franklin, Tennessee
December 15–16	Battle of Nashville, Tennessee
December 21	U.S. forces occupy Savannah, Georgia

1865

January 15	U.S. forces capture Fort Fisher, North Carolina
January 19	U.S. forces begin march from Savannah into South Carolina

February 5–7	Battle of Hatcher's Run or Dabney's Mills, Virginia
February 17	U.S. forces occupy Columbia, South Carolina
	CSA forces evacuate Charleston, South Carolina
February 22	U.S. forces occupy Wilmington, North Carolina
March 3	U.S. Congress passes law establishing the Bureau of Refugees, Freedmen, and Abandoned Lands
March 4	Lincoln's second inauguration
March 19–21	Battle of Bentonville, North Carolina
April 1	Battle of Five Forks, Virginia
April 2	CSA government evacuates Richmond, Virginia
	U.S. forces break through CSA lines at Petersburg, Virginia
	U.S. forces capture Selma, Alabama
April 3	U.S. forces occupy Richmond and Petersburg, Virginia
April 6	Battle at Sayler's Creek, Virginia
April 9	Robert E. Lee surrenders the Army of Northern Virginia at Appomattox Court House, Virginia
April 12	Formal surrender ceremony at Appomattox Court House, Virginia
	U.S. forces occupy Mobile, Alabama
	U.S. forces occupy Montgomery, Alabama
April 13	U.S. forces occupy Raleigh, North Carolina
April 14	John Wilkes Booth shoots Lincoln at Ford's Theater, Washington, D.C.
April 15	Lincoln dies
	Andrew Johnson becomes U.S. president
	U.S. officers meeting in Philadelphia, Pennsylvania, accept constitution for the Military Order of the Loyal Legion of the United States
April 18	William T. Sherman and Joseph E. Johnston sign armistice document
April 26	Sherman and Johnston sign final surrender agreement
April 27	*Sultana* explodes and burns on the Mississippi River
May 1	Decoration Day first observed by African Americans and white abolitionists in Charleston, South Carolina
May 4	CSA forces of the Department of the Alabama, Mississippi, and East Louisiana surrender
May 10	Jefferson Davis captured near Irwinville, Georgia
May 12–13	Battle at Palmito Ranch, Texas, the last land battle of the war
May 23	Grand review of the Army of the Potomac in Washington, D.C.
May 24	Grand review of Sherman's forces in Washington, D.C.
May 26	CSA Army of the Trans-Mississippi surrenders
May 29	Johnson issues Proclamation of Pardon and Amnesty

June 2	CSA General E. Kirby Smith accepts terms of May 26
June 8	U.S. VI Army Corps parades in Washington, D.C.
June 23	CSA General Stand Watie surrenders Cherokee, Creek, Seminole, and Osage troops
	Johnson ends U.S. blockade of CSA ports
June 30	Conspirators in Lincoln assassination plot convicted
July 7	Lincoln conspirators executed
November 10	CSA Captain Henry Wirz hanged for cruelty to U.S. prisoners at Georgia's Andersonville prison
December 18	Secretary of State William H. Seward pronounces operative the 13th Amendment to the U.S. Constitution, abolishing slavery

1866

April 1	First Grand Army of the Republic (GAR) post established, Decatur, Illinois
April 2	Johnson declares insurrection over, except for Texas
August 20	Johnson declares insurrection over in Texas

1868

May 30	GAR begins annual memorial services at soldiers' graves

1879

March 12	North Carolina becomes first Southern state to provide permanent pensions for disabled CSA veterans

1889

June 19	Delegates meet in New Orleans, Louisiana, to establish United Confederate Veterans

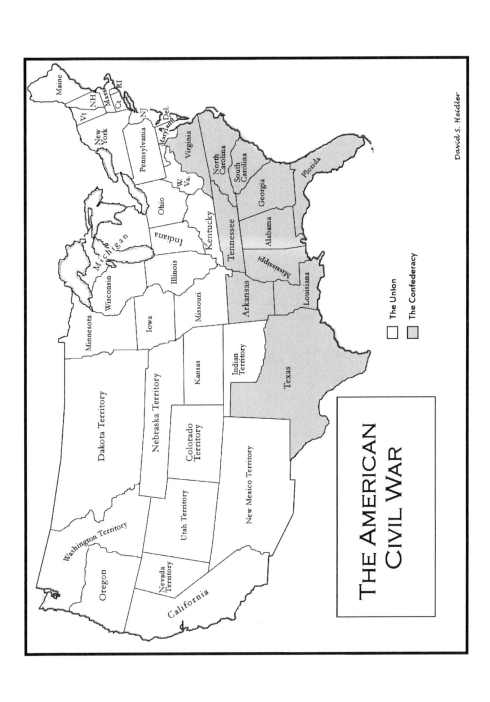

THE AMERICAN
CIVIL WAR

The Union
The Confederacy

David S. Heidler

1 A BLOODY CITIZENS' WAR

CITIZEN-SOLDIERS

At the outset of America's Civil War, necessity and tradition prompted both Northern and Southern governments to rely on local initiative to raise the troops they needed. The United States had a regular army, which the federal government kept whole throughout the war. However, it was not an army ready to engage in a major conflict spread over a large geographical area; in 1861, it consisted of about 15,000 enlisted men, very few of whom left to go south, and 1,080 officers, of which over 300 offered their services to the new Confederacy. In the wake of the firing on Fort Sumter in Charleston harbor by Southern forces on April 12, 1861, and the fort's surrender the next day, the federal government relied on the states for its military force, assigning quotas to them to meet the president's call for 75,000 militiamen to serve for 90 days, a period of time determined by the limits set by a federal law passed in the last century. Congress soon granted the War Department the authority to increase the regular army's numbers by a modest but inconsequential number of men, eventually reaching a total just under 23,000 men. The Confederate Congress planned to establish a small regular army of about 15,000 men, which was a necessary statement of sovereignty and national permanence but one that never captured the enthusiasm of Southern men.

Despite the existence of these regular armies, both governments expected very little from them. They continued to rely on citizen-soldiers throughout the war, and ambitious professionals found higher rank in the new volunteer regiments that came into existence. In March 1861, the Confederate Congress gave President Davis the authority to raise up to 100,000 volunteers for a year's service. After Sumter fell, it authorized the recruiting of more volunteers initially for various lengths of service, and on August 8, 1861, it authorized the president to recruit 400,000 three-year volunteers. Shortly after his initial call for the militia, Lincoln requested additional volunteers for three-year service and, in the wake of the July 1861 disaster at Bull Run, signed legislation for the recruitment of 1 million volunteers for three-year terms. Even after the two governments instituted conscription, however, they continued to rely on the states to play an important role in organizing and giving identities to the volunteer regiments in the field. Indeed, governors in both sections, fond of their authority and protective of states' rights, jealously guarded their roles in fielding their nations' citizen armies.

Both governments looked to their state militias to form a core of their volunteer forces. Embodied as a right of the people in the Second Amendment and as an obligation by legislation throughout the land, militias were rooted in eighteenth-century America's faith in a citizens' army and its distrust of a professional military. It was an impressive force, at least in theory. In 1861, optimistic Northern officials expected to be able to draw on a combined total of state militias reaching almost 2.5 million men. Unfortunately, the militia system had fallen into disrepair, becoming nothing more than ill-equipped, paper organizations unable to muster a fraction of their roll book numbers. By the mid-nineteenth century these militias had become caricatures of martial activity. Their required musters were fine occasions for socializing and carousing with the boys, at least when the boys reported for duty, but they had little to do with military preparedness.

The problems of the old militia system were apparent in its muster rolls, the lack of attention devoted to it by many states, and the equipment states had on hand to deal with military emergencies. In 1861, companies in the United States and the Confederate armies ideally consisted of 100 men, with 10 companies creating regiments of 1,000 men, but in 1860, in the city of Chicago, there were 11 companies of militia that would have been able to field no more than a total of 150 well-turned-out men.[1] In New Jersey, the office of the adjutant general, under whose authority the state militia fell, was no more than a political perquisite that required little effort from a placeholder; the state found the militia useful in dealing with railroad strikes, but the legislature saw no reason to turn it into an organization that could handle serious military threats.[2] In Connecticut, the state militia's arsenals and armament were in poor condition, with many of the weapons being of a Mexican War vintage.[3] And in October 1860, South Carolinians, already thinking about independence, admitted the inefficient state militia would never be able to stand up to aggressive federal action, let alone any slave unrest that might develop in the wake of Lincoln's election.[4]

The hint of a future crisis in late 1860 and early 1861 prompted some politicians to start to repair the damage done by this neglect. Massachusetts had already begun the process. The key to that state's success, however, was the recognition two decades earlier that it was best to rely on an alternative to the old requirements of a universal statutory militia, one that had more appeal to a smaller, dedicated group of men who might actually be eager to participate in some sort of training. In 1840 the commonwealth had declared *voluntary* military companies to be its active militia. The men normally eligible for the old universal, mandatory militia would still need to enroll but would no longer even be bothered with the formality of required drills.[5]

Massachusetts's solution to the militia problem was a realistic one that had occurred or would occur to other states. Most men who wished to participate in martial activities found it more appealing to become part of a volunteer company, and throughout the antebellum period, voluntary military associations remained popular. These volunteer companies initially were not normally part of the statutory militia complement, but states such as Massachusetts, recognizing the problematic nature of their militias, incorporated them into their regular militias to bolster their effectiveness. During the antebellum era, New York, Alabama, and other states reorganized their militias to include the popular volunteer companies. In 1846 the Mexican War provided an opportunity to confirm at least the perception of the value of these companies when citizen-soldiers came together in associations of their own choosing, superseding the contributions of the state militias.

The volunteer companies had many attractive qualities for young men in antebellum America. Their members freely agreed to associate with one another and made their own rules. They socialized at dinners, dances, and drills. They maintained a degree of exclusivity—some more so than others—by carefully guarding entry into their ranks, allowing them to become elite entities in many cities and towns. The 71st New York, for example, was "a swell city regiment" with many rich members that normally admitted "none but native Americans."[6] Thus the companies offered status to those men who joined and provided one of the few regular outlets for male companionship in antebellum America. Even after they became connected with the statutory state militia, volunteer companies maintained a degree of independence exhibited in their continued selective membership, the election of their own officers, and their choice of idiosyncratic and sometimes flamboyant uniforms, for which their members paid. The Little Fork Rangers, a cavalry company organized in 1860 in Culpepper County, Virginia, for example, wore uniforms of red, white, and blue. However, as war approached, companies designed more practical uniforms to replace their outlandish parade dress. After Virginia joined the Confederacy, the Little Fork Rangers donned cadet gray.[7]

The sense of community and the esprit de corps found in the antebellum voluntary organizations would be important as the boys marched off to war. The companies also spent some time in drilling and parading, which would reinforce that identity and add a bit of discipline to their muster. Wesley Brainerd and his friends, members of the Gransevoort Light Guard, a Rome, New York, company and part of the 46th Regiment of the New York State Militia, recalled that the company drilled one or two evenings a week and paraded "on all possible occasions." But the attitude of many peacetime volunteers throughout the states probably followed that shared by Brainerd and his friends, who admitted a certain dilettantish quality to the company. "We were a fancy dress Company of holiday Soldiers," he explained, "comprised chiefly of young men fond of show and with much leisure time on hand."[8] In the end, the many nicely uniformed, well-drilled voluntary associations were only slightly better than the tatterdemalion militia companies at preparing their members for the hard work of real campaigning. None were physically or mentally prepared for more than a short burst of 90-day campaigning.

The popularity of voluntary military associations increased and took on a more serious purpose as the sectional crisis intensified. Northerners and Southerners had been sparring over sectional issues, in particular those issues related to the institution of slavery, since the inception of the republic, but during the 1850s, tensions were reaching a climax. In the wake of the Mexican War, both sections became especially concerned with the expansion of slavery into new territory, and while the Compromise of 1850 produced a short-lived armistice, events would convince many powerful men on both sides that the debate was irresolvable.

Northerners had come to see the South as the home of a conspiracy of slaveholders bent on depriving them of the rights of free men and destroying the nation's free institutions that allowed hardworking individuals to climb up the economic ladder. White Southerners countered with their own fear of a conspiracy to violate their constitutional rights by depriving them of slave property and one that would ultimately promote racial chaos. No greater was the fear of white men in the South than a Haitian-style rebellion that would lead to sexual attacks by unrestrained black men on white women. Furthermore, the attempt to stop slaveholders from carrying their human chattel into the territories was a terrible insult to them and all white Southerners. Nothing seemed to prove more forcefully that Northerners, by depriving white Southerners of their right

Wide awake on the campaign trail in 1860. Local groups from this Republican political organization would form the nucleus of a number of Northern volunteer companies in 1861. (*Library of Congress*)

to property without due process of the law, were intent on relegating them to some type of second-class citizenship. Abolitionist John Brown, who had already earned a reputation for violence by his role in the battles between the forces of antislavery and proslavery settlers in Kansas, also proved to white Southerners that they were not unrealistic in their fears. In October 1859, he raided Harpers Ferry, in western Virginia, the site of a federal arsenal, with the avowed purpose of fomenting a slave insurrection.

The final blow for whites, particularly in the Deep South, where slavery remained a strong institution, came in 1860. The rise of the Republican Party, a political organization that appealed only to Northerners, after 1854 had been troubling to Southerners, but the election of its standard-bearer, Abraham Lincoln, to the presidency was intolerable. It mattered little that Lincoln promised not to meddle with slavery where it already existed. For many white Southerners, it would be only a matter of time before their inferior status in a republic dominated by unsympathetic Yankees would lead to economic ruin and racial anarchy. For men considering secession, the constitution was a means to an end; when it no longer fulfilled its purpose to protect their property and guarantee their happiness, it no longer deserved their allegiance.

It was in this political context that men began to think it wise to oil their weapons and perhaps pay closer attention to the manual of arms. In 1860, for example, Jacksonville, Illinois, men formed three new volunteer companies.[9] In early 1861, Chicagoans from Eastern Europe joined the Lincoln Guards, while the city's Welshmen, Irishmen, and Scotsmen came together in the Highland Guards.[10] Elsewhere across the North in 1860, young men organized themselves into quasimilitary, rudimentary uniformed political associations known as Wide Awakes, with the intention of convincing their neighbors to vote for Lincoln. Cyrus Boyd and a number of his Palmyra, Iowa, friends, all "just young and strong enough to do some tall yelling," associated for that purpose.[11] While not specifically military, these groups formed the core of many Northern volunteer companies that rushed to the colors in 1861. Connecticut veteran Sheldon B. Thorpe might have assigned too much credit to the minimal training that these boys had in preparation for their political rallies, but he believed that it "was of inestimable service to them and others in the ranks of the Union Army."[12]

In the slave states, John Brown's 1859 raid reminded men of the need to organize into military companies to prepare for future probable abolitionist challenges. Around the 1860 presidential election campaign and in its aftermath, however, Southern men began to prepare for war. South Carolinians formed volunteer companies of "Minute Men for the Defence of Southern Rights," expecting that the election of a "black Republican" would lead to sectional difficulties.[13] In addition to preparing for trouble, however, such volunteer associations could act as channels for their members' enthusiastic support for secession. In the northwestern upper piedmont region of South Carolina, for example, small slaveholding yeoman farmers joined vigilance organizations such as the Turkey Creek Minute Men not simply to protect their homes from Republicans, but to promote secession in their neighborhoods.[14]

The reforms of the previous decades and the enthusiasm for volunteering in 1860 and 1861, however, were no guarantees of a universally successful mobilization. When the war came, regiments relied on many of these old associations as their anchors, but their states' needs were greater than the volunteer organizations could satisfy. Also, recruiting was more of an ad hoc affair than the web of antebellum volunteer organizations or legal militia districts would have suggested. Nevertheless, the volunteer units that entered state service provided some sense of order to the chaotic growth of armies during the early days of the war.

In December 1860, South Carolina, where fear of the consequences of Lincoln's election seemed greatest, seceded from the United States, with Mississippi, Florida, Alabama, Georgia, and Louisiana following in January 1861. Texas voted to sever its ties with the old Union on February 1, and within days, representatives of these states gathered in Montgomery, Alabama. The consequence was a new confederation of Southern states, with Jefferson Davis of Mississippi serving as provisional president and Alexander Stephens of Georgia serving as provisional vice president. A year later, both men would assume the same offices in a permanent Confederate government.

During the winter and early spring of 1861, the Deep South states prudently called for volunteers to defend their independence, although it was not yet clear when or even if war would come. They had a purpose and a point to prove that required the backing of military force. Southern states from the East Coast to Texas, with federal installations on their soil, now had to assert themselves or appear to be less than viable political entities.

At this time, the states of the new Confederacy had little difficulty fleshing out old and new volunteer companies. Mississippi's governor requested four regiments of men to serve for a year's time; the men of the state answered the call with sufficient enthusiasm to join enough companies to form twice as many. Men rallied into companies identified by colorful names common among antebellum volunteer units. However, outlandish company names, designed to send chills down the spines of Yankee enemies, soon yielded to the more prosaic alphabetical military designations common to the old regular army, gathered under the numerical designations of regiments identified by their state of origin.

These volunteers soon were joined by members from the upper Southern states that seceded after the firing on Fort Sumter on April 12 and Lincoln's call for volunteers to subdue the "rebellion." First among them was Virginia, which voted to leave the Union on April 17, subject to the approval of a popular vote. In May, Arkansas, Tennessee, and North Carolina followed. Before the end of the year, the Confederate Congress admitted both Missouri and Kentucky into the new nation; governments in exile never did control their states, but divided loyalties at home meant that a significant number of volunteers from those states would serve with Southern forces.

THE WAR COMMENCES, 1861

Members of these various Southern volunteer organizations were eager to prove themselves in combat even if many citizens of the new Confederacy might have wished that the old government would leave them alone. On April 7, 1861, prior to firing on Fort Sumter, Savannah lawyer and politician Francis S. Bartow wrote, "We have rumors of war, but I do not look for it yet." He trusted that "heaven may save us from civil strife" but distrusted the politicians in Washington. Thus he swore to "be in the fight" if the sections came to blows.[15]

Bartow and the other volunteers, however, would soon have to make good on their promise to defend the Confederacy. Secessionists were committed to the new government, but so, too, Lincoln and most Northerners were committed to protecting the integrity of the United States. For Northerners, Americans enjoyed a perpetual union that could not be separated at the whim of disgruntled Southern politicians. There remained Northerners who preferred to let slaveholders leave the Union, believing the country would be better off without them. But others assumed that it would be best not to give in to the desire for compromise—it had not worked in the past—and take a stand for the Union now. On April 5, 1861, Robert Gould Shaw, a member of a prominent abolitionist family who would go on to command the famous black regiment, the 54th Massachusetts, argued that "as for making concessions, it is only patching the affair up for a year or two, when it would break out worse than ever." Each future presidential election would bring similar outbursts from the South, and besides, he argued, the South would never be satisfied with moderate concessions. "Indeed, they would not be content with anything less than a total change of public opinion throughout the North on the subject of slavery, and that, of course, they can't have."[16]

Not all Northerners were so bleak about the possibilities for compromise, but once Confederates fired on the flag at Fort Sumter, there was no turning away from the fight. For Northerners, it was now up to the federal government to enforce its authority on their erring Southern brethren, even it meant violence. Federal forces would have to assume the hard task of invading the rebellious states, compelling the Confederates to defend their states' claims to independence. The fact that Delaware, Maryland, and even Missouri and Kentucky all remained in the United States made the matter of war aims a delicate one for the Lincoln government; it could not risk alienating those states by allowing the abolitionist ambitions of some Northerners to go unchecked. But for the time being, that was not a problem. "Union" would serve as a powerful rallying cry. The war would be over before it could disrupt old social institutions, and one grand battle would bring the defeated rebels back to the old Constitution, or at least so the people believed. Even the more pessimistic Yankees assumed that a year would see the job done or at least agreed with the cautious approach embodied in federal army chief General Winfield

Scott's Anaconda plan. By blockading their ports, cutting the rebellious region in half by capturing control of the Mississippi River, and then moving into the Southern interior, Union forces would strangle the rebels into submission just as the large snake squeezed life out of its prey before devouring it.

Early Battles: Harbingers of Things to Come

During 1861, there were several minor clashes and a few significant ones between Confederate and U.S. troops in the eastern and western theaters. The first major clash of arms in the eastern theater of operations came in July 1861, when federal forces moved into Virginia with the intent of quickly putting an end to Southern foolishness by capturing the Confederate capital, which had moved from Montgomery, Alabama, to Richmond, Virginia. Poorly disciplined Union forces under Irvin McDowell slowly moved into Virginia and, on July 21, 1861, engaged green Confederate forces under Pierre G. T. Beauregard at Bull Run near Manassas Junction. Here Americans witnessed the engagement of armies of a size that seemed remarkable compared to past experiences. McDowell left the defenses of Washington with approximately 35,000 men, and General Beauregard, once joined by General Joseph Johnston after his evasion of U.S. forces in the Shenandoah Valley, had about 30,000 at his disposal. By the end of the day, worn Confederates held the field, while their weary, disorganized enemy retreated into the safety of Washington. The next day, in the capital, Englishman William Russell observed "jaded, dispirited, broken remnants of regiments passing onwards." He was witnessing "the mass of the grand army of the Potomac . . . placing that river between it and the enemy as rapidly as possible." As the rain was falling, helping to prevent chase by an equally weary rebel army, Russell watched "beaten, footsore, spongy-looking soldiers, officers, and all the debris of the army filing through mud and rain, and forming in crowds in front of the spirit stores."[17]

In the wake of the battle, both sides confronted shocking and unprecedented casualty figures, which should have indicated to enlisted men and presidents that this war would be no fleeting moment ending with one grand victory. Compared to future campaigns, the numbers of dead, wounded, and missing would appear to be light, but Americans had not experienced a previous war that had bled them so much. Georgian Francis Bartow had kept his promise to fight the invading Yankees and sacrificed his life in doing so.[18] He was only one of many patriots among the dead, hurt, and unaccounted for. McDowell had lost 2,896 men, including 460 dead, while Beauregard and Johnston suffered close to 2,000 casualties, with 387 dead. During the entire Mexican War of 1846–1848, by way of comparison, of a total of 116,119 regulars and volunteers who served in the U.S. Army, 1,721 were killed in actual fighting or died of their battle wounds; another 4,102 men were wounded in action.[19] No wonder one Confederate soldier concluded shortly after the battle, "I fear this war will become one of extermination."[20]

Both armies now at least had men who knew the meaning of combat. Confederates came away from their victory with a sense that they had proven their superiority over the shopkeepers and laborers of the North. Northerners were chastened by the Battle of Bull Run or Manassas and in need of someone to blame for their defeat. McDowell, the most obvious and perhaps unfair target, lost his command to a young general who had shown some ability to win fights in western Virginia, General George B. McClellan. McClellan would not live up to his own high opinion of himself, becoming but the first general in a long line of disappointing commanders of the United States' most important command

HW, August 3, 1861. *Colonel Hunter's Attack at the Battle of Bull's Run* depicts a portion of the eastern theater's first major engagement. (*Library of Congress*)

in the east, the Army of the Potomac. Nevertheless, he began to turn McDowell's dispirited boys into a disciplined force, one that at least looked like a real army on the parade ground.

Before the end of the year, Union forces in the east experienced another fiasco in Virginia at Ball's Bluff on October 21. Not long afterward, on November 7, down the coast, however, Union forces faired better. Army troops under General Thomas W. Sherman and a naval squadron commanded by Samuel F. Du Pont captured Port Royal, South Carolina, as part of the plan to facilitate the blockade of the Confederate coast. The battle was a good example of successful army-navy cooperation, but the victory did more than give the federal navy safe anchorage. It also led to the Northern army's intimate wartime involvement with an entire community of slaves abandoned by their fleeing rebel masters. It was at Port Royal and its surrounding plantations that Northern soldiers came into contact with one of the most exotic of African American communities. It also became one of the two most significant places, the other being the occupied areas of the Mississippi River Valley, where the government and the army explored policies dealing with Southern slaves that would later shape Reconstruction.

In the theater of war beyond the Mississippi River, on August 10, the U.S. Army added to the humiliation of Bull Run with the withdrawal from the field after the battle at Wilson's Creek, Missouri, the second major fight of the war. There some 5,400 of them engaged over 11,000 Confederates. It was a "very hard Fight," according to Arkansan Tom Spence, who "never saw the like of dead men in life."[21] Union forces lost over 1,300 men, with 258 dead, while Confederate forces lost over 1,200, with 279 dead, sufficient losses to dissuade them from pursuing the retreating federal troops. The casualties in

Missouri as well as in the east during 1861 only hinted at what soldiers would endure as the war continued beyond initial expectations, but for Spence and other participants, the fight offered sufficient clues to how horrible war could become for them.

THE ROAD TO SHILOH: WESTERN SOLDIERS
EXPERIENCE WAR IN EARNEST, 1862

During early 1862 Lincoln's government could take heart in some of the developments in the western theater, where an active general named Ulysses S. Grant was starting to develop a reputation as a fighting soldier. It was in that theater that Union forces faced a Confederate command under Albert Sydney Johnston that covered an area from the Appalachian Mountains into Arkansas in long defensive line across its northern tier. Challenged on a few points, Confederates were particularly embarrassed by the loss of their forts on the Tennessee and Cumberland rivers in Tennessee. The navy subdued Fort Henry on February 6, 1862, and shortly thereafter, not too far away, Grant's men were fighting before Fort Donelson on the Cumberland River. It was here that Grant earned a hero's reputation, promotion to major general, and a new nickname to match his initials when he demanded unconditional surrender from his old army friend Simon Bolivar Buckner, the Confederate officer left in charge of the fort. As Grant later recalled, "The news of the fall of Fort Donelson caused great delight all over the North," while in the Confederacy, "the effect was correspondingly depressing."[22] The victory also led to a reorganization of the western command, bringing federal forces under the control of General Henry Wager "Old Brains" Halleck, a man with a reputation for military scholarship and an unreasonable lack of fondness for his subordinate Grant.

Meanwhile, Albert Sydney Johnston pulled back and consolidated his troops at Corinth, Mississippi, a place convenient for its rail access. On March 6, 1862, farther west, Confederate and U.S. forces confronted each other at Pea Ridge, Arkansas, where they fully engaged the next day. Federal troops finally routed the Confederates on March 8, spoiling rebel chances of returning to Missouri. Also known as the Battle of Elkhorn Tavern, the clash was the largest in the trans-Mississippi Confederacy. The Union victory, however, would be overshadowed, and the battle casualties on both sides would be dwarfed a month later at Pittsburg Landing.

The Battle of Shiloh or Pittsburg Landing in Tennessee was an extraordinarily fierce and bloody engagement, a harsh introduction to war for many new recruits. Grant and his Army of the Tennessee encamped at Pittsburg Landing on the Tennessee River, where they waited for the arrival of all of Don Carlos Buell's Army of the Ohio, a separate command, before moving forward against the Confederates. They did not suspect that the Confederates were preparing to pounce on them. Albert Sydney Johnston and his men surprised the federal forces at nearby Shiloh Church on the morning of April 6 and almost succeeded in driving his enemy into the river but for the fierce resistance of some of the Yankees. During the battle, however, Johnston suffered a wound that bled him to death, and Beauregard assumed command. Beauregard halted the successful attack that night. The next day, he and his men found themselves facing a reinforced enemy that regained its lost ground and forced them from the field. All told, some 65,000 federal soldiers and almost 45,000 Confederates came to the fight. When it was over, they had sustained a total of almost 23,800 casualties, a sobering figure for all who considered it within the context of other American wars, not to mention the earlier battles of 1861 and 1862.

After the battle, James M. Williams of the 21st Alabama correctly judged its intensity: "How the battle of Shiloh is looked upon by the country I do not know," he speculated, "but I believe it to have been one of the fiercest and most deseperately fought conflicts of the whole war."[23] Grant later recalled, however, that the victory gave his men "great confidence in themselves ever after." It was also after Shiloh that Grant, and probably many other Northern soldiers and civilians, came to understand that the Confederacy would not simply collapse after a great battlefield defeat. For Grant, it also meant a change in his tactics. No longer would he refrain from a destructive war; rather, he would set his men about the task of destroying or using what enemy property came within their grasp.[24]

The surrender of the Mississippi River fortification Island No. 10 on April 8 added to Northern optimism, but as the casualty lists of Shiloh became known, citizens on both sides became horrified at the mounting cost of war. Halleck, now in charge on the field after raising Grant to the inconsequential position of his second-in-command, in a slow, deliberate advance eventually captured Corinth, the town to which the defeated Confederates had retreated. He also scattered his great army to pursue several objectives. More important, David G. Farragut and his U.S. naval force ran the fortifications defending New Orleans, Louisiana, on April 24–25, a major blow to the Confederacy and the morale of its people. The Confederates abandoned the important port city, and on May 1 Union general Benjamin Butler and an occupying force took control.

Winfield Scott's anaconda appeared to be cutting the rebellious states through their center, while securing important points along its coast, even though the ailing Mexican War hero had left the army earlier in October 1861. However, the Confederate forces in

The Surrender of Fort Donelson, February 16, 1862. (Library of Congress)

the west were far from finished. During the summer of 1862, Halleck had been called to Washington to take on the roll of general-in-chief of the U.S. Army, which meant that Grant was free of him and back to an independent command that included taking charge of the Army of the Tennessee.

Grant did not do much during the summer after Halleck's departure. However, the Confederates, after Shiloh, challenged Union troops at several points, including Iuka, Mississippi, on September 19 and Corinth, Mississippi, on October 3 and 4, where federal forces checked the rebels. Confederates under Braxton Bragg also launched an invasion of Kentucky, which, on October 4, lifted rebel spirits with the inauguration of a Confederate governor for the state at Frankfort. That attempt to rally Kentuckians to the Confederacy, however, failed to have any lasting effect. At the battle of Perryville on October 8, federal forces under Don Carlos Buell convinced Bragg to retreat to Tennessee. Despite the battle being far from decisive for one side or the other at the end of the day, a cautious Bragg believed the odds were against him.

Many Southerners were bewildered and disappointed by the withdrawal from Kentucky, but soldier George Knox Miller gave Bragg the benefit of the doubt, calling the retrograde movement "judicious." "I am not enough [of a] military genius to give reasons why Bragg fell back, or whether the move was a proper one," wrote Miller. However, he did offer the opinion that it was a "pity" that he could not have held on to his gains. Kentucky, Miller acknowledged, "is of inestimable value to us—so rich, so plethoric with the necessaries of life—what we need above all things."[25] The significance of such a loss of potential resources would become more and more apparent as the war dragged on.

During the latter part of 1862, Grant directed his attention toward Vicksburg, Mississippi, with unpromising results by year's end. The so-called Gibraltar of the Confederacy, a citadel located in a particularly difficult geographic position on a bluff in a bend in the Mississippi River, would now occupy his mind for months to come, into the summer of 1863. If Grant did not realize how difficult a task lay before him, one Iowa soldier certainly did: "The fight at Vicksburg will be a hard one," Charles O. Musser predicted in January 1863, "the rebels are desperate and determined to hold the place."[26]

Also before 1862 expired, on December 31, Confederate and U.S. forces engaged at the Battle of Murfreesboro or Stone's River in Tennessee, where at least George Miller believed he had witnessed some "brilliant achievements." On January 2 they rejoined battle, ending the day with a total of almost 13,000 federal casualties and almost 12,000 Confederate casualties, marking another bloody fight that made some men wonder if such battles could in fact lead to victory for one side or the other. After some additional fighting the next day, Miller concluded that "victory perched upon our banner," but "strange to say," Braxton Bragg repeated his Perryville decision and removed his army from harm's way. Again, some soldiers wondered why the general withdrew at a time when the outcome of the battle was favoring their army, although George Miller correctly assumed that bad weather, exhaustion, and federal reinforcements played a role in the decision. "We have not gone far," an unbent Miller assured a correspondent, "and are preparing for another brush."[27]

BACK EAST: THE VIRGINIA BATTLES OF 1862
AND LEE'S INVASION OF MARYLAND

After assuming command, George B. McClellan, concerned with training his magnificent army, was unable to bring himself to throw his forces at the enemy. Lincoln relieved him of his position as general-in-chief, leaving him in command of the Army of the Potomac, which he finally began to take into the field. He decided against following McDowell's example of moving overland through Manassas Junction to the Confederate capital and, on March 17, began to transport his army by ship to the Virginia peninsula between the James and York rivers, eventually bringing ashore there almost 122,000 men. On the way to their Virginia destination, at least some of McClellan's men assumed they were about to give the lie to secession. Private Warren Lee Goss of Massachusetts later recalled, "The general opinion among us was that we were on our way to make an end of the Confederacy."[28]

Plagued with caution, wet weather, and bad roads, the Army of the Potomac inched its way toward the Confederate capital. Private Goss came to understand in recalling his experiences on the Virginia peninsula that "marching on paper and the actual march made two very different impressions."[29] McClellan's own cautious approach to campaigning did not speed things along. He spent a month besieging Yorktown only to have the rebels retreat, which had given Confederate general Joseph Johnston time to prepare for him as he closed on Richmond. McClellan's advancing army certainly struck fear into the hearts of Richmond residents, many of whom fled the capital, but their defenders were prepared to keep the invaders away from their doors.

About 40,000 Confederates waited for the enemy as the Army of the Potomac made a laborious advance that taxed the patience and the health of its soldiers. Finally, on May 31, the two armies met near Richmond at the Battle of Seven Pines or Fair Oaks, not because of any initiative on McClellan's part, but because he provided an opportunity to the enemy by placing the Army of the Potomac on both sides of the Chickahominy River to the east of Richmond. Over 5,000 Yankees and over 6,100 rebels died, suffered wounds, or went missing during the two days of fighting.

Among the seriously wounded was the Confederate commander, which led to one of the more momentous decisions of the war. Confederate president Jefferson Davis had the good sense to trust Virginian Robert E. Lee, then serving as his military advisor, with Johnston's command. Lee had long served with the U.S. Army before his state's secession but had little to show for his work with Confederate forces during the early months of the conflict. Indeed, he had a bad reputation at this time, thanks in part to failures in western Virginia. With Lee in command of Confederate forces, indecisive fighting continued the next day, not doing much to boost the new commander's reputation. By the time it ended, the casualty figures set a record for fighting in the eastern theater. Once again, the reality of war should have warned Americans that their fight would not be as quick or as easy as some of them had predicted in 1861. However, some Northerners, including those men among McClellan's army, still held on to the belief that victory was imminent.

Lee also once again left himself open to criticism of excessive caution in the aftermath of Seven Pines, but he understood that he could not allow his freshly christened Army of Northern Virginia to fight McClellan's style of entrenching war. Also, he saw opportunity when cavalry officer J.E.B. "Jeb" Stuart, in the course of a bold scouting ride around the enemy, discovered McClellan had poorly positioned his army. For assistance in his confrontation with McClellan, Lee called east from the Shenandoah Valley an aggressive commander, Thomas Jackson, who had been building on a good military reputation first won along with his battle name "Stonewall" at Bull Run. Lee would then have more than a fighting chance, with over 90,000 men under his command facing the cautious McClellan, who tended to multiply the enemy's numbers to highs beyond reason and then act accordingly.

Stonewall Jackson had already harmed McClellan's campaign by maneuvering and fighting in the Shenandoah Valley, beginning with the March 23 battle at Kernstown through the commencement of his move to join Lee on June 17. With a small command of some 16,000 soldiers, Jackson had occupied the attention of over 60,000 federal forces in three armies commanded by mediocre generals and prevented Lincoln from sending the reinforcements that McClellan believed he needed to be successful. He also had worn out his command and probably himself in the process, initially not performing up to his reputation when he joined Lee on the peninsula.

During the Seven Days Battle from June 25 through July 1, Lee proved to be an aggressive commander who would win the admiration of soldiers and civilians alike. Confederates soldiers under his command foiled McClellan's grand plans, forced him to withdraw from before Richmond, and exhausted his army. Union private Warren Lee Goss later concluded that the Confederates could claim the "moral advantage" for having repulsed the federals, but he also believed that the Army of the Potomac had proven itself in hard fighting and had inflicted serious losses on the rebels.[30] Union surgeon J. Franklin Dyer, however, wrote after retreating to Harrison's Landing below Richmond on the James River that "after a week's incessant fighting by day and marching by night we are pretty nearly used up." "We must have more men," he also concluded, "and I am not sure but we shall have to have better generals."[31] The campaign might have bruised the expectations of Northerners, but it also prompted moderate individuals in the North to think in terms of conducting a harder war of the type that McClellan had resisted, perhaps even to the point of attacking the institution of slavery.

New Jerseyan Sam Fox considered the retreat to the James River a victory and, since the army remained close to Richmond, predicted that the federals would capture the rebel capital as soon as McClellan received reinforcements.[32] That would not be the case. Soon after stymieing McClellan on the peninsula, Lee, with his corps commanders Jackson and South Carolina–born and Georgia-raised James Longstreet, a man Lee would later call his warhorse, defeated Union general John Pope and his Army of Virginia in a two-day fight on August 29 and 30 at the old battleground at Manassas Junction. Jackson attempted to press matters on September 1 at Chantilly, where men fought "in torrents" of rain, and the federals, while stopping the Confederate advance, withdrew from the field.

Soldiers were now not surprised by the losses they suffered in such fights, which continued to be severe by any standards of the past. Theodore A. Dodge noted that his regiment, the 101st New York Infantry, made effective use of their weapons as he watched "the poor fellows" across the field fall in "terrible" fashion. Dodge's regiment, however, suffered, too. It started at Chantilly with more than 250 men thanks to the return of stragglers, fought for less than an hour, and left the battle with only 35 fit soldiers. Dodge himself was among the wounded, carried to the rear by two men whose guns "were so wet they could not fire."[33]

It was after this Virginia campaign that Lee decided to take advantage of circumstances and launch an army-sized raid into Maryland. There he hoped to encourage Southern sympathizers to join his cause as well as relieve Virginia of the pressure of war and gather up needed supplies for his army. A great victory along the way might have forced Northerners to ask for peace or at least encourage European nations to recognize the Confederacy. As Northern soldiers, all now under George McClellan's command, set out to confront the enemy, the discouraged private Wilbur Fisk hoped that once the campaign had ended, he would be able to "write of something beside disaster, slaughter, defeat, and skedaddle."[34]

Lee clearly understood his enemy better than McClellan understood Lee. Splitting his forces and counting on the Union general's deliberate, overly cautious approach to war, he sent Jackson to take Harpers Ferry, Virginia. His lieutenant did not disappoint him, capturing significant supplies and 12,500 Yankees. Even after McClellan learned of Lee's plans, he failed to act quickly to attack the divided Confederate army. The federal commander thus allowed Lee, who at first wished to avoid a major collision with the Union army, to gain confidence from Jackson's victory and to gather his troops at Sharpsburg, Maryland, near Antietam Creek in western Maryland, not far from the Potomac River. Jackson even had time to rejoin Lee's army before McClellan launched a series of uncoordinated attacks along Lee's lines that lasted the day. Wasting his superior numbers—he had some 85,000 troops ready for battle—McClellan allowed Lee to exercise a textbook example of the use of interior defensive lines, moving units from his greatly outnumbered army of about 35,000 from one threatened point to another, fending off each enemy assault. When it was all over, one Georgia private judged that he had participated in "the greatest battle that was ever fought on this continent."[35] Indeed, the battle along Antietam Creek, which lasted from dawn to dusk, produced casualties that were horrible, making it the single bloodiest day of the war. At the end of the day, there were close to 23,000 killed, wounded, and missing men, with federal forces suffering about 12,400 of them.

On the morning after the fight, Lee's army still taunted the federals from across that blood-soaked field, and McClellan failed to act. Rebels such as Walter H. Taylor, one of Lee's officers, believed that this situation allowed the Confederates to claim the advantage, pointing out that McClellan "dared not resume the attack the next day." They waited for the Yankees "to lay on," but because McClellan declined to do so, "we quietly left him & came to Virginia, a more hospitable country."[36] Federals, on the other hand, believed that this retreat allowed them to claim victory. Indeed, for the rest of his life, McClellan claimed Antietam as his greatest victory.[37]

Lee's army suffered greatly for its efforts in Maryland, but it was not yet defeated. Antietam once again illustrated that the war would require something more than traditional battlefield victories before one side or the other would give up its cause. Lee planned to regroup across the Potomac and return to Maryland for another encounter with McClellan but realized that his forces were inadequate for such a gambit. Despite Lee's eagerness to reengage the enemy, there were now at least a few Confederates who wondered if such a bloody war could be won on the battlefield. After Antietam, Georgian Ugie Allen remarked to his wife that "we defeat them again and again but like the hordes of Goths and Vandals that laid waste to South Europe; still they come."[38] Allen hoped for a winter's respite from such fighting, as did Lee, who planned to spend the remainder of 1862 resting his worn army before taking on further challenges.

McClellan's so-called victory fell short of being decisive, despite what the general believed, but the battle did have some positive effects for the United States. It prevented Lee from winning his strategic goals, and most important, it provided the opportunity for Lincoln to strike a blow at the Confederacy beyond the battlefield. When, on September 20, Samuel Fiske wrote "that out of the horrors of battle shall arise the blessings of a more secure freedom and stable system of liberal government," he was more prescient than he might have imagined. On September 22, in a preliminary emancipation proclamation, Lincoln warned the rebellious states that he would free their slaves on January 1, 1863, if they did not put down their arms. As with Grant's earlier tactical epiphany after Shiloh, the Emancipation Proclamation moved the war into a new strategic direction that most Americans had not anticipated in 1861. Many Union soldiers might have remained dubious or resentful about emancipation, and the document itself failed to contain the stirring words common to Lincoln's great speeches. Nevertheless, the United States' armies now became armies of liberation with every advance into the Confederacy.

If Americans had not yet come to understand the bloody nature of their war after Antietam, they would have another opportunity to witness its destructive force in Virginia before the year's end. On November 5 Lincoln, again frustrated by McClellan's lack of energy, signed orders that in days would replace him with Ambrose Burnside, a man who was aware of his own military limitations and who lacked enthusiasm for such high command. Burnside should have shared Lee's desire to avoid battle for the time being, but under pressure to use the 120,000-man Army of the Potomac, he moved his forces by mid-November to the Rappahannock River across from the Virginia town of Fredericksburg. Now he had the opportunity to challenge Lee while Stonewall Jackson's corps was in the Shenandoah Valley. However, Burnside waited for long-delayed engineers to bring up pontoon bridges for the river crossing, a circumstance that allowed Lee to gather his troops near the town to meet this threat. When the Army of the Potomac finally crossed the river at a point below the town and at another directly across from it, the Army of Northern Virginia was prepared to challenge its advance.

On December 13, 1862, federal forces unsuccessfully engaged Jackson's corps just to the south of Fredericksburg, where there had been for a time some chance of success, but the bloody fighting just behind the town provided the image of the battle that shocked soldiers and civilians alike. Confederates witnessed "a magnificent sight" as "long lines following one another, of brigade front" assembled across the expanse across from the fortified Confederate position "just where Lee wanted" Burnside to attack, recalled William Owen, a veteran Confederate artilleryman. Then wave after wave of Union troops fruitlessly charged across the exposed ground against Confederates entrenched at Marye's Heights, ending the day "out of sheer desperation" with a bayonet charge.[39]

By the end of the day, Burnside's men endured over 12,000 casualties of killed, wounded, and missing out of the 106,000 who had participated in the battle, while Lee's army had casualties of over 5,300 of the 72,500 soldiers involved in the fighting. Some Union commands were decimated by the fight. Henry L. Abbott of the 20th Massachusetts Infantry told his father that "the regiment, during the few minutes they were engaged, lost about 60 men & 3 officers"; in fact, a few days later, once Abbott added the losses of the December 11 river crossing to his figures, he reported that his regiment of 320 men lost 165 soldiers and 8 officers.[40] Of the 1,200 men of the Irish Brigade that marched on Fredericksburg and attacked Marye's Heights, only 280 reported for duty the next day.[41] No wonder Irish revolutionary, historian, and contemporary David Conyngham concluded, "It was not a battle—it was wholesale slaughter of human beings."[42]

Burnside, whom Henry Abbott believed to be "a noble man, but not a general," considered renewing the battle the next day. His generals changed his mind.[43] Lee considered the state of his own men along with the risk involved in attacking the federals' fortified positions at Fredericksburg and decided not to push back against the enemy. Consequently, on December 14 federal soldiers prepared to retreat across the Rappahanock. The 119th New York left with only food, clothing, and what they could carry, somewhat hindered in the process by the whiskey ration issued the night before. Nevertheless, they and the other defeated troops were safe, with a river between them and Lee by the end of the next day.

Morale in the ranks and at home suffered because of the disaster; men looked to lay blame, and generals and politicians lost the respect of soldiers and civilians alike. Northerners were filled with "indignation…at the slaughter in the mad storming of Fredericksburg batteries," reported Theodore Dodge, "and it does not at all astonish us." Even his mother wrote to him "in high language on the topic." Indeed, Dodge was troubled by the business and wondered, "Why is it we are always defeated? I cannot understand it, for they *do not* fight better than we do." His conclusion was that the Confederates "are *certainly better led* & have I believe more heart in the cause."[44] Men longed for McClellan, and generals plotted against their commander. The best evidence of the flagging morale among enlisted men was the significant increase in desertions as the men contemplated their condition in the winter camps. Soldiers spent the rest of December and part of January in camp, but when Burnside decided to challenge Lee again by outflanking him up the Rappahanock, bad weather and the dirt roads that it turned into quagmires stymied his efforts. This "mud march" began on January 20 and soon ended with the men settling in to winter quarters on January 23 and 24.

CHANCELLORSVILLE TO GETTYSBURG, 1863

On January 25, 1863, Joseph Hooker replaced the hapless Burnside as the army settled in to winter quarters. As Abner Small recalled, the general "took command of an unhappy army, defeated, despondent, ravaged by desertion, unpaid, and stuck in the mud without hope of moving before spring."[45] By the spring of 1863, however, the new commander controlled a force of upward to 150,000 men ready for action, in part because fewer men deserted, thanks to their confidence in Hooker, because of the general's successful efforts at tending to the health of his men in camp and because of other morale-boosting reforms. "Well we have had a good long rest this winter," wrote Massachusetts artilleryman John Chase, "and I think the boys as a general thing are ready and willing to try their hands once more with the Johnnys."[46] When regiments began to move out, soldiers, in good humor, sensed that things would be different this time.

Lee's men, on the other hand, had spent the winter worrying for food and forage, hungry and ragged. The Army of Northern Virginia only had about 60,000 men more or less ready to fend off another Yankee offensive because Lee had held two divisions under James Longstreet in southeastern Virginia to relieve the Fredericksburg area of some supply burden. Hooker employed cavalry to upset Lee's supply lines and also sent some 40,000 men to the point across the Rappahannock from Fredericksburg to suggest

The Attack on the Rebel Works at Fredericksburg by the Centre Grand Division of the Army of the Potomac, on December 13, 1862.—Sketched by Mr. A. R. Waud. (*Library of Congress*)

another attack there, while obscuring his true intentions of taking the remainder of his army upriver to flank Lee. The commander of the Army of the Potomac had a good plan that surprised the Confederates and put his men in a position to win.

Hooker in fact succeeded in fooling Lee. He crossed the Rappahannock and moved into the area of Virginia known as the wilderness, taking charge of the campaign. On April 30, however, despite making good progress, Hooker allowed caution, a trait that his predecessors had had in abundance, to stop his march. That decision allowed Lee to define the course of the imminent battle. Leaving a small force of some 10,000 men at the infamous Marye's Heights to occupy federals at Fredericksburg, he marched at the main Yankee body and, on May 1, convinced Hooker with little fighting to pull into defensive positions at Chancellorsville, an inconsequential former tavern with an outsized name located a short distance to the west of Fredericksburg. There the Army of the Potomac had over 72,000 men ready to meet Lee.

It was early in the morning on May 2 that Lee and his corps commander Stonewall Jackson decided to divide the Confederate army, leaving what was in fact the smaller force to keep Hooker's front busy, while Jackson took the larger body of troops on a round-about march to hit the unprepared federal right flank. Lee thus confronted the main Union army with less than 15,000 men, while the flanking column of Jackson consisted of 33,000. Late in the day, while Lee occupied Hooker's attention, Jackson surprised and scattered the Union troops—*demoralized* was the word a Confederate veteran later used—pushing them back until a strong federal defense and darkness ended the day's fighting.[47]

Lee and Jackson had executed an extraordinary plan that was marred by the corps commander being shot that night by his own men while he was inspecting his lines. Jackson lost his left arm but succumbed to pneumonia, passing away on May 10. The day after Jackson's march, Confederates renewed the fight at Chancellorsville, repulsed federal charges at Fredericksburg before withdrawing, fought troops advancing from Fredericksburg at Salem Church, and once again convinced the enemy to retreat across the Rappahanock River. Casualties for the entire Chancellorsville campaign reached a total of over 17,300 for the Army of the Potomac and over 13,400 for the Army of Northern Virginia.

What had started out as an optimistic campaign that had actually allowed the Army of the Potomac to outwit Lee for a change ended with the great army running away from inferior enemy forces. As usual, soldiers and civilians looked to place blame for the disappointing performance of Hooker's army. The brunt of the criticism fell on Oliver Otis Howard and the German soldiers who made up a part of his XI Corps, which felt the full force of Jackson's attack and collapsed under the pressure. Corps commander Howard deserved criticism, but the ultimate responsibility fell to Hooker. Indeed, many of his officers blamed him for the debacle. Nevertheless, the army did not fall into despair or lose the discipline that Hooker had brought to its ranks. It was a defeated army, not a broken one, that rose to the challenge after Chancellorsville, when Lee and the Army of Northern Virginia again crossed the Potomac River.

The next great encounter of the Army of the Potomac occurred less than two months later. Early in June, Lee began to move. His army fought a major cavalry battle at Brandy Station on June 9, eluded the Yankees, and by the middle of the month, was crossing the Potomac with about 80,000 men in its ranks. Lee was aware of the troubles of western Confederate forces at Vicksburg, Mississippi, and hoped that his advance might draw Union troops east, but he also wished to relieve Virginia of the burden of his army and, with luck, maybe even bring Washington into peace negotiations. This time, Lee did not stop in Maryland, but moved almost unopposed through Pennsylvania, setting off panic in the state capital of Harrisburg.

Hooker failed to impress Lincoln with his efforts to counter the invasion, and the president relieved him of command in the middle of the crisis. On June 28 George Gordon Meade assumed control of the Army of the Potomac. Thereafter, events moved quickly for the new army commander. The next day, forward units of federal cavalry were in the crossroads town of Gettysburg, the general direction in which some 80,000 Confederate and over 100,000 Union troops were now marching.

The three-day battle started on July 1, when some of Lee's soldiers stumbled into Union cavalry scouting west of Gettysburg. Lee had not wished a general engagement. Also, he was not fully apprised of the Union army's disposition. His cavalry commander, Jeb Stuart, had become separated from Lee by Union troops and went off on a wide-ranging ride around the enemy's rear, leaving Lee without a complete view of the enemy's movements. Still, Lee did not turn away from the fight when he discovered the Army of the Potomac's location. He committed his army to battle at Gettysburg, in the afternoon pushing federal units, including O. O. Howard's unlucky XI Corps, from their original positions west and north of Gettysburg. Men of Jackson's old corps once again found themselves "driving the Germans with fearful strength through the town."[48]

At the end of the first day, it appeared that Lee had once again beaten the enemy. However, as Confederate Edmund Patterson noted, "We well knew that one day's work could not decide the contest between two such powerful armies."[49] Fresh troops of both armies were converging on the town, and federal forces had found suitable defensive ground on the hills to the south of the town. Most of Meade's army arrived by the morning

The First Virginia (Rebel) Cavalry at a Halt—Sketched from Nature by Mr. A. R. Waud. Waud was one of the great Northern combat artists of the war. (*Library of Congress*)

of July 2 and developed a strong position, running south from Culp's and Cemetery hills down on Cemetery Ridge to anchor their left flank on two additional hills, Little Round Top and Big Round Top. Across the way to the west, on Seminary Ridge, Lee established his own lines.

Lee's corps commander, James Longstreet, had probably learned the lesson of Fredericksburg all too well. He urged Lee to develop a flanking attack, but the Army of Northern Virginia spent the next two days attempting to dislodge Meade's men with straight-ahead assaults on the high ground. On July 2 Lee failed to break Meade's lines on both the Union left and right flanks, despite fierce fighting and heroic efforts on the part of his men and because of the same on the part of Meade's. On the next day he ordered Longstreet to push against the center of the Union lines on Cemetery Ridge. Despite his objections, after an extraordinary artillery barrage, Longstreet set into motion one of the most famous charges of the war. He sent three divisions against the enemy, but despite his overall command and the participation of two other division commanders, the Virginian George Pickett's name became forever attached to the effort. Confederate officer Walter Herron Taylor proclaimed that Pickett's Charge was "the handsomest of the war as far as my experience goes."[50] Nevertheless, it failed.

"The moment I saw them I knew we should give them Fredericksburg," Major Henry L. Abbott admitted. "So did every body." Abbott's men let a rebel regiment advance "within 100 feet of us, & then bowled them over like nine pins, picking out the colors first." Abbott, his men, and other federal regiments turned back the charge despite Confederate courage.[51] "Night closed the terrible havoc" of battle on July 3, recalled Confederate veteran

The Battle of Chancellorsville—Couche's Corp Forming Line of Battle to Cover the Retreat of the 11th Corps, 20 May, 1863.—From a Sketch by Mr. A. R. Waud. The XI Corps and its German soldiers henceforth were ridiculed by other soldiers as cowards. (*Library of Congress*)

John Casler, "with nothing accomplished, both armies resting on their arms in the same positions they occupied the day before."[52] To get to that unsatisfactory point, it cost Lee over 22,600 casualties, of which over 4,500 were dead. In the end, Lee lost a total of over 27,100 men, taking into consideration the casualties sustained on the march to and from Gettysburg. The Army of the Potomac lost over 22,800 men, of which about 3,150 were dead.

On July 4 Lee's army remained on the field in a defensive position and "waited patiently for the enemy to attack us," reported Walter Taylor, but then withdrew from the field; "Why he [the enemy] did not attempt to intercept us must appear remarkable to those who believe his lies about his *grand victory*."[53] To be sure, there were Yankees who believed that the battle was not yet over and thought they had opportunities to finish the job while Lee was still on the field and while he was in retreat. A disgusted Patrick Guiney of the Ninth Massachusetts believed Meade should have ordered a counterattack after his men had repulsed Pickett; his failure to do so, Guiney believed, "gave us—*another years work*."[54] Samuel Fiske also felt that the army had acquitted itself well but thought Meade should have "follow[ed] up our success with unflinching energy, give him not a moments rest, and use him up entirely before he reaches the Potomac."[55] "The men universally were eager, anxious, panting to be led on to complete the triumph and utterly crush the defeated and despairing enemy," Fiske believed. "They were like hounds on the leash, panting to be let loose."[56]

But there were other men who agreed with Meade's decision to hold back, and in the end, Lee withdrew in bad weather and crossed the Potomac "without the slightest annoyance from the enemy."[57] Indeed, one Confederate veteran and historian later reported, "We never left a battlefield more leisurely, after defeating an enemy on other fields, than we retreated from this."[58] Gettysburg was not a perfect victory for Meade, and Lee's army still had sufficient strength and morale to continue to fight for almost two more years, in part because of his masterful execution of the retreat from Pennsylvania. Furthermore, if Lee's invasion of—or large raid into—Pennsylvania was also designed to add to his ability to feed his army, he enjoyed some success. Assistant quartermaster Charles Bahnson of North Carolina reported that the Confederates "pressed a good many things into service," leaving the area through which they traveled devoid of livestock, fowl, vegetables, wagons, and "everything in fact that could be used by us."[59] Lee's army returned to Virginia with supplies enough to keep his men and their animals in the field for months to come.

Almost immediately, the great battle pricked the curiosity and captured the imagination of Northerners. Casualties still lay on the field, and civilians "came down in their wagons to see the sights, to stroll over the ground, and gaze and gape at the dead and wounded." Setting a course followed by battlefield hucksters well into the future, "one man was found selling pies at twenty-five cents to the poor fellows" who had just fought to save the Union.[60] The sacred and the profane would forever be mixed on what Northerners claimed to be the site of their great victory when part of the battlefield became a cemetery for military dead. Lincoln further sanctified the ground and the cause for which those men had died when, on November 19, 1863, he promised in his short but powerful Gettysburg Address that the nation would witness "a new birth of freedom."[61]

VICKSBURG, 1862–1863

In 1862, Ulysses Grant had failed to capture Vicksburg, the Confederate city on a bluff on the eastern side of the Mississippi that commanded the river with its guns.

"The problem was," Grant later explained, "to secure a footing upon dry ground on the east side of the river from which the troops could operate against Vicksburg."[62] As federal forces had learned in 1862, the terrain made a direct approach from north of the city unfeasible. Port Hudson, Louisiana, another strong point of Confederate resistance over 100 miles south Vicksburg, complicated matters by blocking a river approach from below the city. Aware of these difficulties but intent on his objective, Grant, during the early months of 1863, kept his men busy with efforts to find ways around the citadel's guns. All of them failed to produce progress. Finally, he broke with his supply base, marched his army on the western side of the Mississippi to a point below the city, and then expected to rely on the navy to transport his men across the river to allow them the better southern and eastern approaches to the city.

On April 16, Admiral David Porter ran his ships past the guns of Vicksburg to meet Grant below the city. Then, on April 22, additional vessels, including transports with supplies, followed. In a matter of a few days, Grant was able to transport 24,000 men across the river south of the city. After fighting at Port Gibson on May 1, Grant's army moved eastward, breaking away from its supply lines. It then fought several battles, destroyed Jackson, Mississippi, and after two assaults on Vicksburg's works, settled into a siege.

For many Confederates, the city, its inhabitants, and its defenders became symbols of stubborn resistance against Yankee aggression. On July 4, for example, Mary Jones of Georgia wrote to her soldier son Charles, "Noble Vicksburg! From her heroic example we gather strength to hold on and hold out to the last moment. I can look extinction for me and mine in the face, but *submission* never!"[63] Unfortunately for the Confederacy, Grant's army of 71,000 men had a tight grip on the city, with sufficient resources to hold off any military relief from other Confederate forces. Consequently, the besieged defenders and residents of Vicksburg soon had few alternatives in their larders to mule meat. Pemberton finally decided continued resistance was not worthwhile and, on July 3, met with Grant to discuss surrender. The next day, 29,500 weary, hungry, weak Confederate soldiers surrendered their weapons and received paroles, promising not to fight until they were part of a formal prisoner exchange agreement. They left behind a city that had suffered much during their resistance. Some men from the 25th Wisconsin Infantry entered Vicksburg after the surrender and discovered "a pretty nice place" that had been "badly shot up."[64]

HW, August 1, 1863. *The Surrender of Vicksburg—The Rebels Marching Out and Stacking Arms.—From a Sketch by Mr. Theodore R. Davis.* Davis was another popular battlefield artist. (*Library of Congress*)

Only days later, on July 8, the last hindrance to Union control of the length of the Mississippi River, Port Hudson, surrendered, but Grant had already been thinking of his next move. By the time of Port Hudson's surrender, Sherman was nearing Jackson, Mississippi, the town to which Confederate forces under Joseph Johnston had withdrawn; by June 11 the federals were bombarding its defenses. Confederate forces abandoned the place on the night of July 16. Even so, Grant had little desire to waste time as long as there were enemy troops in the field. Developments father east, however, soon commanded the victorious general's attention.

When Vicksburg finally fell, Charles O. Musser of the 29th Iowa declared that the Union victory meant that "Rebellion is Knocked in a Cocked hat in the west."[65] Throughout the North, people rejoiced, while Confederates believed that the fall of Vicksburg was a national disaster. But as long as there remained viable Confederate forces in the field, there was hope for the South. Alabama soldier James M. Williams, for example, learned of Vicksburg's surrender but admitted that he and his fellow soldiers "are not discouraged, it is the fortune of war, our cause is not fallen; brave hearts and strong arms are left to our Country, and will save it yet."[66]

CHICKAMAUGA AND CHATTANOOGA, 1863

During June 1863, while Grant was besieging Vicksburg and Lee was beginning his northward thrust, Union general William S. Rosecrans finally advanced on Braxton Bragg's forces, which, after the Battle of Murfreesboro, the Confederate general had concentrated in the area around Tullahoma, Tennessee. For the first part of 1863, Bragg had waited for Rosecrans, while Rosecrans had consolidated his own forces at Murfreesboro, about 30 miles from the enemy. Neither army appeared eager to challenge the other, while generals bickered and soldiers foraged, until, by the end of June, they had to take action. Rosecrans finally executed a smart campaign of maneuver, forcing Bragg's army to abandon middle Tennessee and settle in to camp around Chattanooga, deep in the southeastern corner of the state. It was Rosecrans's personal misfortune to move into Tullahoma when word of the more spectacular events at Gettysburg and Vicksburg was exciting the North, preempting the less glamorous news of his almost bloodless victory. Rosecrans's successful campaign cost him fewer than 600 casualties.

To add to his annoyance, the War Department remained unsatisfied and urged Rosecrans to press forward. He did so, moving an army of over 60,000 men, excluding reserves, against what he believed was Bragg's force of about 30,000. Bragg actually had on hand about 37,000 soldiers, but it did not matter. Bragg decided it best to abandon Chattanooga, moving southward into Georgia, where, on September 18, he was near the West Chickamauga Creek, making some contact with Union troops. On September 19, the armies engaged in a battle that grew more serious as the day progressed.

On September 20 the armies resumed the fighting with indecisive results, until James Longstreet, recently arrived from Virginia, exploited a gap in federal lines, which caused panic and retreat among the Union forces. The success made it "a glorious day for our arms," according to Robert Franklin Bunting, a chaplain with Terry's Texas Rangers. Bunting reported that "the proud foe had been driven back at every point"; only nightfall "saved him from a ruinous defeat, if not from annihilation."[67] Certainly Rosecrans's army did not stand before the Confederates, but General George Thomas staved off total disaster by fighting a strong rearguard action until that evening. Thomas earned the sobriquet the "Rock of Chickamauga," and Rosecrans's Army of the Cumberland was

The Army of the Cumberland—The Fourth Corps, under General Gordon Granger, Storming Missionary Ridge.—Sketched from the Left of the Line by Mr. Theodore R. Davis. (Library of Congress)

saved, but the federals now found themselves isolated in their defenses at Chattanooga, with Bragg's men occupying nearby heights. The Battle of Chickamauga had pitted a federal army of about 58,000 effective men against 66,000 Confederates. By the time his army had retreated to Chatanooga, Rosecrans had made up for the low cost of his Tullahoma campaign. His Army of the Cumberland had suffered over 16,000 casualties, while Bragg's Army of Tennessee paid for its victory with almost 18,500 casualties.

Braxton Bragg, who, according to some estimates, now had over 70,000 men at his disposal, settled in to a siege of Chattanooga and the Army of the Cumberland, a force of only about 35,000 effective, beaten, undersupplied men. Bragg's assumption was that his strong position on Lookout Mountain south of Chattanooga and Missionary Ridge to the east as well as on the west bank of the Tennessee River across from the city would allow him to contain and outlast the Yankee defenders. However, he never completely cut off the defenders, and the federal government sent in reinforcements, particularly two corps from the Army of the Potomac, which the War Department believed it could spare since that army was not doing much since Gettysburg.

Probably just as important as reinforcements was a change in the command structure that brought Ulysses Grant to Chattanooga. On October 16, Grant became commander of the Military Division of the Mississippi, which stretched from the river to the eastern mountains, and almost immediately replaced Rosecrans as commander of the Army of the Cumberland with George Thomas. On October 23 Grant arrived to take over affairs in Chattanooga. Within a month of Grant's arrival, federal forces were once again on the offensive. Not only had troops arrived from the east, but by November 15, William T. Sherman's forces were near at hand. On November 23 Grant began to break the siege and, during the two days, drove the enemy from Lookout Mountain and Missionary Ridge. "I felt sorry for General Bragg," wrote Sam Watkins. "The army was routed, and Bragg looked so scared. Poor fellow, he looked so hacked and whipped and mortified and cha-grined by defeat."[68] In fact, on November 30, Bragg resigned his command of the Army of Tennessee, soon to be replaced by Joseph Johnston. Union forces now began to build their strength in Chattanooga, while the Confederates regrouped in northern Georgia with a supply line to Atlanta, the focus of the next part of the federal western campaign.

GRANT'S MOVE INTO THE VIRGINIA WILDERNESS AND ON TO PETERSBURG, 1863–1864

Meanwhile, in Virginia, in November 1863, Meade moved on Lee in what became known as the Mine Run Campaign, only to withdraw the Army of the Potomac into winter quarters. Confederate James Longstreet besieged federal forces in Knoxville, Tennes-see, until early December, when he also withdrew and moved his troops into winter quarters. In early 1864 Sherman marched from Vicksburg and captured Meridian, Mis-sissippi, a rail center, which gave him opportunity to destroy transportation infrastruc-ture. However, the most significant news of this stage of the war was Grant's promotion to lieutenant general in March, a rank not held by an officer since George Washington. Furthermore, he assumed command of all the federal armies, with his former superior Henry Halleck becoming chief of staff. Sherman took Grant's place in the west, where he would continue to forge his reputation as a hard campaigner. Meade remained in command of the Army of the Potomac for the remainder of the war but was overshad-owed by Grant, who made his headquarters in the field with that army and who remade it into his more aggressive image.

Now Grant expected to supervise a coordinated multipronged thrust into the heart of the Confederacy, although the government's political concerns restricted some of his options. In Virginia, in addition to the Army of the Potomac, Union armies would move up the peninsula to Richmond and campaign in the Shenandoah Valley of Virginia. In the west, Union forces would move on and capture Mobile, Alabama. The latter cam-paign was diverted up the Red River in Louisiana. In fact, none of these secondary campaigns proved immediately successful.

From the outset, however, Grant understood that the end of the war would come when federal forces could destroy the two most lethal Confederate armies in the field and make the Southern population aware that their government could not protect it. Lee's Army of Northern Virginia had become the great symbol of Confederate indepen-dence, and as long as it remained in the field, the rebellion had the potential for success. Northerners, including President Lincoln, now in an election year, also assumed that Lee's army had to be defeated if the Northerners were to win the war. Embarrassed by the humiliating way that Lee had handled their eastern generals, they wanted the Army of Northern Virginia beaten. Thus the Army of the Potomac would make it the unrelent-ing object of its attention.

Joseph Johnston's Army of Tennessee was the second army of the Confederacy. In early 1864 it was the defender of Atlanta, the gateway to the southeastern Confederacy. Sherman was to destroy that army and move into the interior to make war on the re-sources necessary for continuing the rebellion.

At the outset of the campaign in Virginia, Grant had at his disposal some 120,000 men. Lee had about 65,000 men on his rolls. Both sides would have to deal with casual-ties that sapped their strength as well as the exhaustion that hurt the effectiveness of their men as the campaign became a relentless one of constant fighting and marching. Grant would always need more men, but for Lee, the sources of manpower were drying up. The men in these two armies saw some of the bloodiest fighting of the war as they grappled, killed, and died on the same ground that their armies had seen on previous campaigns. Despite the familiar landscape, however, many of the Union men as well as their Confederate enemies sensed that this campaign was different from all previous ones. In less than three weeks from the time that Grant moved his army across the Rapidan River, Lee's adjutant Walter Taylor concluded that what was happening in Virginia was "surely the *last* campaign."[69]

On May 4 the Army of the Potomac began the push across the Rapidan River and into the Virginia wilderness. The topography might have diminished the advantage of Grant's superior numbers. However, when the two armies met on May 5 and 6, the undergrowth and forest not only inhibited the invader, but the defender as well, with neither side being able to bring the full force of its power against the enemy. Indeed, after fighting on May 6, Colonel Charles Wainwright wondered if there could have been anything like a plan of battle "in such a dense wilderness."[70] Regardless, the armies fought heroically, but neither one ever really gained a lasting advantage over its enemy.

Lee extracted from the Army of the Potomac during the two days of the battle almost 18,000 casualties at a cost of approximately 11,000 Confederate casualties. Grant's losses were probably heavier since some officers did not make honest reports, and their seriousness was seen in the heavy toll the fighting had taken on the veteran troops. But Grant, always a soldier who learned lessons from his battlefield experiences, absorbed an important one from his first great encounter with Lee: the general he was now facing was not Braxton Bragg.

In the past, such hard fighting, high casualties, and an apparent Confederate victory— Lee had stopped him at the wilderness—prompted Union commanders to retreat to safety to lick their wounds. Grant did not. Perhaps now Lee also had learned a lesson. He, too, was fighting against a different kind of general than he had been used to meeting in Virginia.

On May 7 the Army of the Potomac continued the campaign, leaving behind its unburied dead, moving southeastward, hoping to position itself between Lee and Richmond, or at least tempt Lee into an open battle. As Abner Small reported, "We were bound for Spotsylvania Court House; and so were the rebels, though we didn't know it then."[71] The federals, however, soon learned that to be the case because the Confederates beat them to their destination, in part because of the weariness of the Union troops as well as the difficulties involved with moving the approximately 10 miles through the area. The result was another two weeks of heavy fighting, more casualties, and little to show for all of it. Now, Lee's men began as a matter of course to dig into the earth, while becoming content to allow the federals to attack them.

The two armies engaged in continuous warfare from May 8 through May 21. It was on May 12 that federal forces attacked a "mule shoe" salient, a protrusion north beyond the rest of the Confederate defensive line. That point on the Confederate line earned the name of the Bloody Angle for all of the human destruction that occurred over the course of a fight that lasted from the early morning past midnight.

According to Confederate Walter Taylor, Grant was only "beating his head against a wall" when he attacked their fortifications, something that the general undoubtedly realized.[72] When Grant decided to try to move around Lee, he left with an army that had suffered approximately 18,000 casualties, while having inflicted about 12,000 losses on the Confederates. By this point in the campaign, approximately 60,000 men had become

Major-General Wadsworth fighting in the Wilderness.—Sketched by A. R. Waud suggests the conditions under which both armies fought in the heavily wooded region of Virginia. (*Library of Congress*)

casualty statistics. Yet Spotsylvania reinforced the understanding among Confederates that Grant was not like their previous opposing generals.

Despite the losses at Spotsylvania, the federals had not broken the Confederates, but neither had the Confederates convinced the federals to retreat. Chastened by the losses, however, Grant decided to lure Lee out of his lines to attack him, but failed. Lee's position was too strong for Grant when they faced each other again on May 23–25 at the North Anna River. Indeed, Grant explained to Halleck the day the army withdrew from this face-off that he could neither attack the strong position because it "would cause a slaughter of our men that even success would not justify" nor turn either of the Army of Northern Virginia's flanks because of the topography of the potential battlefield. Grant had to concede that "a battle with them outside of intrenchments cannot be had."[73]

Thus, as before, Lee thwarted the Army of the Potomac, and his men felt they had won another victory. But Grant also assumed that he had had the upper hand, proclaiming that Lee's men were "really whipped." As before, the Union general kept his men moving around right of the Army of Northern Virginia in another attempt to place the federal army between Lee and Richmond.[74]

By now, the Army of the Potomac had suffered casualties amounting to almost 40,000 men. The hard fighting and bloodshed at Cold Harbor, only about 10 miles northeast of Richmond, would add to that amount as men again spilled blood on familiar ground, this time where McClellan had fought during his Peninsula campaign. On June 1 the opposing armies met close to the earlier Seven Days fighting of 1862, but Cold Harbor was remembered foremost for the terrible casualties of the Union frontal assaults of June 3 against the strongest Confederate fortifications they had so far tackled during the campaign.

General Grant's Great Campaign—General Barlow Charging the Enemy at Cold Harbor, June 1, 1864.—Sketched by A. R. Waud. (Library of Congress)

On that day, federal troops began their charge as usual, until they encountered the enemy's heavy fire, which knocked down "files of men...like rows of blocks or bricks pushed over by striking against each other." Many of them gave up the charge and did their best to find protection in hastily dug holes in the ground.[75] By the end of the fighting, Confederate troops believed that because they had again checked the Army of the Potomac, they had won a victory, although the casualties should have alerted them to the dangers of that kind of success; by now, the 1864 Virginia campaign had cost the Army of Northern Virginia a total number of casualties that came to half of the number with which Lee had started in early May. But the cost did not buy anything close to a decisive victory for the Confederates, despite the optimistic assessments of some of them. When, finally, Grant abandoned his positions on June 12, the campaign through Virginia had reached extraordinary casualty totals, with the federals accepting losses of over 55,000 men and the Confederates almost 32,000.

Frustrated at Cold Harbor, Grant decided to take a different tact. He planned to move the army across the James River and cut Lee's supply route by taking Petersburg, considered the back door to Richmond, but also important as the junction of rail lines from the lower Confederacy that brought supplies to Lee. On June 12 the Army of the Potomac began to make its move to the James, using band music to cover the withdrawal as the men slipped away from their positions. The next day, a surprised Lee—a Confederate officer heard the commanding general "was in a furious passion"—learned that the Army of the Potomac was on the move.[76]

Men from the Army of the Potomac almost immediately joined Ambrose Burnside's federal troops, who had been bottled up in the area since Grant had ordered his multipronged offensive, and on June 15 they moved against Petersburg. Lee was determined to hold the important link in his supply line and was, for a time, successful. He also hoped that political developments in the North would come to the Confederacy's assistance if he continued to exact a toll on Grant comparable to that of the fighting in May and June. The Confederates were well aware of Northern discontent with the large casualty lists as well as the hard political position in which Lincoln now found himself. Democrats proclaimed the war a failure, and in August, even Lincoln, who had been renominated by his party earlier on June 8, feared he would not be reelected that November.

All of Grant's efforts to cut off Petersburg in June failed, and his efforts to breach its defenses from June 15 through June 18 cost the federals a loss of almost 10,000 dead, wounded, and missing men. Both armies settled into what became a lengthy siege that lasted into April 1865. Yankee Abner Small concluded that "all through July and halfway through August the chief occupation of our corps was the strengthening of its works in front of Petersburg. We almost came to suspect that the war was degenerating into a digging match."[77]

Throughout the siege, into the spring of the next year, there were episodes of fierce battle. The most spectacular of them was when Union troops dug a mine under the Confederate lines and, on July 30, set off an explosion that, according to Pennsylvanian Henry C. Heisler, threw some rebels 100 feet into the air and others over into the Union lines.[78] The attack that was to take advantage of the explosion and the gap in Confederate defenses it produced, however, turned into a fiasco. Poor preparation, for example, slowed the attack when federal troops did not even clear a way through their own defensive works. Also, the allure of the extraordinary crater attracted the charging Yankees into the pit, where they milled about until the shocked Confederates regained their senses, returned to the place, and took advantage of the confusion. Black troops,

The Cavalry Charge at Winchester, Virginia, September 19, 1864. (Library of Congress)

who had already shown their valor on many a battlefield, had been preparing to lead the assault but were denied that position at the last minute; artillery confused their later attack when they finally went into combat. In the end, the Union army lost almost 3,800 men of the almost 21,000 who participated in the attack known as the Battle of the Crater. But their sacrifice failed to alter the stalemate, further discouraging Northerners about the progress of Grant's campaign.[79]

In the meantime, Lee had sent Jubal Early and his corps into the Shenandoah Valley of Virginia, a significant source of agricultural products, to deal with federals operating there. Early's Confederates stopped the federals and then moved north to defeat Union troops at the Battle of Monocacy in Maryland on July 9, collecting $20,000 from Hagerstown along the way as punishment for earlier Yankee raiding in the Shenandoah. On July 11 Early's men entered the suburbs of Washington but lacked the strength to do much harm against the capital's defenses, withdrawing on July 12. The raid forced Grant to dispatch some of his troops to the area, but Confederates made their way back to Virginia, where, on July 24, they defeated the federals at the Second Battle of Kernstown. Confederate cavalry also raided into Pennsylvania, where they burned down Chambersburg. Grant finally placed a competent and trusted general in charge of federal operations in western Virginia, instructing Phil Sheridan to destroy the logistical value of the valley. Shenandoah Confederates ultimately met defeat at the hands of Phil Sheridan, but their summer of 1864 raiding activities north of the Potomac had not encouraged confidence among Northerners, who were having second thoughts about Lincoln's administration. Lincoln needed good news from his armies, but when he finally received it, it was not from Virginia.

THE ATLANTA CAMPAIGN AND ITS AFTERMATH, 1864

In the spring of 1864, William Sherman told the generals in charge of the three armies under his command in Tennessee to "make immediate preparations for a hard campaign."[80] They did so, and on May 7, 1864, about 100,000 men in the Army of the Cumberland, the Army of the Tennessee, and the Army of the Ohio embarked on their move southward. Their objective was Johnston's Confederate force, which would soon have in its ranks over 60,000 Confederates gathered at Dalton, Georgia, in strong defensive positions. Thus began almost five months of maneuver and battle that fulfilled Sherman's promise.

Sherman made steady progress as his armies moved southward through northwest Georgia. He preferred maneuvering around the enemy because of Johnston's reliance on fortifications; if he could not destroy Johnston in battle at this point in his campaign, he could make certain that the Confederates in Georgia would not be able to send assistance to Virginia. Before May was over, however, Sherman's armies had opportunities to fight, but Johnston continued to rely on calculated withdrawals that brought the war closer and closer to Atlanta.

Johnston, clearly a skilled practitioner of defense and retreat, did not make it easy for the federals. Neither did the rainy weather nor the cavalry that disrupted Sherman's supply line as he tried to sustain his huge army and its tens of thousands of animals. After additional fighting in June, Johnston's army regrouped in defensive works at Kennesaw Mountain, Georgia. On June 27 Sherman, who had grown tired of maneuver, threw his men at the entrenched enemy up a mountain with terrain ideal for hindering their advance. This attempt at a frontal assault under trying circumstances caused by the

General Sherman Reviewing his Army at Savannah.—Sketched by William Waud. (*Library of Congress*)

rugged landscape and oppressively hot weather failed, convincing Sherman and most of the men in his force that attacking Confederate entrenchments straight on was not a good idea.

Sherman failed to achieve his objective at Kennesaw Mountain, but his efforts convinced Johnston to pull out of the defenses there on July 2. Confederates cleverly moved away, while the skeleton detachments left behind made enough noise to convince the federals that Johnston was still in front of them. By now, both armies had suffered significant losses in the campaign, totaling 12,000 for the federals and another 9,000 for the Confederates. The engagements that actually brought the armies together were not as consequential as those that Grant and Lee were fighting at this time. Neither were the casualty figures as appalling as those in Virginia. But such conclusions were just further indications of how bloody 1864 had turned.

Soon, Confederates were holding off Sherman at the Chattahoochie River, not far from Atlanta. The prospects looked good that Johnston's tired army would soon even evacuate Atlanta in another retrograde maneuver. So much retreating, however, did not sit well with the Confederate government, or even with many of Johnston's own officers and men. Consequently, Johnston lost his command to the more aggressive John Bell Hood.

Hood, who assumed command on July 17, quickly lived up to his reputation. He now faced a veteran enemy of some 95,000 men. No longer did he have the natural topographical defenses that Johnston had abandoned on his retreat through northwest Georgia. And the primary purposes for defending Atlanta—that is was an important rail hub with industrial capacities—was no longer operative. At the time of Hood's assumption of command, only one of the city's four railroads was still in rebel hands, and the Confederates had already removed to safety much of the city's industrial infrastructure. Nevertheless, holding Atlanta was important for Southern morale, and Hood acted accordingly. On July 20 he attacked the federals at Peachtree Creek at Buckhead, just north of Atlanta. Sherman suffered almost 1,780 casualties; Hood sustained almost 4,800, suggesting that there was a serious cost involved with an aggressive rebel campaign.

Hood continued to engage Sherman's armies, but in the end, after battles at Atlanta, which cost the Confederates some 5,500 men, and Ezra Church, which brought to Hood's army another 3,000 casualties, he had not much more to show for his efforts, except his tenuous hold on Atlanta. Indeed, veteran Indiana colonel Edward J. Wood, now guarding railroad lines in Sherman's rear, believed that Sherman would soon be in

General Sherman's Grand March through Central Georgia. (*Library of Congress*)

Atlanta.[81] After another fight below Atlanta at Jonesboro on August 31, Hood, his army, and the city they defended were in an untenable position, forcing the Confederates to abandon the city. On September 2 Union forces entered Atlanta, a serious but still not fatal blow to the Confederacy.

The next day, Sherman wrote to Henry Halleck and informed him, "So Atlanta is ours, & fairly won." A couple of days later, the victorious general informed Halleck that he planned to remove the residents of Atlanta from that place, one of several decisions that would earn him white Georgians' lasting hatred. "If the people raise a howl against my barbarity & cruelty," he famously proclaimed, "I will answer that War is War & not popularity seeking." The solution for stopping such harsh treatment was obvious in Sherman's eyes: "If they want Peace, they & their relations must stop war."[82]

Without the need to protect Atlanta, Hood now hoped to move into Sherman's rear and dislodge the Yankees by cutting their supply line. Ultimately, he failed, when Sherman decided he had better things to do than chase him around Georgia and Tennessee. Sherman planned to take "an efficient army of 60, to 65,000 men" into the interior of Georgia. He knew this business was more than a straightforward military campaign that pitted his men against an opposing army. "By this I propose to demonstrate the vulnerability of the South," he explained, "and make its inhabitants feel that war & individual Ruin are synonymous." A week later, he explained to Grant that he expected his forces' "utter destruction of its roads, houses, and people will cripple their military resources." "I can make the march" through the state, he assured Grant, "and make Georgia howl."[83]

On November 15 Sherman's army of over 60,000 select men began its trek. The federals had already destroyed railroads and other property north of Atlanta and, before leaving the captured city, razed upward to 5,000 structures. Now, two army wings cut across the state, feeding off the land, destroying contraband property along the way. The

General Sherman's Advance—Howard's (Fourteenth) Corps Crossing the Chattahoochee, July 12, 1863.—Sketched by Theodore R. Davis. (Library of Congress)

men also had the specific military task of systematically destroying as much of the railroads along their route as they could. Men pulled rails, piled the pitch-soaked pine ties on top of them, set the wood on fire, and then marched on to the next section. Engineers followed behind them, and with special tools bent the white-hot rails into "twisted bar[s] of iron, worthless for any purpose." One soldier recalled that "some regiments even learned to shape the hot rails into forms that resembled the letters 'U.S.'"[84]

The Yankees struck fear into the hearts of civilians, at times deservedly so, but Sherman's men generally refrained from wanton and senseless destruction. Indeed, Sherman restricted the activities of his foragers, allowed men to destroy property only under orders from their corps commanders, and generally tried to reign in the excesses of marauding "bummers," although success in the latter area was not perfect. At the end of the campaign, Sherman estimated that his men had caused $100 million worth of damage, as they ate their way in a 30-mile swath across the state. They also destroyed 100 miles of railroad, confiscated over 10,000 horses and mules, and were the immediate cause of the liberation of "countless numbers of their slaves."[85] Civilians did indeed suffer, even from orderly foraging, but their own protectors also caused them hardship. Confederate cavalry and rebel deserters confiscated foodstuffs for their own use and destroyed property to keep it out of Yankee hands.

The federals encountered little opposition beyond the nuisance of Confederate cavalry as they moved toward an army entrenched at Savannah. On December 10 Sherman's men arrived at that city, but on December 20, even as Sherman was planning his move against the enemy there, the Confederates abandoned the place. The next day, Sherman presented Lincoln "as a Christmas gift the City of Savannah with 150 heavy guns & plenty of ammunition & also about 25,000 bales of cotton."[86]

Sherman now planned to move into the Carolinas to continue his destruction of rebel resources even as he pursued what forces remained arrayed against him. The success of his recent Georgia campaign made him feel confident, no doubt, but it was a confidence shared by his men. Another reason for his confidence in the future was that he knew "that Hood is used up by Thomas."[87]

Sherman had assigned George Thomas to deal with Hood while he marched through Georgia, which he did. Hood's advance into Tennessee led to the November 30 Battle of Franklin, where he failed to break federal lines with his costly head-on attacks. The Union troops withdrew from the field, allowing Hood to claim a victory, but the fight had essentially broken his own army beyond repair. The Confederates lost upward to 7,000 men, including a significant number of the officer corps. As rebel veteran Philip Stephenson recalled, "Franklin was the Waterloo of the Confederacy—the ruin of the army that fought it. It was the death knell of Hood's wild scheme and the South's strangely sanguine hopes."[88] Shortly after Franklin, on December 15–16, at the Battle of Nashville, George Thomas's men defeated Hood's army, turning it into a badly beaten, retreating, and inconsequential fighting force. In January 1865 Hood's men gathered at Tupelo, Mississippi, morale shattered, believing the Confederacy was near its death.

THE FINAL CAMPAIGNS, 1865

While events beyond the Virginia theater provided supporting evidence, it was the fall of Petersburg and Richmond that proved the Confederacy was about to collapse. Once those two cities fell into Union hands, the signs all pointed to success for the federals. At the outset of 1865, Grant had at his disposal over 120,000 men in the vicinity of Richmond and Petersburg, while Lee could draw on some 72,000. Confederate politicians made some effort to discuss peace terms, but in the end, Lincoln would settle for nothing short of unconditional surrender. Grant continued in his efforts to extend his lines to the west around Petersburg but finally had some success when his men engaged the enemy at Five Forks on April 1 and then the next day attacked and breeched the Petersburg lines. The Confederate government abandoned its capital, and on April 3 Union soldiers entered Petersburg and Richmond.

Lee's effort to retreat westward and attempt to join forces with Joseph Johnston came to naught. Fighting at Sayler's Creek on April 6 and the capture of thousands of Lee's hungry men underscored their sense that the end was near. Lee's failure to escape the consequences of these events finally brought about what had eluded the Army of the Potomac over so many campaigns: the capture of the Army of Northern Virginia.

While Grant's men sat in their uncomfortable entrenchments, their comrades to the south continued their march through the southeastern Confederacy. In mid-January and early February 1865, Sherman began his move into South Carolina. Yankee soldiers felt little sympathy for residents of the state, the place they understood to be the start and the heart of the rebellion. It was a soggy march into swampland, but Sherman's men built corduroy roads and bridges that allowed the army to cover ground at a good pace. Along the way, the men destroyed much property, as they were happy to teach the rebels the consequences of flouting the Constitution. On February 17 Sherman's men captured Columbia, which, in the confused situation, suffered greatly when a fire started by drunken soldiers, or Confederates attempting to destroy cotton, or perhaps recently freed prisoners of war and slaves, spread by high winds through the city.

Away from Virginia, Yankees seemed to be having good success shrinking the borders of the Confederacy. On February 22, 1865, for example, the North Carolina port of Wilmington fell into Union hands. Once again, the responsibility for stopping this trend in the southeast fell to Joseph Johnston, but he could do little to turn back his old enemy's relentless march northward. Confederates tried but failed at Averasborough, North Carolina, on March 16, and then again at Bentonville on March 19–21. It was shortly after that fight that both armies learned that the war in Virginia had come to an end and that Abraham Lincoln had been assassinated, dying on April 15. The negotiations of Johnston and Sherman led to a wide-ranging agreement that President Andrew

"Marching On!"—The Fifty-Fifth Massachusetts Colored Regiment Singing 'John Brown's March' in the Streets of Charleston, February 21, 1865. (Library of Congress)

Johnson considered beyond a soldier's authority—too much like a peace agreement and not a military surrender. Johnston finally surrendered to terms much like those accepted by Lee on April 26.

Elsewhere in the Confederacy, during 1865, Union arms continued to make progress, squeezing the life out of the Confederacy. In the Shenandoah Valley, General Phil Sheridan's men engaged in the destruction of enemy property, which would limit what assistance the region could send to Lee. Sheridan had successfully grappled with Confederates under Jubal Early the previous year but finally, on March 2, decisively ended the enemy's resistance in the valley at Waynesboro. There the federals captured most of Early's pathetically small 2,000-man command. Sheridan then rejoined Grant, while the few Confederate survivors of the Valley Campaign joined Lee in time to witness the Army of Northern Virginia's final hours.

In March James Harrison Wilson, who had been George Thomas's cavalry commander, conducted a substantial raid into northern Alabama with about 13,500 well-equipped men, destroying property and eventually capturing Selma on April 2, despite the defense offered by the Confederacy's legendary cavalry man Nathan Bedford Forrest. Not long afterward, on April 12, Wilson's men captured Montgomery, and Mobile, the last significant Confederate city, fell to Union forces under Edward R. S. Canby. Wilson next moved into Georgia, where his men captured towns and learned of the surrender of Lee and Johnston. But they also had the honor of capturing the fleeing Jefferson Davis at Irwinville on May 10. With its two major armies no longer in the field, with no real national civilian leadership, and with minor forces surrendering throughout the month of May, the Confederacy was no more.

NOTES

1. Theodore J. Karamanski, *Rally 'Round the Flag: Chicago and the Civil War* (Chicago: Nelson-Hall, 1993), 71.

2. William J. Jackson, *New Jerseyans in the Civil War: For Union and Liberty* (New Brunswick, NJ: Rutgers University Press, 2000), 40.

3. John Niven, *Connecticut for the Union: The Role of the State in the Civil War* (New Haven, CT: Yale University Press, 1965), 47.

4. Steven A. Channing, *Crisis of Fear: Secession in South Carolina* (New York: W. W. Norton, 1970), 269–71.

5. Marcus Cunliffe, *Soldiers and Civilians: The Martial Spirit in America, 1775–1865* (Boston: Little, Brown, 1968), 222.

6. Josiah Marshall Favill, *The Diary of a Young Officer Serving with the Armies of the United States during the War of the Rebellion* (Chicago: R. R. Donnelley & Sons, 1909), 12.

7. Daniel E. Sutherland, *Seasons of War: The Ordeal of a Confederate Community, 1861–1865* (New York: Free Press, 1995), 38.

8. Ed Malles, ed., *Bridge Building in Wartime: Colonel Wesley Brainerd's Memoir of the 50th New York Volunteer Engineers* (Knoxville: University of Tennessee Press, 1997), 7.

9. Don Harrison Doyle, *Social Order of a Frontier Community: Jacksonville, Illinois, 1825–70* (Urbana: University of Illinois Press, 1978), 232.

10. Karamanski, *Rally 'Round the Flag,* 71.

11. Mildred Throne, ed., *The Civil War Diary of Cyrus F. Boyd, Fifteenth Iowa Infantry, 1861–1863* (Millwood, NY: Kraus, 1977), 13.

12. Quoted in Niven, *Connecticut for the Union,* 39.

13. Channing, *Crisis of Fear,* 269–71; W. Chris Phelps, *Charlestonians in War: The Charleston Battalion* (Gretna, LA: Pelican Publishing, 2004), 17–20.

14. Stephen A. West, "Minute Men, Yeomen, and the Mobilization for Secession in the South Carolina Upcountry," *Journal of Southern History* 71 (February 2005): 75–104.

15. Mauriel Phillips Joslyn, ed., *Charlotte's Boys: Civil War Letters of the Branch Family of Savannah* (Berryville, VA: Rockbridge, 1996), 7–8.

16. Russell Duncan, ed., *Blue-Eyed Child of Fortune: The Civil War Letters of Robert Gould Shaw* (Athens: University of Georgia Press, 1992), 71.

17. William Howard Russell, *My Diary North and South,* ed. Eugene H. Berwanger (New York: Alfred A. Knopf, 1988), 278.

18. Joslyn, *Charlotte's Boys,* 7–8.

19. K. Jack Bauer, *The Mexican War, 1846–1848* (New York: Macmillan, 1974), 397.

20. Randall Allen and Keith S. Bohannon, eds., *Campaigning with "Old Stonewall": Confederate Captain Ujanirtus Allen's Letters to His Wife* (Baton Rouge: Louisiana State University Press, 1998), 19.

21. Mark K. Christ, ed., *Getting Used to Being Shot At: The Spence Family Civil War Letters* (Fayetteville: University of Arkansas Press, 2002), 29.

22. Ulysses S. Grant, *Personal Memoirs of U.S. Grant,* ed. Mary Drake McFeely and William S. McFeely (New York: Literary Classics of the United States, 1990), 214.

23. Here and throughout, all quotations from primary sources are reprinted as originally written by the author, inclusive of errors in spelling and grammar. John Kent Folmar, ed., *From That Terrible Field: Civil War Letters of James M. Williams, Twenty-first Alabama Infantry Volunteers* (Tuscaloosa: University of Alabama Press, 1981), 56.

24. Grant, *Memoirs,* 238–39.

25. Richard M. McMurray, ed., *An Uncompromising Secessionist: The Civil War of George Knox Miller, Eight (Wade's) Confederate Cavalry* (Tuscaloosa: University of Alabama Press, 2007), 93.

26. Barry Popchock, ed., *Soldier Boy: The Civil War Letters of Charles O. Musser, 29th Iowa* (Iowa City: University of Iowa Press, 1995), 17.

27. McMurray, *An Uncompromising Rebel,* 119, 120.

28. Warren Lee Goss, *Recollections of a Private: A Story of the Army of the Potomac* (Scituate, MA: Digital Scanning, 2002), 28.

29. Ibid., 34.

30. Ibid., 68–69.

31. J. Franklin Dyer, *The Journal of a Civil War Surgeon,* ed. Michael B. Chesson (Lincoln: University of Nebraska Press, 2003), 25, 29.

32. Samuel M. Fox to relations, July 6, 1862, Civil War Letters of the Fox Brothers, Primary Source Collection, eHistory, Ohio State University, Columbus, http://ehistory.osu.edu/osu/sources/letters/fox/.

33. Stephen W. Sears, ed., *On Campaign with the Army of the Potomac: The Civil War Journal of Theodore Ayrault Dodge* (New York: Cooper Square Press, 2001), 90–91.

34. Emil Rosenblatt and Ruth Rosenblatt, eds., *Hard Marching Every Day: The Civil War Letters of Private Wilbur Fisk* (Lawrence: University Press of Kansas, 1992), 42–43.

35. Ronald Moseley, ed., *The Stilwell Letters: A Georgian in Longstreet's Corps, Army of Northern Virginia* (Macon, GA: Mercer University Press, 2002), 50.

36. R. Lockwood Tower, ed., *Lee's Adjutant: The Wartime Letters of Colonel Walter Herron Taylor, 1862–1865* (Columbia: University of South Carolina Press, 1995), 44, 45.

37. Stephen W. Sears, *George B. McClellan: The Young Napoleon* (New York: Ticknor & Fields, 1988), 400.

38. Allen and Bohannon, eds., *Campaigning with "Old Stonewall,"* 165.

39. William Miller Owen, *In Camp and Battle with the Washington Artillery of New Orleans* (Baton Rouge: Louisiana State University Press, 1999), 175–93.

40. Robert Garth Scott, ed., *Fallen Leaves: The Civil War Letters of Major Henry Livermore Abbott* (Kent, OH: Kent State University Press, 1991), 149, 150.

41. Lawrence Frederick Kohl with Margaret Cossé Richard, eds., *Irish Green and Union Blue: The Civil War Letters of Peter Welsh* (New York: Fordham University Press, 1986), 2.

42. David Power Conyngham, *The Irish Brigade and Its Campaigns,* ed. Lawrence Frederick Kohl (New York: Fordham University Press, 1994), 343.

43. Scott, *Fallen Leaves,* 152.

44. Sears, *On Campaign,* 110, 123–24.

45. Harold Adams Small, ed., *The Road to Richmond: The Civil War Memoirs of Major Abner R. Small of the Sixteenth Maine Volunteers: Together with the Diary That He Kept When He Was a Prisoner of War* (New York: Fordham University Press, 2000), 80.

46. John S. Collier and Bonnie B. Collier, eds., *Yours for the Union: The Civil War Letters of John W. Chase, First Massachusetts Light Artillery* (New York: Fordham University Press, 2004), 226.

47. John O. Casler, *Four Years in the Stonewall Brigade* (Columbia: University of South Carolina Press, 2005), 145.

48. Sears, *On Campaign,* 304.

49. John G. Barrett, ed., *Yankee Rebel: The Civil War Journal of Edmund DeWitt Patterson* (Knoxville: University of Tennessee Press, 2004), 114.

50. R. Lockwood Tower, ed., with John S. Belmont, *Lee's Adjutant: The Wartime Letters of Colonel Walter Herron Taylor, 1862–1865* (Columbia: University of South Carolina Press, 1995), 61.

51. Scott, *Fallen Leaves,* 188.

52. Casler, *Four Years,* 176.

53. Tower, *Lee's Adjutant,* 61.

54. Christian G. Samito, ed., *Commanding Boston's Irish Ninth: The Civil War Letters of Colonel Patrick R. Guiney, Ninth Massachusetts Volunteer Infantry* (New York: Fordham University Press, 1998), 203.

55. Stephen W. Sears, ed., *Mr. Dunn Browne's Experiences in the Army: The Civil War Letters of Samuel W. Fiske* (New York: Fordham University Press, 1998), 107.

56. Ibid., 113.

57. Jeffrey D. Stocker, ed., *From Huntsville to Appomattox: R. T. Cole's History of the 4th Regiment, Alabama Volunteer Infantry, C.S.A., Army of Northern Virginia* (Knoxville: University of Tennessee Press, 1996), 113.

58. Ibid.

59. Sarah Bahnson Chapman, ed., *Bright and Gloomy Days: The Civil War Correspondence of Captain Charles Frederic Bahnson, a Moravian Confederate* (Knoxville: University of Tennessee Press, 2003), 70–71.

60. Allan Nevins, ed., *A Diary of Battle: The Personal Journals of Colonel Charles S. Wainwright, 1861–1865* (New York: Da Capo Press, 1998), 254.

61. Henry Steel Commager, ed., *The Civil War Archive: The History of the Civil War in Documents* (New York: Tess Press, 2000), 466.

62. Grant, *Memoirs,* 295.

63. Robert Manson Myers, ed., *The Children of Pride: A True Story of Georgia and the Civil War,* abridged ed. (New Haven, CT: Yale University Press, 1984), 383.

64. William H. Mulligan Jr., ed., *A Badger Boy in Blue: The Civil War Letters of Chauncey H. Cooke* (Detroit, MI: Wayne State University Press, 2007), 74.

65. Barry Popchock, ed., *Soldier Boy: The Civil War Letters of Charles O. Musser, 29th Iowa* (Iowa City: University of Iowa Press, 1995), 66.

66. Folmar, *From That Terrible Field,* 115.

67. Thomas W. Cutrer, ed., *Our Trust Is in the God of Battles: The Civil War Letters of Robert Franklin Bunting, Chaplain, Terry's Texas Rangers, C.S.A.* (Knoxville: University of Tennessee Press, 2006), 198.

68. Sam Watkins, *"Company Aytch," or a Side Show of the Big Show and Other Sketches,* ed. M. Thomas Inge (New York: Penguin Putnam, 1999), 94–95.

69. Tower, *Lee's Adjutant,* 162.

70. Nevins, *A Diary of Battle,* 353.

71. Small, *Road to Richmond,* 135.

72. Tower, *Lee's Adjutant*, 160.

73. Grant, *Memoirs,* 569.

74. Ibid., 569–70.

75. Quoted in Jeffrey D. Wert, *Sword of Lincoln: The Army of the Potomac* (New York: Simon & Schuster, 2005), 365.

76. Quoted in Noah Andre Trudeau, *Bloody Roads South: The Wilderness to Cold Harbor, May–June 1864* (Boston: Little, Brown, 1989), 316.

77. Small, *Road to Richmond,* 154.

78. John R. Sellers, ed., *A People at War: Civil War Manuscripts from the Holdings of the Library of Congress* (Alexandria, VA: Chadwyck-Healey, 1989–1990), Henry C. Heisler to sister, July 30, 1864, Henry C. Heisler Papers, reel 49.

79. Russell F. Weigley, *A Great Civil War: A Military and Political History, 1861–1865* (Bloomington: Indiana University Press, 2000), 338–41; Wert, *Sword of Lincoln,* 368–86.

80. William T. Sherman, *The Memoirs of General William T. Sherman* (New York: Da Capo Press, 1984), 2:8.

81. Stephen E. Towne, ed., *A Fierce, Wild Joy: The Civil War Letters of Colonel Edward J. Wood, 48th Indiana Volunteer Infantry Regiment* (Knoxville: University of Tennessee Press, 2007), 190.

82. Brooks D. Simpson and Jean V. Berlin, eds., *Sherman's Civil War: Selected Correspondence of William T. Sherman, 1860–1865* (Chapel Hill: University of North Carolina Press, 1999), 696, 697.

83. Ibid., 729–31.

84. Lyman Richard Comey, ed., *A Legacy of Valor: The Memoirs and Letters of Captain Henry Newton Comey, 2nd Massachusetts Infantry* (Knoxville: University of Tennessee Press, 2004), 212–13.

85. Mark Grimsley, *The Hard Hand of War: Union Military Policy toward Southern Civilians, 1861–1865* (Cambridge: Cambridge University Press, 1995), 174–75, 190–200.

86. Simpson and Berlin, *Sherman's Civil War,* 772.

87. Ibid., 772–74.

88. Nathaniel Cheairs Hughes Jr., ed., *The Civil War Memoir of Philip Daingerfield Stephenson, D.D.: Private, Company K, 13th Arkansas Volunteer Infantry and Loader, Piece No. 4, 5th Company, Washington Artillery, Army of Tennessee, CSA* (Baton Rouge: Louisiana State University Press, 1995), 288.

2 FILLING THE RANKS

RALLYING TO THE COLORS

Martial enthusiasm spread through the Upper South in the wake of the surrender of Fort Sumter and Lincoln's call to put down the rebellion. Meetings, rallies, and calls to arms brought out the men in numbers that would certainly dampen the confidence of Yankee aggressors. Those men who had been happy to remain in the Union as long as the federal government had left alone their cousins in the Deep South now were eager to pick up arms to stop Lincoln's aggressive response to Sumter. In Tennessee, even before formal secession and despite the strong Unionist sentiment in the eastern part of the state, 20 companies of men mustered near Knoxville to defend the Confederacy.[1] Likewise, Virginia's governor John Letcher called out the militia, and companies that had been inactive since the capture of John Brown rapidly formed up to march on the federal arsenal at Harpers Ferry.[2] It was a process repeated throughout the newly seceded states.

The patriotic town meetings that followed in the wake of the firing on Fort Sumter stirred Northern souls just as the call for independence rallied Southerners to their new national banner. Speeches, songs, a Mexican War veteran, and perhaps a woman who audibly regretted her sex for keeping her from defending the flag fueled the enthusiasm of the crowd. Northern town meetings often concluded with men stepping forward to volunteer for companies of soldiers that would be gathered up into regiments organized by their state governments.

Not to be outdone by their new enemies, numerous eager volunteers pressed themselves onto the various military organizations being formed. On April 21, 1861, Josiah Favill went to volunteer his services to a three-month company of the 71st New York, but he discovered that "it was not so easy to join this regiment, as the armory was crowded with men, mostly fine young fellows, all crazy to be enrolled." Fearing he would be left out, he directly approached the company's captain and convinced him "to squeeze me in."[3] Favill was not alone. Men rushed to join companies giving little consideration to anything "beyond the opportunity to go," recalled Wisconsin veteran Rufus Dawes, except for "the fear that some one else would get ahead and crush the Rebellion before they got there."[4] Consequently, volunteers filled their states' initial quotas so rapidly that some governments found it difficult to cope with the martial enthusiasm. The Jasper

Grays of Iowa had to wait over two months before the governor could accept them into the state's volunteer Fifth Iowa Infantry regiment.[5]

Many Northern men thought they would miss out on a grand adventure, given how quickly their states produced their required quotas. If in April or May 1861 they were not accepted into a volunteer company or if their company was not accepted into a regiment, they could find themselves marching home, missing out on the adventure of a lifetime. Such a worry, New Jerseyan Robert McAllister told his wife, "dampens our feelings very much."[6] This concern was not unwarranted, and men went beyond the borders of their home states to find places in regiments. Other patriots agreed to longer enlistment periods to guarantee that they would have a hand in subduing the rebellion. When a Lowell, Massachusetts, company of 90-day men learned that the state was no longer accepting short-term volunteers, they voted to serve for three years.[7] After all, most of these men assumed that the war would be over and they snug before their home fires in the not too distant future.

Other men had no choice but to wait. Ben Hirst and his neighbors in the Rockville, Connecticut, state militia company were prepared to go to war in the spring of 1861 but discovered that they were superfluous soldiers, Connecticut having filled its quota of 90-day men before they could present themselves. Some men tried to find a place in a three-year regiment, but the company itself remained home and met for regular drills, until its members entered the federal service during the summer of 1862.[8] Farther west, in the wake of a patriotic town meeting where "patriotism was effervescent," 30 young men joined the Prescott, Wisconsin, Guards only to learn that the governor did not need them. Unwilling to give up on the war, they "began drilling every day, studied the tactics, erected a liberty pole mounted by a bayonet, pointing south, with the stars and stripes floating from its top." They soon became part of the Sixth Regiment Wisconsin Volunteer Infantry.[9]

In the North and in the South, states and communities relied on local men of reputation and wealth, men with professional stature, men who had some military experience, or ambitious individuals who had a desire for a commission to raise or command new companies and regiments. Governors appointed such luminaries to positions of authority, asked them for advice, promised those who were successful recruiters officer's commissions, or simply accepted their services as a fait accompli when they were volunteered, at times with groups of recruits in tow. Sometimes the process was a bit irregular. Thomas Hyde, then residing in Brunswick, Maine, discovered no recruiting officer in his town. Not to be discouraged in his wish to recruit a company of men in the wake of the First Bull Run, he found a local lawyer to swear him into the United States' service; he then embarked for the state capital to secure official papers.[10]

Some communities relied on resident army veterans to teach them how to prepare their new companies for war. Thus Ulysses Grant provided one of his earliest services to the Union cause by giving the women of Galena, Illinois, "a description of the United States uniform for infantry."[11] States turned to native sons in the regular army to find colonels to organize and train their new regiments. Oliver Otis Howard, for example, took leave from his posting at the U.S. Military Academy to tend to the needs of Maine, soon resigning his regular army commission after learning, as a correspondent told him, that "public opinion" was "unanimous in favor" of him accepting the colonelcy of the Third Maine Infantry.[12]

In the nascent Confederacy, the construction of military organizations followed patterns comparable to the Northern states, from the grand activities of wealthy citizens and large slaveholders to the more prosaic efforts of ambitious local men. In Bainbridge, Georgia, G. W. Lewis, a local tailor, who was the adjutant of the county militia, with "a desire to distinguish himself," set off to raise a company of local men with resources more limited than those of the South Carolina grandee. He hired a wagon, a driver, and a black cook to help him. Packing "an old tent and a couple of drums," he "started out on a tour of the county to induce the few who were yet at home to join his 'company.'" Combining his efforts with those of a prominent local citizen named Augustus Bell, Lewis raised a new company in November 1861 "composed of small schoolboys out for a frolic, old men better suited for consuming rations than fighting, and a few first-class men."[13]

As with their Northern counterparts, Confederate volunteers had a keen desire to get into action; they, too, feared that if they lingered too long at home, they would miss the war. In May 1861, when the men of Edmund DeWitt Patterson's company learned that the governor would not accept any more one-year enlistments, they "immediately reorganized and tendered our services for the war."[14] Charles Trueheart, a Texan and a University of Virginia medical student, "spent months of precious time, money and no small ammount of diligence and patience in fitting myself for a higher position." But he put aside his plans to become an officer by raising troops and joined an artillery unit as a private. "I was too much afraid that another fight would come off without my being in it," he explained to his father in October 1861, "to remain out of active service any longer."[15] Unfortunately, the fledgling central government could not arm all of the enthusiastic volunteers who rushed to the colors, while state governors were already showing a worrisome tendency to keep their resources close to home.

EARLY MOTIVATION TO ENLIST

The recruits of 1861 were caught up in the enthusiasm of the communities in which they lived. They rushed along with their friends into the ranks of the growing armies, sometimes blindly going to war not really understanding the seriousness of the situation and certainly not believing that they would be gone from home for very long.

Some men were naïve, others pragmatic, as they put on the uniforms of their respective causes. Many young men craved the adventure promised by the sounds and sights of war preparation; others were bored with their present situations. Gordon Bradwell, of Bainbridge, Georgia, recalled that he experienced "a very dull summer vacation." Many men had already joined in the spring rush and he and his young school friends "now began to feel lonesome and wanted to go to the war before it should end without their having any part in the 'fun.'" Thus they enlisted, encouraged by thoughts of a "free and easy time in camp."[16]

There were other men who joined because the hard economic times gave them few better opportunities for making a living. In New Jersey, for example, a working man earned less than a private soldier.[17] Indeed, some Yankee prisoners captured at the Battle of Bull Run in July 1861 admitted that they were fighting for the monthly pay.[18] Later, in November, one Union soldier wrote home to his family, "It is no use for you to fret or cry about me for you know if i could have got work i wood not have left you or the children."[19]

Despite the desire for adventure or pay among recruits, there were men who understood their enlistments as a duty to their respective nations. On April 14, 1861, Dick Simpson of South Carolina wrote that his decision to leave college was "no rash act";

rather, he explained, a "feeling of duty urges me to it."[20] Benjamin Baker also believed it was his duty to enlist in the 25th Illinois Infantry, "which as a good citizen I owe to my country, to my friends & to liberty itself."[21] In July 1861, John Quincy Adams Campbell, who became a member of the Fifth Iowa Infantry, explained his noble thinking, also expressing a sense of duty. "I have volunteered to fight this war for the Union and *a government.*" Not desiring glory, he understood "that duty to my country and my God, bid me assist in crushing this wicked rebellion against our government, which rebellion men have instigated to secure their own promotion, to place honor(s), and to secure the extension of that blighting curse—slavery—o'er our fair land."[22]

When all is said and done, early in the war, men probably enlisted for a number of reasons, sometimes not quite understanding their own relative priorities. They might have held frivolous or pragmatic motives even as they tried to make sense of their own noble patriotic feelings. Northern and Southern patriots were moved by their views of secession, slavery, the Constitution, and the nature of liberty. Southerners took up arms to protect their freedom, their homes, their economy, and their right to own slaves. They joined companies to resist Yankee attempts to turn them into second-class citizens. They worried about Republican plans to incite slave unrest or deprive them of access to land in the territories or upset white supremacy. Northerners took up arms to preserve a Union that provided them with the unique benefits of a free-labor society and to stop the Southern slave power from destroying the nation that was the beacon of republican virtue to the rest of the world. Their future and, as Taylor Peirce of Iowa believed, "the happiness and prosperity of our Children" required they put down secession.[23] And there were some Yankees who, early in the war, actually believed that their efforts would bring

SOUTH CAROLINA MEN IN BLUE, SPRING 1861   *Copyright by Review of Reviews Co.*

These officers of the Flying Artillery we see here entering the Confederate service at Sullivan's Island, Charleston Harbor, still wearing the blue uniforms of their volunteer organization. It was one of the state militia companies so extensively organized throughout the South previous to the war. South Carolina was particularly active in this line. After the secession of the State the Charleston papers were full of notices for various military companies to assemble for drill or for the distribution of arms and accoutrements. Number 2 of this group is Allen J. Green, then Captain of the Columbia Flying Artillery (later a Major in the Confederate service). No. 4 is W. K. Bachman, then a 4th Lieutenant, later Captain in the German Volunteers, a state infantry organization that finally entered the artillery service and achieved renown as Bachman's Battery. No. 3 is Wilmot D. de Saussure; No. 7 is John Waites, then Lieutenant and later Captain of another company. After 1863, when the Confederate resources were waning, the Confederate soldiers were not ashamed to wear the blue clothing brought in by the blockade runners.

South Carolina artillerists still wore their blue prewar volunteer company uniforms when they were mustered into the Confederate service in the spring of 1861. (*Library of Congress*)

an end to slavery. In March 1862, Lieutenant Douglas Risley, who was then recruiting in Indiana, assured his parents that "had I a thousand lives, & the laying them down would release a thousand slaves, I would give them."[24]

Men joined, regardless of region, because they believed it was their duty and because they believed their honor was at stake. Some men, living in the shadow of the accomplishments of the Revolutionary generation, considered the war to be a gift in that it provided them with a significant, demanding purpose, perhaps bringing meaning to lives considered mundane and lacking in heroic challenges. The ambitious among them might have wished to position themselves for some future advancement. Or perhaps they wished to win the affection of women or escape their scorn. The Alabama women who in April 1861 promised to provide hoop skirts to shirkers probably touched a nerve among "all those rich young men...who now refuse to respond to their country's call."[25]

Northern and Southern volunteers feared being branded as cowards, and they wished to prove their manhood to themselves, their families, and their communities, even if it resulted in death. In 1861 Marcus Woodcock, the Kentucky Unionist, went off to war claiming to be a patriot, but he also wished "to obtain with my own arms a right to distinction while I should be defending my Country's rights."[26] John W. Chase, a Massachusetts artillery man, told his brother in December 1861 that he enlisted to put down the rebellion; if he failed to do his duty, he would never return home to allow people to brand him a coward.[27] And in September 1861, at the beginning of his diary and his military career, Illinois native Valentine Randolph asked that if found on his body after a battle, the volume be returned to his mother with the inscription, "He died like a man."[28]

WANING ENTHUSIASM

In the North and South, enlistments dwindled by the end of 1861 and, in early 1862, continued to diminish. In the South, as early as 1861, some of the passion to enlist dampened as Confederate policies reinforced expectations for a longer, more burdensome war. Few Southerners had expected the war to drag on much beyond the summer of their victory at Manassas Junction. The Confederate government, strapped by the demands placed on its limited resources, soon promised to equip only those men who volunteered for three years or the duration of the war. It was a policy that alienated men of modest means, who interpreted it as a way of allowing wealthier neighbors the option of taking on a shorter military obligation.

Also, the war itself was taking a human toll, which further sapped the enthusiasm of many men still at home. Even during the early days of the war, inactivity brought second thoughts about the chances for winning the glory that volunteers had expected. As fighting and camp life progressed into 1862, companies shrank because of the inevitable casualties. Soldiers wrote home to their brothers and friends warning them that the army was a difficult life, to be avoided, if possible. Critically, at a time when enlistments lagged and the war appeared to be far from over, those men who had volunteered for one year during the spring of 1861, now tired of camp discipline and the tedium of military life, happily contemplated returning home once their terms expired, well satisfied that they had done their part for the Confederacy. North Carolinian Thomas Fanning Wood noted how "men and officers were equally excited" about the approaching end of their one-year enlistments.[29]

Enthusiasm for Southern independence did not wane, but in some quarters the willingness to leave home to fight for it lessened. In November 1861, for example,

Rudolph Coreth noted that his Texas company consisted of farmers who "only want to defend the coast of Texas."[30] Elsewhere in the Confederacy, able-bodied men still at home were worried about abandoning their farms and businesses for a year of military service, even if they were willing to serve in a local defense force for several months at a time, and there were governors who encouraged them to join state armies that kept men from the front lines. However, the desire to stay close to home made perfect sense to many men and politicians. In Texas, for example, throughout the war men preferred to enlist in the state militia rather than the Confederate service. Believing that their state was too isolated to expect much assistance from Richmond, they took up arms to protect local economies, to guard against slave troubles, to protect a significant coastline, and to patrol the Indian frontier, all legitimate concerns.[31]

In the Northern states, various developments also influenced the eagerness of men to join or not as the war progressed beyond the quick fight so many people had believed it would be. Economic difficulties caused by the sectional crisis might have moved men to enlist in 1861, but by 1862 a growing war economy absorbed workers who otherwise might have contemplated joining. There were Northerners who, by the middle of 1862, had opportunity to reflect on the carnage of battle, and soldiers who had lost their enthusiasm for the close quarters of camp life. In September 1862 New Jersey soldier Peter Vredenburgh warned off his younger brother, at least if he had to serve as an enlisted man. "You had better send him to the state's prison at once," he told his father. "If he expects fun and excitement…he will be most emphatically mistaken."[32]

The bloodbath at Antietam in September 1862 and then, before the end of the year, another at Fredericksburg dampened martial ardor. Both battles seemed to confirm in the minds of many Northerners the inept way in which generals squandered men's lives, another disincentive to enlist. Also, soldiers returning to the North to invalid were advertisements against enlisting. The Michigan quartermaster general noted in his December 1862 report that "when a sick or disabled soldier returns home and tells of the privations endured by him or some of his comrades, recruiting ceases in his neighborhood."[33] Finally, some Northerners were less willing to risk their lives for the expanding Northern war aims, which came to include emancipation by the end of 1862.

In the North, even as early as the end of the summer of 1861, some recruiters ran into difficulties. Companies no longer filled as rapidly as they had, and competition for recruits was more intense. New Yorker Josiah Favill, mustered out of his 90-day regiment, decided that he would return to the military as a commissioned officer, not an enlisted man. To accomplish this end, he learned that he would have to recruit a number of men for the 57th New York Volunteer Infantry. Other men had the same idea, for New York and Brooklyn "were transformed into immense recruiting camps." Tents filled parks and public squares. Flags flew, bands played, speakers exhorted, and "immense colored bills" drew the public's attention to the advantages of joining one or another three-year regiment. However, he realized that "a great change had come over the spirit of the people" since the spring. "Then everybody wanted to go," he concluded. "Now, apparently, most people wanted to stay at home." Having limited success in the metropolis, he traveled up state to Oswego, placed advertisements in the local papers, and recruited about 30 men, who promptly deserted for a locally raised company. Moving on to Poughkeepsie, he had some success in recruiting a handful of men, took ill, and returned home to learn that the city finally yielded the necessary recruits. Clearly he discovered that increased competition for recruits and the waning enthusiasm for the service made the task of earning his commission very hard work.[34]

During 1862 Northerners responded to recruiting rallies in ways that were reminiscent of earlier days, but in fewer and less enthusiastic numbers. Across the country, it took a bit more effort to fill their companies. Abner Small of Maine noted that "recruiting was a discouraging business." In his effort to raise sufficient men to earn an officer's commission, he noted, "I pleaded, cried, swore, and prayed, yet only two patriots were enrolled to my credit."[35] Charles Dana Miller ran into much complacency among the men of western Ohio, where he tried his hand at recruiting. In one town he failed to secure the assistance of patriotic speakers who had been so common at town meetings of 1861. On another occasion at Newark, Ohio, he had the help of drums, flags, speakers, and an applauding crowd, but to no avail. In the end it was a process of signing up one man at a time, not the crowds of volunteers common after Fort Sumter.[36]

Certainly there remained many patriots who, for various understandable reasons, responded to the needs of the country later than some of their neighbors. For some Northerners, particular battle losses or changes in personal situations moved them to enlist, while for others, troubled consciences prompted them to do their duty. Patriotic feelings finally overcame their concerns for the well-being of their families or for their employment obligations. James T. Miller of Pennsylvania joined the army in the fall following the Union fiasco at Bull Run; in early 1862, writing from Camp Reed at Erie, Pennsylvania, he made it clear to his family that he had the heart of a patriot: "i feel that the cause i inlisted is one of the most just and holy that mortal man ever engaged in," he reassured his concerned parents.[37] In the spring of 1862, Samuel Calvin Jones, a young, unmarried Iowa farmer, also admitted that "the feeling had developed that we had a very serious matter on our hands" and his country needed him.[38] For George A. Allen of Massachusetts, it was the October 1861 fight at Ball's Bluff that convinced him to leave his wife and child for the army. His brother had died in that battle, and he was determined to take his place.[39]

For some volunteers, even with an improved economy, the army still offered a job opportunity. In the spring of 1862, Charles Wellington Reed of Massachusetts enlisted as a bugler because he could find no work that would make good use of his musical and drawing talents; in addition, as a musician, he would receive higher pay than that of a regular private and still find time to draw.[40] Not only regular pay, but bounties, too, proved to be strong inducements for many to sign on. In July 1862 the Lincoln government called for an additional 300,000 three-year enlistments, and in August, another 300,000 men for nine months' service. In the wake of the Seven Days Battle, the Philadelphia Corn Exchange, eager to make a contribution to the war effort, offered significant bounties to suitable recruits. Volunteers filled the regiment in 30 days.[41]

Bounties were common inducements offered for military service throughout America's history. During the Civil War they sometimes made the difference for many wavering men and helped recruiters fill their regiments. As early as December 1861, the Confederate government offered a $50 bounty to recruits, an amount increased in early 1864 to $100, paid in greatly devalued Confederate money. States such as Virginia did likewise. Bounties at the outset of the war made a difference for soldiers' families, and men such as Louisianan William Henry King made it clear that soldiers expected the money their government had promised them.[42] However, cash inducements were never as important in the South as they were in the North, perhaps because the Confederate government usually failed to honor bounty promises.

Northern governments much more effectively used cash inducements. Not only did the central government offer bounties for enlisting, but so, too, did states and local communities. Some Northern states also offered extra pay and relief money for families to attract volunteers. Almost immediately after Fort Sumter, Rhode Island offered its volunteers an extra monthly stipend of $12, and Boston gave its soldiers an additional $20. Rochester, New York, and Philadelphia, Pennsylvania, provided funds for soldiers' families. After the Lincoln administration called for three-year volunteers, the federal government also provided a $100 bounty.[43]

As was the case in the South, claiming such bounties, bonuses, and family stipends did not necessarily mean that enlistees were simple mercenaries. Such funds were critical and fair for men who had hesitated to join because of obligations to families, farms, and jobs. For example, two regiments raised in Courtland County, New York, the first in 1861 and the second in 1862 with the help of bounties, shared similar characteristics, but for the fact that the latter regiment had a higher percentage of married men, including a significant number with children. Perhaps bounties eased men's consciences about their family obligations, allowing them to act on their patriotic impulses.[44]

The Northern bounty system, despite its benefits, also created problems. In the summer of 1862, the prospects of a militia draft led to what essentially became bidding wars among communities for recruits so that those communities might avoid the unpleasantness of a draft. Bounty competition placed a financial strain on all levels of government because of the unexpected length of the war. It also brought into the ranks a number of men who played the system as a money-making scheme, skipping away to rejoin another regiment and claim another bounty. By the end of 1862, 100,000 Union men were absent without leave, and many of them had deserted because of the great temptation of claiming another bounty.[45]

CONSCRIPTION

In 1862, in the Confederacy, piecemeal approaches to manpower needs gave way to a new national policy of conscription. Southern politicians concluded that they were not going to be able to rely solely on volunteerism to maintain the defenses of their country. It was a critical time, and those men who had enlisted for one year's service were about to leave the army. As much as one-third of the manpower of Confederate armies consisted of one-year volunteers, so the loss would be crippling. Indeed, South Carolinian Tally Simpson reported on April 15, 1861, while serving in Virginia, that his regiment's one-year term of enlistment had expired the previous day. "To my extreme astonishment," half of the Third South Carolina Volunteers refused to reenlist, despite "an appeal, the most beautiful I ever heard." The men left the army "determined to return home, marching to the music of the enemy's cannon."[46] The central government had to take forceful action to keep its armies in the field, and that meant drafting the men it needed.

On April 16, 1862, the Confederacy became the first of the two governments to resort to conscription. That law extended the service terms of one-year volunteers who would have been free to go home in May 1862 an additional two years and made eligible for the draft men aged 18 through 35, which, the resentful veteran Sam Watkins recalled, made a soldier into a machine. The upper age range of conscription eligibility of that law rose to 45 by a law passed September 27, 1863; another law passed in February 1864 expanded potential draftees to include 17-year-olds as well as men aged 46 through 50, with the intent of using the youngest and the oldest draftees as reserves. Some men resorted to purchasing the services of substitutes to avoid conscription, until their government prohibited the practice in December 1863. As early as June 1862, men were already willing to pay up to $1,000 for a substitute, and wealthy individuals offered upward to twice that amount. Newspaper ads solicited substitutes, and brokers recruited immigrants as replacements, just as their counterparts did in the North. During 1863, estimates from various sources for the number of men serving as substitutes in Confederate armies ranged from a low of 50,000 to a high of 150,000.

Shortly after passage of the conscription act, the government provided for various employment exemptions for certain occupations considered essential for the war effort, including government officials and railroad workers, making the Confederate system less than all-encompassing conscription. In October 1862 it also exempted overseers or owners of 20 or more slaves, a particularly troublesome exemption for those less wealthy families whose men could not qualify, but one that was related to the real fear that Lincoln would use his Emancipation Proclamation to agitate the Confederacy's slaves to rebellion. That particular exemption may well have done more harm than good as it promoted class resentment among nonslaveholders in and out of the army, while contributing to the serious increase in desertions that followed the implementation of conscription. As Sam Watkins later complained, "It gave us the blues; we wanted twenty negroes."[47] Exemptions became more problematical to obtain by the time of the final conscription law of February 1864, but throughout the Confederacy, there were men who took advantage of loopholes in the draft laws with the help of physicians and state politicians, depriving the Confederacy of the soldiers it needed.

On July 17, 1862, President Lincoln signed the Militia Act, which allowed states to draft men for nine months' service, if necessary, to meet an assigned quota, but bounties helped limit—although not eliminate—the need to force men to serve. That law, with its threat of conscription, however, was only a prelude to the Enrollment Act of March 1863, which gave the federal government the power to draft troops. Neither the Militia Act nor the Enrollment Act was as burdensome as either one might have been, and there remained ample opportunities for individuals to avoid conscription when the president used the latter law to call for drafts on four occasions. And Northern states and communities worked hard to avoid the unhappiness of involuntary service, raising more money for bounties and luring men from other communities with ever-increasing financial inducements.

Despite the prospects of financial reward, there remained men who wished to avoid service. They paid commutation fees when the government allowed them during the early drafts and secured substitutes when they no longer had that option. Even the less wealthy could avoid service by joining draft clubs that would pay for substitutes or by tapping into the resources of their communities, which raised funds for substitutes. Almost 4,200 men from New Jersey paid the $300 commutation fee, while almost 5,500 men secured substitutes; the draft lotteries netted only 951 men in that state. In York County, Pennsylvania, the draft brought in 68 men, while 613 paid the $300 commutation fee and 159 others provided substitutes. All told, the summer of 1863 draft drew the names of 292,441 men, with 88,171 of them held to service, but 52,228 paid the commutation fee and another 26,002 furnished substitutes, while only 9,881 draftees actually ended up in the army. Even later drafts were more likely to force men to volunteer or provide substitutes than actually serve as a result of being conscripted. The drafts in the spring of 1864, fall of 1864, and spring of 1865 followed a similar pattern. All four federal draft lotteries produced a total of 776,829 names, with 206,678 obligated to report for induction, but only 46,347 men were actually forced to serve; 86,724 took advantage of commutation, and another 73,607 hired substitutes. In the North, legal draft evasion became as much a part of home front activity as knitting socks for soldiers at the front.[48] Even so, illegal evasion was also part of the Northerners' efforts to avoid service, as men simply failed to answer the call. Some men simply did not report. An approximate 40,000–50,000 men failed to submit to early state drafts during 1861 and 1862, but 161,244 men also failed to submit to the federal calls.[49]

Not only individuals, but entire communities in both regions rose up in opposition to the draft, making it even more difficult to satisfy the armies' needs. In one case, in Randolph County, Alabama, a mob broke into the jail and liberated draft dodgers held there, but the problem was more widespread than one violent outburst would suggest.[50] Many a Southerner, including state officials, agreed with the assessment of the editor of the Raleigh, North Carolina, *Standard,* who believed that the law was "inexpedient, unnecessary, oppressive, and unconstitutional," while others could readily accept the view of Georgians, who considered the 1862 conscription law to be "disgraceful."[51] Thus, in North Carolina, many loyal Confederates resented the added burden, while Unionists resisted to the point that efforts to enforce the draft lead to bloodshed in the western mountain hollows of the state.[52] In the Midwest and in the eastern Pennsylvania mountains, communities sheltered men who chose not to comply with the law. The New York City draft riots of July 1863 were only the most bloody of several collective acts of resistance to conscription.[53]

Despite such resistance, conscription promoted volunteering among men who considered forced service to be dishonorable. In Texas, the 12th Texas Cavalry, organized in 1861, had in its ranks a high proportion of young, eager recruits; two regiments in the same cavalry brigade, organized in 1862, had higher numbers of older men in its ranks, who had decided to join, rather than be subjected to conscription.[54] In the lower Chattahoochee Valley region of Georgia, numerous recruits hastened to enlist before they could fall victim to the first draft law, allowing them to have some say in the units in which they would serve and to be able to collect the $50 bounty.[55] Elsewhere in the Confederacy and in the United States, the threat of conscription encouraged enlistment, even if reluctantly. As John C. Arnold explained, even though he did not care for the hardship of military life, "I am glad that I Enlisted Indeed I am if I would a staid at home I would a bin Drafted Before this I Know I would a Bin."[56]

In the North, continued volunteering diminished some of the need for conscripts. Some regiments, desirous to have their ranks replenished with honest men and not the sort who would allow themselves to be drafted, sent recruiters back to their home states. James M. Randall, for example, along with a number of other officers of the 21st Wisconsin, established recruiting offices in the counties where companies had formed and eventually returned with 127 men. That modest success, he later reflected, "was considered as doing well."[57]

The reenlistment of veterans, the buying of foreign-born substitutes, and the use of African Americans also helped keep the ranks filled with men more willing than draftees. So, too, did the government's call for short-term volunteers to serve for six months in June 1863 and for 100 days in April 1864, which brought in over 16,000 men and over 83,000 men, respectively. In the end, a relatively small number of men actually found themselves forced into military service by conscription. The majority of Union soldiers joined the army or reenlisted even before the federal draft was enacted, while during the federal draft years of 1863 through 1865, only a little over 13 percent of the men brought into the service consisted of conscripts and substitutes. The numbers were higher for the Confederacy, but nowhere close to overwhelming. About 21 percent of the men serving in the Confederate armies were conscripts or substitutes.[58] In the end, men who volunteered, for whatever reasons, sustained the armies.

UNION ARMY VETERAN VOLUNTEERS

The constant quest for new soldiers brought new blood into both Confederate and Union armies, but the easiest way to maintain regimental strength was to keep the men who were already enlisted in the ranks. The problem for both sides became almost immediately apparent as the war outlasted expectations for a quick victory. The Confederacy solved the problem of expiring one-year terms of enlistment by passing its first conscription law, which forced men to stay on beyond their original contracts, although it would continue to face continued manpower needs and the additional problem of desertion.

Northern armies were similarly troubled by the expiration of the 90-day terms of the volunteers of the spring of 1861. Many of those men who had fulfilled their obligations wanted to go home; some simply left when their terms expired, as they were entitled to do. In at least one critical situation in western Virginia, a general begged the 90-day men to stay, but they "laid down their rifles and gear and headed for home." Massachusetts soldier Henry Comey believed, "It was a sorry sight to those of us who intend to stick to it until the Union is saved."[59]

Ninety-day regiments usually returned home in orderly fashion, but entire companies refused to reenlist. Many of the early volunteers considered their duty done or had had enough of the hard army life. In May 1861 James Gillette, for example, promised his parents that he would not reenlist, at least not as a private, because the "physical duties are too severe and the mental too light." At that time he looked "forward to a speedy return home and resumption of my office duties in New York."[60]

There were, however, individuals who were still inclined to serve their country. Politicians and generals understood the value of keeping these "veterans" in the army and urged these short-term volunteers to reenlist for the duration. In some regiments, reluctant men felt the sting of being shamed in front of their old comrades if they decided to forgo continued service, which might have convinced some men to stay in the army. In many cases, 90-day soldiers of 1861 used their limited experience to become non-commissioned officers and commissioned officers. Gillette soon abandoned his plans to return to office work and went on to serve as an officer. And Josiah Favill first went to war as a private in the 71st New York but, on his discharge, made plans to secure a commission. Serving as an officer, he concluded, "will be more to my taste than serving in the ranks."[61]

Reenlisting probably was easier for the first 90-day veterans, considering their belief that they would not need to serve out their three-year contracts. However, the war continued beyond those optimistic expectations, and it became apparent by the summer of 1863 that the army would be mustering out over half of the three-year regiments before the next year of fighting was over. Once again, the federal government attempted to sway decisions to stay in the service by offering bonus money; on June 25, 1863, the War Department authorized bounty payments for reenlistments of three years or the duration. The government hoped additional perquisites would further encourage reenlistment. It offered not only bounties of $400, but 30-day furloughs and free transportation home. Also, if most of a regiment's men reenlisted, the regiment could remain in service identified as a veteran regiment, and the regiment's men could wear red and blue veteran's chevrons.[62]

Regiments had meetings to discuss mass reenlistments. Officers attempted to persuade them to stay in the ranks, making speeches to put some pressure on their men. In other cases, a little peer pressure and the lure of leave worked on the reluctant veterans. In October 1863 Wisconsin soldier William Ray listened to the speeches, but for family reasons hesitated to reenlist. Some of the boys "made considerable sport" of him, but after a talk with his persuasive captain, he changed his mind. "This going home & getting a furlough and getting the Big Bounty," Ray explained, was attractive, but even more so was the fact that "we will belong to the Veteran Corps and have the Badge of Honor to wear."[63]

For some soldiers, there remained the appeal of staying with friends who had shared their hardships and the fear of being left behind as their fellows enjoyed the promised home leave. In January 1864, as the Second Michigan began the process of reenlisting its three-year volunteers, for example, "a considerable number thinking they were likely to be left in the lurch came forward & were sworn." Thus the Second Michigan's "list was soon raised far above the required number."[64] Clearly the additional inducements had an effect on the men. Taking 30 days off from army life, visiting families, and letting off some steam, in addition to collecting some extra money and prestige, provided attractive arguments for some soldiers.[65] In January 1864 Captain Alfred L. Hough, a mustering officer, told his wife of his experience with some of these veterans. "How happy they do look on their way home I expect they will cut up some shindys when they get there," he warned, "but you must bear with them, for they are brave fellows and have only one short month of recreation before returning here to fight more battles and leave some of their number to add to the thousands of graves that now mark the scenes of their former work."[66] Fair warning to the home folk, for when the 76th Ohio arrived at Columbus, the men searched the city "for good food and some fun and almost caused a riot at the theater." When they returned home to Newark, however, they were delighted by the welcome provided by friends and family. One of their officers reported that the men had a fine time during their 30-day leave.[67]

New Yorker Colonel Charles Wainwright noted that these furloughs for unmarried men often meant entanglements with the opposite sex, some that lasted long after their return to the front. "Some four or five hundred dollars cash in hand set the girls wild after the men, so that it was hard work to get clear of them." While some of the men lost their money to women, the "most steady got married." Wainwright believed that "in some companies a third and even a half have been spliced while away."[68]

Once again, these veteran soldiers could have multiple motives for staying on. Illinois veteran John Follett "called an officer a low lived son of a bitch" for soliciting his reenlistment; he avoided any disciplinary action because the officer was "so drunk he could n[o]t resent it." Follett believed his wife and children needed him more than did the army; however, in the end, he reenlisted in part to secure the bounty to add to his family's nest egg. At the same time, he made it clear that he wished to do his patriotic duty and protect the future of a united nation. "If what we have done shall cause our children and our children's children to praise the old flag and love the old union more than they otherwise would have done," he explained to his wife, "we shall be well paid for all we have endured."[69]

Many of the veteran volunteers also understood the symbolic importance of their reenlistments. Iowa soldier George Remley explained that "the willingness of the old

Group of soldiers of Co. G., 71st New York Volunteers, posed in front of tent. (*Library of Congress*)

soldiers to re-enlist must be very disheartening to the rebels. They will find that they can't tire *us* out."[70] Charles W. Gould of New York speculated that reenlistments of veterans "must make Johnny reb feel rather queer to think that 2½ years has not made our boys afraid of them nor discouraged them."[71] And Wisconsin soldier William Ray wrote, "Just think the old troops going in again after having such hard times, it shows our hearts are in the work. The thought will make the Rebels tremble."[72]

Such men might have already decided to reenlist because they were committed to seeing the war through to a Union victory. Elisha Hunt Rhodes admitted he had expected the war to be short, but now that it continued with no end in sight, he expected to stay "to see the end of this wicked rebellion." "The United States need the services of her sons," he concluded. "I feel I owe a duty to my country."[73]

There were those veterans who simply found army life appealing and decided to stay in the service. Rhodes was a patriot, but he admitted that his fondness for the soldier's life contributed to his desire to remain with his regiment.[74] Another soldier reported that officers who had resigned were returning to the service as privates. While acknowledging that patriotism played a role for some of them, he noted that "after they were home a long time something unconquerable drew them back into the army; it was something irresistible that pulled them back into the army. It had become almost second nature for them, a lover of the wild life as it exists in the army." Also, he speculated that army life might have made these men less suitable for the civilian economy. "The second reason that brought these officers back into the army is probably that they spent all their savings," he explained. "Then too, they are too lazy for real work, because the long time in the army, had accustomed them to idleness."[75]

For some Yankees, however, the inducements were not sufficient to convince them to remain in the army. Some men believed that their three-year commitment was sufficient proof of their patriotism. They had done enough, and now it was someone else's turn take up the burden.[76] In January 1864 a veteran reported that there were many soldiers in the Army of the Cumberland who believed that they should not reenlist until the stay-at-homes had joined the army. They still were willing to fight "until the rebellion's last rib is broken." However, they had done some arithmetic and believed that "about one million young men from 18 to 22-years old are sitting at home doing nothing for the grand cause." People at home find it easy to sit by the stove and win battles and criticize armies, he complained, but "when...the call 'to arms' is sent to them, they crawl into their fathers' shirt pockets or hide under the counter." This attitude at home, he explained, was "the main reason" that more men did not reenlist.[77] Indeed, some men, especially professional men and skilled workers, believed it was unfair that they and their families should be facing financial hardship, while others make money from the war.[78] In the end, 136,507 men reenlisted as veteran volunteers.[79]

That number indicated some progress, but many veterans still returned home by the fall of 1864. The government attempted to convince these men to return to the army. In 1864 Union commander Ulysses S. Grant began thinking about an entire corps of veteran soldiers. In October 1864 the War Department put into motion the formation of such a corps, which would consist of men who have served at least two years commanded by officers who had served at least two years, commanded by the popular soldier, General Winfield Scott Hancock. The government still appealed to the mercenary side of the men, despite the prestige involved in belonging to an elite corps. Federal, state, and local bounties could amount to over $1,000 at the peak of federal bounty offers in November 1864. However, the corps never attracted sufficient numbers to become a reality. The army had hoped to recruit 20,000 veterans, but General Hancock's efforts brought back only 4,400 men.[80]

MALINGERERS, INVALIDS, AND DESERTERS

Recruiters, officers, and government officials worked hard to maintain unit strength, but malingerers and invalids who used their wounds to avoid field service hurt their efforts throughout the war. Before battles, soldiers straggled to avoid combat, a problem that Robert E. Lee considered ruinous to his army. After battles they found excuses not to return to their units. In May 1864, for example, a Union report indicated that there were a number of slightly hurt malingerers in the Fredericksburg, Virginia, area, some of whom were suffering from self-inflicted wounds. In such cases, the armies' own provost guards tried to locate the frauds and return them to the fight.[81]

Farther from the front, there were examples of invalided soldiers home on leave using their wounds as excuses to remain away from their units. In September 1863 Captain Samuel Fiske of Connecticut explained to readers of the Springfield, Massachusetts,

Republican that absenteeism greatly reduced the strengths of regiments and hindered the war effort. "It has come to be a thing expected that those who are wounded or sent to the hospital sick, even slightly and temporarily so, are lost to the regiment for the rest of the war in nine cases out of ten," he complained. Furloughed to recover at home, these men were beyond the reach of the authorities, or ready to use their wounds or illnesses to take leave again if they did return to the army. "I hear of men walking the streets of our villages in Connecticut and Massachusetts, and even at work on their farms and in their shops who belong to the United States," Fiske wrote, "and will be back to their companies by and by with some sort of fixed-up certificates, and draw their back pay, and then staying in the service a few weeks, will again fail in their health, get sent to a hospital and try the same over again."[82] Confederate wounded also used the opportunities provided by furloughs home to avoid service. It was only by the end of 1863 that the Confederate government attempted to stop the loss of manpower that attended the liberal medical furlough system.[83]

Closer to the front, in cities such as Louisville and Nashville, Union "hospital bummers" found ways to move from light hospital duty to finding work with staff officers as orderlies or other duty away from their regiments. In such positions they could also earn additional money working at theaters as "scene shifters" or doing other nonmilitary work. At some point, generals would initiate an effort to force these frauds back to their regiments.[84]

The Union War Department eventually dealt with the problem of fraudulent invalids taking on light duty behind the lines by creating, in the spring of 1863, an Invalid Corps, later known as the Veteran Reserve Corps. The organization freed up fit soldiers to serve at the front, while the invalids, many of whom might have turned up among Fiske's malingerers, did useful service as hospital attendants and guards. Indeed, the War Department required enlisted men to serve out their contracts in the Corps, as long as they could perform minimal duty, a regulation that some men considered quite hard. Despite the protests of these disgruntled soldiers, by the end of the summer of 1865, 60,508 enlisted men and 1,096 officers had remained in the army as part of the Veteran Reserve Corps, making an equal number available for active duty. Dressed in sky blue uniform coats, these men would not be mistaken for malingerers when they did duty behind the lines.[85]

A Confederate Invalid Corps, legislated in February 1864, never took a similar well-established form, but the government's effort to keep men in service for light duty probably provided a few thousand men for rear echelon work. Confederate generals also used hurt soldiers to perform provost duty, thereby freeing fit men for battle. In 1863 the Army of Tennessee made a concerted effort, for example, to replace officers working behind the lines with invalids, and in March 1864 Confederate General Leonidas Polk, commander of the Department of Alabama, Mississippi, and East Louisiana, used invalid officers for provost duty.[86]

Malingerers at least kept up the charade of being about to return to their duties. Northern bounty jumpers and resentful Confederates who deserted, on the other hand, made no false pretense about their intentions. Both governments struggled with the problem of desertion as there were always men who tried to avoid service after being conscripted and men who became disenchanted after doing good service. In the Confederacy, Jefferson Davis tried leniency as well as force to bring these deserters back to the army. In August 1863 he offered amnesty to deserters, which did not have the desired results. Subsequently, he ordered General Gideon Pillow to track down and arrest these men, who were doing serious damage to the war effort.[87] Sometimes the army enjoyed success with its dragnet. In July 1863, according to one report, Confederate soldiers in Atlanta raided a theater. They captured some 300 men who lacked proper leave papers and shipped them back to their regiments in Virginia. In November 1864 the Army of Tennessee arrested whatever able-bodied men came within reach of its march.[88] Over the course of the war, Confederate authorities captured and returned to the army a minimum of 33,000 deserters. Nevertheless, desertion remained a problem for the Confederate army and its Union counterpart. By the end of the war, there were at least 103,400 Confederate recorded instances of desertion.[89] At least 200,000 Union soldiers intentionally deserted, although some of these men were repeat offenders and counted more than once. During the war Union officials captured and returned to the army about 80,000 men.[90] Even when taking into account errors and multiple acts of desertion by individuals, the figures indicate a serious challenge to both governments' efforts to keep up the fighting strengths of their armies.

NOTES

1. John D. Fowler, *Mountaineers in Gray: The Nineteenth Tennessee Volunteer Infantry Regiment, C.S.A.* (Knoxville: University of Tennessee Press, 2004), 18.

2. James I. Robertson Jr., *The Stonewall Brigade* (Baton Rouge: Louisiana State University Press, 1963), 4–6.

3. Josiah Marshall Favill, *The Diary of a Young Officer: Serving with the Armies of the United States during the War of the Rebellion* (Baltimore, MD: Butternut & Blue, 2000), 11.

4. Rufus R. Dawes, *A Full Blown Yankee of the Iron Brigade: Service with the Sixth Wisconsin Volunteers,* ed. Alan T. Nolan (Lincoln: University of Nebraska Press, 1999), 6.

5. Mark Grimsley and Todd D. Miller, eds., *The Union Must Stand: The Civil War Diary of John Quincy Adams Campbell, Fifth Iowa Volunteer Infantry* (Knoxville: University of Tennessee Press, 2000), xiv.

6. James I. Robertson Jr., ed., *The Civil War Letters of General Robert McAllister* (Baton Rouge: Louisiana State University Press, 1998), 29.

7. Charles F. Herberger, ed., *A Yankee at Arms: The Diary of Lieutenant Augustus D. Ayling, 29th Massachusetts Volunteers* (Knoxville: University of Tennessee Press, 1999), 11.

8. Robert L. Bee, ed., *The Boys from Rockville: Civil War Narratives of Sgt. Benjamin Hirst, Company D, 14th Connecticut Volunteers* (Knoxville: University of Tennessee Press, 1998), 10–11.

9. Michael H. Fitch, *Echoes of the Civil War as I Hear Them* (New York: R. F. Fenno, 1905), excerpted in Henry Steele Commager, ed., *The Civil War Archive: The History of the Civil War in Documents,* rev. and exp. by Erik Bruun (New York: Tess Press, 2000), 92–93.

10. Thomas W. Hyde, *Following the Greek Cross, or Memories of the Sixth Army Corps* (Columbia: University of South Carolina Press, 2005), 11–12.

11. Ulysses S. Grant, *Personal Memoirs of U. S. Grant and Select Letters, 1839–1865,* ed. Mary Drake McFeely and William S. McFeely (New York: Library of America, 1990), 153.

12. O. O. Howard, *Autobiography of Oliver Otis Howard, Major General United States Army* (New York: Baker & Taylor, 1907), 113.

13. Pharris Deloach Johnson, ed., *Under the Southern Cross: Soldier Life with Gordon Bradwell and the Army of Northern Virginia* (Macon, GA: Mercer University Press, 1999), 19–20.

14. John G. Barrett, ed., *Yankee Rebel: The Civil War Journal of Edmund DeWitt Patterson* (Knoxville: University of Tennessee Press, 2004), 3.

15. Edward B. Williams, ed., *Rebel Brothers: The Civil War Letters of the Truehearts* (College Station: Texas A&M University Press, 1995), 29.

16. Johnson, *Under the Southern Cross,* 19–20.

17. William Gillette, *Jersey Blue: Civil War Politics in New Jersey, 1854–1865* (New Brunswick, NJ: Rutgers University Press, 1995), 161.

18. Randall Allen and Keith S. Bohannon, eds., *Campaigning with "Old Stonewall": Confederate Captain Ujanirtus Allen's Letters to His Wife* (Baton Rouge: Louisiana State University Press, 1998), 14.

19. Quoted in Bell I. Wiley, *The Life of Billy Yank: The Common Soldier of the Union* (New York: Doubleday, 1971), 38.

20. Guy R. Everson and Edward H. Simpson Jr., eds., *Far, Far from Home: The Wartime Letters of Dick and Tally Simpson, 3rd South Carolina Volunteers* (New York: Oxford University Press, 1994), 3.

21. Quoted in Benson Bobrick, *Testament: A Soldier's Story of the Civil War* (New York: Simon & Schuster, 2003), 36.

22. Grimsley and Miller, *Union Must Stand,* 2–3.

23. Richard L. Kiper, ed., *Dear Catherine, Dear Taylor: The Civil War Letters of a Union Soldier and His Wife* (Lawrence: University Press of Kansas, 2002), 24.

24. Douglas Risley to parents, March 15, 1862, Douglas Risley pension file, Civil War Pension Files, Record Group 15, National Archives Building, Washington, DC.

25. G. Ward Hubbs, ed., *Voices from Company D: Diaries by the Greensboro Guards, Fifth Alabama Infantry Regiment, Army of Northern Virginia* (Athens: University of Georgia Press, 2003), 3.

26. Richard Noe, ed., *A Southern Boy in Blue: The Memoir of Marcus Woodcock, 9th Kentucky Infantry (U.S.A.)* (Knoxville: University of Tennessee Press, 1996), 24.

27. John S. Collier and Bonnie B. Collier, eds., *Yours for the Union: The Civil War Letters of John W. Chase, First Massachusetts Light Artillery* (New York: Fordham University Press, 2004), 28.

28. David D. Roe, ed., *A Civil War Soldier's Diary: Valentine C. Randolph, 39th Illinois Regiment,* with commentary and annotations by Stephen R. Wise (DeKalb: Northern Illinois University Press, 2006), 10.

29. Donald B. Koonce, ed., *Doctor to the Front: The Recollections of Confederate Surgeon Thomas Fanning Wood, 1861–1865* (Knoxville: University of Tennessee Press, 2000), 24–25.

30. Minetta Altgelt Goyne, ed., *Lone Star and Double Eagle: Civil War Letters of a German-Texas Family* (Fort Worth: Texas Christian University Press, 1982), 22.

31. Clayton E. Jewitt, *Texas in the Confederacy: An Experiment in Nation Building* (Columbia: University of Missouri Press, 2002), 113.

32. Bernard A. Olsen, ed., *Upon the Tented Field: An Historical Account of the Civil War as Told by the Men Who Fought and Gave Their Lives* (Red Bank, NJ: Historic Projects, 1993), 38–39.

33. Quoted in Robert E. Mitchell, "The Organizational Performance of Michigan's Adjutant General and the Federal Provost Marshal General in Recruiting Michigan's Boys in Blue," *Michigan Historical Review* 28 (Fall 2002): 125.

34. Favill, *Diary of a Young Officer,* 42–43.

35. Harold Adams Small, ed., *The Road to Richmond: The Civil War Memoirs of Major Abner R. Small of the Sixteenth Maine Volunteers: Together with the Diary That He Kept When He Was a Prisoner of War* (New York: Fordham University Press, 2000), 35.

36. Stewart Bennett and Barbara Tilley, eds., *The Struggle for the Republic: A Civil War Narrative by Brevet Major Charles Dana Miller, 76th Ohio Volunteer Infantry* (Kent, OH: Kent State University Press, 2004), 5–6.

37. Jedediah Mannis and Galen R. Wilson, eds., *Bound to Be a Soldier: The Letters of Private James T. Miller, 111th Pennsylvania Infantry, 1861–1864* (Knoxville: University of Tennessee Press, 2001), 7.

38. Samuel C. Jones, *Reminiscences of the 22nd Iowa Infantry: Giving Its Organization, Marches, Skirmishes, Battles, and Sieges, as Taken from the Diary of Lieutenant S. C. Jones of Company A* (Iowa City: Press of the Camp Pope Book Shop, 1993), 5–6.

39. George W. Allen, "Recommendations for a Position in the Veteran Reserve Corps," Letters Received, box 3, Veteran Reserve Corps, Adjutant General's Office, Record Group 110, National Archives Building, Washington, DC.

40. Eric A. Campbell, ed., *"A Grand Terrible Dramma": From Gettysburg to Petersburg: The Civil War Letters of Charles Wellington Reed* (New York: Fordham University Press, 2000), 10, 13.

41. *From Antietam to Appomattox with the 118th Penna. Vols. Corn Exchange Regiment* (Philadelphia: J.L. Smith, 1892), 3–4.

42. Gary D. Joiner, Marilyn S. Joiner, and Clifton D. Cardin, eds., *No Pardons to Ask, nor Apologies to Make: The Journal of William Henry King, Gray's 28th Louisiana Infantry Regiment* (Knoxville: University of Tennessee Press, 2006), 15.

43. Eugene C. Murdock, *One Million Men: The Civil War Draft in the North* (Madison: State Historical Society of Wisconsin, 1971), 154–69; Fred Albert Shannon, *The Organization and Administration of the Union Army, 1861–1865* (Gloucester, MA: Peter Smith, 1965), 2:50–99.

44. Edmund J. Raus Jr., *Banners South: A Northern Community at War* (Kent, OH: Kent State University Press, 2005), 225.

45. James W. Geary, *We Need Men: The Union Draft in the Civil War* (DeKalb: Northern Illinois University Press, 1991), 15.

46. Everson and Simpson, *Far, Far from Home,* 114.

47. Armstead L. Robinson, "In the Shadow of Old John Brown: Insurrection Anxiety and Confederate Mobilization," *Journal of Negro History* 65 (Autumn 1980): 283, 293–94; Sam Watkins, *"Company Aytch," or a Side Show of the Big Show and Other Sketches,* ed. M. Thomas Inge (New York: Penguin Putnam, 1999), 31.

48. Geary, *We Need Men,* 114–15, 145–46; Gillette, *Jersey Blue,* 158–59; Murdock, *One Million Men,* 178–217, 356; Mark A. Snell, "'If They Would Know What I Know It Would Be Pretty Hard to Raise One Company in York': Recruiting, the Draft, and Society's Response in York County, Pennsylvania, 1861–1865," in *Union Soldiers and the Northern Home Front: Wartime Experiences, Postwar Adjustments,* ed. Paul A. Cimbala and Randall M. Miller (New York: Fordham University Press, 2002), 69–115.

49. Geary, *We Need Men,* 98.

50. David Williams, *Rich Man's War: Class, Caste, and Confederate Defeat in the Lower Chattahoochee Valley* (Athens: University of Georgia Press, 1998), 130.

51. W. Buck Yearns and John G. Barrett, eds., *North Carolina Civil War Documentary* (Chapel Hill: University of North Carolina Press, 1980), 133; Williams, *Rich Man's War,* 130.

52. John C. Inscoe and Gordon B. McKinney, *The Heart of Confederate Appalachia: Western North Carolina in the Civil War* (Chapel Hill: University of North Carolina Press, 2000), 111–14; Philip Shaw Paludan, *Victims: A True Story of the Civil War* (Knoxville: University of Tennessee Press, 1981).

53. Joan E. Cashin, "Deserters, Civilians, and Draft Resistance in the North," in *The War Was You and Me: Civilians in the American Civil War,* ed. Joan E. Cashin (Princeton, NJ: Princeton University Press, 2002), 262–85; Grace Palladino, *Another Civil War: Labor, Capital, and the State in the Anthracite Regions of Pennsylvania, 1840–68* (Urbana: University of Illinois Press, 1990), 95–120; Adrian Cook, *The Armies of the Streets: The New York City Draft Riots of 1863* (Lexington: University Press of Kentucky, 1974).

54. Anne J. Bailey, *Between the Enemy and Texas: Parsons's Texas Cavalry in the Civil War* (Fort Worth: Texas Christian University Press, 1989), xv.

55. Emory M. Thomas, *The Confederate Nation, 1861–1865* (New York: Harper and Row, 1979), 152–54; Geary, *We Need Men,* 4–5; Bell I. Wiley, *The Life of Johnny Reb: The Common Soldier of the Confederacy* (Garden City, NY: Doubleday, 1971), 125–27; Gary W. Gallagher, *The Confederate War: How Popular Will, Nationalism, and Military Strategy Could Not Stave Off Defeat* (Cambridge, MA: Harvard University Press, 1997), 32; Paul D. Escott, *After Secession: Jefferson Davis and the Failure of Confederate Nationalism* (Baton Rouge: Louisiana State University Press, 1992), 80–83, 116–22; Williams, *Rich Man's War,* 129.

56. John R. Sellers, ed., *A People at War: Civil War Manuscripts from the Holdings of the Library of Congress* (Alexandria, VA: Chadwyck-Heakey, 1989–1990), John C. Arnold to wife [Mary Ann] and family, August 2, 1864, reel 1.

57. James M. Randall Diary, chapter 11, eHistory, Ohio State University, Columbus, http://ehistory.osu.edu/osu/sources/letters/randall/.

58. Geary, *We Need Men,* 81, 83–85, 133.

59. Lyman Richard Comey, ed., *A Legacy of Valour: The Memoirs and Letters of Captain Henry Newton Comey, 2nd Massachusetts* (Knoxville: University of Tennessee Press, 2004), 18.

60. Sellers, *A People at War,* James J. Gillette to parents, May 15, 1861, James Jenkins Gillette Papers, reel 32.

61. Favill, *Diary of a Young Officer,* 41.

62. Shannon, *Organization and Administration,* 2:62; Mark M. Boatner III, *The Civil War Dictionary,* rev. ed. (New York: David McKay, 1988), 870; Wiley, *Life of Billy Yank,* 342–43.

63. Lance Herdegen and Sherry Murphy, eds., *Four Years with the Iron Brigade: The Civil War Journal of William Ray, Company F, Seventh Wisconsin Volunteers* (Cambridge, MA: Da Capo Press, 2002), 222–23, 243–44.

64. Stephen W. Sears, ed., *For Country, Cause and Leader: The Civil War Journal of Charles B. Hayden* (New York: Ticknor & Fields, 1993), 351–52.

65. John David Smith and William Cooper Jr., eds., *A Union Woman in Civil War Kentucky: The Diary of Frances Peter* (Lexington: University Press of Kentucky, 2000), 183; Grimsley and Miller, *Union Must Stand,* 142.

66. Robert G. Athearn, ed., *Soldier in the West: The Civil War Letters of Alfred Lacey Hough* (Philadelphia: University of Pennsylvania Press, 1957), 174.

67. Stewart Bennett and Barbara Tilley, eds., *The Struggle for the Life of the Republic: A Civil War Narrative by Brevet Major Charles Dana Miller, 76th Ohio Volunteer Infantry* (Kent, OH: Kent State University Press, 2004), 141, 143, 146–48.

68. Allan Nevins, ed., *A Diary of Battle: The Personal Journals of Colonel Charles S. Wainwright, 1861–1865* (New York: Da Capo Press, 1998).

69. John M. Follett to wife, January 6, 16; February 12, 1864, Follett Brothers Letters, eHistory, Ohio State University, Columbus, http://ehistory.osu.edu/osu/sources/letters/follett_brothers/.

70. Julie Holcomb, ed., *Southern Sons, Northern Soldiers: The Civil War Letters of the Remley Brothers, 22nd Iowa Infantry* (DeKalb: Northern Illinois University Press, 2004), 123.

71. Robert F. Harris and John Niflot, comps., *Dear Sister: The Civil War Letters of the Brothers Gould* (Westport, CT: Praeger, 1998), 115.

72. Herdegen and Murphy, *Four Years with the Iron Brigade,* 223.

73. Robert Hunt Rhodes, ed., *All for the Union: The Civil War Diary and Letters of Elisha Hunt Rhodes* (New York: Vintage Books, 1992), 127–28.

74. Ibid.

75. Joseph R. Reinhart, trans. and ed., *Two Germans in the Civil War: The Diary of John Daeuble and the Letters of Gottfried Rentschler, 6th Kentucky Volunteer Infantry* (Knoxville: University of Tennessee Press, 2004), 66.

76. Rhodes, *All for the Union,* 119; Jennifer Cain Bohrnstedt, ed., *Soldiering with Sherman: The Civil War Letters of George F. Cram* (DeKalb: Northern Illinois University Press, 2000), 108.

77. Reinhart, *Two Germans,* 41.

78. Comey, *A Legacy of Valour,* 165–66.

79. Geary, *We Need Men,* 81.

80. Shannon, *Organization and Administration,* 1:90–91; David M. Jordon, *Winfield Scott Hancock: A Soldier's Life* (Bloomington: Indiana University Press, 1988), 169, 170–74.

81. U.S. War Department, *The War of the Rebellion: A Compilation of the Official Records of the Union and Confederate Armies,* series 1 (Washington, DC: Government Printing Office, 1891), 36(1):235.

82. Stephen W. Sears, ed., *Mr. Dunn Browne's Experiences in the Army: The Civil War Letters of Samuel W. Fiske* (New York: Fordham University Press, 1998), 172–73.

83. Mark A. Weitz, *More Damning Than Slaughter: Desertion in the Confederate Army* (Lincoln: University of Nebraska Press, 2005), 265.

84. Jennifer Cain Bohrnstedt, ed., *While Father Is Away: The Civil War Letters of William H. Bradbury* (Lexington: University Press of Kentucky, 2003).

85. Paul A. Cimbala, "Union Corps of Honor," *Columbiad* 3 (Winter 2000): 59–91.

86. H. H. Cunningham, *Doctors in Gray: The Confederate Medical Service,* 2nd ed. (Baton Rouge: Louisiana State University, 1960), 42–43; Kenneth Radley, *Rebel Watchdog: The Confederate States Army Provost Guard* (Baton Rouge: Louisiana State University Press, 1990), 19–20, 25–26, 29.

87. Escott, *After Secession,* 129–30.

88. Radley, *Rebel Watchdog,* 204–5.

89. Weitz, *More Damning Than Slaughter,* ix, 288.

90. Geary, *We Need Men,* 15; Ella Lonn, *Desertion during the Civil War* (Lincoln: University of Nebraska Press, 1998).

3 THE MEN IN THE RANKS

YOUNG CITIZENS IN THE RANKS

By the end of the war, perhaps 2.1 million men served in the armies of the United States for varying amounts of time, while upward toward 900,000 men had served in the Confederate forces. For the most part, these men were representative of the general demographics of their regions. They were young, native-born men who may have seen the war as an opportunity as well as a cause or an adventure. The Civil War was a young man's war, with the bulk of the men being in their twenties, and given their youth, not as well established in society as their elders. For example, at the outset of the war, the earliest volunteers from Courtland County, New York, were young, single men in their early twenties who were just about to embark on life's adventures or had just begun their journey to independent living. More slightly older family men from Courtland joined in 1862, which would be common elsewhere as the war progressed.[1]

The demographics were similar in the Southern states. The overwhelming majority of Confederate soldiers from Ashe County in western North Carolina were young, unmarried men who still lived with their parents and, in these cases, were probably not as critical to the financial well-being of their households. In 1861, young men with an average age of 23 filled the ranks of the 15th Mississippi Infantry. The majority was made up of single men with not much property to leave behind or with little family inheritance in their futures. They were restless young men, eager for the change and opportunity offered by the war. In the spring of 1861, Greensboro, Alabama's, volunteer company's composition reflected the social and economic patterns of the larger community. When the company marched off to war after Fort Sumter, however, it resembled the Mississippi regiment. It had fleshed out its ranks with new members, the majority of them still in the process of becoming something in their communities. These men perhaps viewed the war as a way to make a place for themselves in the world.[2]

What was true for Greensboro's young men was true for the majority of recruits in the North and the South. Most Northern soldiers were farmers or farm laborers and skilled or unskilled workers. There were smaller numbers of men from professional and white-collar positions in the ranks, which would be expected in a young army of men. As for the Confederate armies, even with the various exemptions contained in the conscription laws, soldiers reflected the social and economic aspects of Southern society. Northern and Southern soldiers expressed bitterness about those fit individuals who stayed home; draft exemptions provoked resentment among Southern soldiers; and the way wealthier soldiers interacted with their so-called inferiors led to occasional class antagonism in both armies. However, on the whole, the burden of fighting spread itself across Northern and Southern society in fairly equitable ways. The war had a harder impact on the poorer soldiers, who may have resented the further deterioration of their economic situations, but that did not mean that wealthier men did not fight.[3]

Armies, however, could have different mixes of various socioeconomic qualities, giving the organizations distinctive characteristics—or at least the perception thereof. Even within armies, there were regional distinctions that could lead to friction. Soldiers and civilians, for example, generally considered the western armies to contain rougher,

A Yankee Volunteer, Aug. 10, 1863 by Edwin Forbes depicts a tough-looking veteran soldier. (*Library of Congress*)

less disciplined men. The Confederate Army of Tennessee claimed to have a harder time on the battlefield than its Virginia counterpart because the eastern army did not have as tough a Union foe. But even within that army, some regiments appeared coarser than others. The Sixth Arkansas and Terry's Texas Rangers, for example, did not have the polish of some of the sophisticated units from the more settled Gulf Coast.[4]

There were always exceptions to the general demographic patterns. A few hundred women hid their sex, put on uniforms, and fought as men. The greater diversion from the norm consisted of perhaps 76,000 soldiers in both the Confederate and the Union armies who were mere boys. Some of these youths convinced their parents to allow them to serve; many lied about their age to meet the requirement that they be 18 years old.[5] Sixteen-year-old Irish-born Florence Garen had been living on his own for some time and had even rode with the Pony Express; he had no difficulty convincing officers of a Minnesota cavalry company that he was 18.[6] A persistent 16-year-old, Henry Matrau, had a little more difficulty. He had to travel far afield from his Michigan home to find a place where he was not known to join the Union army. He had no luck in Chicago, but he finally enlisted in Beloit, Wisconsin.[7]

Robert Braswell, a 14-year-old boy from Fort Valley, Georgia, did not resort to such tactics, but stubbornly informed his mother of his desire to enlist. She allowed him to go off to war in the company of his 17-year-old brother Samuel, and the volunteer company they joined had no problem with the brothers' youthfulness.[8] Other company officers, especially in the Confederate service, probably had similar feelings about underage volunteers. In the Confederacy, especially as the war dragged on, youngsters as well as older men more fit for retirement than combat found thier way into the Confederate service. In the Northern states, the pressing obligations of government-imposed quotas and the draft probably convinced many officials to take the word of young volunteers who claimed to be 18.

Even among the typical young men in the ranks, there was some diversity. Some Northerners fought with the Confederate armies; many Southerners from slaveholding states fought for the Union. The Union forces had an important immigrant component, but even Confederate armies had some ethnic diversity. And black Americans enrolled in sufficient numbers in the Union army to make a difference in the campaigns of the last two years of the war.

REBEL YANKEES, SOUTHERN UNIONISTS

The Confederate cause appealed to some Northern men, and a few Democrats believed it to be their duty to do more than stay in the loyal opposition. New Jersey soldier Jacob Wadling had a brother who traveled south to join the Confederate army because he believed in the patriotism of the rebellious Southerners, while George G. Junkin of Pennsylvania, who had some family connections in Virginia, also fought for the Confederacy because he believed in the Southern cause.[9] Henry Lane Stone resided in southern Indiana with his Unionist family, who had come from Kentucky. He had a brother who had enlisted in the Union army, but at the outset of the war, he went south, perhaps rebelling against his parents as much as the Lincoln government.[10] And Michigander Harry Eells was not particularly surprised to learn that an acquaintance who had always been "an independent fellow" was in the rebel army.[11]

Some of these northern Confederates probably fought for the Southern cause out of romantic idealism, a commitment to states' rights, or hatred for the so-called tyranny of the Lincoln administration. Most Yankees in the Southern ranks, however, were probably men who had moved to the South prior to the war, married, and established business and family connections as well as emotional ties with their new home states. David Nance's family moved to Texas when he was still a child; in 1861 he believed that states should have the right to decide whether to remain in the Union, consequently volunteering to support that view.[12] Charles F. Bahnson, son of a Moravian minister, was a native of Pennsylvania but had moved with his family to Salem, North Carolina, as a nine-year-old boy. While he had returned north to Philadelphia to study the jeweler's trade, he eventually enlisted in the Confederate army.[13] Twenty-one-year-old Maine native Edward W. Drummond moved to Savannah in 1859, secured employment, and married a Georgia girl; after the war started, he entered the Confederate army.[14] And Hiram Williams, a native of New Jersey and a sojourner in the Midwest, settled in Alabama in 1859; he disliked Republicans as much as he did fire-eating Southerners but threw in his lot with the Confederacy.[15] The numbers of antebellum immigrants combined with ideologically sympathetic Northerners who moved in 1861 and fought for the Confederacy could add up. A surprising 2,000 Pennsylvanians, either antebellum or post-Sumter transplants, fought in Virginia regiments.[16]

The Confederacy found more support among border state men, where loyalties divided entire communities and families. Maryland, Delaware, Missouri, and Kentucky were slave states but remained within the Union. Nevertheless, some 20,000 white Marylanders and 30,000 Missourians cast their lots with the Confederacy. Kentucky contributed its famous five-regiment "Orphan Brigade" to the 35,000 men who served the Confederate cause from that state, while Delaware added about 1,000 more. Even so, the United States enrolled larger numbers from this conflicted region. Maryland provided about 35,000 white men and Delaware another 10,000, while Kentucky's white population contributed approximately 50,000 and Missouri's approximately 80,000.[17]

Loyalty to the Union, however, extended beyond the border states deep into the South, much to the consternation of Confederate officials. Loyal Union men joined Northern armies in significant numbers because they opposed secession, or at least the men who supported the disruption of the Union.[18] Tennessee, with its strong loyalist population in the eastern part of the state, contributed an estimated 42,000 soldiers to the Union army. Some of those men risked retribution when they crossed into Kentucky early in the war to enlist; others joined when opportunities presented themselves as the Union army advanced across the state. Despite the danger to family and property left behind, all told, about 100,000 white Southerners from every state of the Confederacy wore the blue uniform, including men from the western Virginia counties that became a new loyal state. The Confederate army lost access to what amounted to about 10 percent of its total manpower numbers because men from rebel states decided to fight for the Union cause.[19] In addition to these Southerners, approximately 5,000 rebel prisoners of war joined the Union army and fought on the western frontier rather than remain in camps.[20]

Such a mixing up of loyalties could not escape notice, nor could the divisions that it caused among families. "This is the most singular war for separating families," Michigander Henry Eells concluded in July 1862. Eells had the opportunity to become acquainted with a number of Southerners after he had been captured at Shiloh, and "a great many of them," he reported home, "asked after friends and relatives as near as brothers that they had in the Northern army."[21]

TURNCOATS

Along with the principled individuals who abandoned the states of their nativity, there were both a few Confederate and U.S. soldiers who chose to do so to avoid imprisonment. Both sides actively recruited among the prisoners of war, with only modest success. Lieutenant Freeman Bowley, a young Union officer in a black regiment who became a prisoner of war, recalled his own experience when a Confederate officer tried to convince him to join a "Foreign Legion." The officer promised that he and other Yankees who joined would work away from the front and become part of the regular army of the Confederacy after the war. Bowley cursed the officer, but a number of enlisted men accepted the offer. They, in fact, used it as a ploy to escape imprisonment, as did other Yankee prisoners who agreed to the terms, but were quickly recaptured and executed by their Confederate jailers.[22]

Union recruiters had better luck with Confederate prisoners of war who agreed to "swallow the eagle," despite the disdain that such actions generated among their fellow Southern captives. Initially, the War Department opposed using captured Confederates, although some prisoners of war took an oath of allegiance and found themselves integrated into Northern units. But in the fall of 1864, the government began a serious recruiting effort among captured Confederates. The resulting volunteers, or "repentant rebels," as General Benjamin Butler called them, filled the ranks of six regiments of U.S. volunteers with approximately 6,000 men—including some Northern-born and some foreign-born soldiers—because they could no longer endure prison or had lost their enthusiasm for the Confederate cause. There were numbers of prisoners who wished to avoid being exchanged and forced into unfamiliar Confederate companies or returned to the Confederate service when they deemed the cause close to being lost. Some Southerners may have hoped to find an opportunity to escape and return home, but service on the western plains probably complicated achieving that goal. In the end, on average, the former Confederates deserted only at a rate slightly higher than their counterparts in other Northern volunteer regiments. Regardless of their reasons for turning their coats, these "white-washed rebs" or "galvanized Yankees" freed up an equal number of federal soldiers to fight their former Confederate comrades. The "transfugees," as a friend of Butler dubbed them, served in the west, although the First U.S. Volunteer Infantry Regiment manned positions in Norfolk and Portsmouth, Virginia, shortly after its organization. However, when members of the First saw combat again, it was against an Indian foe.[23]

ETHNIC AMERICANS

Immigration into the United States slowed as the sectional crisis came to a head, but the U.S. Army also benefited in this area more than its Confederate counterpart. The Northern government did its best to encourage this immigration, with some success. The Republican administration, for example, passed the May 1862 Homestead Act, which provided 160 acres of land to settlers, and, in July, passed legislation that provided citizenship to immigrants who resided in the United States for one year and served in the army. Such welcoming actions probably contributed to the increased numbers in immigration in the North. Word of multiple bounties also might have tempted potential immigrants, and there were professional soldiers and doctors who migrated to both sections after the war had started to sharpen their skills. But men generally did not come to the United States determined to join the army; rather, the war created economic conditions that attracted them. Employment was just as important to immigrants during the war as it had been before, and as it became after the conflict. The result was that despite the slowing of immigration at the outset of the war, a total of 800,000 people made it to the United States, despite the unsettled nature of the times.[24]

Some of these new arrivals found themselves in the army because substitute brokers took advantage of them or because they were conscripted, but despite some notable opposition to the draft among the Northern Irish community, many immigrants willingly joined the army. The Southern states, with its slave economy, were never as hospitable a place for immigrants before the war and appeared to be even less so after hostilities commenced. During the war the Richmond government seemed to put greater effort into trying to convince European governments to discourage emigration to the North than into convincing individuals to come to the Confederacy. Consequently, both sections relied more on the ethnic populations already within their borders.

There was no uniform response to secession and war within the established Northern and Southern ethnic communities, but many foreign-born residents, particularly the Irish and the Germans, who made up the majority of that population, decided to defend their new homes. They joined Confederate and Union armies for all of the reasons that their native-born counterparts enlisted, from patriotism and love of liberty to a need for adventure or to satisfy their own economic interests. In Massachusetts Ferdinand Dreher, formerly of Baden and, in 1861, a new American citizen, had been involved in the revolutionary movement of 1848; for him, raising German troops for the Union cause was another stage in his fight for freedom.[25] There were other ethnic Americans who agreed with him.

Irish immigrant Peter Welsh made it clear to his family that he had joined a just and glorious cause when he joined the Union army. Southerners were absolutely wrong in their rebellion, he assured his family. The war, he explained to his wife, "is the first test of a modern free government in the act of sustaining itself against internal enemies and matured rebellion." The world awaited its outcome, knowing that if the United States failed to maintain itself, "then the hopes of milions fall and the desighns and wishes of all tyrants will succeed." For Welsh, the United States was this free government not hindered by a hereditary aristocracy, one that allowed freedom of conscience and one that provided the best chance for the advancement of all the people. He reminded his father-in-law that the Irish-Americans "have a claim a stake in the nation and an interest in its prosperity." Furthermore, it was the United States that had provided a home for "thousands of the sons and daughters of Irland" who had "come to seek a refuge from tyrany and persecution at home." Thus they have "a vital interest in the preservation of our national existence the perpetuation of our institutions and the free and untrammeled exicution of our laws."[26] Welsh clearly grasped the benefits of Northern free-labor ideology, and few men argued their merits better.

In Louisiana, however, many Irishmen joined the Confederate service because economic difficulties before the war had thrown them out of work on the state's levees; during 1862 they and their German neighbors in New Orleans also joined the Union occupying army, until the city's labor market began to absorb their numbers.[27] Advertisements designed to bring men into the ranks, especially as the war bloodily progressed, emphasized the financial benefits of service, just as they did for nonethnic recruits. The Illinois Scotch Regiment, for example, advertised that recruits would earn $13 a month and be entitled to a $100 bounty at the end of the war. Furthermore, it informed potential recruits that Congress was considering providing each volunteer with 160 acres of land.[28] Recruiters would not have wasted ink on such things if they did not matter, but as with American-born recruits, Northern and Southern ethnics probably held to a number of motives. They also enlisted out of a sense of obligation and duty to their new homes as well as out of a desire to prove themselves worthy of acceptance by their neighbors.

Despite their presence in the Union armies, ethnic Northerners never enlisted in numbers that fully reflected their place in the population.[29] Nevertheless, the Union armies benefited significantly from the enlistment of foreign-born Northerners, including Frenchmen, Englishmen, Italians, and Canadians. German Americans, however, comprised the largest number of recruits, with 200,000 men, surpassing the Irish, who contributed over 150,000. Immigrant recruits and those recruits born of immigrant parents contributed mightily to the Union cause, making up 25 percent of the Union armies. Foreign-born Confederates, however, made up only 9 percent of the men and officers of the Southern armies, in large part because the Southern states' slave-dominated staple crop economy had not been able to compete with the Northern free-labor economy in attracting foreigners before and during the war.[30]

Immigrants had had their own ethnic volunteer companies before the war, and they continued to join exclusively ethnic regiments after Fort Sumter. Before the war in 1859, Scots immigrants and men of Scots heritage organized and dominated the ranks of the New York's 79th Regiment of the state militia, which in its entirety answered Lincoln's call to arms. After Sumter, New York Germans filled 20 infantry regiments, two cavalry regiments, and five artillery batteries, while Irish in Massachusetts filled two regiments.[31]

Foreign-born men and their sons enlisted in distinctly ethnic regiments because they felt comfortable doing so, a sentiment well recognized by recruiters. In Cleveland, Ohio, Thomas F. Galway, an Irish Catholic, for example, joined the Hibernian Guards, because he felt at home with the unit, rather than another company he had first visited that day of his enlistment.[32] Irish recruiting posters played on such sentiments. They often promised potential volunteers that they would have access to priests, something the men could not depend on if enrolled in any other volunteer regiment. Recruiters also promised that the volunteers would serve under men who understood their needs. When recruiters pursued Germans, they did so with German-language broadsides, speeches made in German, and the understanding that the enlistees would serve under German-speaking officers. Irish recruiting posters also emphasized in bold print the distinctly Irish names of the officers who would lead the volunteers. One Massachusetts broadside promised recruits that they would "be led to the battle-field by officers of your own ancient race, who have proved themselves inferior to no others of our grand army." "Come with us and our *IRISH HERO*, CORCORAN," solicited another, just to make that point very clear.[33]

Recruiters obviously did not hesitate to play on ethnic pride in their efforts to convince men to join. "IRISHMEN To the Rescue!" called out one broadside. It promised that their service would "cast a bright ray of glory on the GREEN FLAG! and the unconquerable nationality it represents."[34] In April 1861, when Wisconsin Governor Alexander W. Randall urged Norwegians to enlist, he played on the idea that the brave "spirit of the Fatherland" would prompt them to take up arms; he also attempted to shame them by noting that Germans and Irishmen were rushing into the ranks to defend their new home.[35] Such appeals, however, did not mean universal ethnic segregation. Many Northern ethnics probably already felt comfortable in their communities and leavened many locally recruited companies and regiments with their presence. When Benjamin Hirst left Connecticut for the war in August 1862, he recalled that his company's "good byes were given in almost every language spoken in Europe."[36]

The Confederacy had its own ethnic companies and regiments, too. Before the war, immigrants participated in distinctly ethnic volunteer companies, just as their Northern counterparts did. In Charleston, South Carolina, Scots immigrant James Campbell joined the Union Light Infantry; because of its membership, Charlestonians also knew it as the Scotch Company or the Charleston Highlanders. The Confederate Army of Tennessee had four ethnic regiments, consisting of two Irish regiments from Tennessee, a Louisiana regiment made up of Irish and German companies, and another Louisiana regiment that was a mélange of French, Spanish, German, Italian, Chinese, and Irish soldiers. Mobile, Alabama's, Emerald Guards, mostly from Ireland, marched off to war wearing green uniforms. Alabama also fielded a company of Scotch Guards. Notably, Texas contributed several German units, despite the general Unionist sentiment among their communities, as well as Irish, Poles, and Mexicans. And Louisiana, where more than one-third of the South's immigrant population resided, also brought into the Confederacy's service many ethnic recruits.[37]

Adding to the ethnic mix and the numbers of the Civil War armies were the American Indians who chose to join the fray on one side or the other. Approximately 20,000 Indians served in the Union and in the Confederate military. Again, young Indian men shared all the motivations of their European American counterparts, from a desire to break the routine in their lives to the need for employment. Austin George, a Connecticut Pequot who served in a black regiment, enlisted because antebellum difficulties and wartime circumstances hurt his prospects for earning a living at whaling.[38] But more complicated group circumstances also influenced Indians' decisions to fight. Tribal politics, relationships with white governments, and calculated moves for survival as a people brought Indians into the war on one side or another. Western Cherokees, for example, contributed men to both armies because they had their own internal political conflict that split the tribe.[39]

AFRICAN AMERICANS

After Lincoln's call to arms, free African Americans in the North shared their white neighbors' eagerness to put down the rebellion. They offered their voluntary companies to the cause, and some men set out to form new fighting organizations for that purpose. The Hannibal Guards of Pittsburgh, Pennsylvania, volunteered for duty in the state's militia. "Although deprived of our political rights," they petitioned, "we yet wish the government of the United States to be sustained against the tyranny of slavery."[40] In October 1861 a black medical doctor from Michigan offered to raise up to 10,000 black troops, preferably to fight as sharp shooters, but also willing to act as guerrillas.[41] These men understood that the war, at its heart, was a war against slavery, "which is the cause of all our trouble," according to an ex-slave residing in Canada.[42] In 1861, unfortunately for these black patriots, white Northerners had not yet reached that conclusion. Consequently, for the time being, the war remained a white man's fight, excluding blacks from state and federal service, a reality that had its legal foundation in federal law.

Despite this sentiment, there were a few black men who breached the enforced borders of a white man's army early in the war. African American Nicholas Biddle, from Pottsville, Pennsylvania, went to the capital's rescue in April 1861 as a member of the Washington Artillerists. And in 1862 Henry Ford Douglas, a black Chicago minister, joined the 95th Illinois Volunteer Infantry.[43] Other blacks served as white men or in some irregular association with a regiment. At the outset of the war, William H. Johnson, a free-born native of Virginia residing in Norwich, Connecticut, served with the Second Connecticut Infantry but was not mustered into the service. He would also later serve with the white Eighth Connecticut. He and several other so-called proscribed Americans, probably associated with the Eighth Connecticut as servants, formed the "Self-Defenders of Connecticut," with the understanding that sooner or later, the nation would call on African American men to aid "in this struggle for liberty." Johnson and two other Connecticut blacks became the organization's officers.[44]

The bloody circumstances of a war that dragged on beyond anticipation led many Northerners to reconsider their stand on black soldiers. Even Negrophobes came to accept that African Americans, who in their minds were the root cause of the war, should share in the burden of death. During 1862, as the nation moved toward emancipation, Congress passed the Second Confiscation Act and the Militia Act, both of which pointed to the enlistment of black troops. After the promulgation of the Emancipation Proclamation on January 1, 1863, there was no longer any serious question about the Union army using African Americans to fill its ranks. The 1864 conscription law even made "all able-bodied male colored persons, between the ages of twenty and forty-five years, resident in the United States" subject to the draft.[45] Thus African Americans would become a critical component of the Northern war machine.

During 1862, freemen and ex-slaves in Kansas, Louisiana, and South Carolina joined newly formed black regiments, not entirely with the support or the satisfaction of the federal government. After the beginning of 1863, however, Northern state governments, pressed to fill quotas, courted the African American population with heretofore unseen vigor within their state boundaries and beyond. The first Northern black regiment, the 54th Massachusetts, came into existence early that year, and soon, Northern governors were competing for black volunteers. From its inception the 54th Massachusetts drew blacks into it ranks from across the North. Lieutenant E. N. Hallowell and other recruiters found some of the regiment's earliest volunteers among the black population of Philadelphia as well as New Bedford, Massachusetts. By the spring of 1864, A. P. Dunlop reported that he was recruiting black troops for the 54th and 55th Massachusetts in Maryland and Tennessee. Almost all of the men who enlisted in the 55th Massachusetts came from out of state, especially Ohio, Pennsylvania, and Virginia.[46]

Massachusetts was not alone in relying on far-flung recruiting. African American Martin Delany, for example, recruited in Illinois for Connecticut and Rhode Island regiments. Indiana, Illinois, and other states attempted to ward off this poaching to preserve the black male population for their own 1863 quotas. Those midwestern states had much larger populations of black men on which to draw than indicated by their 1860 census data because of the large numbers of escaped slaves who had entered their borders early in the war. The earliest Illinois enlistees in Company A of what would become the 29th U.S. Colored Infantry were recent arrivals to the state, many having been runaway slaves. Some of those men went on to recruit for the regiment in Missouri.[47]

Recruiting African Americans, in many respects, was no different from recruiting white men. In December 1863, for example, wealthy members of the Union League Club of New York City raised money to sponsor a black New York regiment.[48] Recruiters for the 54th Massachusetts and other regiments approached black leaders for assistance and held rallies to excite the enthusiasm of local black populations.[49] Ohio recruiters held meetings at which prominent black residents and government officials gave speeches.[50] Illinoisan James T. Ayers, who, in 1863, was recruiting in Alabama, employed all the tactics that recruiters used to lure white men into the ranks. Some of

Ayers's counterparts, especially among substitute brokers, were not necessarily as honest as he in their dealings, sometimes promising extravagant bounties or tricking black men into enlisting by other means.[51] For example, a New York paper reported substitute brokers kidnapping blacks after plying them with drink. Likewise, an Ohio black soldier complained to Abraham Lincoln about how he had expected to enlist for a year and collect a $200 bounty, only to have the recruiter dull his senses with liquor and sell him as a substitute. There were substitute brokers who threatened black men with arrest if they did not enlist, and some soldiers who carried out similar threats. In December 1863, in Virginia, soldiers were "making arrests of Colored Citizens," according H. S. Beals, a white missionary, "for the purpose of compelling them to volunteer in the U.S. Service." In January 1864 John Banks, a black Virginia soldier, confirmed the charge. He described how he ended up in the service as an unwilling volunteer, forced to join at gun point by the military. "I did not dare to remonstrate," he explained, "but accepted the five dollars bounty and my uniform and clothing and performed the duty of a soldier."[52]

There were some problems, however, that were unique to enlisting blacks, both for the recruiters and the recruits. Recruiting for black regiments, as an officer of the 54th Massachusetts later reported, "was attended with much annoyance." Lieutenant Hallowell and the other Massachusetts agents recruiting in Philadelphia had to collect their volunteers in secret, keep them in small groups, and get them aboard trains to Massachusetts "one at a time... or under the cover of darkness," all "to avoid molestation or excitement." Also, recruiters had to deal with whites who ridiculed them and harassed their families for their associations with black regiments. As for the black men who joined, they, too, suffered ridicule and violence at the hands of "white rowdies, or pretended citizens." In June 1863, in Washington, D.C., blacks in uniform were attacked on the streets and could not count on the local police for assistance.[53]

States, eager to meet their quotas, competed with one another for black enlistees in the occupied parts of the Confederacy as well as among the refugees in the North. Also, the federal government's efforts added to the success of bringing African Americans into the ranks. During 1863 Adjutant General Lorenzo Thomas, for example, was very successful in his efforts to raise black troops in the Mississippi River Valley.[54] In the end, former slaves contributed significantly to the Union cause. Estimates of the numbers of blacks serving in the U.S. Army during the war vary, with numbers ranging from around 179,000 upward to over 186,000. Of the lower figure, over 102,000 came from the Confederacy, with almost another 43,000 coming from the slave border states. Most of these enlistees from the slave states had probably recently been slaves, which suggests that the bondsman could legitimately claim to have participated in his own emancipation.

Northern free blacks and Southern contrabands enlisted for all the reasons their white counterparts did, including for the state and local bounties that were available to them. African Americans also understood from the start that they had to prove that they were just as good, if not better, than white men at war to earn a place as citizens when peace came. Black recruiter Sergeant Milton Holland told a group of Ohio blacks, when trying to convince them to enlist, that there was good reason to "sacrifice home comforts": "you will win the respect of the whole nation."[55] Blacks knew that the war's outcome would greatly shape their future as well as the future of their families, their communities, and their race. Black Massachusetts soldier James H. Gooding made it clear when he proposed that there were only two outcomes to the war: "one is slavery and poverty and the other is liberty and prosperity." Black men, therefore, had to take an active role in securing the positive outcome or forever face ridicule for not helping

Band of the 107th U.S. Colored Infantry at Fort Corcoran, Arlington, Virginia. When given the opportunity, African Americans helped fill the ranks of the Union army. (*Library of Congress*)

bring about the end of slavery. As Gooding explained, "the least false step, at a moment like the present, may tell a dismal tale at some future date."[56] But the risks they assumed were greater than those of their white counterparts. If captured, they could end up being enslaved or executed for participating in a slave rebellion.

Even slaves, who may have relished the thought of avenging the wrongs of slavery by fighting their former masters, understood the larger, noble consequences of their enlistments. Their actions and sacrifices indicated their commitment to the cause of freedom. Some border state slaves, among them Kentuckian Elijah Marrs and 27 black men, risked their lives traveling through hostile country to join the Union army.[57] Contraband Solomon Bradley gave up a good job on a steamer to join the army in South Carolina. "I could not stay there," he explained. "In Secesh times I used to pray the Lord for this opportunity to be released from bondage and to fight for my liberty, and I could not feel right as long as I was not in the regiment."[58] For Samuel Cable, a private in the 55th Massachusetts, crushing "this ungodly rebellion" would have personal consequences: his wife was still enslaved. "I am a soldier now," he wrote to her in 1863, "and i shall use my utmost endeavors to strike at the rebellion and the heart of this system that so long has kept us in chains."[59]

The Confederate government never committed itself to tapping into the manpower reserves of its black population for soldiers until it was much too late to matter. The Confederacy relied on thousands of blacks to perform support duties that ranged from playing music to building defenses.[60] But using free blacks and slaves as laborers and servants was one thing; sanctioning the arming of black men was another matter. The idea of an armed black man challenged the very nature and meaning of the Confederacy.

If the Confederate government welcomed black men into its armies, William W. Holden, editor of the *North Carolina Standard,* explained in October 1864, "it will proclaim by such an act that the white men of the Confederate States are not able to achieve their own liberties."[61] The ideological contradiction of armed black men was simply too difficult to circumvent until March 1865, when the Confederacy agreed to enlist slaves.

There were, nevertheless, free blacks in the Southern states who sought places in the Confederate service. The Louisiana Native Guards of New Orleans, over 900 elite free men of color, volunteered for the state militia; after the fall of the city, only 108 of them joined the Union Army's First Regiment of Native Guards.[62] In March 1863, in South Carolina, free black John Wilson Buckner was able to join an artillery regiment, despite state law forbidding the arming of blacks, because of his family's good reputation. There were probably some free people of color who passed for white and enlisted to complete their racial transition.[63]

There were no black regiments regularly mustered into the Confederate army. Groups of black men, slaves and free, however, helped to defend their communities on an ad hoc basis, while individual black slaves probably came to the aid of masters on the battlefield, even though the Confederate government did not sanction such actions. Some Union soldiers, for example, claimed to have witnessed blacks fighting against them. Kentucky Unionist Marcus Woodcock reported to have come across a black man "clothed armed and equipped in Confederate custom."[64] New Jerseyan Alfred Bellard recorded the killing, in April 1861, of a black Confederate picket in Virginia.[65] And Lieutenant Charles H. Brewster claimed that in April 1862, near Warwick Court House, Virginia, where he was stationed, two regiments of black men attacked the Union picket line. He noted that "it is a notorious fact that the rebels have any quantity of niggers in their service" and that "our pickets have seen them and have shot them."[66]

Some of these black Confederates possibly fought willingly, but local commanders, in spite of government policy, forced blacks to take up arms against the Yankees. For example, African American John V. Givens noted that in Virginia, in July 1861, he encountered free blacks fighting in Confederate uniform "that were pressed into the rebel service." Forty black deserters had been "forced to leave their families" by the Confederates. They wished to join the Union ranks, "but how disappointed they were when they found that they could not fight in our ranks against their oppressors."[67] Some willing black men may very well have been found in the Confederate ranks. They became fine symbols for the postwar Lost Cause, but their contribution to the secession was negligible compared to what their brothers accomplished for the Union.

FAMILY, FRIENDS, AND NEIGHBORS

Ethnic regiments provided just one type of opportunity to march off with companions who had common cultural and social bonds. Most volunteers who enlisted in locally raised companies and state regiments would not go off to war with strangers. It was practically guaranteed that recruits who joined units raised during the first two years of war would find many familiar faces in the ranks because of the local nature of recruiting. Neighboring towns or counties provided companies of men for a common regiment, as did Iowa City and surrounding Johnson County, whose citizens filled the ranks of the 22nd Iowa Infantry.[68] Those soldiers who had been members of antebellum volunteer companies probably took comfort in knowing that they had old comrades at their sides, as did members of new organizations recruited within various communities.

The process might not have guaranteed a certain amount of personal ease within the organizations, but it certainly made it likely. Rockville, Connecticut's, volunteers made "a very harmonious company, all of its members being more or less acquainted with each other before enlisting."[69]

In both Northern and Southern communities, personal bonds encouraged friends and relatives to accompany one another into the service. Henry Graham, a young New Yorker, enlisted with several college friends.[70] Beloit College in Wisconsin contributed 12 students and alumnae to a company in the Second Wisconsin.[71] And 40 students from Middlebury College in Vermont, presumably all sharing some degree of familiarity, enlisted together.[72] The phenomenon was equally pronounced in the South. In March 1861, for example, Georgian Billy Braswell and his friend Tom Massee traveled to Macon together to join a volunteer company, expecting to be among the first to stand up to Yankee threats.[73]

Indeed, Northern and Southern companies frequently contained not only friends, but also brothers and cousins, fathers and uncles, not a surprising phenomenon given the communal source of so many of the units. Numerous groups of brothers joined companies that would make up the 37th North Carolina Infantry, and Ben Hirst went to war with his two brothers as well as his friends and neighbors from Rockville, Connecticut.[74] Brothers Dick and Tally Simpson, along with several paternal cousins, joined a South Carolina company before the firing on Sumter, while Samuel Lowry joined a South Carolina company in which two of his uncles were officers.[75] It was also a common occurrence in Virginia's famous Stonewall Brigade, in which one company served as the military home to 18 men from one family.[76]

Even within the more impersonal borders of larger towns and cities, men had participated in various associations based not only on ethnicity, but also on employment and politics, that provided the army with groups of volunteers that had already had a sense of common identity. Recruiters in Philadelphia filled 90-day companies with men already acquainted with one another in fire companies, factories, and at least one university department.[77] The Republican Wide Awakes, from cities such as Hartford,

Company F, 114th Pennsylvania Infantry (Zouaves). (*Library of Congress*)

Connecticut, was another antebellum group that could transfer its loyalties to the army; these political activists provided a core for the recruiting of volunteers in Connecticut in 1861.[78] Less formal urban connections also played their part. Virginian William W. Parker, a Richmond physician, recruited for his artillery company among his patients' families; parents knew him well enough to trust their boys with him.[79]

PHYSICALLY FIT AND UNFIT RECRUITS

Most recruits were, for the most part, young and fit specimens, certainly fit for soldiering. Nevertheless, many men with less than adequate health ended up in the ranks. As many as 25 percent of Union soldiers recruited during the first year of the war should have been rejected for medical reasons; the Confederate army probably held at least a like percentage of men not fit for soldiering.[80] Camp life and campaigns would eventually take a toll on such recruits, although many a healthy youth fell victim to the unusual circumstances produced by both. Still, some unfit men who died might have lived if their armies had prevented them from joining in the first place.

One of the first tests that these men should have faced in their transition from civilian life to military life, just to be sure of their fitness for the rigors of war, was the physical examination. That generally was not the case in the Confederacy. At the outset of the war, Confederate mustering officers appeared to have little concern for the health of volunteers. If a man looked healthy, his company officers deemed him to be so. As one Arkansas volunteer explained, "We were not subjected to the indignity of being stripped and examined"; rather, he and his fellow recruits "were accepted into the military service upon our own assurance of being in fit condition."[81] In May 1861 Louisianan William Henry King witnessed how a careless surgeon named Roan certified that he had examined recruits after giving them only a cursory look. If a man failed to volunteer any evidence of a physical disability, he passed the surgeon's exam; if he complained about an ailment, he found the surgeon amenable to excusing him. As far as King could tell, Dr. Roan did not care one way or another because he received his pay regardless of the outcome of the exam.[82]

Only later, in 1862, did the Confederate government require physicals for recruits. Such examinations remained perfunctory and tolerant of many flaws. If a man appeared to be able to do civilian work with one eye, or some deafness, or missing fingers, he could, according to the authorities, perform military duty.[83] The least fit, however, probably soon fell ill as they began camp routine and either ended up discharged or dead.

Union recruits might receive a cursory examination by local physicians before they enlisted or soon thereafter, but the U.S. War Department required regimental surgeons to examine every recruit in a fairly thorough manner. In 1861 Massachusetts surgeon J. Franklin Dyer conscientiously spent his early days in the army examining recruits, "rejecting such as were found unfit."[84] When African American recruits for the 54th Massachusetts arrived at Readville, they received a "most rigid and thorough" medical examination, with nearly one-third of their number being rejected as unfit for the service. "As a consequence," Massachusetts's surgeon general bragged, "a more robust, strong, and healthy set of men were never mustered into the service of the United States."[85] That may well have been the case, but it certainly was not the norm for many other Yankee regiments.

Union volunteers generally had medical experiences much less thorough than those given the recruits by Dyer or the Readville surgeon. In 1861 New Jersey recruits gathering at the state capital of Trenton answered a series of questions posed by doctors concerning their health. "If the questions were answered in the affirmative and he had no reason to doubt it," volunteer Alfred Bellard recounted, "he would give us a thump on the chest, and if we were not floored nor showed any signs of inconvenience, we were pronounced in good condition and ordered to fall in on the other side of the room, where while waiting for the examination to end, we amused ourselves by grinning at each other."[86] One New Jersey recruit noted that the surgeon dismissed seven men from his company, but only two for health reasons; the others were either too young or too short.[87]

In June 1861 Rufus Robbins, a private in the Seventh Massachusetts Infantry, described his company's experience as perfunctory at best: "The examination was a short one. Not more than half an hour for the whole company," he explained. It consisted of a surgeon asking if a man "was a well hearty man."[88] Such lax examinations led to the mustering of many an unfit man and even a number of fit women into the army. Sarah Edmonds, at the time known as Private Franklin Thompson, gave the examining surgeon a strong handshake and passed muster.[89] In another case, a surgeon performed an eye exam by simply asking a recruit named A. B. Buckles if he could see, and the soldier replied in the affirmative. Had the surgeon asked Buckles if "he could see well out of both eyes," which he could not, the outcome of the physical would have been different.[90]

Later in the war, Union regiments might have devoted more time to examinations, but the standards were fairly lax given the desperate need for men. The 1862 militia draft law, for example, required significant disability to prevent a man from being inducted. Later, in 1863, John King described a procedure at Camp Fuller, in Rockford, Illinois, that provided a thorough examination of the recruits, but also one that gave the surgeons one final opportunity to keep a man in the ranks. "We had all been taken separately and alone into a tent before a surgeon, stripped, examined, and all who were found wanting were rejected," a soldier reported. "But now came another examination in a different form. We stood in what is called open ranks, each surgeon examining the soldiers as he passed. One examined the eyes, another the limbs, and still another strong, robust surgeon examined the physical abilities of every soldier." The latter phase of the examination involved having a surgeon attempt to jerk a man out of the ranks. If the soldier held his place, he passed. Surgeons considered the recruits who could not stand up to their tugging to be too weak to serve. Even so, the rejected men went through one last physical review: "The best were sent back to the ranks and puny ones were sent home to their mothers."[91]

NOTES

1. James W. Geary, *We Need Men: The Union Draft in the Civil War* (DeKalb: Northern Illinois University Press, 1991), 88; Bell I. Wiley, *The Life of Johnny Reb: The Common Soldier of the Confederacy* (Garden City, NY: Doubleday, 1971), 330–31; Edmund J. Raus Jr., *Banners South: A Northern Community at War* (Kent, OH: Kent State University Press, 2005), 12, 225.

2. John C. Inscoe and Gordon B. McKinney, *The Heart of Confederate Appalachia: Western North Carolina in the Civil War* (Chapel Hill: University of North Carolina Press, 2000), 75; Ben Wynne, *A Hard Trip: A History of the 15th Mississippi Infantry, CSA* (Macon, GA: Mercer University Press, 2003), 39–40; G. Ward Hubbs, *Guarding Greensboro: A Confederate Company in the Making of a Southern Community* (Athens: University of Georgia Press, 2003), 101.

3. James M. McPherson, *Ordeal by Fire: The Civil War and Reconstruction,* 3rd ed. (Boston: McGraw-Hill, 2001), 386–87; Geary, *We Need Men,* 89.

4. Larry J. Daniel, *Soldiering in the Army of Tennessee: A Portrait of Life in a Confederate Army* (Chapel Hill: University of North Carolina Press, 1991), 11–22.

5. David Williams, *A People's History of the Civil War: Struggles for the Meaning of Freedom* (New York: New Press, 2005), 192.

6. Kurt D. Bergemann, *Brackett's Battalion: Minnesota Cavalry in the Civil War and Dakota War* (St. Paul: Minnesota Historical Society Press, 2004), 8.

7. Marcia Reid-Green, ed., *Letters Home: Henry Matrau of the Iron Brigade* (Lincoln: University of Nebraska Press, 1993), vii, 3.

8. Scott Walker, *Hell's Broke Loose in Georgia: Survival in a Civil War Regiment* (Athens: University of Georgia Press, 2005), 8.

9. William Gillette, *Jersey Blue: Civil War Politics in New Jersey, 1854–1865* (New Brunswick, NJ: Rutgers University Press, 1995), 135; Christian B. Keller, "Keystone Confederates: Pennsylvanians Who Fought for Dixie," in *Making and Remaking Pennsylvania's Civil War,* ed. William Blair and William Pencak (University Park: Pennsylvania State University Press, 2001), 1–2.

10. Amy E. Murrell, "Union Father, Rebel Son: Families and the Question of Civil War Loyalty," in *The War Was You and Me: Civilians in the American Civil War,* ed. Joan E. Cashin (Princeton, NJ: Princeton University Press, 2002), 358–91; Amy Murrell Taylor, *The Divided Family in Civil War America* (Chapel Hill: University of North Carolina Press, 2005), 13.

11. John R. Sellers, ed., *A People at War: Civil War Manuscripts from the Holdings of the Library of Congress* (Alexandria, VA: Chadwyck-Healy, 1989–1990), Henry Eells to friends, July 11, 1862, Samuel Henry Eells Papers, reel 24.

12. B. P. Gallaway, *The Ragged Rebel: A Common Soldier in W. H. Parsons' Texas Cavalry, 1861–1865* (Austin: University of Texas Press, 1988), 1–2, 8, 13.

13. Sarah Bahnson Chapman, ed., *Bright and Gloomy Days: The Civil War Correspondence of Captain Charles Frederic Bahnson, a Moravian Confederate* (Knoxville: University of Tennessee Press, 2003), xi–xiii.

14. Roger S. Durham, ed., *A Confederate Yankee: The Journal of Edward William Drummond, a Confederate Soldier from Maine* (Knoxville: University of Tennessee Press, 2004), xiv–xv.

15. Lewis N. Wynne and Robert A. Taylor, eds., *This War So Horrible: The Civil War Diary of Hiram Smith Williams* (Tuscaloosa: University of Alabama Press, 1993).

16. Keller, "Keystone Confederates," 262, n. 3.

17. McPherson, *Ordeal by Fire,* 166–73; William C. Davis, *The Orphan Brigade: The Kentucky Confederates Who Couldn't Go Home Again* (Mechanicsburg, PA: Stackpole Books, 1993).

18. Margaret M. Storey, *Loyalty and Loss: Alabama's Unionists in the Civil War and Reconstruction* (Baton Rouge: Louisiana State University Press, 2004), 18–55.

19. Richard Nelson Current, *Lincoln's Loyalists: Union Soldiers from the Confederacy* (Boston: Northeastern University Press, 1992), 32, 46–49, passim.

20. Michèle Tucker Butts, *Galvanized Yankees on the Upper Missouri: The Face of Loyalty* (Boulder: University Press of Colorado, 2003).

21. Sellers, *A People at War,* Henry Eells to friends, July 11, 1862, Samuel Henry Eells Papers, reel 24.

22. Keith Wilson, ed., *Honor in Command: Lt. Freeman S. Bowley's Civil War Service in the 30th United States Colored Infantry* (Gainesville: University Press of Florida, 2006), 176.

23. Charles W. Sanders Jr., *While in the Hands of the Enemy: Military Prisons of the Civil War* (Baton Rouge: Louisiana State University Press, 2005), 275; Butts, *Galvanized Yankees,* 29–63, passim; Alvin M. Josephy Jr., *The Civil War in the American West* (New York: Vintage Books, 1991), 314; Robert M. Utley, *Frontiersmen in Blue: The United States Army and the Indian, 1848–1865* (Lincoln: University of Nebraska Press, 1967), 308, passim; D. Alexander Brown, *The Galvanized Yankees* (Urbana: University of Illinois Press, 1963), 1–10, passim.

24. Martin W. Öfele, *German-Speaking Officers in the U.S. Colored Troops, 1863–1867* (Gainesville: University Press of Florida, 2004), 52; Phillip Shaw Paludan, *A People's Contest: The Union and Civil War, 1861–1865,* 2nd ed. (Lawrence: University Press of Kansas, 1996), 284–85; Ella Lonn, *Foreigners in the Confederacy* (Gloucester, MA: Peter Smith, 1965), 163.

25. Richard F. Miller, *Harvard's Civil War: A History of the Twentieth Massachusetts Volunteer Infantry* (Hanover, NH: University Press of New England, 2005), 10–11.

26. Lawrence Frederick Kohl, ed., with Margaret Cossé Richard, *Irish Green and Union Blue: The Civil War Letters of Peter Welsh* (New York: Fordham University Press, 1986), 64–67, 100–4.

27. Terry L. Jones, *Lee's Tigers: The Louisiana Infantry in the Army of Northern Virginia* (Baton Rouge: Louisiana State University Press, 1987), 7; James G. Hollandsworth Jr., *The Louisiana Native Guards: The Black Military Experience during the Civil War* (Baton Rouge: Louisiana State University Press, 1995), 14–15.

28. William L. Burton, *Melting Pot Soldiers: The Union's Ethnic Regiments* (New York: Fordham University Press, 1998), 66.

29. James M. McPherson, *Battle Cry of Freedom: The Civil War Era* (New York: Oxford University Press, 1988), 606.

30. James I. Robertson Jr., *Soldiers Blue and Gray* (Columbia: University of South Carolina Press, 1988), 27–29.

31. Terry A. Johnston Jr., ed., *"Him on the One Side and Me on the Other": The Civil War Letters of Alexander Campbell, 79th New York Infantry Regiment and James Campbell, 1st South Carolina Battalion*

(Columbia: University of South Carolina Press, 1999), 4–5, 8; Eugene C. Murdock, *One Million Men: The Civil War Draft in the North* (Madison: State Historical Society of Wisconsin, 1971), 306–7.

32. Sellers, *A People at War,* Entry for April 14, 1861, Thomas F. Galway Diaries, reel 28.

33. R. Reinhart, ed. and trans., *Two Germans in the Civil War: The Diary of John Daeuble and the Letters of Gottfried Rentschler, 6th Kentucky Volunteer Infantry* (Knoxville: University of Tennessee Press, 2004), xxix. See Burton, *Melting Pot Soldiers,* 61–65, for Irish and German recruiting posters.

34. Burton, *Melting Pot Soldiers,* 61, 62, 65.

35. Ella Lonn, *Foreigners in the Union Army and Navy* (Baton Rouge: Louisiana State University Press, 1951), 59.

36. Robert L. Bee, ed., *The Boys from Rockville: Civil War Narratives of Sgt. Benjamin Hirst, Company D, 14th Connecticut Volunteers* (Knoxville: University of Tennessee Press, 1998), 12.

37. Johnston, *"Him on the One Side,"* 2–3; Daniel, *Soldiering,* 18–19; Wiley, *Life of Johnny Reb,* 109–10, 322–23; Dean B. Mahin, *The Blessed Place of Freedom: Europeans in Civil War America* (Washington, DC: Brassey's, 2002), 59; Jones, *Lee's Tigers,* 5–7.

38. Laurence M. Hauptman, *Between Two Fires: American Indians in the Civil War* (New York: Free Press, 1995), 148–49.

39. Anne J. Bailey, *Invisible Southerners: Ethnicity in the Civil War* (Athens: University of Georgia Press, 2006), 24–46.

40. James M. McPherson, *The Negro's Civil War: How American Blacks Felt and Acted during the War for the Union* (New York: Vintage Books, 1991), 19–20.

41. Ira Berlin, Joseph P. Reidy, and Leslie S. Rowland, eds., *Freedom: A Documentary History of Emancipation, 1861–1867,* Series 2, *The Black Military Experience* (Cambridge: Cambridge University Press, 1982), 79.

42. Ibid., 82.

43. Edwin S. Redkey, ed., *A Grand Army of Black Men: Letters from African-American Soldiers in the Union Army, 1861–1865* (Cambridge: Cambridge University Press, 1992), 9–10, 24.

44. Redkey, *A Grand Army,* 10; Donald Yacovone, ed., *Freedom's Journey: African American Voices of the Civil War* (Chicago: Lawrence Hill Books, 2004), 90–93.

45. Fred Albert Shannon, *The Organization and Administration of the Union Army, 1861–1865* (Gloucester, MA: Peter Smith, 1965), 2:164.

46. Luis F. Emilio, *A Brave Black Regiment: The History of the Fifty-fourth Regiment of Massachusetts Volunteer Infantry, 1863–1865,* 2nd enlarged ed. (New York: Da Capo Press, 1995), 9–11; Virginia Matzke Adams, *On the Altar of Freedom: A Black Soldier's Civil War Letters from the Front* (Amherst: University of Massachusetts Press, 1991), xviii; A. P. Dunlop to Col. M. N. Wisewell, April 29, 1864, Letters Received, box 14, Veteran Reserve Corps, Provost Marshal General Records, RG 110, National Archives Building, Washington, DC; Noah Andre Trudeau, ed., *Voices of the 55th: Letters from the 55th Massachusetts Volunteers, 1861–1865* (Dayton, OH: Morningside House, 1996), 13.

47. Edward A. Miller Jr., *The Black Civil War Soldiers of Illinois: The Story of the Twenty-ninth U.S. Colored Infantry* (Columbia: University of South Carolina Press, 1998), 10, 12, 15–19; C. Peter Ripley, Roy E. Finkenbine, and Paul A Cimbala, eds., *The Black Abolitionist Papers,* Vol. 2, *Canada, 1830–1865* (Chapel Hill: University of North Carolina Press, 1986), 520–22.

48. Berlin et al., *Black Military Experience,* 107.

49. Emilio, *A Brave Black Regiment,* 10; Berlin et al., *Black Military Experience,* 89.

50. Versalle F. Washington, *Eagles on their Buttons: A Black Infantry Regiment in the Civil War* (Columbia: University of Missouri Press, 1999), 15–16.

51. John Hope Franklin, ed., *The Diary of James T. Ayers: Civil War Recruiter* (Baton Rouge: Louisiana State University Press, 1999), xxvii, 2, 6; Murdock, *One Million Men,* 289.

52. Murdock, *One Million Men,* 289; Berlin et al., *Black Military Experience,* 111–12, 138–40.

53. Emilio, *A Brave Black Regiment,* 9–10; McPherson, *Negro's Civil War,* 180–82.

54. Michael T. Meier, "Lorenzo Thomas and the Recruitment of Blacks in the Mississippi Valley, 1863–1865," in *Black Soldiers in Blue: African American Troops in the Civil War Era,* ed. John David Smith (Chapel Hill: University of North Carolina Press, 2002), 249–75.

55. Washington, *Eagles on their Buttons,* 14.

56. Adams, *On the Altar of Freedom,* 5, 13, 19.

57. Bruce Levine, *Confederate Emancipation: Southern Plans to Free and Arm Slaves during the Civil War* (New York: Oxford University Press, 2006), 79.

58. Quoted in Keith P. Wilson, *Campfires of Freedom: The Camp Life of Black Soldiers during the Civil War* (Kent, OH: Kent State University Press, 2002), 1.

59. Yacovone, *Freedom's Journey,* 110–11.

60. Walker, *Hell's Broke Loose,* 32.

61. Robert F. Durden, *The Gray and the Black: The Confederate Debate on Emancipation* (Baton Rouge: Louisiana State University Press, 1972), 95.

62. Lawrence Lee Hewitt, "An Ironic Route to Glory: Louisiana's Native Guard at Port Hudson," in Smith, *Black Soldiers in Blue,* 78–79; Hollandsworth, *Louisiana Native Guards,* 1–11.

63. Michael P. Johnson and James L. Roark, *Black Masters: A Free Family of Color in the Old South* (New York: W. W. Norton, 1984), 307.

64. Kenneth W. Noe, ed., *A Southern Boy in Blue: The Memoir of Marcus Woodcock, 9th Kentucky Infantry (U.S.A.)* (Knoxville: University of Tennessee Press, 1996), 95.

65. David Herbert Donald, ed., *Gone for a Soldier: The Civil War Memoirs of Private Alfred Bellard* (Boston: Little, Brown, 1975), 56–57.

66. David W. Blight, ed., *When This Cruel War Is Over: The Civil War Letters of Charles Harvey Bristol* (Amherst: University of Massachusetts Press, 1992), 117–18.

67. Yacovone, *Freedom's Journey,* 93–97; Ervin L. Jordan Jr., *Black Confederates and Afro-Yankees in Civil War Virginia* (Charlottesville: University of Virginia Press, 1995), 222–26.

68. Samuel C. Jones, *Reminiscences of the 22nd Iowa Infantry: Giving Its Organization, Marches, Skirmishes, Battles, and Sieges, as Taken from the Diary of Lieutenant S. C. Jones of Company A* (Iowa City: Press of the Camp Pope Bookshop, 1993), 7.

69. Bee, *Boys from Rockville,* xvi–xxviii, 5, 12.

70. Sellers, *A People at War,* Entries for October 27, 1862, and November 6, 1862, Henry Graham Journal, reel 37.

71. Jeffrey D. Wert, *A Brotherhood of Valor: the Common Soldiers of the Stonewall Brigade, C.S.A. and the Iron Brigade, U.S.A.* (New York: Simon & Schuster, 1999), 22.

72. Jeffrey D. Marshall, ed., *A War of the People: Vermont Civil War Letters* (Hanover, NH: University Press of New England, 1999), 19.

73. Walker, *Hell's Broke Loose,* 6, 8.

74. Michael C. Hardy, *The Thirty-seventh North Carolina Troops: Tar Heels in the Army of Northern Virginia* (Jefferson, NC: McFarland, 2003), 12; Bee, *Boys from Rockville,* 5, 12.

75. Guy R. Everson and Edward H. Simpson Jr., eds., *Far, Far from Home: The Wartime Letters of Dick and Tally Simpson, 3rd South Carolina Volunteers* (New York: Oxford University Press, 1994), 3; DeWitt Boyd Stone Jr., ed., *Wandering to Glory: Confederate Veterans Remember Evans' Brigade* (Columbia: University of South Carolina Press, 2002), 11–12.

76. James I. Robertson Jr., *The Stonewall Brigade* (Baton Rouge: Louisiana State University Press, 1978), 21.

77. J. Matthew Gallman, *Mastering Wartime: A Social History of Philadelphia during the Civil War* (Cambridge: Cambridge University Press, 1990), 12.

78. John Niven, *Connecticut for the Union: The Role of the State in the Civil War* (New Haven, CT: Yale University Press, 1965), 39.

79. Robert K. Krick, *Parker's Virginia Battery C.S.A.,* 2nd rev. ed. (Wilmington, NC: Broadfoot, 1989); Gary W. Gallagher, ed., *Fighting for the Confederacy: The Personal Recollections of General Edward Porter Alexander* (Chapel Hill: University of North Carolina Press, 1989), 162.

80. Wiley, *The Life of Billy Yank: The Common Soldier of the Union* (Garden City, NY: Doubleday, 1971), 23; Wiley, *Life of Johnny Reb,* 245.

81. Quoted in Wiley, *Life of Johnny Reb,* 245.

82. Gary D. Joiner, Marilyn S. Joiner, and Clifton D. Cardin, eds., *No Pardons to Ask, nor Apologies to Make: The Journal of William Henry King, Gray's 28th Louisiana Infantry Regiment* (Knoxville: University of Tennessee Press, 2006), 11.

83. Wiley, *Life of Johnny Reb,* 245; H. H. Cunningham, *Doctors in Gray: The Confederate Medical Service,* 2nd ed. (Baton Rouge: Louisiana State University Press, 1960), 163–65.

84. J. Franklin Dyer, *The Journal of a Civil War Surgeon,* ed. Michael B. Chesson (Lincoln: University of Nebraska Press, 2003), 2.

85. Emilio, *A Brave Black Regiment,* 19–20.

86. Donald, *Gone for a Soldier,* 5.

87. Bradley M. Gottfried, *Kearny's Own: The History of the First New Jersey Brigade in the Civil War* (New Brunswick, NJ: Rutgers University Press, 2005), 6.

88. Ella Jane Bruen and Brian M. Fitzgibbons, eds., *Through Ordinary Eyes: The Civil War Correspondence of Rufus Robbins, Private, 7th Regiment, Massachusetts Volunteers* (Westport, CT: Praeger, 2000), 29.

89. Lauren Cook Burgess, ed., *An Uncommon Soldier: The Civil War Letters of Sarah Rosetta Wakeman, Alias Pvt. Lyans Wakeman, 153rd Regiment, New York State Volunteers, 1862–1864* (New York: Oxford University Press, 1995), 3.

90. Donald C. Elder III, ed., *A Damned Iowa Greyhound: The Civil War Letters of William Henry Harrison Clayton* (Iowa City: University of Iowa Press, 1998), 7.

91. Claire E. Swedberg, ed., *Three Years with the 92d Illinois: The Civil War Diary of John M. King* (Mechanicsburg, PA: Stackpole Books, 1999), 7–8.

4   GOING OFF TO WAR

GOOD-BYE TO FAMILY AND FRIENDS

In 1861, recruits did not expect to be away from home for long when they joined their companies, but they still prepared in some way to enter into their new way of life. Husbands bade farewell to wives and children, giving them instructions for conducting home life and business while they were gone. Young men listened to words of wisdom given by concerned parents and took leave of family, friends, and sweethearts. No doubt there were many boys who married their beloveds before they left for the war, as did the Illinois private "who thought best to take to himself a wife."[1] But prudent individuals such as East Tennessee Confederate Daniel Miller disappointed their fiancées by postponing their nuptials for more propitious times.[2]

Early in the war, young men left home excited about their new adventure, with little worries about long separations, mutilation, or death. But the more thoughtful among them probably had to adjust to the unsettling feelings that accompanied leaving loved ones. Louisianan William Henry King noted in his diary that he wept when parting with his wife and children. "I shall ever remember the scene," he recorded, "for I then felt what I shall never be able to express in words."[3]

Wisconsinite John Henry Otto, a German immigrant, recalled the melancholy of the men in his company as they set out for war. "One could not help but to put the question to himself," he wrote, "Will I ever see this place and home again?" On the train he roused the company, driving away the blues with a German war song.[4] But even when men left home with what appeared to be light hearts, they might very well have been doing their best to "dispel sad feelings," as some Louisiana recruits did with their "gayety." "We sought to drown trouble in mirth," one of them recalled.[5]

Men made peace with family members as they prepared to go to war, not wishing to leave behind any hard feelings, or at least tried to explain their actions to concerned relatives. Sons tried to reassure parents by making it clear that enlistment was not an impulsive act. Confederate soldier David Pierson apologized to his father for "leaving so suddenly" but informed him that he did so "after a calm and thoughtful deliberation."[6] And 18-year-old Frank Rieley of Ohio, who had run away from home, leaving his parents worried and searching for him in local Cleveland encampments, alerted his family to his whereabouts. Not exactly apologizing, but still feeling an explanation was in order, he wrote to them from Camp Worcester, at Monroeville, Ohio, informing them that he had no regrets about his decision to enlist. It was his duty, he explained, and one that surpassed his obligations to them.[7]

Once committed to go to war, men busied themselves, as one Louisianan recorded, making "the necessary preparations for the exchange of home comforts for the trials and tribulations" of a soldier.[8] They arranged their affairs, collected their essential items, and prepared themselves psychologically for their new lives. New Yorker Henry Graham spent time preparing to leave for the army by rereading letters from a soldier friend, which gave him an idea of what to expect in camp life, and by packing his personal gear, including his checkers and chess men, "so that we shall not be wholly destitute of rational amusement."[9]

Kentucky Unionist Marcus Woodcock planned on packing something more lethal. After he enlisted he immediately ordered a Bowie knife "without which a soldier's equipment was then considered very imperfect," a large piece of steel favored by many a new Southern-born soldier. Woodcock also devoted time to less bloodthirsty concerns, as did so many other young men. He wrote letters and tended to personal business. "I was in a continued whirl of excitement during the whole evening," he noted. He returned to his company the next morning to the sound of friends urging him to be careful.[10]

Some young men exhibited their naïve perceptions of war-making by the things they thought to carry with them. Mississippian David Holt bemusedly recalled the long list of items, including a Bible and a volume of Shakespeare, he "absolutely toted" to Virginia.[11] Arkansan William E. Bevens recalled that he and his fellow recruits expected to "take our trunks and dress suits." His captain, however, "nearly paralyzed us by telling us . . . to take only one suit, a woolen top shirt and two suits of underwear."[12]

No one gave Connecticut soldier Ben Hirst such good advice. He gathered up a full load of equipment ranging from books, foodstuffs, assorted items of clothing, patent medicine, and an engraved silver flask of whiskey to "a pious book or two to read when we got settled down in camp."[13] Soldiers ended up carrying 40–50 pounds of equipment; unsurprisingly, much of their superfluous gear would soon litter roadways, as they became veteran campaigners who valued light packs. As Pennsylvanian Allen Landis later reported to his parents in 1863, the men in the veteran regiments discarded "everything but the clothing upon their backs."[14]

Many of these new soldiers took advantage of daguerreotype shops and had their pictures made for their families either before or shortly after they left home. Iowa's Jasper Grays even posed for two company pictures.[15] Sitting for such portraits was a novel experience for most soldiers, but the act also had a sober purpose. As one soldier later wrote about his picture, "If anything happens [to] me you can Keep it in memory of me."[16]

THE RENDEZVOUS

At the height of the secession crisis, many Southern companies rushed off to invest federal property or man defenses, while after the firing on Fort Sumter, Northern troops made their way south to defend Washington or other critical points endangered by rebel threats. At a time when both Northerners and Southerners expected a short war and men volunteered for 90 days' service, state authorities were more concerned with moving men quickly to the front. In the wake of the first rush of the summer of 1861, however, many new recruits made the transition from civilian to military routine at rendezvous camps in their home states, where signs of their former lives were close at hand and where officers were just learning how to impose rigid discipline on the erstwhile civilians.

Frequently, the new soldiers first met their comrades at a designated place near their homes at an appointed time. Southern companies milled about the town squares of county seats or camped at plantations of prominent men while waiting to be mustered into state service or for orders to move on to centralized camps. Northern companies acted in similar fashion or congregated at urban armories before they settled into rendezvous camps set up by state governments on land that once had been farms and county fairgrounds. In the case of the 40th New York, the men had to endure bunking and drilling in an old, cramped ironworks in Manhattan and then in another uncomfortable building, a flour mill, north of the city in Yonkers before they pitched their tents in an open field overlooking the Hudson River.[17] At some point along the way from the first gathering to their relocation to the rendezvous camps, the volunteers added their names to descriptive lists for their companies (which would maintain a record of their service throughout their term of enlistment), swore an oath, were mustered into the service, and received uniforms and other military equipment, including weapons, when they were available.

The initial gathering places of many of the men, still so close to home, did not encourage discipline or even allow a clean break with civilian life. During the spring of 1861, volunteers in the 28th Louisiana Infantry expected their colonel to allow them to go home to harvest their crops, while the volunteers soon to become part of the 13th Texas Cavalry gathered at a camp near Crockett in Houston County, where they visited saloons, friends, and family members.[18] Colonel Oliver Otis Howard, a veteran of Regular army training, was disturbed by the visible lack of discipline when he first met his new regiment encamped on the statehouse grounds at Augusta, Maine. He wondered if the men understood the deadly nature of their enterprise, such was the festive atmosphere of the encampment. The camp's population, he recalled, was swollen with wives, sweethearts, and parents of soldiers, "but notwithstanding the seriousness of the occasion, there was more gala excitement than solemnity." Indeed, he noted, "Many soldiers were even jubilant; some had been drinking and some were swearing." All were talking of a short campaign of a few months' duration, so the new colonel did his best to bring a sober note to the assembled troops, warning them to prepare for war, not a "holiday."[19] Regardless of the discipline he and other officers tried to impose, Howard's men and recruits throughout the land found opportunities to say good-bye one more time before heading off to larger or more distant rendezvous camps, with the orations of politicians, the sobs of family, and the cheers and fanfare of the local citizens ringing in their ears.

States generally had one or more conveniently located rendezvous camps at which new regiments were formed. Such camps required an expanse of land near adequate transportation routes that could contain large numbers of men. In the North, that meant facilities near urban centers, with good roads and railroad connections sufficient to hold at least the four to eight regiments that the federal government expected to assemble at the state camps. At the outbreak of the war, for example, volunteers inundated Harrisburg, Pennsylvania, a place with good transportation connections; Pennsylvania governor Andrew G. Curtin had them establish camp on the local fairgrounds north of the capital city.[20] Indeed, fairgrounds often served the purpose well, but officials used whatever was available.

Louisiana established Camp Moore in a barren spot 80 miles above New Orleans, where most of the state's troops destined for campaigns in the east entered army life.[21] Louisiana officials wisely located the place away from the temptations of the fabled port city, but many camps were situated near state capitals, county seats, and population centers, where supplies and transportation could be easily had. The process of getting to these camps—for some new soldiers, the farthest they had ever traveled from home—provided many inexperienced recruits with the novelty of traveling by rail or boat through unfamiliar countryside. Soldiers already at a Texas camp found train arrivals a call for celebration; they soon took advantage of the transportation to enjoy the novelties of Houston on a regular basis.[22] Georgia boys fresh off upcountry farms traveled to Savannah, not only experiencing new life in military camps, but also the charms of a city for the first time. Some were impressed, while others found the town, its residents, and its climate disappointing.[23]

The earliest arrivals at rendezvous camps frequently had to fend for themselves and then perhaps also prepare for those men who would follow them. Louisiana soldier William Henry King recorded that his regiment had to clear ground for their tents at their regimental camp and that "filth of the most disgusting kinds had to be moved."[24] When Alfred Bellard and his comrades arrived at Trenton, New Jersey's, Camp Olden at nine o'clock in the evening, they pitched tents "with a great deal of swearing," their progress hindered by their inexperience.[25] The First and Fourth Iowa Cavalry regiments rendezvoused at an empty field, were issued building materials, and proceeded to construct their shelter, an experience they shared with the 33rd Iowa Infantry.[26] But even when soldiers found shelter awaiting them, they could be disappointed. Horace Emerson complained that the "damn Shanties" at Camp Randall did little to keep them or their bunks dry.[27]

The need for shelter for ever-increasing numbers of soldiers was also apparent at Elmira, New York. Elmira had suitable rail facilities to move men to the rendezvous, but the factory initially designated as the soldiers' barracks quickly proved to be inadequate. Over 6,000 soldiers arrived at the camp within the first month of its existence; men filled the barracks for which officials had contracted and also took up residence in other available large buildings in the town, including churches.[28]

Camps were indeed crowded places. Elmira quickly constructed shelter capable of holding thousands of soldiers, and within less than three months of the firing on Fort Sumter, 9,500 recruits had passed through the camp.[29] In late 1861, there were 15,000 men at the St. Louis, Missouri, Benton rendezvous, and the barracks, where men slept in bunks "three tiers high," were drafty affairs in which coal smoke provoked constant coughing among the men. A Minnesota cavalry trooper called the crowded Benton Barracks "truly a most execrable place."[30] So many men crammed into confined spaces turned camps into especially foul-smelling places. Camp Holmes, located near Austin, Texas, according to Theophilus Perry, had an odor "that is sickening after one has been absent from there awhile." But all camps in Perry's estimation "will smell badly" no matter "how nice they are kept."[31]

Recruits found the press of humanity to be disturbing and the lack of privacy to be troubling. Nevertheless, there were some recruits who discovered that the camps provided a tonic to cure the boredom of civilian life. The newfound freedom of the rendezvous camp also encouraged mischievous—if not outright—bad behavior. Soldiers at Louisiana's Camp Moore might have been living far from the pleasures of the city of

New Orleans, but they found ways to obtain liquor to liven up camp life.[32] Camp Randall, Wisconsin, was home to clever Yankee volunteers who, in May 1861, escaped the compound, became drunk, and engaged in a gunfight with the proprietor of the brewery, who was defending his stock.[33] Matters did not improve as the war progressed. In 1862, at Camp Curtin, Pennsylvania, for example, soldiers unhindered by discipline "rushed the guards to go bathing in the river."[34] Also in 1862, volunteers from the Keokuk, Iowa, camp engaged in a serious brawl with drunken firemen who had harassed convalescing soldiers in the town hotel. In the evening, 300 men from the camp returned to "finish the job." They could not find any of the firemen, so they went to the theater instead.[35] Such were the social opportunities had by new soldiers camping near a town.

One of the causes of the early difficulties between soldiers and townsfolk was the fact that the rendezvous camps lacked much during the chaotic early months of the war, including food and discipline. After Fort Sumter, Connecticut volunteers arrived at New Haven to find inadequate shelter and limited cooking facilities awaiting them. The initial camp location was less than ideal because officials dismissed offers by owners of other lots who hoped to turn the newly arrived soldiers into a profitable entertainment for the local residents by selling tickets to the drills. They rose to the challenge and within a short time quartered two regiments at a park in the town's suburbs and a third on fairgrounds some distance away, at Hartford. At New Haven, 50 recruits still lacking proper rations, and having not yet internalized military discipline, went absent without leave from the First Regiment to rustle up a proper meal. The unhappy situation was not simply the consequence of inexperience on the part of commissary officers. Officials contracted with business men to the feed the soldiers, who dealt with subcontractors, who did their best to squeeze profit out of the allocations provided for provisions by skimping on what they provided for the men.[36]

Other camps had comparable problems that reflected the difficult nature of mustering new armies for the war. New recruits at Camp Trousdale in Tennessee, for example, suffered from poor food, bad sanitation, and lack of equipment.[37] At the Burlington, Iowa, rendezvous, John Quincy Adams Campbell recorded that the food left such a poor impression on some of the men that they "kicked over the table and raised quite a breeze," while also noting that diarrhea was "a prevailing disease in camp."[38]

While in their first camps, some of the new recruits still enjoyed the society of local women, who used their domestic skills to help ease this difficult transition of volunteers to military life. Jacksonville, Illinois, women sewed and baked for the new soldiers at Camp Duncan, first coming together in church groups that developed into voluntary associations.[39] The women from Keokuk, Iowa, brought cakes to soldiers at the training camp, enjoying the break in their own daily routines by witnessing the drills, a practice that wives, daughters, and curious women would continue across the North throughout the war.[40]

Not to be outdone by the enemy, Southern women also did their part, feeding body and spirit with their presence at the camps. When, in April 1861, Alabama's Greensboro Guards gathered in town to offer their services to the Confederacy, they waited for orders, drilled, visited with friends and family, and ate well thanks to "the ladies" who supplied the soldiers "with every delicacy."[41] At the Asheville, North Carolina, camps, women brought food to the troops but also amused them by singing "Dixie" and engaging in a feminine version of military drill. Soldiers from one company listened to a rousing speech from one of their female visitors, paraded about the town square, and enjoyed cheers and flowers offered by the ladies.[42]

Some recruits who watched their fellows thoroughly enjoying themselves with such activities might admit that they were not yet soldiers. "We were, perhaps, becoming too comfortable with camp life," Henry Comey reported prior to leaving Massachusetts for Washington, D.C., in July 1861.[43] "We think now that playing soldier is a grand thing," John Henry Cowin, a Greensboro, Alabama, volunteer, also wisely observed, "but let's see the end of the twelve months, wonder how we will then like it."[44]

Despite the relatively short stay at these rendezvous camps, ranging from several weeks to a couple of months, it was at such places that Northern and Southern regiments began to take shape. There were regiments that moved from their rendezvous directly to the front, but depending on circumstances, other units continued the transition from civilian life to military life at larger camps of instruction such as the Benton Barracks in St. Louis and the numerous camps near Richmond and Washington. It was a transformation that was never entirely impressed on the civilian volunteers, but it was usually at these camps that the recruits began to understand that they were no longer civilians. It was a process that at least eventually forced men to understand that "not everything can be done according [to] ones own will and with full personal liberty."[45]

EARLY TRAINING

Few men, including those who had paraded with antebellum volunteer companies, had had much experience with the military on the scale that suited the larger organizations and serious purpose now required of them. Given how men received commissions, not many of the recruits had the benefit of well-trained officers to indoctrinate them into the mysteries of military service. Men elected by recruits and commissioned by governors were not necessarily well versed in tactics and discipline. Furthermore, many of the volunteers who became company leaders had little understanding of the nature of their duties. Nineteen-year-old Elisha Hunt Rhodes was proud of his election to first sergeant in a company of the Second Rhode Island Infantry in the spring of 1861 but admitted "just what a First Sergeant's duty might be I have no idea."[46]

At local camps and at the rendezvous, however, some volunteers benefited from the experiences of Mexican war veterans, foreign-trained officers, and military academy cadets and graduates, but there were simply not enough of such men to go around. Regimental commanders were aware of the lack of experience of new officers and did their best to correct it. North Carolinian Charles Bahnson's colonel drilled new officers an hour each day, even while the officers continued to drill their new recruits.[47] And Robert Gould Shaw established a school for the officers of the 54th Massachusetts.[48]

Not only did these men need to learn how to lead on the battlefield, they also had to know how to keep up with the army paperwork that would become their constant companion. Tri-folded documents, multiple copies of forms, and properly kept regimental books and muster rolls would have an impact on the effectiveness and morale of a unit. Furthermore, paperwork errors could plague a soldier and his family when the volunteer ended his service either as a veteran or a casualty. As Thomas Wentworth Higginson later noted in 1864, "One wrong spelling in a muster-roll may beggar a soldier's children ten years after the father has been killed in battle."[49]

Some of the more conscientious officers modestly realized they were as green as their men and tried to correct their deficiencies by perusing the standard military texts of the day. One North Carolina officer drilled his company during the day while studying all night, while Ohioan Alvin Voris studied his manuals in the evenings, keeping one drill lesson ahead of his men.[50] New Yorker Josiah Favill recorded, during the early days of training his men at a Staten Island rendezvous, "After dark I devoured the army regulations, and the book of tactics, and was proud and happy indeed."[51] By midsummer of 1861, such study was important if a Yankee volunteer officer wished to keep his position; after the fiasco at Bull Run, the U.S. Congress initiated a system of examination of officers that could lead to the removal of incompetent men.[52]

Both Northern and Southern units suffered from a lack of uniformity in how these new officers drilled their men. But despite their inexperience, conscientious commanders tried to do their best. The better company officers drilled the men to the point where they had some sense of what it was like to carry themselves as "real soldiers."[53] The smart ones understood the critical nature of having good noncommissioned officers assist them in their work. The wisest of them understood that long days of drill curbed mischief among enlisted men too tired to get into trouble. And William Vermillion believed that six to eight hours of drill for the men at Keokuk, Iowa, would keep them healthy.[54]

In 1861, tenderfoot horse soldiers learned to sit in their saddles, especially Yankee city boys like those in the Sixth Pennsylvania Cavalry, who had never ridden before signing up.[55] Texas cavalrymen, long familiar with horses, spent the better part of the day training because even if they could stay in their saddles, neither they nor their mounts had experience at soldiering. Colonel Henry McCulloch appointed special officers to supervise the training of his Texas horsemen's drill, while Colonel William H. Parson, aware of the dangers of idleness among soldiers, had his Texas troopers go beyond the usual drill and ride their horses through a course of jumps that included fences and ditches.[56]

In 1862 the 12th Illinois Cavalry lacked mounts; they kept busy drilling on foot and learning the lore of soldiering, which was in fact the common practice among new Yankee

Photograph of Washington, 1862–1865, view of the defenses of Washington. Photograph of 1st Connecticut Artillery drilling at Fort Richardson. (*Library of Congress*)

troopers. By the end of the summer of 1861, officials provided horses for Union cavalry volunteers who had previously had to bring their own. Thus the Illinois volunteer Yankee cavalry and most of their comrades had the added burden of breaking and training newly issued horses, but Confederate troopers continued to have the advantage and the responsibility of bringing familiar mounts with them, as their cavalry service required.[57]

New artillerymen also picked up the rudiments of working their equipment. Some of the men who had been in well-known antebellum volunteer artillery companies, such as those Louisianans in New Orleans's Washington Artillery or Virginia's Portsmouth Light Artillery and the Norfolk Light Artillery Blues, had had some prewar familiarity with their guns, caissons, and limbers; others had none and would need considerable drill.[58] Presumably, the 70 volunteers from Virginia's Shenandoah Valley who voted to organize as the Rockbridge Artillery would need training, and they received it at the hands of the Reverend William Nelson Pendleton. Fortunately, Pendleton, a West Point graduate, was able to use Virginia Military Institute's cannon to break in his company.[59] Other new Confederate batteries gathered at the old fairgrounds near Richmond, Virginia, then known as Camp Lee, in late 1861 through the spring of 1862 to learn the artillery drill. William Parker's boys spent almost two months there polishing their skills and waiting for equipment, although because of a shortage of ammunition, they and their companion batteries probably had not much chance of firing their guns before leaving the camp.[60]

Infantrymen drilled, sometimes for the better part of the day, as did Lyman Holfield at Wisconsin's Camp Randall.[61] Men who would serve in the 37th North Carolina Infantry drilled for five hours each day while at their Camp Fisher rendezvous.[62] Black soldiers in the 22nd U.S. Colored Troops drilled most of the day, with noncommissioned officers spending extra time in classes studying their own particular duties.[63] Despite all of this martial activity, Yankee officer Alvin Voris still believed the entire time devoted to training new soldiers before moving to the front was inadequate.[64]

Some men learned how to fire their weapons, although marksmanship training was difficult for some units that lacked the equipment or the time. New Confederate recruits at Camp Trousdale, Tennessee, trained with anything that resembled a rifle but the rifle itself. The problem of arming the Southern recruits at the outset of the war was serious. Officers detached members of the 28th Louisiana Infantry to return to their homes to requisition weapons from the civilian population, but William Henry King puzzled over the efficacy of the move. Not only would it leave home folks defenseless, but "what benefit can they be to us without ammunition?"[65]

Yankees also had some problems with equipping their men and training them to handle the weapons they received. For a while, the 22nd Iowa drilled with "wooden guns and swords of their own manufacture."[66] Another Yankee regiment left Camp Randall on August 1, 1861, with no rifles, arriving at Baltimore with only half the men armed; finally, on September 1, the regiment was fully outfitted with weapons.[67] After arriving in camp in Washington, D.C., Charles Harvey Brewster found it remarkable when the 10th Massachusetts actually engaged in skirmish drill with blank cartridges, "which we have not done before."[68] And when Alvin Voris's regiment arrived in Virginia in January 1862 after their training at Camp Chase, Ohio, he reported that half of the "innocent creatures...cannot yet make any practical use of a gun."[69] In the end, many officers probably agreed with Thomas J. Morgan, a commander of black troops, when he noted after his troops were sent into the field without much training that they "so learned to soldier by soldiering."[70]

Confederate recruits were certain that each one of them could easily handle at least five Yankees in a fight. Such an assumption might have left them dubious about the need to engage in routine training exercises, especially when most of them believed, in the spring of 1861, that the war would be over within months.[71] Yankee recruits also were reluctant participants in all of this drilling, so eager were they to end the war with one "good, sound drumming" of the enemy, an attitude that revealed their uninitiated view of the trials they were about to face as soldiers. As Wisconsin John Henry Otto, then a sergeant and formerly a Prussian soldier, unsuccessfully tried to explain to his men, "drumming" the rebels was a fine idea, but "there were two parties in the game, and that the party who were prepared best and know how to obey orders would do the drumming part."[72]

Officers at times made some interesting subjective observations about which men in the ranks most readily adapted to the rigors of drill and military discipline. Officers of black soldiers frequently commented on the ease with which their men, particularly the ex-slaves, took to the regimentation of soldiering, although some were perceptive enough to understand that their men worked hard at soldiering because their freedom and the future of their race depended on their performance. But such judgments were not confined to black recruits. John Henry Otto saw a soldierly advantage held by some men because of their prewar work routines. "The best men always were mechanics and farmers and laborers," he judged. Students, clerks, and other office workers and the sons of influential families had a "conceited pride"; they believed that "they stood far above all order and discipline." "But few of them," he concluded, "made good soldiers."[73] The German soldier was an observant drillmaster. The better soldiers might very well have been the individuals already used to discipline and hierarchy in their earlier work lives.

Most white Northern and Southern volunteers had had little experience with being commanded about by others; many, especially in Southern units, resented it. In the fall of 1861, for example, planters in one Texas company found that military regimentation was "repugnant to them, of which they make no secret."[74] But some Northern men, such as the Connecticut factory workers from Rockville, might have adapted to the discipline of drill much more readily than other soldiers who had experienced less regimented lives before enlisting. Their long, regulated days of machine tending under the supervision of foremen combined with the understanding that they all needed to work as a team if the factory were to produce goods might have already acquainted them with taking orders, doing tedious tasks, and thinking of themselves as part of a team. Such experience they could readily transfer to their army service, a decided advantage over their high-spirited, self-important, but undisciplined counterparts in both armies.[75]

In the end, experience would prove to be the best teacher for the new soldiers, but at least the rendezvous camps provided the occasion for beginning the recruits' psychological adjustment to military ways, including the machine-like discipline that citizens initially found difficult to accept. Drill and discipline awakened many recruits to the fact that the army was making them into something different from what they had been before the war. Yankee Warren Goss later recalled that hard drill substituted "blind, unquestioning obedience to military rules," in place of "methods of action and thought common to citizens."[76] Indeed, some men compared soldiering to being a "volunteer slave," others an inmate in a penitentiary.[77] Men also commonly referred to their transformation into a machine, an "automaton," as Confederate Sam Watkins later wrote, to do the bidding of "a good, bad, or indifferent engineer."[78] It was a sentiment shared by Yankees, too. In September 1862 Stephen F. Fleharty found that the men of the

102nd Illinois Infantry at Camp McMurty, Knoxville, Illinois, were "gradually being moulded into the form of a disciplined army. Yet it takes time to learn to be a machine!"[79]

CITIZENS ADJUST TO SOLDIERING

Elisha Hunt Rhodes's early days in the Second Rhode Island revealed the naïveté of many a new soldier who resisted the early efforts to impose military discipline on him. When Rhodes transferred to another company, he reverted from his sergeant's rank to that of private. "As I did not know much about sergeants or privates and cared less," he admitted, "I was satisfied." Since the regiment was still located near Rhodes's home, he expected to be able to go home at night, "but the Captain said that I was a soldier and must sleep in the Armory." He and his fellows were upset by their confinement. "As we were still citizens we claimed the right to do as we pleased." Nevertheless, Rhodes was promoted to "Eight Corporal." "This made me feel all right towards the Captain, but just what an Eight Corporal had to do I did not know. And why I should be eight I did not at the time understand." By early June, when Rhodes and his comrades bedded down in their quarters, he noted, "We did not howl all night either, for we found that as we were now regularly mustered into the U.S. Service we couldn't do as we pleased."[80] In Rhodes's case, signing the muster roll sparked some understanding of the new situation in which he and his comrades found themselves.

Rhodes and his friends were not alone in how they initially resented the military's treatment of them. But sooner or later, most recruits came to accept their new situations. "We are now soldiers, citizens no longer," George Cram came to understand at Camp Childs, Chicago.[81] For some men, that realization came when they traveled to rendezvous camps or camps closer to the front. Some resented the fact that they could not travel in comfort, as a civilian might expect, even if they could afford to do so. A sergeant of the 76th Ohio "felt the mortification of being forced below my social level" when he boarded a steamer in Cincinnati and watched as some "socially inferior" officers settled into cabins, while the men had to make do "on the deck or in the hold."[82] Recruits boarding their transport vessel at Hartford, Connecticut, expected to be able to purchase first-class tickets. The enlisted men learned, however, that that was not their prerogative. "Gradually," one of their numbers later recalled, "they were finding out they were no longer citizens, but on their way to war."[83]

For many Southern recruits, such treatment stung. In May 1861, three companies of Arkansas soldiers boarded a ship for Memphis, Tennessee, and learned that they were at the mercy of officers who had separated themselves from the enlisted men. "We are all kept down on deck, have no place to sleep and nothing to eat," Alex Spence complained. "The officers of our Company do not seem to study the wants of their men, without the men are treated like *free and white men* ought to be." He predicted that some of the men would refuse to continue on to Virginia "without they have guarantees that they will be treated better." As for himself, Spence planned to ask the officers to allow him to pay for his own passage from Memphis to Virginia "so that I can fare like *white men* ought."[84]

Given the nature of recruiting early in the war, Civil War companies generally reflected the community connections and hierarchies common before the war, thus allowing soldiers to begin their wartime days taking along some sense of familiar social relationships to the strange new setting of military camp. Alabama's Greensboro Guards, a volunteer company in existence since the 1820s, went to war as a unit sharing a common community identity, which for about half the men also meant recognizing the antebellum bonds enjoyed by local slaveholding families.[85] The 15th Mississippi Infantry contained companies recruited from the same communities, and its leadership cadre consisted of the more prominent individuals from those communities.[86] But all of these men, despite any deference they might have shown to members of their antebellum communities, had grown up used to their democratic traditions.

New recruits, Yankees or rebels, were used to having their say as civilians. These new soldiers were American citizens steeped in the lore of independence and equality for white men. Some, including those who had yet to reach voting age, had enthusiastically participated in electoral campaigns, and all expected to cast votes for their local, state, and national leaders in the future. They had voluntarily joined the army and had willingly given up some of their freedom, but even soldiers who respected their communities' social hierarchies and the accomplishments of their betters considered themselves to be free men and no one's slaves. Confederates in one Louisiana company, for example, threatened not to move until they had received their promised bounty money. As one of the men recorded in his diary, it was not "simply fifty dollars we were contending for"; rather, they did not like being "swindled" by officers who had made a promise to them. "*Against wrong & for right,* we started out to contend," he explained, "then, why go abroad to correct evils before correcting those which exist in our midst?"[87]

Recruits expected their officers to tend to their rights, and many of them expected to have a say in how they participated in the war. That same company of Louisianans deprived of their bounty had earlier voted against being attached to the 28th Louisiana Infantry. When their leaders ignored the wishes of the men, the officers felt the need to appease the "disaffected" with "better places" to maintain harmony in the company.[88] Also, not only did Georgia's Pulaski Volunteers select their officers, as was the common practice at the time, but they petitioned their governor for a place in the regiment of their choice.[89] Union Kentuckians also felt at ease making their displeasure known to generals when they discovered that promises made at enlistment went unfulfilled. In the fall of 1861, as free men, they had agreed to serve in an artillery company soon disbanded but assumed that they were being abused by authority when they were assigned to infantry against their will. They claimed the right in a petition to General Don Carlos Buell to select "whatever branch of service was most suitable to our several tastes and inclinations."[90]

Recruits in the Pulaski Volunteers and other organizations had that sense of equality reinforced when men first selected their officers. These elections might not have been as free and open as some soldiers might have wished—some recruiters secured promises of support from men as they built their companies and regiments—but they underlined the sense that enlisted men were not inferior to officers and that officers were not naturally superior to enlisted men. This might especially be the case where men actively courted the votes of their comrades. Louisiana soldiers, for example, engaged in a very active electoral campaign at Camp Moore; so, too, did members of the First New Jersey Cavalry, who split their support between two lieutenant colonels, both claiming to be the legitimate winner of the election.[91] Texan James Bates remarked on "the tricks & turns & electioneering schemes of the candidates," which "would afford infinite amusement" if the matter did not have such serious consequences.[92] Later in the war, South Carolinian Tally Simpson confessed that these elections brought out the worst in his fellow soldiers when an election failed to go his way. Some of his fellow South Carolinians, "the most consummate villains…I ever knew," had promised to vote for him and then failed to do so. "We live and learn," he concluded, "and each day I lose confidence in mankind."[93]

While some elections were contentious and competitive, others ratified the positions of men who had already assumed leadership roles in raising companies and regiments or who had been promised commands by the politicians.[94] Regardless, the men scrutinized and analyzed the abilities of those individuals who would lead them into battle. In 1862 John King of Illinois noted that "every man in the regiment had his private opinion" of the men standing for positions as regimental officers. "Not one of them was so good that you could not find something faulty, neither were they so bad that you could not find something to commend," he concluded.[95] "Officers were not gods to us," Down Easter Harold Adams Small explained, "they were studied most critically and their capacities were closely measured."[96] Indeed, it took time for some men to realize that officers controlled all moments of their lives. One Nantucket recruit in the 20th Massachusetts in camp at Readville made it clear that he was his own man when he responded to efforts to stop him and his fellows from taking a swim: "Why shouldn't a man go where he pleased when his day's work was done . . . without asking leave of any God-damn officer?"[97]

Union and Confederate officers attempted to impose cleanliness, uniformity, and an orderly appearance on their men even as they trained them to fight; they tried to keep their men from swearing, and in general, they imposed on them to behave well. All such efforts on their part could earn them the unfair reputation of being martinets, especially among the new recruits still resisting discipline. Critical soldiers commented on the rigid nature of officers, men who might have been their neighbors or business associates only a few short months before they had enlisted. Abner Small came "to be conscious of the immensity of icy space between the officers and the rank and file." Now, he understood, "friendly neighbors in civilian life, one spreading manure and the other cleaning fish, were now immeasurably apart."[98] Robert K. Beecham noted that when he enlisted in the Second Wisconsin in May 1861, he "was all unaware of the wide and almost impassable gulf that yawns between the enlisted soldier and commissioned officers." He soon learned the lesson when an officer severely chastised him for not removing his hat in the presence of an officer. "I was only a country boy of 23 years and imagined that no soldier of the republic was a menial, and that I had no call to uncover while standing in his presence; but the noble colonel, knowing that such unsoldierly conduct, if not at once rebuked and eradicated, would lead to the defeat of our armies in the field and the overthrow of the republic, said to me very firmly," to take off the hat in the presence of his superiors. The experience damped his spirits, but he became determined not to forget the nature of the American soldier if he ever became an officer, promising to retain "sufficient manhood and common sense to treat a private soldier as a gentleman and as an American citizen."[99]

The gap between soldier and officer dawned on other men where camp discipline was most strict. Men admitted that they no longer could claim all the rights of free men. In June 1861 New Yorker Charles W. Gould was training at Camp Scot on Staten Island. He informed his sister that despite the pleasant location, he was unable to enjoy it; rather, he was "bound down by riged laws under the control of officers who do with soldiers as they wish." He and his fellow soldiers suffered from cold, heat, and numerous inconveniences, "besides with little more freedom than the slave. The pleasures of heaven would I think pass unenjoied by us were they here."[100] In the fall of 1862 Illinoisan George F. Cram was at Camp Childs, Chicago, under the control of "very strict" and uncaring officers. Submission to the will of officers, he admitted the following month after arriving in Kentucky, had turned him and his comrades into new creatures.

"We are now soldiers," he explained, "citizens no longer."[101] Another soldier, John M. King, noted the same change after he arrived at Camp Fuller, Rockford, Illinois. "I had been in school and my mind was active," he lamented, "but now the mind had nothing to do but to obey."[102]

LEAVING RENDEZVOUS CAMPS

One of the last local public ceremonies that the new soldiers experienced before leaving for the seat of war was the flag presentation by the women of the community. By passing on national and regimental flags often made by their own hands or purchased with funds they had raised, women charged their men to protect the nation and their homes. They imbued those pieces of cloth with a sense of honor and an identity that reached back to their hearths. To disgrace the colors of the regiment by cowardly or immoral behavior would shame the entire community. At one such occasion, the "prominent women of Boston," including some officers' wives, presented the Second Massachusetts Infantry with a national flag before a large crowd. A local politician representing the women reminded the men that the flag's "folds will never be stained, that they will ever wave foremost among the foremost where duty and honor call." That evening, Henry Comey and his friends, members of the regiment, vowed to defend the flag with their lives and "promised each other that it would never fall in battle or be disgraced, regardless of our personal sacrifices."[103]

It was often after such ceremonies that the men broke camp for the rendezvous or left their rendezvous for sites near the front. Early in the war, they did so in a festive style. Men might have pondered the deadly purpose of their new calling, but the excitement of travel probably kept most soldiers' minds off melancholy thoughts, as communities fed them, celebrated them, and hailed them as heroes as they moved closer to the fight, just as communities had done as the men had traveled to their first rendezvous. In the spring of 1861, John Henry Cowin of Alabama found that the people he and his comrades encountered on their travels from Greensboro to Selma, Alabama, happily catered to their needs. And when they finally departed for Virginia, they encountered along the way ladies "cheering us on, waving flags, throwing us boquets, pieces of poetry &c."[104]

Northerners treated their heroes in a similar fashion. Henry Comey encountered "at every station along the way, from Boston to Groton, Connecticut, people" who "gathered to wish us well and wave small American Flags." As his Massachusetts regiment traveled through Pennsylvania, they continued to meet cheering citizens, and "in many places a drink and victuals were brought to us by the ladies of the area."[105]

Despite such celebration, newly enlisted men traveled in ways that reminded them of the reality of military life. Iowan A. F. Sperry recalled that his regiment packed onto a river steamer "like freight in a boat, which afterward became so familiar that nothing better was expected."[106] Such style of travel also reminded them of what they had learned in camp: officers had a better life than they had. When brothers Lycurgus and George Remley left the Benton Barracks for Rolla, Missouri, they "crowded into cattle cars fixed up with rough board seats," while their officers rode in "a first class passenger car."[107]

Of course, as the war progressed long beyond its expected conclusion, not all soldiers shared in the enthusiastic farewells that the volunteer companies and regiments experienced. Excitement diminished as the war ground on, and soldiers leaving for the front had become an ordinary sight. Northern voluntary associations soon replaced

Regimental musicians provided the martial music for men marching off to war. (*Library of Congress*)

spontaneous roadside feasts with regular "soldiers' rests" that lasted throughout the war to provide some refreshment and comfort to the traveling Billy Yank.[108] It might also have appeared to civilians that the latecomers to the war did not deserve much celebration.

In the South, conscription officers gathered up men in small groups and then sent them off to special camps of instruction in the various states. Ideally the men would receive physical examinations and some training in the camps, but too often, the desperate manpower needs of the Confederate armies meant that the camp commander quickly dispersed them to established units. Not only did the men miss the fanfare showered on the volunteers, but they also missed the companionship of friends and neighbors. Confederate conscripts could ask to be assigned to companies that had been recruited from their neighborhoods, and the military bureaucrats would comply if they deemed it practicable. However, the need to fill regiments meant men were likely not to have their wish, which angered them and encouraged desertion.[109]

Northern substitutes and conscripts also made their way to the front in a similar fashion, first stopping at conscript camps for some instruction, although officials probably expected veterans to introduce replacements in the art of soldiering. Northerners generally assumed that conscripts and substitutes were not as dedicated to the cause as were the earlier volunteers and thus were not as trustworthy to keep their pledges to serve. Indeed, the actions of these individuals confirmed much of what the civilians thought of them. In Connecticut, substitutes attempted to burn down the conscript camp at New Haven, attacked their guards while escaping from the New Haven and New London camps, and leaped from the moving trains to cheat the government of their service.[110]

It was not surprising, then, to find conscripts and substitutes under heavy guard at rendezvous camps and en route to the front. Indeed, one Invalid Corps guard reported that after losing some substitutes to desertion, "We now keep them as closely confined as prisoners with pieces loaded, so that they would have rather a disagreeable time of it to get away."[111] However, Frank Wilkeson's experiences vividly illustrate the approach taken by the Northern military not only toward conscripts and substitutes, but toward late-arriving volunteers as well.

In 1863 Wilkeson, a young New Yorker, joined the 11th New York Battery at Albany when he was not yet 16 years old. As his unit was in Virginia, the authorities deemed it best policy to keep the volunteer in the heavily guarded penitentiary building, a place he shared with "eight hundred or one thousand ruffians." He remained in "this nasty prison for a month," during which time he had his patriotism and his person abused by the bounty jumpers who made up most of the inmates. The entire crowd of men marched through the streets chained and under bayonet guard, heckled by street urchins and mocked by the people who witnessed the scene, finally ending up herded into the hull of a transport vessel. Such treatment led the volunteer to wonder "musingly if I were a patriot or simply a young fool."[112]

The conscripts and substitutes with whom Frank Wilkeson traveled deserted when they could, but even the volunteers of 1861 and 1862, while determined to make it to the war, made some mischief along the way. In June 1861 Louisiana soldiers heading for Richmond from Pensacola, Florida, hijacked their train, uncoupling the last car, which happened to contain their officers. They ran drunken riot in Montgomery, Alabama, until their abandoned superiors arrived and beat some discipline into the men. On the rails to Richmond, the men continued to behave badly, killing an officer, uncoupling cars, and then repeating their Montgomery antics in Columbia, South Carolina. Another group of Louisiana men smuggled liquor on board their train at a stop in Tennessee, broke into liquor stores in the town, rioted, chased officers into a hotel, and set fire to the building. These wild Louisianans were a unique group of men, but behavior of this sort was not unknown elsewhere among Northern and Southern soldiers.[113]

As some men made their way to camps closer to the battlefields of the war, they began to ponder the immensity and danger of their undertaking. In October 1862, when Vermonter George R. Benedict arrived at Washington, he was struck by the fact that his regiment was only a small "part of the big army of the Republic."[114] John McCandish King Jr.'s mind drifted to more sober thoughts as he made his way to the front after leaving the rendezvous camp at Rockford, Illinois. While bound for Chicago and eventually the war, he considered what lay before him. "What was going to be our future?" he wrote. "We were going out for the express purpose of shooting men and other men were coming out on the other side of the line for the express purpose of shooting us." Travel and novel scenery kept his mind off further melancholy thoughts, as undoubtedly they did for other men on their way to the front.[115] But they could not for long ignore the very purpose for which they had joined the army.

NOTES

1. David D. Roe, ed., with commentary and annotations by Stephen R. Wise, *A Civil War Soldier's Diary: Valentine C. Randolph, 39th Illinois Regiment* (DeKalb: Northern Illinois University Press, 2006), 11.

2. John D. Fowler, *Mountaineers in Gray: The Nineteenth Tennessee Volunteer Infantry Regiment, C.S.A.* (Knoxville: University of Tennessee Press, 2004), 17.

3. Gary D. Joiner, Marilyn S. Joiner, and Clifton D. Cardin, eds., *No Pardons to Ask, nor Apologies to Make: The Journal of William Henry King, Gray's 28th Louisiana Infantry Regiment* (Knoxville: University of Tennessee Press, 2006), 1–2.

4. David Gould and James B. Kennedy, eds., *Memoirs of a Dutch Mudsill: The "War Memories" of John Henry Otto, Captain, Company D, 21st Regiment Wisconsin Volunteer Infantry* (Kent, OH: Kent State University Press, 2004), 6.

5. Joiner et al., *No Pardons to Ask,* 5.

6. Thomas W. Cutrer and T. Michael Parrish, eds., *Brothers in Gray: The Civil War Letters of the Pierson Family* (Baton Rouge: Louisiana State University Press, 1997), 13.

7. David D. Van Tassell, with John Vacha, *"Beyond Bayonets": The Civil War in Northern Ohio* (Kent, OH: Kent State University Press, 2006), 46.

8. Joiner et al., *No Pardons to Ask,* 1.

9. John R. Sellers, ed., *A People at War: Civil War Manuscripts from the Holdings of the Library of Congress* (Alexandria, VA: Chadwyck-Heakey, 1989–1990), entries for October 27, 1862, and November 6, 1862, Henry Graham Journal, reel 37.

10. Richard Noe, ed., *A Southern Boy in Blue: The Memoir of Marcus Woodcock, 9th Kentucky Infantry (U.S.A.)* (Knoxville: University of Tennessee Press, 1996), 18–24.

11. Thomas D. Cockrell and Michael B. Ballard, eds., *A Mississippi Rebel in the Army of Northern Virginia: The Civil War Memoirs of Private David Holt* (Baton Rouge: Louisiana State University Press, 1995), 66.

12. Daniel E. Sutherland, ed., *Reminiscences of a Private: William E. Bevens of the First Arkansas Infantry, C.S.A.* (Fayetteville: University of Arkansas Press, 1992), 7.

13. Robert L. Bee, ed., *The Boys from Rockville: Civil War Narratives of Sgt. Benjamin Hirst, Company D, 14 Connecticut Volunteers* (Knoxville: University of Tennessee Press, 1998), 12.

14. Sellers, *A People at War,* Allen Landis to parents, February 13, 1863, Allen Landis Papers, reel 58.

15. Mark Grimsley and Todd D. Miller, eds., *The Union Must Stand: The Civil War Diary of John Quincy Adams Campbell, Fifth Iowa Volunteer Infantry* (Knoxville: University of Tennessee Press, 2000), 4.

16. Sellers, *A People at War,* James Kelaher to cousin, January 21, 1863, Kelaher Letter, reel 57.

17. Robert Knox Sneden, *Eye of the Storm: A Civil War Odyssey,* ed. Charles F. Bryan Jr. and Nelson D. Lankford (New York: Free Press, 2000), xiii.

18. Joiner et al., *No Pardons to Ask,* 17; Thomas Reid, *Spartan Band: Burnett's 13th Texas Cavalry in the Civil War* (Denton: University of North Texas Press, 2005), 14.

19. Oliver Otis Howard, *Autobiography of Oliver Otis Howard, Major General United States Army* (New York: Baker & Taylor, 1908), 1:117–18.

20. William J. Miller, *Civil War City, Harrisburg, Pennsylvania, 1861–1865, the Training of an Army* (Shippensburg, PA: White Mane, 1990), 5.

21. Terry L. Jones, *Lee's Tigers: The Louisiana Infantry in the Army of Northern Virginia* (Baton Rouge: Louisiana State University Press, 1987), 8.

22. Anne J. Bailey, *Between the Enemy and Texas: Parsons's Texas Cavalry in the Civil War* (Fort Worth: Texas Christian University, 1989), 11–12.

23. Scott Walker, *Hell's Broke Loose in Georgia: Survival in a Civil War Regiment* (Athens: University of Georgia Press, 2005), 9–11.

24. Joiner et al., *No Pardons to Ask,* 15.

25. David Herbert Donald, ed., *Gone for a Soldier: The Civil War Memoirs of Private Alfred Bellard* (Boston: Little, Brown, 1975), 6.

26. Stephen Z. Starr, *The Union Cavalry in the Civil War,* Vol. 1, *From Fort Sumter to Gettysburg, 1861–1863* (Baton Rouge: Louisiana State University Press, 1979), 114; A. F. Speery, *History of the 33d Iowa Infantry Volunteer Regiment, 1863–6,* ed. Gregory J. W. Urwin and Cathy Kinziger Urwin (Fayetteville: University of Arkansas Press, 1999), 6–7.

27. Quoted in Jeffrey D. Wert, *A Brotherhood of Valor: The Common Soldiers of the Stonewall Brigade, C.S.A., and the Iron Brigade, U.S.A.* (New York: Simon & Schuster, 1999), 22.

28. Michael P. Gray, *The Business of Captivity: Elmira and Its Civil War Prison* (Kent, OH: Kent State University Press, 2001), 2.

29. Ibid., 2–4.

30. Kurt D. Bergemann, *Brackett's Battalion: Minnesota Cavalry in the Civil War and Dakota War* (St. Paul, MN: Borealis Books, 2004), 15–16.

31. M. Jane Johansson, ed., *Widows by the Thousand: The Civil War Letters of Theophilus and Harriet Perry, 1862–1865* (Fayetteville: University of Arkansas Press, 2000), 35.

32. Jones, *Lee's Tigers,* 11.

33. Wert, *A Brotherhood of Valor,* 24.

34. Quoted in Fred Albert Shannon, *The Organization and Administration of the Union Army, 1861–1865* (Gloucester, MA: Peter Smith, 1965), 1:179.

35. Donald C. Elder III, ed., *Love amid the Turmoil: The Civil War Letters of William and Mary Vermillion* (Iowa City: University of Iowa Press, 2003), 16–17.

36. John Niven, *Connecticut for the Union: The Role of the State in the Civil War* (New Haven, CT: Yale University Press, 1965), 49–54.

37. Sumner A. Cunningham, *Reminiscences of the 41st Tennessee: The Civil War in the West,* ed. John A. Simpson (Shippensburg, PA: White Mane, 2001), 4.

38. Grimsley and Miller, *Union Must Stand,* 4.

39. Don Harrison Doyle, *The Social Order of a Frontier Community: Jacksonville, Illinois, 1825–70* (Urbana: University of Illinois Press, 1978), 232.

40. Charles F. Larimer, ed., *Love and Valor: The Intimate Civil War Letters between Captain Jacob and Emeline Ritner* (Western Springs, IL: Sigourney Press, 2000), 26.

41. G. Ward Hubbs, ed., *Voices from Company D: Diaries by the Greensboro Guards, Fifth Alabama Infantry Regiment, Army of Northern Virginia* (Athens: University of Georgia Press, 2003), 3.

42. John C. Inscoe and Gordon B. McKinney, *The Heart of Confederate Appalachia: Western North Carolina in the Civil War* (Chapel Hill: University of North Carolina Press, 2000), 71–72.

43. Lyman Richard Comey, ed., *A Legacy of Valour: The Memoirs and Letters of Captain Henry Newton Comey, 2nd Massachusetts* (Knoxville: University of Tennessee Press, 2004), 9.

44. Hubbs, *Voices from Company D,* 3.

45. Gould and Kennedy, *Memoirs of a Dutch Mudsill,* 8.

46. Robert Hunt Rhodes, ed., *All for the Union: The Civil War Diary and Letters of Elisha Hunt Rhodes* (New York: Vintage Books, 1992), 5.

47. Sarah Bahnson Chapman, ed., *Bright and Gloomy Days: The Civil War Correspondence of Captain Charles Frederic Bahnson, a Moravian Confederate* (Knoxville: University of Tennessee Press, 2003), 25.

48. Luis F. Emilio, *A Brave Black Regiment: The History of the 54th Massachusetts, 1863–1865,* 2nd enlarged ed. (New York: Da Capo Press, 1995), 23.

49. Quoted in Fred Albert Shannon, *The Organization and Administration of the Union Army, 1861–1865* (Gloucester, MA: Peter Smith, 1965), 1:154.

50. Michael C. Hardy, *The Thirty-seventh North Carolina Troops: Tar Heels in the Army of Northern Virginia* (Jefferson, NC: McFarland, 2003), 20; Jerome Mushkat, ed., *A Citizen-Soldier's Civil War: The Letters of Brevet Major General Alvin C. Voris* (DeKalb: Northern Illinois University Press, 2002), 22.

51. Josiah Marshall Favill, *The Diary of a Young Officer: Serving with the Armies of the United States during the War of the Rebellion* (Baltimore: Butternut & Blue, 2000), 44.

52. Shannon, *Organization and Administration,* 1:186.

53. Favill, *Diary of a Young Officer,* 44.

54. Elder, *Love amid the Turmoil,* 16.

55. Eric J. Wittenberg, ed., *"We Have It Damn Hard Out Here": The Civil War Letters of Sergeant Thomas W. Smith, 6th Pennsylvania Cavalry* (Kent, OH: Kent State University Press, 1999), 3.

56. Stanley S. McGowen, *Horse Sweat and Powder Smoke: The First Texas Cavalry in the Civil War* (College Station: Texas A&M University Press, 1999), 18; Bailey, *Between the Enemy and Texas,* 9, 13.

57. Samuel M. Blackwell Jr., *In the First Line of Battle: The 12th Illinois Cavalry in the Civil War* (DeKalb: Northern Illinois University Press, 2002), 9–11; Starr, *From Fort Sumter to Gettysburg,* 132–33, 139–40.

58. Nathaniel Cheairs Hughes Jr., *The Pride of the Confederate Artillery: The Washington Artillery in the Army of Tennessee* (Baton Rouge: Louisiana State University Press, 1997), 3–4; Larry J. Daniel, *Cannoneers in Gray: The Field Artillery of the Army of the Tennessee,* rev. ed. (Tuscaloosa: University of Alabama Press, 2005), 5; Jennings Cropper Wise, *The Long Arm of Lee or the History of the Artillery of the Army of Northern Virginia with a Brief Account of the Confederate Bureau of Ordnance* (Lynchburg, VA: J. P. Bell, 1915), 112.

59. Wert, *A Brotherhood of Valor,* 19.

60. Robert K. Krick, *Parker's Virginia Battery C.S.A.,* 2nd rev. ed. (Wilmington, NC: Broadfoot, 1989), 13–15, 19.

61. Sellers, *A People at War,* Lyman Holford, "A Record of the Doings and Adventures of a Volunteer in the U.S.A.," undated entry, Diary, Lyman C. Holford Papers, reel 50.

62. Hardy, *The Thirty-seventh North Carolina Troops,* 19.

63. Versalle F. Washington, *Eagles on their Buttons: A Black Infantry Regiment in the Civil War* (Columbia: University of Missouri Press, 1999), 27–28.

64. Mushkat, *A Citizen-Soldier's Civil War,* 22.

65. Joiner et al., *No Pardons to Ask,* 17.

66. Samuel C. Jones, *Reminiscences of the 22nd Iowa Infantry: Giving Its Organization, Marches, Skirmishes, Battles, and Sieges, as Taken from the Diary of Lieutenant S. C. Jones of Company A* (Iowa City: Press of the Camp Pope Bookshop, 1993), 8.

67. Sellers, *A People at War,* Holford, "A Record of the Doings."

68. David W. Blight, ed., *When This Cruel War Is Over: The Civil War Letters of Charles Harvey Brewster* (Amherst: University of Massachusetts Press, 1992), 50.

69. Mushkat, *A Citizen-Soldier's Civil War,* 24.

70. Quoted in Dudley Taylor Cornish, *The Sable Arm: Black Troops in the Union Army, 1861–1865* (Lawrence: University Press of Kansas, 1987), 243.

71. Richard Lowe, ed., *A Texas Cavalry Officer's Civil War: The Diary and Letters of James C. Bates* (Baton Rouge: Louisiana State University Press, 1999), 8.

72. Gould and Kennedy, *Memoirs of a Dutch Mudsill,* 4–5.

73. Ibid.

74. Minetta Altgelt Goyne, ed., *Lone Star and Double Eagle: Civil War Letters of a German-Texas Family* (Fort Worth: Texas Christian University, 1982), 23.

75. Bee, *Boys from Rockville,* xx–xxiv.

76. Warren Lee Goss, *Recollections of a Private: A Story of the Army of the Potomac* (Scituate, MA: Digital Scanning, 2002), 17.

77. Claire E. Swedberg, ed., *Three Years with the 92d Illinois: The Civil War Diary of John M. King* (Mechanicsburg, PA: Stackpole Books, 1999), 58; William C. Harris, ed., *"In the Country of the Enemy": The Civil War Reports of a Massachusetts Corporal* (Gainesville: University Press of Florida, 1999), 64–65.

78. Sam Watkins, *"Company Aytch," or a Side Show of the Big Show and Other Sketches,* ed. M. Thomas Inge (New York: Penguin Putnam, 1999), 8.

79. Philip J. Reyburn and Terry L. Wilson, eds., *"Jottings from Dixie": The Civil War Dispatches of Sergeant Major Stephen F. Fleharty, U.S.A.* (Baton Rouge: Louisiana State University Press, 1999), 45.

80. Rhodes, *All for the Union,* 6, 9.

81. Jennifer Cain Bohrnstedt, ed., *Soldiering with Sherman: The Civil War Letters of George F. Cram* (DeKalb: Northern Illinois University Press, 2000), 11.

82. Stewart Bennett and Barbara Tilley, eds., *The Struggle for the Republic: A Civil War Narrative by Brevet Major Charles Dana Miller, 76th Ohio Volunteer Infantry* (Kent, OH: Kent State University Press, 2004), 14.

83. William H. Relyea, *16th Connecticut Volunteer Infantry,* ed. John Michael Priest (Shippensburg, PA: Burd Street Press, 2002), 8.

84. Mark K. Christ, ed., *Getting Used to Being Shot At: The Spence Family Civil War Letters* (Fayetteville: University of Arkansas Press, 2002), 5–6.

85. G. Ward Hubbs, *Guarding Greensboro: A Confederate Company in the Making of a Southern Community* (Athens: University of Georgia Press, 2003), 96–97.

86. Ben Wynne, *A Hard Trip: A History of the 15th Mississippi Infantry, CSA* (Macon, GA: Mercer University Press, 2003), 41–42.

87. Joiner et al., *No Pardons to Ask,* 31.

88. Ibid., 9, 11.

89. Mark V. Wetherington, *Plain Folk's Fight: The Civil War and Reconstruction in Piney Woods, Georgia* (Chapel Hill: University of North Carolina Press, 2005), 113.

90. Quoted in Gerald J. Prokopowiczm, *All for the Regiment: The Army of the Ohio, 1861–1862* (Chapel Hill: University of North Carolina Press, 2001), 21.

91. Starr, *From Fort Sumter to Gettysburg,* 100–1; Jones, *Lee's Tigers,* 8–10.

92. Lowe, *A Texas Cavalry Officer's Civil War,* 7.

93. Guy R. Everson and Edward H. Simpson Jr., eds., *Far, Far from Home: The Wartime Letters of Dick and Tally Simpson, 3rd South Carolina Volunteers* (New York: Oxford University Press, 1994), 172.

94. Wert, *A Brotherhood of Valor,* 24.

95. Swedberg, *Three Years with the 92d Illinois,* 8.

96. Harold Adams Small, *The Road to Richmond: The Civil War Memoirs of Major Abner R. Small of the Sixteenth Maine Volunteers: Together with the Diary That He Kept When He Was a Prisoner of War* (New York: Fordham University Press, 2000), 8.

97. Quoted in Richard F. Miller, *Harvard's Civil War: A History of the Twentieth Massachusetts Volunteer Infantry* (Hanover, NH: University Press of New England, 2005), 36–37.

98. Small, *Road to Richmond,* 13.

99. Michael E. Stevens, ed., *As If It Were Glory: Robert Beecham's Civil War from the Iron Brigade to the Black Regiments* (Madison, WI: Madison House, 1998), 143–44.

100. Robert F. Harris and John Niflot, comps., *Dear Sister: The Civil War Letters of the Brothers Gould* (Westport, CT: Praeger, 1998), 2–3.

101. Jennifer Cain Bohrnstedt, ed., *Soldiering with Sherman: The Civil War Letters of George F. Cram* (DeKalb: Northern Illinois University Press, 2000), 7, 11.

102. Swedberg, *Three Years with the 92d Illinois,* 9.

103. Comey, *A Legacy of Valour,* 8.

104. Hubbs, *Voices from Company D,* 4.

105. Comey, *A Legacy of Valour,* 11–12.

106. A. F. Sperry, *History of the 33d Iowa Infantry Volunteer Regiment, 1863–6,* eds. Gregory, J. W. Urwin and Cathy Kunzingen Urwin (Fayetteville: University of Arkansas Press, 1999), 8.

107. Julie Holcomb, ed., *Southern Sons, Northern Soldiers: The Civil War Letters of the Remley Brothers, 22nd Iowa Infantry* (DeKalb: Northern Illinois University Press, 2004), 7.

108. Theodore J. Karamanski, *Rally 'Round the Flag: Chicago and the Civil War,* (Chicago: Nelson-Hall, 1993), 100; J. Mathew Gallman, *Mastering Wartime: A Social History of Philadelphia during the Civil War* (Cambridge: Cambridge University Press, 1990), 127, 129.

109. Albert Burton Moore, *Conscription and Conflict in the Confederacy* (New York: Macmillan, 1924), 114–16; Ella Lonn, *Desertion during the Civil War* (Lincoln: University of Nebraska Press, 1998), 15.

110. Niven, *Connecticut for the Union,* 90.

111. Capt. N. C. Warrens to Col. E. B. Alexander, November 5, 1863, Second Regiment Veteran Reserve Corps, Regimental Papers, Adjutant General's Office, Record Group 94, National Archives Building, Washington, DC.

112. Frank Wilkeson, *Turned Inside Out: Recollections of a Private Soldier in the Army of the Potomac* (Lincoln: University of Nebraska Press, 1997), 2–20.

113. Jones, *Lee's Tigers,* 14–19.

114. Eric Ward, ed., *Army Life in Virginia: The Civil War Letters of George G. Benedict* (Mechanicsburg, PA: Stackpole Books, 2002), 39.

115. Swedberg, *Three Years with the 92d Illinois,* 1–10.

5 DAILY CAMP LIFE

MORE DRILL

As time passed and the war did not end as quickly as expected, the routines of camp life came to dominate much of the soldiers' existence. Union and Confederate soldiers trained at camps closer to the front before they tasted combat and then returned to encampments after the horrors of battle had passed. In April 1862 James Williams, of the 21st Alabama and a survivor of the Battle of Shiloh, even admitted to feeling at home in such a place "when I came back from that terrible field, weary, wet, and heart-sick."[1] For many commanders, however, battle exhaustion was no excuse for relaxing discipline. Consequently, even as soldiers attempted to restore themselves, they spent much of their time dealing with the routines and monotony of military life.

Lulls in fighting allowed generals to put their entire commands through the paces of various large-formation drills. Units at times engaged in various competitions, divisions participated in grand reviews, and corps even participated in mock battles. Sometimes officers sounded false alarms and watched their men scramble about striking their tents, packing their baggage, and falling into marching order as quickly as possible. Soldiers might have found such activity exciting, but in the end they spent the better part of their days performing routine drill.

For officers, rounds of drills, training exercises, and parades were essential for military effectiveness and discipline. Thus conscientious officers and martinets alike drilled their men to instill that necessary discipline. But soldiers found it all very trying. Perhaps their reluctance to submit to the discipline of drill resulted from the fact that it reminded them that they were no longer free men. Throughout the war, men repeated the lesson they had first learned at the rendezvous. In March 1863 Illinois soldier John M. King judged that being a soldier was akin to being a "volunteer slave." "In an army the private soldier loses all individuality," King reported. Furthermore, "he is no longer a man in the light of the Republic. He has no opinion that will ever be heard, much less heeded. It is his duty to obey and never be heard." But at least King acknowledged that all of the drill and discipline had a purpose. After all, he admitted, "war is a dreadful calamity at best, and in order to get men to be hurled up to the very cannon's mouth at the command of one man—each man must volunteer to become a willing slave."[2]

Officers in charge of black troops understood the necessity of disciplining and training former slaves, but they also recognized that they were doing more than simply making them soldiers. There were those officers who commanded their men with undisguised racism, but the best of the abolitionist officers believed they were making black men into new Americans. Ironically, even as their white counterparts complained that army life turned them into "voluntary slaves," black soldiers worked under white officers who expected to exorcise servile traits from their men. In late 1862 Thomas Wentworth Higginson, colonel of the First South Carolina Volunteers, a black regiment, praised the way his men learned their drill, as his officer not only put them through the manual of arms, but also skirmishing drill and target practice. Such soldiering, Higginson believed, would give the former slaves under his command self-respect, thus forever changing their lives. "The better the soldiers they become," he noted, "the more they are spoiled for slaves."[3] Indeed, the men understood how their performance in even mundane duties could change not only themselves, but the way people viewed them. In August 1863 Corporal James Henry Gooding of the 54th Massachusetts explained that the regiment was "bound to live down all prejudice against its color, by a determination to do well in any position it is put."[4]

It was in camp through the normal military routine that companies integrated and trained new arrivals to their regiments. The recruits, conscripts, and substitutes became the students of the veterans, who frequently took advantage of their ignorance and made their lives difficult, forgetting that they, too, had once been green. The Second Massachusetts Infantry received some new men while in camp on the Chattahoochie River in Georgia; in the middle of the campaign, the officers had "to work on them the whole time," requiring two drills a day.[5] "The period of seasoning with these poor fellows was very severe," recalled Confederate surgeon Thomas Wood Fanning about the new men. "His veteran comrades had little sympathy for men who had to be dragged into war, for which they had volunteered, and they treated them as inferiors." But eventually, new men made successful transitions to army life and joined in the community of their companies. James P. Sullivan of the Sixth Wisconsin recounted the difficulty he had breaking in a new set of men in late 1864. He noted two in particular who were clumsy in drill, with awkward steps and tempers worn by their frustrating experiences. Both, in the end, "proved to be good soldiers."[6]

It was, however, conscripts and the Northern bounty men who drew the particular scorn and disdain of Northern veterans. In August 1863 Fifth New Jersey veterans were "all anxious to see the Conscrips or $402.00 men," as they planned to "have a great lot of fun with them."[7] For most volunteers, conscription marked a soldier with "an everlasting disgrace."[8] And in the eyes of the old soldiers, bounty men were contemptible characters. One officer characterized them as "*poor, mean, contemptable scoundrels* whom you can never get into battle."[9] Perhaps this prejudice had sound origins and thus encouraged the veterans to consider training the bounty men a waste of time. A veteran Northern regiment fighting before Petersburg discovered that the bounty men sent to fill its depleted ranks were an embarrassment to the cause. Warren Lee Goss recalled that they "deserted in such numbers that the enemy jokingly sent word, that, as they had most of the regiment over on their side, they thought we had better send them over the regimental colors."[10]

BUILDING SHELTER IN CAMP

Summer camp life generally meant the convenience, if not comfort, of living out of doors or under canvas. A well-laid-out camp with rows of tents away from the fighting filled some soldiers with contentment hard to imagine. "It is a splendid sight to stand off a piece from an encampment in the still hours of the night, when every thing is quiet and still and the moonshines out in full splendor upon white rows of tents, all systematically arranged," wrote Pennsylvanian Allen Landis in September 1862, probably happy to be where he was after the Antietam campaign. "I was gazing upon our encampment last evening, when nothing was to [be] heard save the soft tread of the lonely sentinel as he paces his lonesome beat, and I thought to myself, were this all of a soldiers life, what is more pleasant?"[11]

Winter changed the nature of camp life, however, and soldiers devoted a good bit of time to making their habitats as snug as possible. The type of structures soldiers built depended on the location of their regiment, the available materials, and their own energy. During the winter of 1862–1863, Louisianans in Virginia resorted to digging holes in the ground, covering them with whatever material was available.[12] Many soldiers did better than the Louisianans but still kept it simple, as did those men who added tenting to roof a low foundation of logs. Others engaged in more elaborate building projects. Soldiers constructed small log huts, roofed with canvas or wood, depending on the amount of energy the occupants wished to expend, and sometimes floored with wood and furnished with improvised pieces of lumber and discarded boxes. Men improvised with their tents, strengthening their walls with various materials to help them withstand the weather, adding cellars and chimneys for additional comfort. Some men wisely dug trenches around their tents to facilitate drainage.

Yankees and rebels begged homefolk to send along nails and other building supplies, or they made do with what they had at hand. Massachusetts bugler Charles Reed noted that the Virginia mud was troublesome, but he and other men found use for it, making bricks from the muck and employing it as "first rate mortar" in the construction of their chimneys.[13] In the wake of the 1861 Virginia campaign, members of New

Gen. Hooker's Division, 8th N.J.V. March 1862: Examples of the snug wooden structures built by soldiers for their winter encampments. (*Library of Congress*)

Petersburg, Va. Sutler's tent, 2d Division, 9th Corps. (*Library of Congress*)

Orleans's Washington Artillery "had learned to handle the axe with skill," as they filled the air with "the ring of their axes and falling of trees…the livelong day."[14] Soldiers eager to stay warm multiplied that activity by thousands, and forests disappeared under their axes.

Winter camp construction could bring out the creative nature of some men who wished to make residences attractive, despite their military purposes. During early 1863 a New Jersey regiment at Camp Fitzhugh Farm in Virginia, probably bored with camp life, produced "a magnificent camp." The soldiers constructed "archways" over the camp's streets made of evergreens with company designations at their top and paved the way to their commander's tent with additional branches.[15] Farther south, black troops also showed their ability to improvise with the materials at hand as well as the pride they had in their camp by the structures they built. In December 1863 Thomas Wentworth Higginson reported that the First South Carolina Volunteers built a "picturesque" camp of "screens & shelters of light poles, filled in with the gray moss that hangs from live oaks everywhere." Higginson admitted, "I have always had rather a knack at these decorative matters, but the men lead me entirely & get up just what they please, within certain restrictions."[16]

CAMP DUTIES

When not drilling or looking to their shelter, men performed "the thousand commonplace duties of the soldier."[17] Privileged Southerners might have slaves accompany them into the army to make camp life more comfortable, and Confederates used blacks when they could to do heavy work. Northerners also hired "contrabands," as they called runaway slaves, to give them a hand with cooking, washing clothes, and other camp chores as well as to serve the army in the capacity of carpenters, teamsters, and laborers. But there were camp duties that most soldiers simply could not escape.

In October 1861, in camp outside of Washington, Wisconsin infantryman William Ray lived a "pretty busy" camp life: "get up when the drum beats, fall in, answer role call, get breakfast, scour guns, black shoes, comb head to keep tangles out, keep lice out, wash socks, wash shirts and writing and various things to[o] numerous to mention" were all part of his routine.[18] Those "various things" probably included the housekeeping choirs such as chopping wood, carrying water, digging latrines or "sinks," and a multitude of other tasks, some quite heavy labor, all known collectively as fatigue duty. Even the Sabbath could not abate these necessary routines. In August 1862 Sergeant William Winters of the 67th Indiana Volunteers informed the home folks that at Camp Jackson at Munfordville, Kentucky, Sunday "is the same as any other day. almost the only difference is we know that it is the sabath there is the same noise, bustle, and confusion as on any other of the seven."[19]

In May 1862 Wilbur Fisk reported to the folks back in Vermont that camp duties came in fits and starts, but when they came, a soldier "may be called upon to perform all that his physical powers can possibly accomplish, and often his power of endurance yields to exhaustion, and he is obliged to stop ere his task is complete."[20] No wonder veterans developed a particularly bad attitude toward such work. "In most cases," Theodore Dodge of Massachusetts explained, "the older a Regiment gets, the more unwilling it is to do fatigue duty, and the less work can be got out of the men."[21]

Specialized soldiers had additional routine duties beyond those of infantrymen to occupy their time. Engineers in camp practiced building fortifications and drilled with pontoon bridges, but also built hospitals and tended to bridges. They maintained their equipment and cared for their animals, training them to their tasks when necessary. Cavalry troopers, artillerymen, mounted infantry, and officers also had the added responsibility of feeding and caring for their mounts. Field artillerymen had additional duties that consumed more time than those of the average infantryman. They looked after their cannon, carriages, wagons, and other accoutrements as well as a large complement of horses, which required shelters during winter weather. Feeding the animals essential to a field artillery battery in and of itself was a significant task. In June 1862 Parker's Virginia Battery had to provide 56 horses and 4 mules with an individual ration of 16 pounds of hay and fodder every day.[22]

Of all the distasteful camp jobs that a soldier might attempt to avoid, guard duty struck many soldiers as "the hardest part of soldiering."[23] When enlisted men landed jobs or earned promotions to noncommissioned ranks that excused them from guard duty, they considered it a stroke of good fortune. Indeed, guard duty was sufficiently distasteful that officers used it as punishment. Guard duty kept men in or on the fringes of camp, standing in front of headquarters or at entrances to camp or walking its perimeter. Men on picket duty guarded encampments from some distance and were the first line of defense against an enemy attack, an early warning system designed to alert their comrades of imminent danger. Pickets shared the discomfort of camp guards and more, sometimes having to return to their picket lines after only a brief respite back at their camps. Wesley Brainard, a Union engineering officer, expressed the opinion that "if there is any one thing more disagreeable than any other thing in a Soldiers life [it] is the performance of Picket Duty."[24]

Picket duty technically permitted little relaxation and required constant readiness to the point where "no man is allowed to take off his boots, coat or any part of his clothing while he sleeps," with his weapon always nearby.[25] And yet, in 1862 in Virginia, such duty along the Rappahannock River in the wake of the bloody fighting at Fredericksburg provided Yanks and rebs with the diversion of "good natured" talks. Despite orders against consorting with the enemy, one Union officer believed that there was some benefit in talking instead of engaging in "miserable picket firing, which really does no good, and helps neither side."[26]

Unsurprisingly, if there were distasteful jobs awaiting them, there were soldiers—"beats," shirkers, or malingerers—"who would by hook or by crook" do their best to avoid the duty. Some found sick call the perfect opportunity for avoiding hard duty, giving even the youthful volunteer a chance for "playing old soldier" by conjuring up fraudulent illnesses in an effort to avoid camp work. Some found ways to allow the more conscientious soldiers to do most of a detail's assignment. Some "would waste a great deal of time and breath maligning the government or their officers for requiring them to do such work," always explaining that they were soldiers, not laborers, who had enlisted to fight.[27]

Most soldiers, however, performed their camp routine even as it wore on their spirits. Some soldiers lost track of the days marked by repetitive duty. Other bored soldiers succumbed to homesickness as they plodded through their boring chores. And in January 1864, a Yankee soldier reported from his winter camp in Tennessee that there was nothing to occupy him from one meal to the next meal. "The forenoon is spent poke, poke, poking around," he explained, "till the appetite says it is dinner time."[28]

FOOD

Dinnertime, indeed, was an important event in the daily lives of soldiers, and as the war progressed, food occupied an increasingly significant part of the men's thoughts. One Confederate veteran remembered eating to be "more than a convenience; it was a comfort which rose almost to the height of a consolation."[29] There were times when federal

Camp scene, showing Company kitchen, ca. 1860–1865. (*Library of Congress*)

soldiers suffered from hunger, but Confederates especially came to appreciate the food they had and did not have. This was particularly a concern when their army, pressed for supplies even early in the war because of a poor commissary system, cut their rations from the amount prescribed in U.S. Army regulations. Crop failures and the reluctance on the part of planters to turn over their cotton fields to food crops complicated the supply difficulties. By the end of the war, expectations in the ranks of the Army of Tennessee had dropped so low that one Confederate was simply happy to have some sweet potatoes and sorghum syrup to break the months of monotonous dining.[30]

Samuel W. Fiske of Connecticut pronounced a soldier's life to be a hungry life.[31] Thus the men dwelled on the subject of food and came to understand that one of their foremost duties was to fill their bellies, even forgoing the niceties of table manners in the process. In 1862 Confederate soldier Leonard Ives straightforwardly described the situation to his brother: "I am fast becoming every inch a soldier and have arrived at the point where the great object of life is to get something to eat," he explained. "Never lose an opportunity and where I have a chance stuff till I can just move, and only regret not being able to eat more."[32] Later, in 1864, John Arnold, a Pennsylvania soldier, noticed how enthusiastically the men approached their food while at the Camp Curtin rendezvous. They "puts me in mind as iff thare ware about Thirty hungray horgs In one pen and the trough onely Big anough for about three to get in," he reported.[33]

No wonder men always wrote home about their gastronomical desires. They made it plain that civilians should send them useful food items such as Borden's condensed milk and jellies instead of silk handkerchiefs and other things that only weighed them down. North Carolinian John Anglin did not beat around the bush when, in April 1862, he mailed his brother a list of the things he expected him to bring along on his next visit, advising him that he was not limited to those items and could "get other good things that I haven't mentioned."[34]

Fall in for Soup: Soldiers line up for their rations. (*Library of Congress*)

Civilians obliged their boys by sending packages of food to the camps to help feed soldiers, "toothsome remembrances of friends and relatives," as one Union veteran recalled.[35] During the early years of the war, before hardship reached deep into the Confederacy, express companies did a good business transporting packages of food to men at the front; boxes also arrived by the wagonload in Yankee camps, which considerably raised the spirits of the men.[36] Soldiers still in need could purchase food from nearby farms or, if they lacked money, as did poor Louisiana privates fighting in Virginia in late 1862, simply help themselves to what bounty was available.[37]

Soldiers, if they had pocket money, also had opportunities to purchase supplies from sutlers. These merchants, who followed the armies—some soldiers would have said preyed on the armies—drew scorn from men who viewed them as dishonest sharpers, men who "would take a man[']s heart and sell it," according to Massachusetts artilleryman John Chase.[38] In the eyes of New York engineer John Westervelt, they were a "most miserable set of wretches"; Westervelt believed that all such men "should be drafted and placed at the front and used as targets for the enemy to fire at."[39]

AMUSEMENTS

Aside from eating or thinking about eating, soldiers broke the boredom of camp life by amusing themselves in any number of ways. When stationed near cities, towns, and villages, men could invite ladies to camp for dances. Men like Michigander Charles Hayden, on garrison duty in Kentucky, amused himself by flirting with local girls.[40] Some Yankees were able to develop platonic relationships with members of the opposite sex, even in hostile territory. Federal soldiers occupying Southern towns socialized with local women, once the ladies became convinced of their gentlemanly character; some of the women even became romantically involved with the occupiers. In Nashville alone, 174 soldiers gave up their bachelor status, marrying local women.[41]

Fortunate soldiers on duty near cities also received permission to leave camp to see the unusual sights of the nearby communities. Yankees stationed near Washington visited the city "on a tour of curiosity" of the various government buildings during the day and attended plays in the evening.[42] As occupiers, Yankees stationed in Southern towns from Vicksburg, Mississippi, to Beaufort, South Carolina, enjoyed what the towns had to offer in the way of amusements ranging from racetracks to bordellos.[43]

Confederates encamped near towns also took advantage of the local entertainment. Even small communities provided diversions from the routines of camp. In May 1862, men from the 21st Georgia visited mountain communities, where they danced and sang with the civilians, while on occasion they visited the local apple brandy still.[44] The dangers presented by civilian communities, in particular, the availability of alcohol, meant that commanders preferred to keep their men under the close supervision of camp. Thus it was in camp that the men had to while away most of their free time.

Since so many of the volunteers of 1861 and 1862 went to war with family and friends, soldiers had easy comrades near at hand with whom they could socialize. Also, if a solitary volunteer tented with "a good crowd," he was likely to make friends, which would keep up his spirits.[45] Soldiers visited friends and family in other companies and regiments and used peacetime associations to maintain former or cultivate new friendships. Confederate Marion Fitzpatrick, for example, expected to attend Masonic lodge meetings while in camp, which would provide him with the familiar brotherhood of the antebellum lodge.[46]

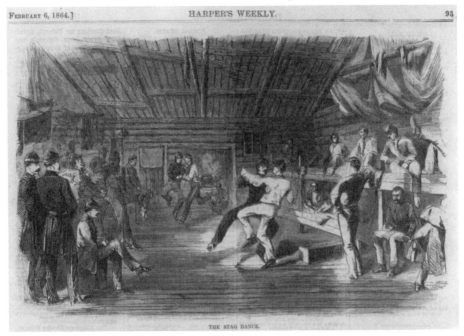

THE STAG DANCE.

The Stag Dance: Soldiers improvised when no women were available. (*Library of Congress*)

Men had several other ways to occupy their time, depending on their inclinations and talents. Bored bullies picked fights. Imagined or real insults as well as individual acts of violence stoked tension between units that could erupt into a full-fledged "skirmish."[47] But most men preferred peaceful pastimes such as corresponding with their families and friends, who learned much about battle, camp life, slaves, and the exotic Southern landscape from the soldiers. Some soldiers also wrote to their local hometown papers, amusing themselves in a purposeful way by keeping civilians apprised of the progress of their hometown boys, including, as one Connecticut soldier explained, "random sketches of things that seem most striking, most *uncivil,* and out of the way of our ordinary peaceful life."[48]

African American James Henry Gooding provided the editors of the New Bedford *Mercury* with news of the 54th Massachusetts, but the majority of black volunteers were handicapped in this area by their illiterate slave past.[49] When possible, they attempted to correct this deficiency by using their free time to attend schools in their camps and spent their evenings studying their lessons, sometimes with the assistance of their literate comrades. The wife of Colonel James Beecher of the 35th U.S. Colored Troops recalled that "whenever they had a spare moment, out would come a spelling-book or a primer or a Testament, and you would often see a group of heads around one book."[50]

Soldiers read and discussed books and newspapers, played games, put on theatrical performances, held formal debates, fished, trapped small game for their supper pots, kept pets, and amused themselves as best they could with the resources at their disposal. Men "shot marbles, danced, played ball, played cards, chess, back-gammon, drafts, etc." and spiced their days by playing practical jokes on each other and sometimes on their officers.[51] They watched local slaves and contraband perform song and dance, and holidays, such as Christmas and St. Patrick's Day, also broke the routine of camp life.

Pickets trading between the lines by Edwin Forbes illustrates one of the ways that soldiers broke the monotony of the duty. (*Library of Congress*)

Soldiers with musical talent shared their skills with their fellow soldiers, providing pleasant diversions for the men. Massachusetts bugler Charles Reed formed a vocal quartet to spend "enjoyable evenings" more privately with a "quiet little sing now and then."[52] African American soldiers especially relaxed to the group singing around their campfires that helped build up their camaraderie. They favored spirituals, but secular songs were also part of their repertoire; indeed, the men frequently improvised songs that commented on current events and concerns.[53]

Regimental bands gave concerts when they could, but much of the musical entertainment was more intimate. One company of the 74th New York Infantry valued musical entertainment so much that its members took up a collection to purchase instruments for a string band.[54] Soldiers welcomed banjo pickers, fiddle players, and bone rattlers, who seemed to be common fixtures in every regiment. But one truly innovative entertainer provoked special comment from a soldier. He was an accomplished mimic and, accompanied by a banjo picker, entertained the men by imitating "every bird you can think of and dancing with a cup of water on his head."[55]

Those soldiers with artistic talent sketched their environs, sometimes illustrating the letters they sent home with renderings of camp life. Charles Wellington Reed in fact turned his artistic talent into a business, making hundreds of dollars by producing lithographs as well as maps of the Gettysburg battlefield, while soliciting subscriptions for his work among his fellow soldiers and selling his work back home in Massachusetts.[56] Indeed, some men less talented than Reed found that they could best employ their spare time engaged in developing small enterprises. Vermont soldier Wilbur Fisk made extra money by selling various and sundry items to other soldiers, while Joseph Lester sold newspapers and stationery in camp, grossing on average about three dollars a day. He also took on selling tobacco and, at one point, in August 1864, reported that he "made as near as I can come at it since I began about One Thousand dollars, all of which I have in current funds."[57]

Despite the hard duties associate with camp life, men also enjoyed athletic competitions and physical activity. In the winter, when they became tired of sledding or building snowmen, they had snowball fights, which could turn into sizeable battles. In nice weather, soldiers swam when near water and played various games. Soldiers enjoyed all sorts of physical activities and competitions. Baseball, however, held a particular place among American soldiers, both Northern and Southern. In April 1863 Trenton, New Jersey, native George Fox reported that at his camp near Falmouth, Virginia, "Base Ball is all the rage and when ever the weather permits the fields around here are filled with men playing ball." Soldiers formed various team configurations, sometimes with officers playing enlisted men and men from different regiments forming "nines" to compete with one another.[58]

POLITICS

Soldiers complained about being kept in the dark about the progress of the war and spent a good bit of their camp time discussing current events in an effort to correct that deficiency. The common spread of rumor was probably why soldiers appreciated the skill of men who could sift the fact from fancy and bring them the real news. New Yorker Frank Wilkeson recalled that the enlisted men had a system for distributing information that was better than official announcements. Certain men took it on themselves to stroll through the camps, gathering up information at one campfire and passing it on at others. "The enlisted men knew of defeats and successes long before they were published in general orders," Wilkeson explained. "The truth is that the privates of the army...never believed a report that was published from head-quarters, unless it corresponded with the information the 'camp-walkers' had gathered." Wilkeson and his comrades welcomed the camp walkers but closely watched them as they often combined their news gathering and sharing activities with the theft of their hosts' belongings.[59]

Beyond mere gossip, political discussions entertained the soldiers while giving news gathering and socializing serious purpose. The men were not reticent about expressing their views when it came to the various issues of the day. Confederate soldiers held political meetings to argue about current events, while more privately, men discussed the relative merits of their generals and political leaders. In the Army of Tennessee, for example, men discussed the conscription act that kept them in the army; according to Sam Watkins, they "cursed the war," "cursed Bragg," and "cursed the Southern Confederacy" because of it. When they learned of the exemption for planters with 20 slaves, they complained about the "rich man's war, poor man's fight." In the aftermath of Perryville and Murfreesboro, their commander, Braxton Bragg, became "the laughing stock of the whole army" and subject to their invectives when he refused to grant them leave.[60] Beyond their generals and their own situations, men discussed the Northern commitment to the war and Yankee politics, criticized their politicians, worried about economics, and wondered about Unionist feelings among the people back home. In July 1863 Arkansan Theophilus Perry reported that the soldiers who reflected on his state's politics opposed "the noisey men," "these base demagogues and hypocrites" and "white livered" politicians who "desire less war."[61]

Most Yankee soldiers, to one degree or another, engaged in political discourse, particularly before the presidential election of 1864. That election, in the minds of many Union soldiers, was more than anything a referendum on whether the nation would stop the war short of complete victory. But federal troops were not passive players in this democratic drama. As they made clear on more than one occasion, when they were chafing under the discipline of "despotic" offices, they were citizens first and foremost and claimed citizenship's responsibilities as well as its privileges.

Discussions about the coming presidential election of 1864 added a degree of seriousness to the soldiers' socializing. During the fall at Knoxville, Marcus Woodcock reported that "the soldiers had been gradually bringing themselves into campfire discussions in regard to the future Presidential Canvass, though that event was yet some distance off." Nevertheless, Woodcock continued, "The soldier had no better way of employing his time than to think, and his condition naturally led him to calculate who should be the next President and how the soldiers' condition was to be affected by his election."[62]

As early as the summer, they began to have sharp discussions about potential candidates and soon could talk of nothing else; as the election drew near, they held meetings to express their views. In October 1864, while campaigning in Georgia, Colonel Edward J. Wood reported that "politics have agitated" his Indiana regiment "for the last few days."[63] Iowan George Remley also noticed that in his camp, "the Presidential question is exciting considerable interest among the soldier and animated discussions upon the merits and demerits of the several candidates are becoming more frequent every day." Colonel Wood had discovered that his Indianans were strong for Lincoln, while Remley also found there was little room for equivocating about the war. "The soldiers as a class are 'true as steel,'" he explained, "and will show at the coming election that they can fight for their country with *ballots* as valiantly as they do with *bullets*." Indeed, there were regiments in which Democrats supported George B. McClellan, the former commander of the Army of the Potomac running against Lincoln, but in Remley's case, none of his comrades could empathize with any politician that represented the slightest antiwar sentiment.[64]

Soldiers who associated themselves with the Democratic party came in for ridicule from their Republican comrades. George Cram of the 105th Illinois Infantry was embarrassed to admit that there were McClellan men in his regiment, but "they are weak-kneed cowards who want him elected merely to stop the fighting so they may not have to endanger their worthless necks anymore."[65] And Iowan Taylor Peirce informed his wife that "all good soldiers are in for Lincoln"; only the Irish and poorest soldiers were McClellan men.[66]

No wonder many a soldier excoriated hometown Copperheads, while doing his best to influence voters back home. Abial Edwards of Maine informed his sweetheart that he had no respect for peace Democrats. "They only serve to make the soldier Truer to his country than ever before," he explained. "I detest them and their principals."[67] In letters home and in petitions to their communities, Republican soldiers assured their families and their neighbors that Lincoln and his allies were their only choice. Ohioan Sam Evans urged his father to "do all within your power" for Lincoln and his Democratic vice presidential running mate Andrew Johnson, running together on what was now technically called the Union ticket. "On their election," he warned his father, "hangs the hopes of an honorable conclusion of this war."[68] Some soldiers acted collectively as regiments in their efforts to bring to bear their influence on the home folks. The 19th Iowa

Infantry "adopted a series of resolutions a short time ago assuring the people of Iowa and all others that we give the government our undivided support," explained William Clayton. "We enlisted for the purpose of aiding in putting down this infernal rebellion and we intend to do so," he continued. "I have heard a number of the regiment express their views in regard to these northern *traitors* [the antiwar Democrats] for they are nothing else and always there is ten times the hatred towards the northern traitors there is to those who are in arms against us."[69]

When election day came, in Vermonter Wilbur Fisk's camp, "the boys instead of huddling into their tents, driven there by the cold, are gathered in knots in their company streets discussing politics and other grave questions of the hour, and performing the by no means unimportant duty of casting their votes for men and principles that are to govern our country through another period of four years."[70] Given the opportunity, Union soldiers across the battlefront did as Fisk's comrades and voted. Thousands of soldiers pocketed furloughs and traveled home to have their say at their local polling stations; other soldiers mailed their ballots home; and many of them, such as Maine soldier Abial Edwards, proudly cast their ballots for Lincoln "in the field."[71] Indeed, 19 Northern states allowed their soldiers to cast ballots from their camps, and over a quarter of a million men did so. An overwhelming majority of these men, much greater than Lincoln's majority in the civilian popular vote, confirmed their commitment to the war effort by voting for their commanders-in-chief. As Wilbur Fisk explained after learning of his brigade's majority turnout for Lincoln, "Soldiers don't generally believe in fighting to put down treason, and voting to let it live."[72]

RELIGIOUS ACTIVITIES

Soldiers and civilians, North and South, believed that a victorious army had to be a virtuous, Christian army. Consequently, there was concern that camp life not allow men to stray from the religion that would bring them victory. Many soldiers took advantage of the opportunities offered to them to keep on the right path, thus making an effort to maintain their religious sensibilities. Along with their hometown newspapers and the popular sensational novels of the day, soldiers had access to all sorts of religious reading material. Many left home with Bibles in their packs. Organizations such as the U.S. Christian Commission, with the material assistance of the American Bible Society and the American Tract Society, distributed religious reading material—including thousands of bibles, hymnals, books, and religious newspapers—to soldiers. The Bible Society, for example, supplied 1,500 New Testaments to one New York regiment at its rendezvous. The donation prompted a formal presentation of the books to the mustered regiment, with citizens and clergymen present. General Dan Sickles completed the ceremony with a speech about "the power of God and the accountability of men and nations" to impress on the recipients the significance of the gift.[73]

Confederate churches also developed a specialized religious press to help keep soldiers moral, disciplined, positive, and well behaved. The Bible Society of the Confederate States was not particularly successful in adding scripture to the soldiers' pack because of the poor publishing facilities in the South, but the American Bible Society and foreign groups donated and sold on easy terms Bibles to the Confederacy. With access to scripture, men were able to spend camp time engaged in Bible study groups.[74]

Regimental chaplains also did their best to encourage the men to live good lives. Their Sunday preaching entertained as well as edified their soldier congregations. Even so, some Yankees, bored with the humdrum preaching of white chaplains, wandered over to the camps of their black counterparts to witness their services. African American soldiers held regular and enthusiastic religious meetings, frequently without the benefit of appointed chaplains and usually with some popularly selected exhorter. There were white soldiers and chaplains who found black religion too exotic and strange, but others enjoyed the "colored preachers." "They preach excellent sermons," one Yankee reported, "and they attract the boys more than our own preachers. They have great talent."[75]

Chaplains also touched the lives of the men in other ways besides delivering their Sunday sermons. For example, they counseled men through hard times. New York chaplain Joseph Hopkins Twichell reported that "from a sick baby at home, to the fears of a court martial here, everything is brought to me." He had "almost hourly opportunities to comfort, admonish, reprove or encourage," receiving as thanks "many hearty blessings" from the men.[76] Other chaplains might have won the esteem of some men by performing social services, such as carrying home pay, for soldiers and their families when possible. But some selfish, lazy, and sanctimonious chaplains earned the disdain of men who found them worthless appendages to the army. Nevertheless, even the unpious among them could be helpful to the men. Charles Hayden, a Michigan soldier, believed his chaplain to be "cool, calculating, [and] deceitful." However, he has "good authority on the practical affairs of life provided he will tell the truth." Consequently, Hayden kept "on the right side of him."[77]

As the war progressed beyond the expected quick victory, soldiers came to devote more of their time to public displays of religion beyond the usual Sunday service; in both armies, there were times when revivals spread through the regiments. As early as January and February 1862, one New York regiment experienced a minor religious awakening. It first started with a trickle of backsliders and sinners presenting themselves at the chaplain's tent and then manifested itself in subsequent prayer meetings conducted by the soldiers.[78] But it was during 1863 that revivals spread through the Confederate armies, resulting in increased religiosity and new chapel buildings scattered through camps, raised up by the faithful in part because of denominational efforts to increase religion, in part because of defeats at Gettysburg and Vicksburg, in part because of the evangelic roots of soldiers.[79]

WICKEDNESS IN CAMP

Religion kept many a soldier on the righteous path. Nevertheless, there remained soldiers who were skeptical of the enthusiasm with which their comrades embraced their faith. And there always remained some men who gave in to temptation. In January 1862 Union soldier Milton McJunkin wrote home explaining there were only "two grades" in the army: one that tries "to serve god and live as they would at home" and "another class ... who think that as they are away from home they will act as bad and be as ornry as they can as their friends are not here to see it and likely will never find out."[80] In November 1862 George Cram, a 21-year-old soldier with the 105th Illinois Volunteer Infantry, also found evidence of men in his Galatin, Tennessee, camp abandoning the right living that they might have maintained as civilians. "A great many of the boys are not what they were at home," he reported. Later, in February 1864, he found that bad behavior caused "much demoralization in the army and thousands of young men here are ruined," although he still considered himself a gentleman capable of returning to polite civilian society. "I have never been tempted to follow the vices of camp and cannot see how one who has any respect for himself or his friends at home can so degrade themselves as many do."[81]

Falling short of terrible vice, healthy young men could not help but to fantasize about the opposite sex. Michigander Charles B. Hayden's comments suggested how easily soldiers' thoughts could turn to women. Noting an abundance of fig trees while campaigning in Mississippi, he found that his comrades "could not forget even amid their toils that there was a time (so says tradition) when a single fig leaf was all that concealed the charms of woman." Because of the biblical connection, men "caressed the leaves" and discussed "the fitness of Eve's choice for her first & at that time her only garment." Some of the men were unhappy because the foliage was "the first article used to conceal her loveliness." Despite such criticism, other men "soon suggested that the concealment was so slight that her charms half concealed, half disclosed were more exciting than if seen in their full glory." In the end, Hayden concluded that "Eve did not think that her simple efforts at dress making & modesty would be discussed by her boys after so many years."[82]

Soldiers' innocent speculation about the female form moved beyond the limits of good behavior learned at home when men sang bawdy songs, wrote erotic poetry, and told blue stories. They also read pornographic literature and viewed pornographic prints. An advertisement in a Chattanooga, Tennessee, newspaper, for example, offered Union soldiers images of the "handsomest woman in the world," a picture described as "rich, rare & racy." Indeed, Northern businesses mailed catalogs offering a wide range of pornographic materials to soldiers, presumably because they believed there was a demand for the articles.[83]

Men not satisfied with voyeurism eagerly frequented brothels to satisfy their erotic cravings. Even before leaving the North, Charles Hayden noticed a tendency on the part of the soldiers to seek out women of questionable virtue. In May 1861 he concluded that "if the men pursue the enemy as vigorously as they do the whores they will make very efficient soldiers."[84] Consequently, bordellos became common in cities and towns when soldiers were present. Washington, D.C., had a plethora of brothels sporting such names as "the Ironclad" and "Madam Russel's Bake Oven," while Richmond, Virginia, the heart of the God-fearing Confederacy, had houses that catered to the baser instincts of its defenders.[85]

Civil War soldiers free from the civilizing, restraining influence of good women and home not only transgressed the sexual boundaries of chaste civilian life. Out of sight and earshot of pastors and mothers, they also swore, played cards, and greedily drank whatever liquor they could obtain. Officers tried to stop such activities because they feared these bad habits would hurt discipline, and courts-martial punished men who, used to the easy flow of profanity, directed their foul language at officers. Robert E. Lee issued orders against the "vice" of gambling, but those men intent on cardplaying, dice throwing, holding raffles, and running horse or lice races found ways to continue their betting games. Even innocent and healthful games could not escape the soldiers' habit of wagering. When New Jerseyan George Fox reported on the outcome of baseball games, he noted that bets on the winning team were in the range of $100 to $200.[86]

More than anything else, the misuse of alcohol contributed greatly to the soldiers' bad—and sometimes deadly—behavior in camp. Chaplain Joseph Hopkins Twichell considered it to be "the worst evil among both officers and men." The majority of men in his New York regiment, he lamented, thought "that getting drunk is rather commendable."[87] Theodore Dodge found it "astonishing how soon men will get drunk in camp when they get a chance. They can't be moderate."[88] That certainly was the case of some jolly Arkansan Christmas revelers; celebrating the holiday, "two commissioned officers, four non-commissioned officers, and twenty-seven privates" became too drunk to stand up for the evening's dress parade.[89]

Officers concerned that drink would erode discipline did their best to control the use of liquor. Some of them tried to organize temperance societies for their comrades and men. Other officers tried to crack down on the consumption of liquor by prohibiting it among their men and confiscating unauthorized supplies of spirits. Despite such efforts, soldiers who wanted drink became quite resourceful in outsmarting their superiors. Smuggling and hiding liquor rose to an art form in the soldiers' camps. Confederates camping near Fredericksburg, for example, hid their refreshment in barrels of oysters.[90] A truly thirsty Northern veteran stationed in Virginia during the winter of 1864 stole a case of whiskey from a sutler, buried it in a heaping pile of horse manure, and escaped detection at the hands of officers bent on disciplining the culprit. He soon retrieved the drink, reburied it in a more accessible place when the coast was clear, and later enjoyed his prize with his friends.[91]

Officers who worried about the effects of alcohol were not being overly cautious: liquor had a terrible effect on camp discipline. Drunks wandering through the Virginia camp of the 40th New York Infantry required an entire company of men to put down their disturbances.[92] Those drunken soldiers were disruptive, but in the case of another New York regiment, one drunk encouraged another to shoot one of their comrades. He did, and the victim died. Also, the "depredations and cuttings up" of drunken soldiers spilled over into the nearby civilian populations, which was "just punishment," according to Chaplain Twichell, "for giving soldiers liquor."[93]

Such bad behavior required firm discipline, which, for breaches of military decorum fueled by liquor as well as other various and sundry offences, ran the gamut of punishments, limited only by the creativity of officers. "When a man was very drunk or abusive, a bayonette or piece of wood was placed in his mouth and a string tied behind his ears kept in a position, seating him on the ground with his knees drawn up to his body," one Yankee soldier explained. "A piece of wood is run through his legs, and placing his arms under the stick on each side of his knees, his hands are then tied in front, and he is secure as a traped rat."[94] Confinement to the guardhouse seemed tame by comparison. In the end, however, perhaps the most constructive lesson for drunken bad behavior was forcing the offending parties to do their duty while still recovering from their sprees. The hungover Arkansas Christmas revelers had to march the next morning under the threat of court-martial if they failed to keep up with the rest of the regiment. On another occasion, officers forced pickets from the First Arkansas, who had managed to smuggle a considerable amount of liquor to their post, to drink it all on an empty stomach while marching back to their camp. In this case, however, the punishment failed to achieve its disciplinary purpose; the parched officers joined in, finding the drink "so good they did not let it go in a hurry."[95]

SOLDIERS' HEALTH IN CAMP

Many soldiers reassured the home folks that camp life agreed with them and that the rugged military routine set them up in prime physical condition. But camp life could be hard on the health of soldiers, leaving them with chronic problems that followed them into peacetime. Crowds of unseasoned men from the countryside not immune to common diseases came down with all sorts of communicable ailments from the time they first gathered in their encampments. Officers attempted to have new recruits vaccinated for smallpox, but soldiers became infected with numerous other diseases. New recruits were especially vulnerable in their first camps, where measles became a particular problem. Even old soldiers suffered from camp illnesses that ranged the entire diagnostic spectrum, although dysentery, diarrhea and digestive problems, fevers primarily caused by malaria, and respiratory problems, particularly bronchitis, were most common. As one Connecticut soldier discovered during the fall of 1862, "in camp it is *cough, cough, cough all night long from one end of the line to the other.*"[96]

From their earliest days in military camps, Northerners and Southerners witnessed the effects of disease and acknowledged the toll it took on themselves and their comrades. Camp diseases not only affected individuals' health and morale, but hurt the fighting strength of the armies. The Confederate army encamped at Corinth after the Battle of Shiloh endured more casualties in less than two months there than it had suffered at Pittsburg Landing; thousands of cases of diarrhea and dysentery took their toll on the physical and mental well-being of the men.[97] Confederate Silas Grisamore recalled that after Shiloh, his own regiment "was reduced to about 300 men fit for duty, in an aggregate of near 700" because of illness.[98] Indeed, sickness killed more men than enemy bullets and hurried along the demise of wounded men who otherwise might have recovered. Confederate officer James B. Griffin acknowledged this situation when he admitted, "I honestly believe that the battle itself is about the least of dangers, to which the Soldier is exposed."[99]

The very nature of camp life created the conditions that produced so much illness among the armies. A monotonous diet lacking in vegetables or other fresh foods brought on scurvy, a connection that was not lost on physicians and soldiers' relief agencies. Indeed, the disease manifested itself in ways that could lead an officer to assume that the suffering soldier was a lazy shirker; the bleeding gums and loose teeth, however, proved otherwise, as did the sores and other symptoms well known to regimental surgeons.

Proper diet brought men back to health, as medical men and many soldiers understood. In April 1863, before the Battle of Chancellorsville, members of the ambulance corps of the Army of Northern Virginia went out on a mission to collect wild onions and watercress to supplement the soldiers' diets in an effort to combat illness.[100] Yankee George Cram, whose company had some men suffering from scurvy, avoided the disease by eating blackberries.[101] But scurvy or no, there were untold other health hazards in camp that were more likely to lay low a volunteer than an enemy's bullet.

Human and animal waste, contaminated drinking water, and offal from butchered animals all combined with poor sanitation to create the unhealthful conditions that plagued armies. At times, officers compounded the problem by selecting poor campsites, without an eye to their potential health problems. Thomas Fanning, a North Carolinian who later became a surgeon, noted that his regiment's South Carolina campsite was poorly selected, but even after they relocated to a better site, the "imprudent" men themselves continued to create sanitary problems that resulted in sickness.[102]

Fanning's comrades were not alone in their bad habits. Federal and Confederate soldiers, despite medical supervision, often made matters worse for themselves with their poor camp hygiene. Peter Vrendenburg put the worse light on camp life to discourage his younger brother from enlisting as a private soldier by describing the filthy, crowded conditions of the soldiers' sleeping quarters. "He will have to sleep in his clothes," he informed his father, "nestled close in with 10 or 12 dirty-lousy devils who probably have not washed or changed their clothing in a month or two."[103] Despite the purpose of his letter, he was not off the mark. In July 1862 Georgian Ugie Allen reported from Virginia to the home folks about lice and other problems: "Thare is not a man in the regiment but what have had them. The fact is thare are men in our company that are actually being eat up by them. They are sucking their life's blood out of them."[104]

Lice, flees, and other vermin thus plagued soldiers in camps where men might lack either soap or the inclination to do laundry and bathe. Samuel Fiske of Connecticut reported that "the first observation every man would make...is that the soldier's life is an eminently dirty one."[105] Yankee George M. Cram confirmed Fiske's assessment, reporting that "soldiers seldom wash more than their noses and fingernails." While he bathed regularly, he found that the doctors disapproved of his habit, "so a great many of the boys go weeks and some months without washing their bodies." It was Cram's opinion that "one half of the deaths in the army are caused by filth."[106]

Military policy apparently controlled the lice problem to the point where neither Union nor Confederate soldiers suffered the typhus that the creatures spread in epidemic proportions in European regiments of the day. But while soldiers could hunt down "critters" and discard vermin-infested clothes, they could not escape viruses and bacteria. Military surgeons had limited tools at their disposal for dealing with the maladies caused by those unseeable enemies, and common practices often did little to aid the suffering soldier. Bowel ailments prompted treatments that included the use of castor oil and other laxatives as well as various opiates. In October 1862 Iowa soldier Lycurgus Remley was plagued by diarrhea; the doctor treated him with morphine, a purgative, quinine, and whiskey, while suggesting he would also dose him with "blue mass pills" consisting of mercury "to rouse" his liver.[107] Because most of the soldiers who had bouts of diarrhea came back to health in several days, surgeons considered such treatments a success and persisted in their use.

Confederate surgeons, troubled by wartime shortages, did no better than their Yankee counterparts. They could resort to herbal and other natural remedies or make do with whatever their pharmacies had on hand. Surgeon William Taylor asked the men of the 19th Virginia Infantry one question at sick call, regardless of the nature of the complaints: "How are your bowels?" "In one pocket of my trousers I had a ball of blue mass, in another a ball of opium," he reported. "If they were open, I administered a plug of opium; if they were shut, I gave a plug of blue mass."[108]

Many soldiers thought it wise to avoid regimental surgeons; they believed it best to allow nature to take its course because they had little faith in their doctors' abilities. Alabaman A. D. Beck pronounced his battalion's surgeon "one of the sarriest Doctors...you ever saw. He cant tell the chill and fever from the head ache."[109] Robert Patrick, a Louisiana soldier, believed that the "treatment of ignorant, sap-headed physicians" did him more harm than his undiagnosed illness. Patrick accused surgeons of administering uniform and large doses medicines to patients, regardless of their illness, "until they either kill the individual or ruin his constitution for life."[110]

Not only the treatment, but the hospitals in which the men found themselves could also be unpleasant and something they tried to avoid. Even doctors questioned their value and also wondered about the worth of military medicine. "Very little can be done for a man while he lies upon the ground with typhoid fever, attended by incompetent nurses," assistant surgeon Daniel M. Holt noted. "When I order one to hospital, it seems almost equivalent to ordering his grave dug."[111]

DEATH IN THE CAMPS

With illness so prevalent, soldiers saw death walk among them even when they were away from the battlefield. In May 1862 Alabaman Grant Taylor reported that measles

Funeral march by Alfred R. Waud depicts a common event in the camps of both armies. (*Library of Congress*)

had serious consequences among the troops, bringing a death to the camp almost every day.[112] It was little different for Northern men. In January 1863 New York assistant surgeon Daniel Holt glumly told his wife that at their Fredericksburg camp, "Death is upon our track, and almost every day sees its victim taken to the grave." The toll was heavy, he reported, "and still the avenger presses harder and harder claiming as his victim the best and fairest of the men."[113]

In November 1861 John Sewell Anglin wrote about the common occurrence of death in camp at Manassas, Virginia, and the ceremony that accompanied even a lowly private's demise:

> Every day or so we hear the Band commence playing a sad burial tune very suddenly. We know then that some poor boy's spirit has departed and presently we see the 'Band' gradually appearing from out of some companies street, followed by a small corpse bearing the last remains of some poor soldier in a plain pine coffin....And in a few moments we see them gradually disappearing wending their way around a hill to the original forest, a short sad tune played slowly and the corpse is born into the grave there to remain until the resurrection of the dead. Well that is the only and last tribute of respect paid to the dead.[114]

These funerals became so much a part of camp life that soldiers soon took them in stride. In September 1862 Yankee soldiers participated in the ceremonial burial of one of their own. Yet, on their return to camp, Elisha Rhodes reported, "Everything went on as usual...as if nothing had happened, for death is so common that little sentiment is wasted. It is not like death at home."[115] Indeed, Charles Muser admitted that funerals occurred "so frequent that we are a getting used to it."[116] Camp death contributed to that hardening that made men "insensible to grief—or compassion." As Kentucky Confederate Edward Guerrant reasoned, "Death is nothing here, where so many die & all are liable to it."[117]

CONNECTIONS WITH HOME

Soldiers who could ignore camp funerals pondered the notion that the war was changing them. They lived hard and dirty. They watched friends die, while they themselves killed. Military experience was foreign to their earlier lives, but it was becoming their normal way of existing. Thoughtful men, such as South Carolinian Tally Simpson, worried that "inactivity, indolence and various other things have very nearly reduced me to the lamentable state of a nontalkative Quaker." Nothing roused him from his "stupor," except dinner or roll call.[118] And William Craig concluded that the war's influences would not be easily shaken. "This rebellion will be the ruination of thousands of men," Craig warned his wife. "They have become hardened to everything." A soldier, he noted, "will get so weary that he cares for nothing."[119]

Men understood that their hardening was partially the fault of their lack of contact with the home. Thus it became all the more important that the soldiers stay in touch with the civilizing influences in their lives: their wives, their families, their sweethearts.

Married men never completely gave up their role as the head of the family, nor did fathers abdicate the responsibilities of raising their children. Husbands advised their wives about business matters and agricultural concerns, while fathers instructed their children in how to live a good life. Soldier sons argued with their parents, while they also courted their old sweethearts or looked for new ones as they longed for the company of women. What happened at home was important to the men at the front, and it had an impact on their ability to deal with the military task at hand. Even the illiterate soldiers, single and married, did their best to keep in touch with their families and sweethearts through the good graces of their educated comrades and officers.

Soldiers had rare opportunities to go on furlough from their companies to visit their families, while during some quiet times, relatives visited them in camp. But for most of their service, men stayed connected to their home through the post. Sending and receiving letters became an important diversion and mail call a happy diversion from camp routine. In April 1863 Tally Simpson received a cheerful letter from his aunt, which "thoroughly aroused" him from his lethargy.[120]

When men did not receive mail regularly, they became both angry and sad. They begged and even demanded that their families be more diligent in keeping in touch with them. Soldiers who felt neglected chided wives, family members, and friends in hopes

Headquarters, 50th New York Engineers, Petersburg, Va. depicting the attention to detail noted by many letter writers and diarists when discussing their long-term encampments. (*Library of Congress*)

of spurring them on to greater literary efforts. Without correspondence, men felt cut adrift from home and kept in the dark about the everyday events in the lives of those people most dear to them.

There were good reasons for soldiers to worry when they did not hear from loved ones. On the Northern and Southern home fronts, there was no respite from the ordinary concerns and tragedies of life for soldiers' families. Financial hardship, sickness, and death did not pass them by. There was real hardship in the Confederacy, as inflation and hunger taxed soldiers' families and Yankees campaigned across the land. Soldiers worried about unruly slaves and what horrors might result from unsupervised black men roaming the countryside. All of this turmoil near home troubled Confederates who had enlisted to fight for the safety of their homes.

If an absence of letters caused anxiety, the arrival of news from home did not always bring relief. Unsettling news placed soldiers in the unhappy situation of knowing about family crises but not being able to do anything about them. Texan Will Neblet's wife, Lizzie, reported the state of their farm in some detail, but in April 1863 lamented, "Oh Will you don't know how heavily the burden & responsibility rests upon me of having things done which are highly necessary outside of the farm, and my fear that the negros will not support themselves, and I know so little about farming." Lizzie, coming a bit unhinged, pleaded with her husband "for God's sake" to hire a substitute and return home "even if it takes half we have" because, she reasoned, "what would the world full of money be to me if you were dead." Even after she regained some composure, she continued to lament her situation; far from encouraging her soldier in his fight, she continued to express her worries for his safety and remarked, "Oh I feel like dying in despair almost like you were gone forever."[121]

News about their families enduring financial hardship was especially troubling to the men who had been good providers before the war. Businessmen and landlords failed to take pity on Northern soldiers' families, and morale suffered as the men placed blame on uncaring relatives, creditors, profiteers, or government officials. Pennsylvanian John Arnold, whose pay was overdue as he campaigned in the bloody Virginia wilderness during the spring of 1864, complained about a merchant who refused to give his wife credit. The merchant had a cold heart because, Arnold reasoned, he was a copperhead and "cant any Thing Better be expected of such a man."[122] Such financial exploitation and the apparent war profiteering of home-front businessmen embittered soldiers who worried about their families. In November 1862 George Squier, writing to his wife, Ellen, from Indianapolis, bitterly complained about how everyone was out to get money "whethe[r] it be defrauding the Government or the private soldier who leaves his family and friends, sunders ties, sacrifices his little means for the good of his country."[123]

In June 1862 Georgian Samuel A. Burney longed to comfort his wife in her illness. That concern probably contributed to rethinking his commitment to the cause; he asked his wife to explore the possibility of finding a substitute for him. "I know that a man that gets a substitute is not generally thought well of," he admitted to her; "that makes no difference to me I see that others are for themselves and I intend to be for myself hereafter."[124] In March 1863, when young Tennessean William Hackworth heard that "soldiers had taken all the corn in the valley there without respect of persons," he revealed a conflicted commitment to the Confederate cause. He advised his parents and siblings to let him know honestly if they were suffering for want of food because, he assured them, "I feel like I would do you justice my contry justice and my god justice to come home and make bred for you although I feel like it was my duty to fite for my home." Hackworth, however, remained in Nathan Bedford Forrest's cavalry and sent home money to help his family endure "this lonsom and trubblesom world."[125] Later in the war, many Confederate soldiers simply left the ranks to take care of the needs of their families, believing such action justified because their government had broken a generally assumed agreement that they would care for their families. Many men may have had the intention of returning once they had settled their business at home, but the disruption in the ranks had a negative impact on the Confederate armies' ability to conduct their own business.[126]

Most soldiers who stuck it out in the ranks of the armies probably felt that they were being most useful in securing their families' well-being, short of winning the war, when they sent home money. Despite distance, they could still act as heads of families, and men were quite diligent in their efforts. William Craig of the 116th Illinois told his wife that "some say they don't think anything about home...but I thank God it makes me proud to get a dollar to send to my dear wife and baby."[127] At one point in the war, men from Iowa's Third Cavalry sent money to the home of Samuel Miller, a prominent Keokuk citizen, whose wife delivered the funds to the various families; into the future, the cavalrymen continued to use the Miller residence as a place where their wives could collect their husbands' pay.[128] And in January 1863 New York chaplain Joseph Hopkins Twichell transported about $10,000 of his regiment's pay to the home folk.[129] Armies, however, deprived men of that connection with home when paymasters appeared only on rare occasions. "Eleven months have now passed away and still we are without pay," complained one soldier from the black 55th Massachusetts. "How our families are to live and pay house-rent I know not."[130] No wonder Chaplain Twichell accused the government of being beyond "all reason and humanity in a matter which seriously affects the welfare of thousands [of] poor people." Furthermore, the absent paymaster was simply "miserable policy." "Men will lose confidence in an Administration which does not keep its promises to women and children," the chaplain predicted.[131]

Sending money home was but one way to reserve a claim to the chair at the head of the table, and family men found other opportunities to act as the patriarch. Soldiers did their best to assert some control over the well-being of their families by filling the letters they wrote with advice to wives and children. Many soldiers refused to give up their responsibilities as parents and continued to cultivate a close relationship with their children through this correspondence. Frustrated by their inability to be involved in the everyday events of their lives, they wrote directly to their children, instructing them the best they could from their distant camps.

Men were especially precise in detailing advice to wives back home. When William Craig sent some money home to his wife, he advised her to live on the funds and "don't expose yourself as long as it will last." He also ordered her "to drink good coffee" and tell him "whether you drink it or not."[132] Men instructed their wives in child-rearing duties as well as all other aspects of home life, from handling financial matters to fattening up and slaughtering the livestock and tending their gardens. Women responded admirably, collecting debt, slaughtering hogs, and raising children, which probably pleased those men who expected their wives to hold down the home front, stand on their own two feet, and prepare themselves for a future that might not include their husbands.

There were, however, some soldiers who worried that their wives might become too independent. In June 1863 Midwesterner William Vermilion warned his wife to be prepared to accept his authority when he returned. "You may think Dollie you will do as you please when we get to living together again. All this time you are your own boss,

Wash day near Fort Slocum, Washington, D.C. On occasion wives visited
their enlisted husbands in camp. (*Library of Congress*)

but just wait. We will have military law when I get there," he explained. He may have
been joking, but he did give fair warning that he planned to reassert himself as head of
the household after the war.[133]

The worry that war and the absence of men at home might upset the sexual hierarchy touched other soldiers. Illinois Sergeant George Cram chastised his mother for her
efforts to win the vote for women. "Two years in the army leads one to think still more
that ladies should be ladies and not meddle with the contentions of men," he argued.
"Let the women teach their children to be honorable, honest statesmen, and the girls social and rational women," he advised, explaining that such actions would have a greater
impact on creating good politics. Women, Cram concluded, should keep to their special
sphere and let the men handle the "strifes and contentions of the political world."[134]

Wives accepted practical advice from their husbands, and parents listened to their
maturing sons, but they, too, sent advice back to their men and boys, especially in their
effort to keep them on the righteous path. Civilians worried a good bit about the impact
of camp life, and war in general, on their soldiers and tried to remind them of their responsibilities and their civilian values. They urged their men to trust God and live good
lives. Wives warned their men to avoid the vices common to army life. Fathers and
mothers also urged their sons to live in God's grace, to do their duty to their country,
and to acquit themselves as men.

George Cram's direction to his politically inclined mother, however, suggested that
soldier sons, once inexperienced youths but now away from constant parental supervision, were maturing and developing opinions of their own that would forever alter their
relationships with their parents. Young soldiers did not hesitate to make their views
about the home front, and especially politics, known to their elders. They also kept

their parents aware of their hardships and accomplishments as well as their battle experiences. In the process, they forced their parents to reconsider their perceptions of their children. Young sons assumed responsibilities as noncommissioned and company-grade officers. Boys became men as they endured the hardships of war, and their parents had to recognize the change. For example, Sam Evans of Ohio, who became an officer in a black regiment, moderated his racist Democratic father's views about the future role of blacks in a reunited America.[135] Also, in some cases, soldiering led to a reversal of family roles. It was money set aside by Yankee James Randall from his army pay that, in 1863, allowed his father to move onto land provided by the Homestead Act.[136]

As war progressed, soldiers found the separation from family, and especially wives, difficult to endure. Young men might have enjoyed the freedom of camp, but those soldiers who had experienced the adult comforts of home life expressed their longing for their families. In May 1861 Sergeant Valentine G. Barney of Vermont reported how he missed his home life. "I tell you Maria I never before realized so forcibly the comforts of a home and the kindness and goodness of my loveing Wife and children as at the present," he explained. "I hope and trust that I may be more attentive to them in the future than I have been in the past."[137] A very depressed Wright Vinson badly missed his Georgia home, promising his wife, "When I get home I will kiss you and hug you and doo any thing you want mee to doo."[138] The separation from his wife led Michigander John Paddington to promise her that he would be a much better husband on his return from war. He could not keep his pledge, falling on the first day of Gettysburg, but in the January before he died, he told her that he "little thought a man could have such thrilling feelings for a Woman as I have for you."[139]

Men tried in their own delicate way to express the sexual desires they had for the women they had left behind. In January 1863 Alabaman Grant Taylor told his wife that when he conjured up an image of her in his mind, he yearned "to press those silent lips to mine and hear those sweet words of love fall from them once more."[140] In late 1862 Wright Vinson dreamt of hugging his wife but woke up to find himself "hugging the boys." He expressed his desire to lie next to her because he knew he "wold sleep warm and more than that... cold hug up with" her. No wonder Vinson began to think about deserting because, he explained to his wife, "I never wanted to gow home as bad in my life as I doo now." For Vinson, his life was miserable and he "had just as soon die as to live."[141]

Unmarried men also thought of the fairer sex back home. They daydreamed, perhaps wishing "to go corting and squeaze some of the girls," as one North Carolinian confessed, "for I no that they would like to be squeazed a little."[142] The reason Tally Simpson was so pleased to hear from his aunt was that she sent him news about a young woman in whom he had an interest. "So sail in, give me a lift occasionally, and always keep me posted on how the wind blows," he instructed her, especially since Simpson was worried that the object of his affection might already be engaged to another young man, something he wished his aunt to clarify.[143]

The more fortunate among these young soldiers had women with whom they could correspond, sometimes with more than just literary amusement on their minds. Louisiana soldier Rufus Cater clearly had more than a passing platonic interest in his female correspondent, cousin Fannie Cater. "You cannot easily imagine Dear Cousin what solace I find in your letters," he informed her. "They serve for encouragement, for consolation, for thought. They cheer me in sadness, they come to me in loneliness, bringing hope & comfort and a *joy* in the assurance that [throu?] sunshine and storm I have yet a friend."[144] Some men warned young ladies not to forget them for local lads. Former slave Bob, a member of the 30th U.S. Colored Infantry, told his girl Tilley "how he thought of her day and night...and that he didn't want to hear of any of the young fellows from the other plantations calling around to see her."[145]

Northern soldiers placed newspaper ads requesting letters from young women who desired to correspond with young men in the army. Many men, even some who were married, found the game amusing, but others looked on it as a serious way to identify potential mates.[146] Other soldiers conducted lengthy correspondence with familiar girls who eventually became their wives. John Emory Bryant married his former student and wartime correspondent Emma Spalding before the end of the conflict; Ohioan Dwight Corry, while he felt the need to remain a single man until "peace is established and the government has no more need of soldiers," married his correspondent "friend Hattie" shortly after war's end, in October 1865; Abial Edwards needed more time but got around to marrying his correspondent Anna Conant in 1869.[147] In the end, the connections with family, friends, and sweethearts through the mail, even when strained with anxiety, went a long way to remind soldiers that there was something beyond their rugged camp life.

NOTES

1. John Kent Folmar, ed., *From That Terrible Field: Civil War Letters of James M. Williams, Twenty-first Alabama Infantry Volunteers* (Tuscaloosa: University of Alabama Press, 1981), 57.

2. Claire E. Swedberg, ed., *Three Years with the 92d Illinois: The Civil War Diary of John M. King* (Mechanicsburg, PA: Stackpole Books, 1999), 57, 58.

3. Christopher Looby, ed., *The Complete Civil War Journal and Selected Letters of Thomas Wentworth Higginson* (Chicago: University of Chicago Press, 2000), 48, 50, 68, 106 (quotation).

4. James Henry Gooding, *On the Altar of Freedom: A Black Soldier's Civil War Letters from the Front*, ed. Virginia M. Adams (Amherst: University of Massachusetts Press, 1991), 54.

5. Lyman Richard Comey, ed., *A Legacy of Valour: The Memoirs and Letters of Captain Henry Newton Comey, 2nd Massachusetts* (Knoxville: University of Tennessee Press, 2004), 179–80.

6. William J. K. Beaudot and Lance J. Herdegen, eds., *An Irishman in the Iron Brigade: The Civil War Memoirs of James P. Sullivan, Sergt., Company K., 6th Wisconsin Volunteers* (New York: Fordham University Press, 1993), 132–34.

7. George W. Fox to Charlie Fox, August 8, 1863, Civil War Letters of the Fox Brothers, eHistory, Ohio State University, Columbus, http://ehistory.osu.edu/osu/sources/letters/fox/.

8. John M. Follett, to wife, February 21, 1863, Follett Brothers Letters, eHistory, Ohio State University, Columbus, http://ehistory.osu.edu/osu/sources/letters/follett_brothers/.

9. James I. Robertson Jr., *The Civil War Letters of General Robert McAllister* (Baton Rouge: Louisiana State University Press, 1998), 574.

10. Warren Lee Goss, *Recollections of a Private: A Story of the Army of the Potomac* (Scituate, MA: Digital Scanning, 2002), 328.

11. John R. Sellers, ed., *A People at War: Civil War Manuscripts from the Holdings of the Library of Congress* (Alexandria, VA: Chadwyck-Heakey, 1989–1990), Allen Landis to parents, September 27, 1862, Allen Landis Papers, reel 58.

12. Terry L. Jones, *Lee's Tigers: The Louisiana Infantry in the Army of Northern Virginia* (Baton Rouge: Louisiana State University Press, 1987), 140.

13. Eric A. Campbell, ed., *"A Grand Terrible Dramma": From Gettysburg to Petersburg: The Civil War Letters of Charles Reed Wellington* (New York: Fordham University Press, 2000), 56.

14. William Miller Owen, *In Camp and Battle with the Washington Artillery of New Orleans* (Baton Rouge: Louisiana State University Press, 1999), 68.

15. Robertson, *The Civil War Letters of General Robert McAllister,* 277.

16. Looby, *Complete Civil War Journal and Selected Letters of Thomas Wentworth Higginson,* 179.

17. Carlton McCarthy, *Detailed Minutiae of Soldier Life in the Army of Northern Virginia, 1861–1865* (Lincoln: University of Nebraska Press, 1993), 31.

18. Lance Herdegen and Sherry Murphy, eds., *Four Years with the Iron Brigade: The Civil War Journal of William Ray, Company F, Seventh Wisconsin Volunteers* (Cambridge, MA: Da Capo Press, 2002), 8.

19. Steven E. Woodworth, ed., *The Musick of the Mocking Birds, the Roar of the Canon: The Civil War Diary and Letters of William Winters* (Lincoln: University of Nebraska Press, 1998), 1–3.

20. Emil Rosenblatt and Ruth Rosenblatt, eds., *Hard Marching Every Day: The Civil War Letters of Private Wilbur Fisk, 1861–1865* (Lawrence: University of Kansas Press, 1992), 23.

21. Stephen W. Sears, ed., *On Campaign with the Army of the Potomac: The Civil War Journal of Theodore Ayrault Dodge* (New York: Cooper Square Press, 2001), 218.

22. Robert K. Krick, *Parker's Virginia Battery C. S. A.*, 2nd rev. ed. (Wilmington, NC: Broadfoot, 1989), 23.

23. Donald C. Elder III, ed., *A Damned Iowa Greyhound: The Civil War Letters of William Henry Harrison Clayton* (Iowa City: University of Iowa Press, 1998), 32.

24. Ed Malles, ed., *Bridge Building in Wartime: Colonel Wesley Brainerd's Memoir of the 50th New York Volunteer Engineers* (Knoxville: University of Tennessee Press, 1997), 133.

25. Swedberg, *Three Years with the 92d Illinois*, 67.

26. Charles F. Herberger, ed., *A Yankee in Arms: The Diary of Lieutenant Augustus D. Ayling, 29th Massachusetts Volunteers* (Knoxville: University of Tennessee Press, 1999), 87.

27. John D. Billings, *Hardtack and Coffee: The Unwritten Story of Army Life* (Lincoln: University of Nebraska Press, 1993), 95–107, 173–75; Mark H. Dunkelman, *Brothers One and All: Esprit de Corps in a Civil War Regiment* (Baton Rouge: Louisiana State University Press, 2004), 79–81.

28. Quoted in Bell I. Wiley, *The Life of Billy Yank: The Common Soldier of the Union* (Garden City, NY: Doubleday, 1971), 53.

29. McCarthy, *Detailed Minutiae*, 74.

30. Larry J. Daniel, *Soldiering in the Army of the Tennessee: A Portrait of Life in a Confederate Army* (Chapel Hill: University of North Carolina Press, 1991), 62–63.

31. Stephen W. Sears, ed., *Mr. Dunn Browne's Experiences in the Army: The Civil War Letters of Samuel W. Fiske* (New York: Fordham University Press, 1998), 3.

32. Sellers, *A People at War*, Leonard Ives to Joseph C. Ives, September 25, 1862, Joseph Christmas Ives Collection, reel 57.

33. Ibid., John C. Arnold to wife and family, March 10, 1864, John Carvel Arnold Letters, reel 1.

34. Ibid., John S. Anglin to brother, April 18, 1862, John S. Anglin Letters, reel 1.

35. *From Antietam to Appomattox with the 118th Penna. Vols. Corn Exchange Regiment* (Philadelphia: J. L. Smith, 1892), 157.

36. Bell I. Wiley, *The Life of Johnny Reb: The Common Soldier of the Confederacy* (Garden City, NY: Doubleday, 1971), 99; Billings, *Hardtack and Coffee*, 220.

37. Jones, *Lee's Tigers*, 140.

38. John S. Collier and Bonnie B. Collier, eds., *Yours for the Union: The Civil War Letters of John W. Chase, First Massachusetts Light Artillery* (New York: Fordham University Press, 2004), 27.

39. Anita Palladino, ed., *Diary of a Yankee Engineer: The Civil War Story of John H. Westervelt, Engineer, 1st New York Volunteer Engineer Corps* (New York: Fordham University Press, 1997), 16.

40. Stephen W. Sears, ed., *For Country, Cause and Leader: The Civil War Journal of Charles B. Hayden* (New York: Ticknor & Fields, 1993), 326.

41. Stephen V. Ash, *When the Yankees Came: Conflict and Chaos in the Occupied South, 1861–1865* (Chapel Hill: University of North Carolina Press, 1995), 219–220; Thomas P. Lowry, *The Story the Soldiers Wouldn't Tell: Sex in the Civil War* (Mechanicsburg, PA: Stackpole Books, 1994), 83.

42. Campbell, *"A Grand Terrible Dramma,"* 48.

43. Ash, *When the Yankees Came*, 77, 91–92.

44. Kenneth E. Olson, *Music and Musket: Bands and Bandsmen of the American Civil War* (Westport, CT: Greenwood Press, 1981), 188.

45. Sellers, *A People at War*, Allen Landis to parents, Jan. 1, 1863, Allen Landis Papers, LC, reel 58.

46. Jeffrey C. Lowe and Sam Hodges, eds., *Letters to Amanda: The Civil War Letters of Marion Hill Fitzpatrick, Army of Northern Virginia* (Macon, GA: Mercer University Press, 1998), 100.

47. Elder, *A Damned Iowa Greyhound*, 16–17; Mary E. Kellog, comp., *Army Life of an Illinois Soldier, Including a Day-by-Day Record of Sherman's March to the Sea: Letters and Diary of Charles W. Wills* (Carbondale: Southern Illinois University Press, 1996), 27.

48. Joel Craig, ed., *Dear Eagle: The Civil War Correspondence of Stephen H. Bogardus, Jr. to the Poughkeepsie Daily Eagle* (Wake Forest, NC: Scuppernog Press, 2004); Rosenblatt and Rosenblatt, *Hard Marching Every Day*; Sears, *Mr. Dunn Browne's Experiences*, 3.

49. Gooding, *On the Altar of Freedom*, 54.

50. James M. McPherson, *The Negro's Civil War: How American Blacks Felt and Acted during the War for the Union* (New York: Vintage Civil War Library, 1991), 215.

51. Donald B. Koonce, ed., *Doctor to the Front: The Recollections of Confederate Surgeon Thomas Fanning Wood, 1861–1865* (Knoxville: University of Tennessee Press, 2000), 13; Daniel E. Sutherland, ed., *Reminiscences of a Private: William E. Bevens of the First Arkansas Infantry, C.S.A.* (Fayetteville: University of Arkansas Press, 1992), 35.

52. Campbell, *"A Grand Terrible Dramma,"* 67.

53. Keith P. Wilson, *Campfires of Freedom: The Camp Life of Black Soldiers during the Civil War* (Kent, OH: Kent State University Press, 2002), 147–75; Thomas Wentworth Higginson, *Army Life in a Black Regiment* (New York: W. W. Norton, 1984), 187–213.

54. Sellers, *A People at War,* Felix Brannigan to sister, October 29, 1861, Felix Brannigan Papers, reel 4.

55. Barbara Bentley Smith and Nina Bentley Smith, eds., *"Burning Rails as We Pleased": The Civil War Letters of William Garrigues Bentley, 104th Ohio Volunteer Infantry* (Jefferson, NC: McFarland, 2004), 50.

56. Campbell, *"A Grand Terrible Dramma,"* 168–69, 181–85, 194, 257, 306.

57. Rosenblatt and Rosenblatt, *Hard Marching Every Day,* viii; Sellers, *A People at War,* Joseph Lester to father and sisters, June 5, August 16, 1864, Joseph Lester Collection, reel 58.

58. George W. Fox to Charlie Fox, April 23, 1863, Civil War Letters of the Fox Brothers, eHistory, Ohio State University, Columbus, http://ehistory.osu.edu/osu/sources/letters/fox/; George B. Kirsch, *Baseball in Blue and Gray: The National Pastime during the Civil War* (Princeton, NJ: Princeton University Press, 2003), 28–47.

59. Frank Wilkeson, *Turned Inside Out: Recollections of a Private Soldier in the Army of the Potomac* (Lincoln: University of Nebraska Press, 1997), 52–54.

60. Sam Watkins, *"Company Aytch," or a Side Show of the Big Show and Other Sketches,* ed. M. Thomas Inge (New York: Penguin Putnam, 1999), 31; Daniel, *Soldiering in the Army of Tennessee,* 128–29.

61. M. Jane Johansson, ed., *Widows by the Thousand: The Civil War Letters of Theophilus and Harriet Perry, 1862–1864* (Fayetteville: University of Arkansas Press, 2000), 148.

62. Kenneth W. Noe, ed., *A Southern Boy in Blue: The Memoir of Marcus Woodcock, 9th Kentucky Infantry (U.S.A.)* (Knoxville: University of Tennessee Press, 1996), 272–73.

63. Stephen E. Towne, ed., *A Fierce, Wild Joy: The Civil War Letters of Colonel Edward J. Wood, 48th Indiana Volunteer Infantry Regiment* (Knoxville: University of Tennessee Press, 2007), 200.

64. Julie Holcomb, ed., *Southern Sons, Northern Soldiers: The Civil War Letters of the Remley Brothers, 22nd Iowa Infantry* (DeKalb: Northern Illinois University Press, 2004), 160.

65. Jennifer Cain Bohrnstedt, ed., *Soldiering with Sherman: The Civil War Letters of George F. Cram* (DeKalb: Northern Illinois University Press, 2000), 140.

66. Richard L. Kiper, ed., *Dear Catherine, Dear Taylor: The Civil War Letters of a Union Soldier and His Wife* (Lawrence: University Press of Kansas, 2002), 263.

67. Beverly Hayes Kallgren and James L. Crouthamel, eds., *"Dear Friend Anna": The Civil War Letters of a Common Soldier from Maine* (Orono: University of Maine Press, 1992), 108.

68. Robert F. Engs and Corey M. Brooks, eds., *Their Patriotic Duty: The Civil War Letters of the Evans Family of Brown County, Ohio* (New York: Fordham University Press, 2007), 301.

69. Elder, *A Damned Iowa Greyhound,* 54.

70. Rosenblatt and Rosenblatt, *Hard Marching Every Day,* 273.

71. Kallgren and Crouthamel, *"Dear Friend Anna,"* 108.

72. Rosenblatt and Rosenblatt, *Hard Marching Every Day,* 276.

73. Peter Messent and Steve Courtney, eds., *The Civil War Letters of Joseph Hopkins Twichell: A Chaplain's Story* (Athens: University of Georgia Press, 2006), 22–23.

74. Wiley, *Life of Johnny Reb,* 176–79; Gardiner H. Shattuck Jr., *A Shield and Hiding Place: The Religious Life of Civil War Armies* (Macon, GA: Mercer University Press, 1987), 85.

75. Sellers, *A People at War,* John G. Jones to parents and brothers, November 21, 1863, John Griffith Jones Correspondence, reel 57.

76. Messent and Courtney, *Civil War Letters of Joseph Hopkins Twichell,* 70.

77. Sears, *For Country, Cause and Leader,* 320.

78. Messent and Courtney, *Civil War Letters of Joseph Hopkins Twichell,* 88–89, 93.

79. Wiley, *Life of Johnny Reb,* 180–85.

80. Richard Sauers, ed., *The Bloody 85th: The Letters of Milton McJunkin, a Western Pennsylvania Soldier in the Civil War* (Daleville, VA: Schroeder, 2000), 15.

81. Bohrnstedt, *Soldiering with Sherman,* 22, 73.

82. Sears, *For Country, Cause and Leader,* 334.

83. Lowry, *Story the Soldiers Wouldn't Tell,* 48–60; Wiley, *Life of Billy Yank,* 255–56.

84. Sears, *For Country, Cause and Leader,* 4.

85. Lowry, *Story the Soldiers Wouldn't Tell,* 61–87.

86. George W. Fox to Charlie Fox, April 23, 1863, Civil War Letters of the Fox Brothers, eHistory, Ohio State University, Columbus, http://ehistory.osu.edu/osu/sources/letters/fox/.

87. Messent and Courtney, *Civil War Letters of Joseph Hopkins Twichell,* 69, 81.

88. Sears, *On Campaign,* 100.

89. Daniel E. Sutherland, ed., *Reminiscences of a Private: William E. Bevens of the First Arkansas Infantry, C.S.A.* (Fayetteville: University of Arkansas Press, 1992), 53.

90. Ibid., 59.

91. Billings, *Hardtack and Coffee,* 229–30.

92. Robert Knox Sneden, *Eye of the Storm: A Civil War Odyssey,* ed. Charles F. Bryan and Nelson D. Lankford (New York: Free Press, 2000), 4–5.

93. Messent and Courtney, *Civil War Letters of Joseph Hopkins Twichell,* 81, 93.

94. David Herbert Donald, ed., *Gone for a Soldier: The Civil War Memoirs of Private Alfred Bellard* (Boston: Little, Brown, 1975), 27–28.

95. Sutherland, *Reminiscences of a Private,* 55.

96. Robert L. Bee, ed., *The Boys from Rockville: Civil War Narratives of Sgt. Benjamin Hirst, Company D, 14th Connecticut Volunteers* (Knoxville: University of Tennessee Press, 1998), 29–30.

97. George G. Kundahl, *Confederate Engineer: Training and Campaigning with John Morris Wampler* (Knoxville: University of Tennessee Press, 2000), 144.

98. Arthur W. Bergeron Jr., *The Civil War Reminiscences of Major Silas T. Grisamore, C.S.A.* (Baton Rouge: Louisiana State University Press, 1993), 51.

99. Judith N. McArthur and Orville Vernon Burton, eds., *A Gentleman and an Officer: A Military and Social History of James B. Griffin's Civil War* (New York: Oxford University Press, 1996), 147.

100. Koonce, *Doctor to the Front,* 74.

101. Bohrnstedt, *Soldiering with Sherman,* 48.

102. Koonce, *Doctor to the Front,* 19, 22.

103. Bernard A. Olsen, ed., *Upon the Tented Field: An Historical Account of the Civil War as Told by the Men Who Fought and Gave Their Lives* (Red Bank, NJ: Historic Projects, 1993), 39.

104. Randall Allen and Keith S. Bohannon, eds., *Campaigning with "Old Stonewall": Confederate Captain Ujanirtus Allen's Letters to His Wife* (Baton Rouge: Louisiana State University Press, 1998), 129.

105. Sears, *Mr. Dunn Browne's Experiences,* 3.

106. Bohrnstedt, *Soldiering with Sherman,* 27, 48.

107. Holcomb, *Southern Sons, Northern Soldiers,* 10.

108. Michael A. Flannery, *Civil War Pharmacy: A History of Drugs, Drug Supply and Provision, and Therapeutics for the Union and Confederacy* (Binghamton, NY: Pharmaceutical Products Press, 2004), 216–17.

109. Thomas W. Cutrer, ed., *Oh What a Lonesome Time I Had: The Civil War Letters of Major William Morel Moxley, Eighteenth Alabama Infantry, and Emily Beck Moxley* (Tuscaloosa: University of Alabama Press, 2002), 41.

110. F. Jay Taylor, ed., *Reluctant Rebel: The Secret Diary of Robert Patrick, 1861–1865* (Baton Rouge: Louisiana State University Press, 1959), 88.

111. James M. Greiner, Janet L. Coryell, and James R. Smither, eds., *A Surgeon's Civil War: The Letters and Diary of Daniel M. Holt, M.D.* (Kent, OH: Kent State University Press, 1994), 63.

112. Ann K. Blomquist and Robert A. Taylor, eds., *This Cruel War: The Civil War Letters of Grant and Malinda Taylor, 1862–1865* (Macon, GA: Mercer University Press, 2000), 25.

113. Greiner et al., *A Surgeon's Civil War,* 63.

114. Sellers, *A People at War,* John Sewell Anglin to parents, November 27, 1861, John Sewell Anglin Letters, reel 1.

115. Robert Hunt Rhodes, ed., *All for the Union: The Civil War Diary and Letters of Elisha Hunt Rhodes* (New York: Vintage Books, 1992), 75–76.

116. Barry Popchock, ed., *Soldier Boy: The Civil War Letters of Charles O. Musser, 29th Iowa* (Iowa City: University of Iowa Press, 1995), 27.

117. William C. Davis and Meredith L. Swintor, eds., *Bluegrass Confederate: The Headquarters Diary of Edward O. Guerrant* (Baton Rouge: Louisiana State University Press, 1999), 40.

118. Guy R. Everson and Edward H. Simpson Jr., *Far, Far from Home: The Wartime Letters of Dick and Tally Simpson, 3rd South Carolina Volunteers* (New York: Oxford University Press, 1994), 215.

119. W. S. Craig to Levica Craig, June 23, 1863, William Samuel Craig Letters, eHistory, Ohio State University, Columbus, http://ehistory.osu.edu/osu/sources/letters/craig/.

120. Everson and Simpson, *Far, Far from Home,* 215.

121. Erika L. Murr, ed., *A Rebel Wife in Texas: The Diary and Letters of Elizabeth Scott Neblett, 1852–1864* (Baton Rouge: Louisiana State University Press, 2001), 94–95.

122. Sellers, *A People at War,* John C. Arnold to wife, May, June 5, 1864, John Carvel Arnold Letters, reel 1.

123. Julie A. Doyle, John David Smith, and Richard M. McMurry, eds., *This Wilderness of War: The Civil War Letters of George W. Squier, Hoosier Volunteer* (Knoxville: University of Tennessee Press, 1998), 20.

124. Nat Turner, ed., *A Southern Soldier's Letters Home: The Civil War Letters of Samuel Burney, Army of Northern Virginia* (Macon, GA: Mercer University Press, 2002), 184–85.

125. William Hackworth to father, mother, brothers and sisters, March 18, 1863, Hackworth Collection, eHistory, Ohio State University, Columbus, http://ehistory.osu.edu/osu/sources/letters/hackworth/.

126. Mark A. Weitz, *More Damning Than Slaughter: Desertion in the Confederate Army* (Lincoln: University of Nebraska Press, 2005), 44–45, 49–50, 56–85.

127. W. S. Craig to wife, October 8, 1862, 1863, William Samuel Craig Letters, eHistory, Ohio State University, Columbus, http://ehistory.osu.edu/osu/sources/letters/craig/.

128. Michael A. Ross, *Justice of Shattered Dreams: Samuel Freeman Miller and the Supreme Court during the Civil War Era* (Baton Rouge: Louisiana State University Press, 2003), 62.

129. Messent and Courtney, *Civil War Letters of Joseph Hopkins Twichell,* 211.

130. Noah Andre Trudeau, ed., *Voices of the 55th: Letters from the 55th Massachusetts Volunteers, 1861– 1865* (Dayton, OH: Morningside House, 1996), 81.

131. Messent and Courtney, *Civil War Letters of Joseph Hopkins Twichell,* 205.

132. W. S. Craig to wife, October 8, 1862, 1863, William Samuel Craig Letters, eHistory, Ohio State University, Columbus, http://ehistory.osu.edu/osu/sources/letters/craig/.

133. Donald C. Elder III, ed., *Love amid the Turmoil: The Civil War Letters of William and Mary Vermillion* (Iowa City: University of Iowa Press, 2003), 149–50.

134. Bohrnstedt, *Soldiering with Sherman,* 137.

135. Joseph T. Glatthaar, "Duty, Country, Race, and Party: The Evans Family of Ohio," in *The War Was You and Me: Civilians in the American Civil War,* ed. Joan E. Cashin (Princeton, NJ: Princeton University Press, 2002), 332–57.

136. Chapter 19, James M. Randall Diary, eHistory, Ohio State University, Columbus, http://ehistory.osu.edu/osu/sources/letters/randall/.

137. Jeffrey D. Marshall, ed., *A War of the People: Vermont Civil War Letters* (Hanover, NH: University Press of New England, 1999), 26.

138. Scott Walker, *Hell's Broke Loose in Georgia: Survival in a Civil War Regiment* (Athens: University of Georgia Press, 2005), 61.

139. Coralou Peel Lassen, ed., *Dear Sarah: Letters Home from a Soldier of the Iron Brigade* (Bloomington: Indiana University Press, 1999), 10, 11, 21, 61, 77.

140. Blomquist and Taylor, *This Cruel War,* 152.

141. Walker, *Hell's Broke Loose,* 59, 61.

142. Christopher M. Watford, ed., *The Civil War in North Carolina: Soldiers' and Civilians' Letters and Diaries, 1861–1865,* Vol. 1, *The Piedmont* (Jefferson, NC: McFarland, 2003), 145.

143. Everson and Simpson, *Far, Far from Home,* 215–16.

144. Sellers, *A People at War,* Rufus W. Cater to Fannie S. Cater, November 8, 1862, postscript November 12, 1862, Douglas J. and Rufus W. Cater Papers, reel 11.

145. Keith Wilson, ed., *Honor in Command: Lt. Freeman S. Bowley's Civil War Service in the 30th United States Colored Infantry* (Gainesville: University Press of Florida, 2006), 82.

146. Patricia L. Richard, " 'Listen Ladies One and All': Union Soldiers Yearn for the Society of Their 'Fair Cousins of the North,' " in *Union Soldiers and the Northern Home Front: Wartime Experiences, Postwar Adjustments,* ed. Paul A. Cimbala and Randall M. Miller (New York: Fordham University Press, 2002), 143–81.

147. Ruth Douglas Currie, ed., *Emma Spauding Bryant: Civil War Bride, Carpetbagger's Wife, Ardent Feminist, Letters and Diaries, 1860–1900* (New York: Fordham University Press, 2004), 8–77; Kallgren and Crouthamel, *"Dear Friend Anna,"* 149; Dwight H. Cory to Hattie Rice, November 6, 1864, Dwight Henry Cory Letters and Diary, eHistory, Ohio State University, Columbus, http://ehistory.osu.edu/osu/sources/letters/cory/.

6　APPROACHING BATTLE

A DESIRE TO FIGHT

Lieutenant Thomas Galway of the Eighth Ohio Volunteer Infantry found all of the correspondence sent by soldiers to hometown newspapers that touted their eagerness to engage the enemy to be hogwash. Those "blatant asses in the ranks," along with the usual journalistic crowd that followed an army, were "of course egregious liars." Galway admitted that "an army is full of real heroes"—excluding those bombastic letter writers—"but in the mass, soldiers like better to eat, drink and be merry, than to march and fight."[1] Veteran soldier John C. Arnold probably would have agreed. In May 1864, after some hard fighting in the Virginia wilderness, Arnold admitted not being concerned for his own life; however, he also noted that "I still would sooner not here anything about fighting for it always Costs a grate many lives."[2]

Yet there were always inexperienced Confederate and Union soldiers as well as some of their more seasoned compatriots who considered the commencement of a campaign a welcome change from camp life. Men bound to extended periods of quiet soon came to the conclusion that despite their games, gambling, and other shenanigans, camp life and drill were "wearisome" and "tedious." The men longed "for an adventure of some kind," as did the volunteers of the Ninth Illinois Infantry, who, early in the war, while encamped at Paducah, Kentucky, were "spoiling for a fight."[3]

Complementing the desire to break the boredom of camp life was the new soldiers' fear that they would entirely miss the entire affair if they did not meet the enemy soon. The general belief that the war would not last long fueled the concern and made men anxious for combat. Early in the war, novice soldiers expected and hoped for a great battle that would bring about the destruction of the enemy's will to continue to fight. But soldiers also worried the spectacular conclusive fight would take place without them. The 15th Mississippi Infantry spent the early weeks of the war in camp at Corinth, Mississippi. When the men discovered that there had been a battle at Bull Run, they became quite concerned that they would entirely miss the war, forced to return home untested and humiliated by their failure to fight.[4] Sam Watkins and his fellow western Confederates also feared the consequences of the victory at Manassas. They became "frenzied with excitement" but feared they "would have to return home without even seeing a Yankee soldier." "We thought at that time that we would have given a thousand dollars to have been in battle," he later recalled, "and to have had an arm shot off, so we could have returned home with an empty sleeve."[5]

Frequently, the unseasoned soldiers' eagerness to fight was accompanied by a sense of unwarranted confidence, bravado, or naïveté, common sins of the young men who disproportionately filled the ranks of both armies. Confederate soldiers, such as those in the 15th Mississippi Infantry, held it as an article of faith that spirited, virile Southerners could easily outfight Northerners.[6] Arkansas infantry "boast too much about what they will do," which worried Alex Spence that "when it comes to acting they will not be found there."[7]

Yankees also came to war with some inflated self-confidence. New Yorker Theodore Dodge found the untested soldiers on Virginia's peninsula in the spring of 1862 believing that "they are just going out to fire at the Rebels, who at once run away." He was sure, however, that experience would alter their assumptions. "When they have been into one or two actions," he cautioned, "they will find that turning out to fight is not so pleasant a duty."[8] Indeed, a lieutenant in the 77th Illinois Infantry who had given the impression that "he would tear the confederacy all to pieces in a little while" changed his mind after the Battle of Arkansas Post on January 11, 1863; he "was one of the first to resign when we got to where rebel bullets begun to sing around in a careless manner."[9]

CONTEMPLATING THE BATTLE

Soldiers prepared to move out from their camps by cooking several days' worth of rations, gathering up their essential equipment, stuffing cartridges into their pockets, and perhaps dashing off a letter home. Rumors as "thick as blackberries," false starts, or long delays eventually gave way to the march, with the men shouldering packs much lighter than when they first set off for their rendezvous camps as enlistees, sometimes leaving behind a jumble of equipment on their old campgrounds.[10] Once on the march, rumors persisted in part because generals saw little need to keep enlisted men apprised of their grand plans. As Charles Musser, a 20-year-old Iowa farm boy, noted, "A Soldier does not know where he is a going till he gets there and then he dont know hardly."[11]

Some men afraid or sick of combat certainly did what they could to avoid the inevitable battle. A Union surgeon complained about "loafers and malingerers" who appeared at his hospital pleading that they were too ill to fight and the "coffee boilers" who were "straggling in the woods."[12] A Confederate doctor noted that "some of the trifling men had a trick of deliberately shooting off a finger or thumb, so as to avoid the battles."[13] Soldiers deserted, skulked, and straggled as they marched to battle, but most men in the ranks, and especially veterans, accepted commands to prepare for a fight with a sense of duty or fear of dishonor or a commitment to their comrades that outweighed other emotions. Experience also brought a degree of gravity that had been missing during the earliest marches. Michigander Charles Hayden suggested in the spring of 1863 that old soldiers in his regiment will go into fight now "with the dogged obstinacy of veteran troops having a prescribed duty to perform & not with the hilarity & confidence which used to characterize our movements."[14]

As the men approached the enemy, they probably became more nervous—and perhaps more thoughtful—than usual. Members of the 15th Mississippi heard hunters' shots in the night while encamped in Tennessee, rallied for a fight, and were disappointed; it took the men days to calm down.[15] Others thought of what might happen to them if they did indeed meet the enemy. South Carolinian Berry Benson recalled that many of his comrades on the eve of an expected fight asked friends to send messages to their families if they were killed, part of the "forethought and preparation" for battle that included soldiers reviewing favorite biblical passages "for comfort and encouragement." These religious soldiers Benson remarked, were "foremost in the charge and rearmost in retreat,"[16] having found it easier to risk their lives for their cause once they had made peace with their maker.

Such a realistic awareness of the possibility of death, however, could turn into morbid foreboding, which caused some men to foretell their imminent demise. During the Atlanta campaign, a wounded Confederate soldier rejoined his Arkansas regiment, gave his watch to a comrade, and predicted that he would be killed in battle that day. He did not fear his death, he assured his friend, because he was a Christian and expected soon to find refuge in heaven. He died in an assault on Union fortifications.[17]

The more self-reflective soldiers also wondered about battle and how they and their fellow soldiers would perform when the time came to fight. In May 1861 Alex Spence was concerned that the men in his Arkansas regiment would break and run, as an Arkansas cavalry regiment did in 1847 during the Mexican War at Buena Vista; "if it does," he warned, "I never want to go back to Clark County."[18] In Virginia, in July 1861, when rebel Edmund Patterson accepted his issue of cartridges, he began to awaken to "the reality of war." "In the first place," he admitted, "it looks as if someone is to be hurt....These are the first 'Cartridges' that I have ever seen, and is it possible that we are actually to *kill men. Human Beings?* That these cartridges were made purposely for one poor mortal to shoot at another?" He finally accepted that "this is war, and how hardened men must become."[19]

It could not have escaped Patterson or other soldiers that their enemies also held instruments that might be the means of their own deaths. They hoped that they would face such a prospect in a way that would not shame themselves or the home folk. Yankee sergeant John Follett expressed common concerns when he wrote to his wife in March 1863, promising that "if we do have a battle I shall try to act as you would have me, and you and the children shall never have cause to be ashamed of my memory."[20]

MARCHING TO THE FIGHT

Fighting required marching, and campaigns generally required a good deal of it. Generals attempted to outwit their counterparts, shift troops within a theater to counter threats, and send troops great distances to assist other armies. Indeed, a soldier's life required more time and effort to get to a fight than to engage in one. Sergeant John Follet reported that between January 14 and February 21, 1863, he and other Illinois infantry marched over 400 miles.[21] Soldiers on these marches might not know where they were heading, and even when they understood their objectives, the campaign could become a frustrating exercise. John C. Arnold spent much time during the summer of 1864 chasing after Confederate Jubal Early's army. "The Rebs will Bee some outher place and so they will keep us Running around all somer," he reported to his wife. "I wish wee could Ketch them Some place and Kill every Son of a Bitch."[22]

Fighting the Landscape

Along the way to battle, no season seemed willing to spare the men hardship. Soldiers encountered rain and muddy roads, heat and dusty roads, and all sorts of inconvenient terrain. Iowan George Remley, campaigning near Vicksburg in June 1863, lamented that a Northern civilian could "not even imagine the enervating effect that the hot and sultry weather of the Southern climate, has upon one's system."[23] Once summer passed, winter brought its own difficulties. Southern weather did not guarantee frozen ground, and the soldiers suffered for it. The Army of the Potomac's winter "mud march" shortly after its defeat at Fredericksburg was only the most famous of the hard winter treks soldiers made. In February 1863, Sergeant Follett began his march into the Vicksburg campaign trudging through mud in rain and snow.[24] Also in February, members of the Eighth Georgia Infantry set off on their own march from Fredericksburg that had them first wading through upward of nine inches of snow and then enduring a soaking rain that turned the roads into a muddy morass.[25]

Rugged terrain in the east and the west forced soldiers to fight the landscape while they marched to fight the enemy. Ohio volunteer William Bentley did "some big marching" in Tennessee "through an almost unbroken forest for 70 miles"; at times, the men "had to march *indian* fashion for 2 or 3 miles along foot paths."[26] Vermonter Wilbur Fisk and his fellow Yankees left the roads to the artillerymen and traversed "fields, brooks, ditches and fences, through woods that are almost impenetrable, and trough mud holes that are very penetrable indeed, making a mile's marching with a heavy knapsack on one's back, and a pair of tired legs under his body, not the easiest thing in the world to accomplish." Another march of 20–25 miles left the Vermonters exhausted. "I don't know exactly how far we marched," Fisk reported, "but the choking dust and heat

A pontoon boat, essential for bridging rivers during a campaign. This one belongs to the 50th New York Engineers. (*Library of Congress*)

and the many crooked turns we made, made the march doubly difficult." Furthermore, "those last miles were doled out in suffering by inches," leaving muscle and bone worn and weary. Fisk and his compatriots bedded down at 10 o'clock that night and rose at 4 o'clock in the morning to start the marching all over again.[27]

Trying to Find Comfort on the March

No wonder soldiers, regardless of the circumstances of their travels, continued to do their best to moderate the hardship that had become so much a part of their lives. "The central idea of a soldier is to make himself as comfortable as possible," John King of Illinois confirmed in December 1863. "The soldier centers his weak energies on keeping his clothing as dry as possible, plans how to make the best bed he can, how to cook and get the best meal he can, and how to care for his horse so that he will hold his flesh. All other subjects are but secondary affairs and many soldiers overlooked many things that under more favorable circumstances would have been scrutinized with much interest."[28]

Comfort on campaign, where camp resources might be beyond reach, usually required some improvisation. In January 1863 John G. Jones, a Wisconsin volunteer in Sherman's Army of the Tennessee, marched off from Memphis to burn a bridge. They arrived at their destination too late to perform the task and bedded down for the night. "There were warehouses full of cotton within twenty five yards of us, so you can imagine that we had a very soft bed that night," Jones reported. "I never slept better than I did on a bale of cotton."[29] John Westervelt and members of the First New York Engineers campaigned on Folly Island, South Carolina, in April 1863. After one wearisome march,

Throwing up earthworks prevent a night attack by Alfred R. Waud. As the war dragged on and casualties grew, soldiers in both armies dug entrenchments even when they would be encamped for only a short time during a campaign. (*Library of Congress*)

he and some other men "pulled out our jack knives" and "cut a hole under the brush" for a sleeping compartment. They then lined the place with palmetto leaves "by pressing them against the top and sides forming an arch making a neat and comfortable place to sleep."[30]

Food and water, of course, took a prime place on any list of necessary campaign comforts. Soldiers tended to their bellies whenever they could. Soldiers—and especially Confederate soldiers—came to realize that they could not always depend on commissary stores being at the right place at the right time. Members of the 56th Georgia Infantry embarked on "a campaign of three months almost incessant marching, day and night, part of the time with nothing to eat and no water to drink."[31] Even Yankees suffered on occasion, as did sergeant John Follett, who, during his muddy march during the winter of early 1863, on occasion had to forego rations.[32]

The need for water on a hot summer day in July 1861 was one reason why the untested Union troops marching toward Bull Run frequently broke ranks, regardless of their officers' efforts to maintain discipline.[33] The desire to quench a soldier's thirst on the march could drive men to consume what they never would consider touching under better circumstances. Marshall Twitchell of Vermont recalled trying to drink water on the Virginia peninsula in 1862 that was "so thick with mud and droppings from mules and horses that sucking it through our teeth, there was as much filth left in the cup as there was water which we had been able to drink."[34]

Clashing with Civilians

Confederates fighting in their own land could count on the population to help fill their commissary needs when civilian supplies were available and the population shared them with the soldiers. But regardless of the civilians' generosity or lack thereof, rebel soldiers assumed that the Confederacy had to feed them one way or another. They were not above conscripting and roasting the civilian pig that happened on their camps, nor did they hesitate to requisition chickens when their own stores were low, sometimes even when civilians suffered from their actions. Tennessean Sam Watkins recalled how he and some comrades stole a hog from an impoverished Confederate family; on another occasion, he and a friend filled their packs with sweet potatoes from a farmer's field.[35] Other Confederates on the march were not above harvesting a cornfield or orchard when their stomachs required it. Confederate soldiers could strip the countryside clean and were well aware that they caused as much devastation to the people's resources as did their enemies. In early 1863, cavalry, hungry after raiding into Missouri, stole livestock from Confederate civilians in Arkansas, and in 1864, desperately hungry Texas cavalry resorted to stealing food.[36] By the end of the war, foraging was such a problem in some areas of the Confederacy that the people feared their own men as much as they feared the Yankees.

When Confederates had an opportunity to take food from Yankees, they felt no qualms. After the Gettysburg campaign, North Carolinian Charles F. Bahnson, an assistant quartermaster, reported that Lee's army did not spare the Pennsylvania countryside, taking back to Virginia a sufficiency of food, livestock, and other useful things. The men denuded the countryside of fences, he told his father, but farmers need not worry about animals getting into their fields "for we left but little stock to run around & destroy crops."[37]

Yankees on campaign were never reluctant to forage food and feed in rebel territory. Sherman's march through Georgia became famous for its foraging activity, but living off of the enemy was common in other theaters and during other campaigns. In 1864, in the Shenandoah Valley, Bay State soldier John Chase reported, "Enjoyed the trip up the valley much for we took any thing we could get hold of to eat."[38] Indeed, he boasted to his brother, "I never lived better in my life." Iowan George Remley shared the experience in a prosperous part of Louisiana and concluded, "It may truly be said of us that we live on the fat of the land."[39] No wonder one of Sherman's company officers judged that "words cannot describe" what an invading army could do to the countryside.[40]

Men might pity the enemy civilians, but they also assumed that Confederates had brought these circumstances on themselves; foraging was part of a rebel's punishment for trying to destroy the Union. As Army of the Potomac veteran Warren Lee Goss explained the process, "Our army...was like a swarm of locusts, destroying every green thing except the people who had rebelled against the thrift and content conferred by a good government." Each may need not have taken much, he noted, to strip the land when they were part of a large force. "I don't think we were very hard with these people," he continued, "yet their fences fast melted away into camp-fires, and their chickens and turkeys and geese into goodly messes, to the satisfaction of those who had endured hardships to restore such as these blessings of an undivided country."[41]

Commanders and staff officers imposed rules to bring order to this activity, but men ignored them when they found the restriction to be inconvenient. Gottfried Rentschler of the Sixth Kentucky Infantry of the United States explained that on his march through Tennessee to Knoxville, officers attempted to keep foraging an orderly process, assigning squads from each regiment in two divisions for daily patrols to farms some distance from the line of march, where they would "'press' provisions for their regiment," leaving receipts with the accommodating farmer, noting also the man's politics. Nearby farms were supposed to be searched carefully, with the men removing "mainly everything that was useful to move or to carry or that could be prepared for nourishment." Despite efforts to bring order to foraging, men continued to act in a disorderly way. "The scream of hunted and chased-down chickens and geese often drowned out the thousand steps of the troop and clatter of the wagons following on the dry streets," he noted, regretting that the uncivilized behavior of the soldiers was closer to looting than to the orderly foraging the staff officers had in mind.[42] George Remley also noted that in Louisiana, authorized foraging parties regularly combed the countryside, and orders were supposed to prevent "private foraging." Nevertheless, he and his fellow Iowans ignored orders and ate well because "the guards being soldiers and sympathetic creatures cannot always see things in the same light that Gen'l Banks does."[43]

Physical Effects of Marching

Some soldiers claimed that the marching made them fit and fine specimens of manhood. Other men loathed the blistering of their feet, the thirst, the troublesome weather, and untold additional discomforts; some of these men endured with the help of whiskey or opium, if available.[44] Regardless of how men felt about marching, any campaign involving long treks had an impact on their combat effectiveness. Hard marches led to straggling, something that plagued Lee's Army of Northern Virginia during the Antietam campaign of 1862.[45] Even when men boasted of their marching abilities, as did Ohioan William Bentley, who walked with his regiment from the eastern theater over the mountains into Tennessee during the summer of 1863, the men paid a price. Bentley's reassurances not withstanding, his regiment's clothing was in such a desperate state of disrepair that commanders declared it unfit for duty.[46]

Fighting-and-marching campaigns especially took their toll on the men involved. The demands of Grant's spring 1864 campaign through the Virginia wilderness put an extraordinary strain on the Army of the Potomac, as it experienced "some severe marching" and "some hard battles."[47] Soldiers of the 110th Ohio, for example, skirmished, fought battles, stood picket, and marched, all of which reduced their ranks from 550 men to about 200 effective soldiers.[48] But Stonewall Jackson's campaign in the Shenandoah Valley during May and June of 1862 provided one of the best examples of what hard campaigning could do to an army, even when it was an apparently victorious one.

Jackson and his men became heroes of the Confederacy for the tactical brilliance of the campaign that included marching 400 miles to engage multiple Yankee formations. At the same time, however, that campaign ground the men down and wore them out. The physically demanding marching and maneuvering did more harm to Jackson's army than the actual fighting. The famous Stonewall Brigade and Jackson's Louisiana Brigade suffered noncombat losses upward to 30 percent.[49] By this time, Jackson's old brigade had earned the name "Jackson's Foot Cavalry" for their ability to march hard and fast. One veteran later boasted, "We could break down any cavalry brigade on a long march."[50]

Such tramping, however, had consequences. When Jackson's men moved east after their valley campaign, they continued to suffer from such punishing activity. Some of them simply dropped out on the march because of exhaustion. "Myself and several hundred others from our brigade, like our broken down horses were left behind to graze, and recruit up our exhausted frames; or clericaly speaking energies," wrote Ujanirtus "Ugie" Allen, a Georgia soldier who had campaigned with Jackson in the valley. "The fact is your humble servant was completely worn out; and was compelled to stop."[51]

Hard marching, no matter how brilliantly executed, meant soldiers often arrived at the battle already worn out. On May 1, 1863, Illinoisan John Follett and comrades fought at the Battle of Port Gibson, Mississippi, after an arduous march carrying over 50 pounds of equipment while foregoing sleep for some 30 hours.[52] And an Alabaman at Chancellorsville noted that his exhausted and hungry comrades had been marching all the day before they engaged the enemy as well as on the day of their fighting, which contributed to their disorganization on the field.[53]

Reaching Their Destinations by Trains and Ships

Thousands of soldiers gained some respite from the march by traveling to their destinations by rail or sea, but even when provided with such transportation, the men experienced inconvenience, discomfort, and danger. Rail travel was not always easy or pleasant for soldiers. At the start of the war, while there was an accepted standard gauge of—or distance between—the rails, there remained a number of other gauges in use throughout the land, which could disrupt travel. That situation proved to be a minor problem, but the Confederacy suffered from the lack of a true rail system that united the various states. For example, it was common for one railroad company's lines simply to end without being connected to another company's track. That reality was more problematic for the smooth flow of troops and caused serious delays, as men waited at the end of one line for a second rail company to produce the necessary rolling stock for their transport. The Confederacy attempted to correct this problem, all the while running into states' rights arguments and other shortsighted commercial concerns. But even Yankees arriving in Philadelphia, where three rail lines remained unconnected until 1863, experienced the delays resulting from uncoordinated antebellum commerce.[54]

When men finally boarded trains, they found them crowded and uncomfortable, especially when they traveled in boxcars. Men who decided that it was more pleasant riding on the roofs of the cars died from falls or other accidents. There was always the danger that a train would derail, causing injury and death to the passengers, and even in federal-occupied regions in Tennessee, Kentucky, and elsewhere, Yankee trains risked attack from guerillas and Confederate cavalry.[55]

Ships could be even worse than the railcars. They were as pestilential a place as any rendezvous camp, allowing disease to spread among the men confined to the tight quarters. In July 1862 Massachusetts native Theodore Dodge remarked on the crowded, filthy conditions on board the ship that was transporting his regiment to the Virginia peninsula. He concluded that "transports are worse than camps, dirty, crowded, & with nothing to eat or drink."[56] And in January 1863, an Iowa soldier reported that his regiment contained "a Sicker Set of men Soldiering you never Saw" when it arrived in Mississippi after a journey by ship.[57]

Seeing New Parts of the Country

Despite all of the difficulties, campaigning soldiers encountered curious things that made their hard lives a bit more interesting. Confederates rarely campaigned beyond the borders of their country, but when they did, they commented on what they saw, sometimes with amazement. Prior to the Battle of Gettysburg, they lived off the Pennsylvania countryside and remarked on the rich farms that fed them so well. It was there that Charles Bahnson saw "many things of interest."[58] South Carolinian Tally Simpson found it remarkable that he saw no blacks during his march to Gettysburg, but he was more taken with how even the common farmers appeared to be prosperous. "They are fine livers," he wrote. "But they are abolitionists, and that kills the thing dead in my eyes." Simpson's comrades appeared to have concurred and directed their anger at the Pennsylvanians in the way of their march. "The most of the soldiers seem to harbor a terrific spirit of revenge," he reported, "and steal and pillage in the most sinful manner."[59]

Campaigning through and then occupying parts of the Confederacy allowed Yankees to come to know what they considered quite a different, even exotic, and in some parts a beautiful land. Charles Hayden found Mississippi to be a fairly extraordinary place while campaigning there in June 1863. It was, however, "not very pleasing" to his eyes." Bad water, stumpy hills, canebrakes, woods thick with underbrush, and trees draped with moss marked the land. The moss especially "gives to everything a sort of dull somber appearance." The place "looks old, very old," he concluded, "as though everything was on the decline." The fauna also astonished him, and not in a pleasing way: "There are some *alligators,* a good many snakes, lizards everywhere, plenty of mosquitoes, flies, bugs, tarantulas, horned frogs & other infernal machines too numerous to mention." He especially worried about the snakes and the lizards because "they say" that those creatures in the woods "tumble down on your head every few steps." But as Hayden became used to his surroundings, he warmed to them. About a week later, he admitted that the country was not as bad as he first assumed, especially because there were not "so many snakes or other infernal machines as was represented." To be sure, "the alligators eat some of the soldiers," but that problem was easily rectified. "If the soldiers would keep out of the river," Hayden noted, "they would not be eaten."[60]

While some Northerners found the Southern climate a new and delightful experience, especially in the spring, others found the summer heat unbearable. For George Remley, however, it was Texas's fickle weather that did not suit him. "Give me a country, like Iowa, where there is cold enough to make it pay a person to get used to it," Remley complained. "Here one day it will be so warm the 'boys' go about with their coats off and perhaps the next day will be cold enough to 'freeze the horns off a muley cow.' "[61]

The Southern people themselves provoked comment from the curious Yankees who came on them in their campaigns and afterward in their occupation duties. Sometimes guerrilla warfare and the killing of foragers provoked retaliation against civilians and nurtured hatred toward the enemy. In northern Mississippi, during the Vicksburg campaign, for example, soldiers arrested suspected guerillas, confiscated civilian property, fouled food stores with human waste, and distributed the dresses of white women to slaves.[62] But in relatively peaceful encounters, campaigning soldiers exhibited a curiosity about the people that matched their curiosity about the land.

Yankees Meet White and Black Southerners

Sometimes the soldiers developed favorable opinions of the people they met; other times they did not. In the spring of 1864, while campaigning in Virginia, private Warren Lee Goss encountered a young lady from a Unionist family who had gone to school in the North; needless to say, he found her to be "more intelligent than most of the Southern girls I had, thus far, met." Goss also encountered a poor white man who, despite the fact that he had sons in the Confederate army, was skeptical about the "great folks" dragging them into a war. Goss pronounced him a man with "unusual common-sense when speaking of the war—a fact quite new to my experience with ordinary Virginians."[63]

On the other hand, Daniel R. Larned, who spent much of his letter-writing efforts trying to explain the Southern people to his family, found that the poor whites he encountered in North Carolina were "on a *par* with the negroes—the worst contemptible set I ever looked on." When he was in Knoxville, he also found amusement in listening to the area's peculiar dialect. He told his sister that "they say '*Youans*' for you & '*heans*' for *he*." Larned was particularly surprised by the habits of "two young ladies, one of them rather pretty and quite sociable, but seeing them chewing a dipping-stick and spitting tobacco juice rather detracts from their charms."[64]

White Southerners prompted soldierly curiosity, but slaves were especially exotic creatures to many Yankees who might never have had any contact with the Confederacy's peculiar institution. Soldiers commented on how the slaves were helpful and friendlier than whites but also noted their poverty and remarked on their ignorance. Daniel R. Larned was particularly critical of the contrabands he encountered in North Carolina. In March 1862 he explained to his sister that "they are amusing, yet disgusting—their character, and representatives by the negro minstrels are correct to the life." Not one, he judged, would compare with the poorest of the free blacks of the North.[65]

Sometimes, however, the men were surprised by what they discovered of the black character. Massachusetts soldier Silas Browning visited the slave quarters and sugar house on a Louisiana plantation. While there, he had the opportunity to converse with some of the black workers. "I was very much supprised at the intelagience of thoes that I saw," he admitted. "There was an old man that gave me a discription of the process of Making Sugar and he dun it as inteligentley as most Northern White men would have given a discription of their Farmes." He concluded that there was no need to worry about the end of slavery. "The more I see of the Neggroes the more I am convinced that thay will take care of them Selves."[66]

So, too, was Wilbur Fisk surprised by the accomplishments of a free black he encountered while campaigning in Virginia. In a letter to his local Vermont newspaper, he used the man's life as an argument for emancipation. "This man had never been a slave, and has consequently possessed many advantages that are denied slaves," he wrote in August 1863; "but if his superiority to the common negro is attributable mainly to freedom, it only furnishes an argument against this institution of bondage that all the sophistry of the infernal regions cannot overthrow." Furthermore, he argued, "If the soul of the African has sufficient elasticity to rise to such a height, when released from the pressure of slavery, it must be a fearful responsibility for a nation to keep them down. This nation has run the risk, and is reaping the consequences."[67]

At times, when soldiers witnessed the results of the power wielded by white masters over their chattels, they became outraged, and even came to accept the necessity of emancipation. Certainly not all soldiers were or became radical abolitionists, and many of them chafed under the war aim thrust on them by Lincoln's Emancipation Proclamation. Still, there were men who were appalled by what they saw and others who questioned the morals of a people who held humans in bondage. Firsthand experience changed any number of soldiers' attitudes about slavery and convinced them that the war had to end the institution. Sherman's men, on their march to the sea and through the Carolinas, exhibited the range of what soldiers thought about black people; by the end of the campaign, the men had witnessed the worst of slavery, the best of black life, and the grateful attitudes of the contrabands they met along the way. Such encounters softened the hearts of many of a man toward the South's slaves.[68]

During the Vicksburg campaign, Joseph Lester was astonished by the wealth in land and slaves that he witnessed. But he was especially surprised by the skin color of many of the bondsmen. The plantation slaves, "instead of being pure blacks, are in many cases as white as I am." Light skin, however, did not earn these slaves any special consideration, as "these are all treated alike. Whipped and driven." He was also shocked by the way that slave owners sold off their own children, born to their women slaves, "and all the while witnessed by the White wife with complacency." "Such are their Morals!" he concluded. "Can God smile upon such conduct? Will he prosper them or us if we wish to perpetuate such a System? I believe not."[69] Rufus Kinsley of Vermont also was troubled by the consequences of miscegenation. In one particular case, a planter fathered offspring with his own three children and then sold them. "Verily slavery *is* profitable," Kinglsey concluded.[70]

Rufus Kinsley's experiences while stationed in New Orleans in 1862 led him to conclude that he had seen "enough of the horrors of slavery to make me an Abolitionist forever." Along with the incestuous behavior, he came on torture apparatus, including whips, thumbscrews, stocks, and balls and chain, that suggested the various positions in which whites fastened unruly slaves, "those who had been guilty of loving liberty more than life, but had failed in their efforts to obtain the coveted boon." On several occasions, he freed runaways from the various contraptions their owners used to try to keep them on the plantation. He concluded, again with irony, "Verily this picture presents positive proof that the slave is happy and contented with his lot."[71]

Assisting the March: Staff Work

Moving soldiers along to combat was a substantial network of support staff that copied, recorded, and circulated orders. Specialists such as quartermasters, commissary officers, engineers, and signal corpsmen also did essential work outfitting soldiers, securing transportation and bringing food and other supplies up to the front, providing officers with maps, sending visual and telegraphic signals, and building corduroy roads and bridges to make the terrain passable. Even if they did not always employ it wisely, generals had staff assistance to help them make sure their armies were able to meet and defeat the enemy. Specialty officers, such as medical officers, quartermasters, and engineers, kept commanding generals informed as to their armies' strength and health, the status of equipment and stores, the progress of the enemy, expenditures, and all other necessary details for maintaining a fighting force, producing significant amounts of paperwork. These officers required clerks, guards, and other attendants to help them do their jobs.

Even regimental commanders had staff assistance to deal with record keeping and quartermaster and commissary matters, while company commanders made use of adjutants and clerks in the running of their organizations. These were essential positions in armies, where superiors required multiple copies of reports; the recording of letters sent and received, along with any endorsements made on the original documents; the maintenance of the personal records of individual soldiers; and mountains of other paperwork, all of which ended up in numerous bound books or bundles of trifolded forms neatly tied with the ubiquitous red string or "tape." Thus any number of smart young officers oversaw the shuffling of paper for regimental commanders, while enlisted men with good penmanship or stenographic skills served as clerks, taking dictation and copying and recording the various orders that set an army in motion down to the lowest level of command.

Clerks, according to William H. Bradbury, who was one himself, were the "most intelligent and impertinent" of the office workers, holding down what many enlisted men considered to be desirable berths. Bradbury, an Englishman by birth and an experienced businessman in his early thirties on his enlistment in the 129th Illinois Infantry, did his best to make sure his superiors knew of his talents, which were considerable. He was well educated in practical office skills such as handwriting, arithmetic, and "phonography," or shorthand, which made him a perfect candidate for clerical duties. Through the war he worked for several Union generals in the western theater.[72]

Assisting the March: Mapmaking

Any soldier with draftsman's skills who could help armies correct their deficient and unreliable map collections, a consequence of the inadequate mapping of the Southern states before the war, could find himself working for a topographical officer. Officers understood that knowledge of the topography of the region through which their men must advance was critical, especially given the large size of Civil War armies. The published maps that they might find proved to be inadequate, and the prewar civilian maps, lacking sufficient detail for military purposes, frustrated many an officer. Thus commanders always had need for more and better maps.[73]

Given this situation, both armies needed men who not only could survey the lay of the land, but reproduce that information for its officers. Union Lieutenant John R. Meigs, serving as the chief engineering officer for Brigadier General Benjamin F. Kelley in the Department of West Virginia, in September 1863 reported that "there will be plenty of work in the field for all the topographers" that he could secure, as long the weather allowed it.[74] Confederates were equally deficient in maps and were hindered by their inability to duplicate the maps they produced.[75] Thus there were opportunities for men such as Private Robert Knox Sneden. Sneden, a member of the 40th New York Infantry, impressed General Samuel P. Heintzelman's topographer, Captain William Heine, who had the volunteer detached to his staff. Captain Heine scouted the Virginia landscape, gathering intelligence that would find its way onto maps that Sneden and other draftsmen at headquarters compiled and copied for various commands to assist them in placing pickets, conducting reconnaissance patrols, and preparing troop movements. At one point, three generals squabbled over having him attached to their staffs.[76]

Sneden and other talented men did admirable work. William Bradbury noted that men like Sneden drew and colored "those minute and beautiful maps illustrative of every foot of country over which our armies have passed." These cartographers also produced linen lithographs, photographs, and tracings of their maps all under less-than-ideal working conditions for the use of officers in an army on the move in ways that would allow even officers ignorant of map reading to make sense of the land over which they traveled. "Long before Sherman left Atlanta," Bradbury reported, "I saw a skillful draughtsmen (all private soldiers) busy at work with fine pens and delicate pencil-brushes delineating the cities of Macon and Columbus, with their approaches, fortifications, &c. and gradually introducing the intervention of topography, as fast as deserters, refugees or scouts furnished the information."[77]

At the outset of the war, the Army of Northern Virginia developed a cartographical operation that used lithography to make maps for distribution not only to its own officers, but to other armies as well. Also, engineering officers on the scene of field operations supervised the production of maps as needed, with draftsmen painstakingly reproducing the finished product. However, demand for maps meant that artistic renderings often gave way to more perfunctory work. Officers required maps to deal with the immediacy of campaigns and battles. Consequently, Confederate engineers sketched rough charts of enemy positions on the scene. Also, the need for maps meant that soldiers with steady hands traced what maps existed for wider distribution. During the spring of 1864, engineering sergeant Carter N. B. Minor spent a good deal of his time at regimental headquarters tracing maps.[78] As the war progressed, Confederate mapmakers simply did not have sufficient tools at their disposal to make fine maps throughout the war, and even their Union counterparts suffered at times for want of color.[79]

THE COMFORTS AND FRUSTRATIONS OF STAFF WORK

Enlisted men on detached duty from their regiments could live in relative comfort, while also making extra money, once their office work was done for the day. William Bradbury, who had himself pushed hard to land an office job safely away from the fighting, reported in April 1865 that a high proportion of the clerks in General George Thomas's headquarters were from the 15th Pennsylvania Cavalry. These were men from the elite class of Philadelphia society, who "are better satisfied to perform clerical duties, to which they had been trained, and 'crush the rebellion' seated at a desk in some elegant mansion, than to scour over the mountains of Tennessee" in search of rebels.[80]

After some rigorous field service, in November 1864, artist Charles Reed secured a position as a cartographer with the Fifth Corps's headquarters. His new working conditions made him "as comfortable as a 'bug in a rug'" while he continued to find time to work on his lithograph business.[81] Watchmakers, tailors, and other soldiers with useful skills also plied their civilian trades during their off-duty hours. All of them risked earning the jealousy or scorn of some of the other soldiers for being "head-quarters bummers" who had an easy, safe assignment, but having the opportunity to make hundreds of dollars doing what they had done in civilian life probably eased the sting of the name-calling.[82]

Even an unskilled, lowly private who impressed an officer with his military bearing or dedication could benefit from relatively safe headquarters assignments. Georgian William Stillwell missed the bloody fighting at Antietam because his brigade commander, for whom he was serving as a headquarters guard, left him behind to look after his belongings. Later, at Fredericksburg, Stillwell watched the battle from afar, spending his time guarding his general and looking after his baggage; at Chancellorsville he again guarded baggage, with the additional duty of arresting shirkers from the battle.[83]

Despite the perquisites, staff and specialty work was not without its own difficulties. Quartermaster officers, for example, frequently had to go to great lengths to provide for the men in the ranks. Texan Theophilus Perry found his duties as acting brigade quartermaster to be a weighty burden that kept him from corresponding with his wife. "Everything is in a hurry to get the Brigade in good condition to move, when called upon," he explained to her in September 1862.[84] Once engaged, the quartermaster's duties became even more demanding. During the Virginia peninsula campaign, Minnesotan and assistant quartermaster officer Captain William G. Lu Duc performed heroically under difficult circumstances that went beyond the comfortable duties his counterparts experienced at the large supply depots behind the lines. He not only made

Clerks at the Army of the Potomac Headquarters, Brandy Station, Virginia. (*Library of Congress*)

sure his regiments had their necessary ammunition, but took on engineering work to keep the army moving. Along the way, he dealt with muddy and sometimes obstructed roads, swamps, heat, the lack of maps, a drunken wagon master who threatened him with a pistol, and the usual army bureaucracy. He also performed the duties of chaplain, conducting the burial service for his best teamster.[85]

In the Confederate army, there was always the frustration of not having what one needed to do a job. In 1862 John Morris Wampler delayed commencing his assignment as a topographer for the Confederate army at Corinth as he dealt with the quartermaster's requirements to obtain a horse; he also had to borrow necessary tools of the trade to conduct his survey of the terrain because the engineering department had none.[86] Just as frustrating was the typical bureaucratic mentality up the chain of command that required proper forms for all paperwork. In February 1863 Massachusetts native and regimental adjutant Theodore Dodge wrote a "very voluminous report" and sent it on to headquarters, only to have it returned with the blank forms appropriate for such a document. With the help of "two good writers detailed" to him, Dodge had the report copied and sent off. "This is just a sample of how things are done," he recorded in his journal. "Instead of giving out blanks in the first place, they wait till the reports are sent in, and then send the blanks for them to be copied upon."[87]

There were no guarantees that staff work and headquarters duty would always be comfortable and free of risk. Paper shuffling did not always keep staff officers and headquarters soldiers out of harm's way. Commanders used engineering officers to scout enemy positions before and during engagements, placing them close to the enemy. Clerks, such as Kentuckian Edward Guerrant, came under fire as they copied the orders of officers on the field of battle and carried dispatches.[88] Theodore Dodge sustained a serious leg wound on the battlefield at Chantilly on September 1, 1862, and had his ankle shattered on the first day of Gettysburg, which resulted in the amputation of the lower part of his leg.[89] And Henry Klock, former schoolteacher and adjutant for the Ninth Illinois Infantry, was wounded twice, once at Shiloh and again at Corinth.[90]

While Robert Sneden spent much of his time in comfortable headquarters surroundings drafting his maps, he shared in the hardships of the 1862 Virginia peninsula campaign. Also, in November 1863, Sneden came under artillery fire while studying the ground at the Kelly's Ford, Virginia, battlefield. Granted, this was not the same as participating in battle, but there were real risks for headquarters men who worked just behind the front lines. Sneden, along with a number of headquarters clerks, became the captive of John Singleton Mosby's partisan rangers.[91] Young John R. Meigs not only tended to typical engineering duties, such as supervising the construction of railroad blockhouses and mapmaking, but in December 1863, rode with cavalry raiders into Confederate territory to disrupt a rebel railroad. He later campaigned in the Shenandoah Valley, supervising the destruction of Confederate property; it was there, in October 1864, while performing his duties, that he was killed by guerrillas.[92]

ENGINEERING DUTY

John Meigs's experiences as an engineer were not unusual. Throughout the war, the officers and men who engaged in engineering duties as their armies campaigned and closed with the enemy shared the hardships and dangers of regular combat troops. Both Confederate and U.S. armies had some, but never enough, dedicated companies and regiments of pioneers and engineers on campaign. In April 1861 the U.S. Army had one company of engineers totaling 150 men. In 1862 George McClellan moved over 120,000 men in his Army of the Potomac to the Virginia peninsula to begin his campaign to capture Richmond; there were only about 2,000 regular and volunteer engineers accompanying the army. When Ulysses Grant began his move against Vicksburg, he did so with only three engineering officers and no engineering regiments or companies. And the Confederate armies were in worse shape when it came to having access to these specialized soldiers.[93]

Pioneering organizations that cleared the way for moving armies were created in the field by commanding officers, who drew on skilled men already at their disposal, while the Confederate and the Union engineering corps were eventually established by statute. The engineering troops in the field generally performed more complex duties such as bridge building, with pioneers performing many tactical jobs involving ax and shovel work. The Army of Northern Virginia established pioneer units consisting of men who could handle the tools required for keeping an army in motion, and in March 1863 the Confederate government authorized the establishment of regiments of engineers that included the necessary mechanics and artificers to do bridge building, carpentry, and other skilled work. The federal army had engineering units in the regular army and eventually was granted the authority to incorporate volunteer engineer regiments into their formations.[94]

Throughout the war, however, there remained a good deal of improvisation, and all of these technical and legal distinctions were confused by plan and necessity. Ulysses Grant, for example, found that the resources of a citizen army were not always clearly

Topographical Engineers, Camp Winfield Scott, Yorktown, Virginia vicinity, May 2, 1862. These men helped to provide the Union army with essential maps during the Peninsula campaign. (*Library of Congress*)

marked by formal organizational arrangements. At Vicksburg, and elsewhere through-out the war, Grant later claimed, "I found that volunteers could be found in the ranks and among the commissioned officers to meet every call for aid whether mechanical or pro-fessional."[95] Indeed, Grant created an ad hoc engineering organization as he campaigned against Vicksburg, using officers with engineering knowledge to train soldiers in the necessary work. Earlier, in 1862, Union General George McClellan also improvised and created an engineering organization in his Army of the Potomac without the approval of Congress, which later, in 1863, accepted his work. At the tactical level, while on campaign, the distinctions between the limited number of engineers and the pioneers were blurred, with pioneers performing all sorts of duties identified with engineering troops and engineering troops wielding shovels and axes, when required. Also, western Confederate forces were relaxed in how they described the various men employed in engineering tasks, further confusing matters.[96]

Additional blurring of distinctions came when infantrymen often found themselves working as bridge builders or doing the heavy shovel work of pioneers to meet the needs of a campaign, without any change of their status. During the Vicksburg campaign, for example, regular infantry did their share of canal digging, part of Grant's effort to facilitate his army's approach to the Confederate citadel, as well as entrenching work once they forced the enemy into the city's defenses. At Vicksburg, soldiers with civilian backgrounds in mining found themselves back at their old trade, tunneling shafts under Confederate lines. Their Pennsylvania counterparts in the Army of the Potomac about a year later dug the tunnel under Confederate lines at Petersburg, Virginia, that prepared the way for the bloody Battle of the Crater.[97]

Prudence dictated that ordinary infantrymen pick up their shovels and produce some protection for themselves, regardless of the presence of engineers or pioneers. "Whenever we stop, even for a few hours, in the vicinity of the enemy fortifications of some kind are thrown up," reported Iowa soldier George Remley, who was campaigning with Sheridan in the Virginia valley; "logs, stones and everything available are brought up into requisition." Remley's Confederate foes did the same, making everyone wary of initiating a frontal assault.[98]

Engineers, however, were generally prepared for all sorts of duty, putting their shoulders to the tasks their officers required of them. In April 1863 the 50th New York Volunteer Engineers set off with pontoon trains as well as "working parties" who carried picks, shovels, and axes, which all men of the regiment would use as circumstances dic-tated; the engineers, also armed as infantry, were to construct corduroy roads, as neces-sary, on the march route.[99] John H. Westervelt, an enlisted man who served with the First New York Volunteer Engineers in South Carolina and Virginia, built lookout towers, cut roads through thick growth for artillery, and made gabions and facines, despite the fact that the regiment's primary purpose was working with pontoon bridges. He also built furniture for officers and performed what he called "humbug work" such as repairing wagons, "which as Pontooners we have no business to do."[100]

Because of their limited numbers, engineering troops were valuable and expected to save themselves for their assigned duties. In April 1863, on Folly Island, scouts alerted Union troops of a possible enemy threat; in preparation to meet the Confederates, the "engineers now fell in the rear and the infantry front for battle."[101] Nevertheless, on occasion, engineering troops entered the battle fray as infantry. Indeed, engineers not only practiced handling pontoons, bridge building, road building, and making defensive works while in camp, but also drilled as infantry. The editor of a Rome, New York, paper

50th New York Volunteer Infantry engaged in road-building on the North Anna River during Grant's Overland campaign in May 1864. (*Library of Congress*)

that ran a recruiting notice for an engineering company explained that the men would also be trained in infantry tactics, including skirmishing and scouting.[102]

Despite their limited numbers, engineering and pioneering troops did hard and important service on campaign and frequently came under enemy fire, even when performing their specific duties. Union engineering troops did yeoman work in bridge building for McClellan during the Virginia peninsula campaign. At the start of the campaign, they repaired and built numerous small and large bridges, improved inadequate roads, and, in the case of the 50th New York Engineers, milled their own lumber in the bargain; for their exhausting work in aiding McClellan's withdrawal, the *New York Times* dubbed them "iron men."[103] Later, in December 1862, Yankee engineers at the Battle of Fredericksburg grappled with the laborious and dangerous duty of bridging the Rappahannock in the face of enemy fire that left many of their number dead. They failed to complete the task opposite Fredericksburg until Michigan and Massachusetts infantry rowed pontoons from one of the bridges across the river and dispersed the enemy snipers. A newspaper correspondent reported that once free of the enemy's fire, the engineers "laid hold with a will, plunging waist-deep into the water, and working as men work who are under inspiration." Their efforts then allowed their infantry comrades to engage in a terrible battle.[104]

CAVALRY RECONNAISSANCE

Related to the critical importance of engineers and topographers for helping soldiers arrive at the right place at the right time was the work of cavalry troopers, who acted as the immediate eyes of their armies. Given their mobility, troopers were ideally situated to do the work of topographers and assist an army's mapmakers. On the Virginia peninsula in 1862, officers of the Third Pennsylvania Cavalry, for example, "penetrated the region between the Chickahominy and the James, taking bearings and making notes," which in turn produced a map of the region of significant detail.[105]

Cavalry also provided more immediate assistance for a marching army in its efforts to get to the fight. Union cavalry officer William Woods Averell explained that "on the march, cavalry forms in advance, flank and rear guards and supplies escorts, couriers and guides." In the forward position, troopers acted as "antennae to mask" an advancing column's "movements and to discover any movement of the enemy." These activities certainly did not keep them from battle.[106] Sherman's infantry, for example, had such an easy march through Georgia because his cavalry was so effective in keeping Confederate general Joe Wheeler's troopers away from them, which involved a number of clashes along the way. Cavalry also came into contact with the enemy when it had to protect the army's retreat.

Troopers who dreamed of the glorious charges of the Napoleonic years soon discovered that generals found their value in another kind of employment. Saber-wielding horse soldiers clashing with one another and with infantry did not disappear from the Civil War battlefield. But times were changing, and cavalrymen found themselves engaged in other, less glamorous duty. As Averell later noted, cavalry "has long since ceased to be a projectile, except against cavalry."[107] Commanders deployed them as raiders, used them as mounted infantry and counterguerilla forces, had them work as a shield to hide their armies' movements, and assigned them to guard supply lines.

Generals also understood that their cavalry were valuable additions to their intelligence-gathering needs, a task troopers performed as a routine matter throughout the war. For example, in 1862, on the Virginia peninsula, Confederate Jeb Stuart's cavalry ride around the Union army confirmed Lee's suspicions about McClellan's weaknesses; later, the rebel horse soldiers probed Union lines along the Rappahannock in February 1863 and helped Lee to determine his next move. John Buford's cavalry provided important intelligence to the Union army before the Second Battle of Bull Run in August 1862. And Confederate horsemen in Georgia did their best to find out where Sherman was heading with his armies. After the Battle of Antietam, the 12th Illinois Cavalry spent a good bit of their time on picket duty, patrolling the Maryland countryside and observing the Potomac River crossings, an intelligence-gathering duty that would have proven critical if Confederates had attempted another invasion.[108]

Cavalry troopers shared the hardships of the campaigning infantry, without the problem of sore feet, but with the added burden of worrying about their mounts. Whether fighting or scouting, active duty took its toll on horses, just as it did on men. During the winter months of 1862–1863, west of the Mississippi, Confederate cavalry troopers lost few horses in combat but significant numbers to lameness and sickness; vigorous service simply wore out horse flesh. This was a particular burden to the rebel trooper, who had to provide his own mount.[109] The Union army remounted its cavalry, but troopers also experienced problems with diseased and tired horses. Members of the 12th Illinois Cavalry, for example, participated in Stoneman's spring 1863 raid and came back with high spirits and worn down mounts, while at the beginning of 1865, many men who were to join in Union general James H. Wilson's raid were still without mounts, having already worn them out campaigning.[110]

NOTES

1. John R. Sellers, ed., *A People at War: Civil War Manuscripts form the Holdings of the Library of Con gress* (Alexandria, VA: Chadwyck-Healey, 1989–1990), entry for July 12, 1863, Thomas F. Galway Diaries, reel 28.

2. Ibid., John C. Arnold to wife and family, May 28, 1864, John Carvel Arnold Letters, reel 1.

3. Marion Morrison, *A History of the Ninth Regiment Illinois Volunteer Infantry, with the Regimental Roster* (Carbondale: Southern Illinois University Press, 1997), 15, 17, 20–37; John Kent Folmar, ed., *From That Terrible Field: Civil War Letters of James M. Williams, Twenty-first Alabama Infantry Volunteers* (Tusca-loosa: University of Alabama Press, 1981), 52.

4. Ben Wynne, *A Hard Trip: A History of the 15th Mississippi Infantry, CSA* (Macon, GA: Mercer University Press, 2003), 50.

5. Sam Watkins, *"Company Aytch," or a Side Show of the Big Show and Other Sketches,* ed. M. Thomas Inge (New York: Penguin Putnam, 1999), 9.

6. Wynne, *A Hard Trip,* 50.

7. Mark K. Christ, ed., *Getting Used to Being Shot At: The Spence Family Civil War Letters* (Fayette-ville: University of Arkansas Press, 2002), 7.

8. Stephen W. Sears, ed., *On Campaign with the Army of the Potomac: The Civil War Journal of Theo-dore Ayrault Dodge* (New York: Cooper Square Press, 2001), 15.

9. Terrence J. Winschel, ed., *The Civil War Diary of a Common Soldier: William Wiley of the 77th Illinois Infantry* (Baton Rouge: Louisiana State University Press, 2001), 26, 26n.

10. Sellers, *A People at War,* Joseph Lester to father and sisters, June 5, 1864, Joseph Lester Collection, reel 58; John D. Billings, *Hardtack and Coffee: The Unwritten Story of Army Life* (Lincoln: University of Nebraska Press, 1993), 337, 342.

11. Barry Popchock, ed., *Soldier Boy: The Civil War Letters of Charles O. Musser, 29th Iowa* (Iowa City: University of Iowa Press, 1995), 19.

12. J. Franklin Dyer, *The Journal of a Civil War Surgeon,* ed. Michael B. Chesson (Lincoln: University of Nebraska Press, 2003), 164.

13. Donald B. Koonce, ed., *Doctor to the Front: The Recollections of Confederate Surgeon Thomas Fan-ning Wood, 1861–1865* (Knoxville: University of Tennessee Press, 2000), 108.

14. Stephen W. Sears, ed., *For Country, Cause and Leader: The Civil War Journal of Charles B. Hayden* (New York: Ticknor & Fields, 1993), 320.

15. Wynne, *A Hard Trip,* 51.

16. Susan Williams Benson, ed., *Berry Benson's Civil War Book: Memoirs of a Confederate Scout and Sharpshooter* (Athens: University of Georgia Press, 1992), 16–17.

17. Daniel E. Sutherland, ed., *Reminiscences of a Private: William E. Bevens of the First Arkansas Infan-try, C.S.A.* (Fayetteville: University of Arkansas Press, 1992), 187–91.

18. Christ, *Getting Used to Being Shot At,* 7.

19. John G. Barrett, *Yankee Rebel: The Civil War Journal of Edmund DeWitt Patterson* (Knoxville: University of Tennessee Press, 2004), 6.

20. John M. Follett to wife, March 28, 1863, Follett Brothers Letters, eHistory, Ohio State University, Columbus, http://ehistory.osu.edu/osu/sources/letters/follett_brothers/.

21. Ibid.

22. Sellers, *A People at War,* John C. Arnold to wife and family, July 13, August 7, 1864, John Carvel Arnold Collection, reel 1.

23. Julie Holcomb, ed., *Southern Sons, Northern Soldiers: The Civil War Letters of the Remley Brothers, 22nd Iowa Infantry* (DeKalb: Northern Illinois University Press, 2004), 76–77.

24. John M. Follett to wife, February 21, 1863, Follett Brothers Letters, eHistory, Ohio State University, Columbus, http://ehistory.osu.edu/osu/sources/letters/follett_brothers//.

25. Warren Wilkinson and Steven E. Woodworth, *A Scythe of Fire: Through the Civil War with One of Lee's Most Legendary Regiments* (New York: HarperCollins, 2002), 207.

26. Barbara Bentley Smith and Nina Bentley Baker, eds., *"Burning Rails as We Pleased": The Civil War Letters of William Garrigues Bentley, 104th Ohio Volunteer Infantry* (Jefferson, NC: McFarland, 2004), 69.

27. Emil Rosenblatt and Ruth Rosenblatt, eds., *Hard Marching Every Day: The Civil War Letters of Pri-vate Wilbur Fisk, 1861–1865* (Lawrence: University Press of Kansas, 1992), 223, 229–30.

28. Claire E. Swedberg, ed., *Three Years with the 92d Illinois: The Civil War Diary of John M. King* (Mechanicsburg, PA: Stackpole Books, 1999), 157.

29. Sellers, *A People at War,* John G. Jones to parents, January 2, 1863, John Griffith Jones Correspon-dence, reel 57.

30. Anita Palladino, ed., *Diary of a Yankee Engineer: The Civil War Story of John H. Westervelt, Engi-neer, 1st New York Volunteer Engineer Corps* (New York: Fordham University Press, 1997), 2–3.

31. Scott Walker, *Hell's Broke Loose in Georgia: Survival in a Civil War Regiment* (Athens: University of Georgia Press, 2005), 33 (quotation).

32. John M. Follett to wife, February 21, 1863, Follett Brothers Letters, eHistory, Ohio State University, Columbus, http://ehistory.osu.edu/osu/sources/letters/follett_brothers/.

33. William C. Davis, *Battle at Bull Run: A History of the First Major Campaign of the Civil War* (Baton Rouge: Louisiana State University Press, 1981), 93.

34. Ted Tunnell, ed., *Carpetbagger from Vermont: The Autobiography of Marshall Harvey Twitchell* (Baton Rouge: Louisiana State University Press, 1989), 41.

35. Watkins, *"Company Aytch,"* 108–9, 196.

36. Stephen B. Oates, *Confederate Cavalry West of the River* (Austin: University of Texas Press, 1961), 55.

37. Sarah Bahnson Chapman, ed., *Bright and Gloomy Days: The Civil War Correspondence of Captain Charles Frederic Bahnson, a Moravian Confederate* (Knoxville: University of Tennessee Press, 2003), 70–71.

38. John S. Collier and Bonnie B. Collier, eds., *Yours for the Union: The Civil War Letters of John W. Chase, First Massachusetts Light Artillery* (New York: Fordham University Press, 2004), 361.

39. Holcomb, *Southern Sons, Northern Soldiers,* 795.

40. Charles F. Larimer, ed., *Love and Valor: Intimate Civil War Letters between Captain Jacob and Emeline Ritner* (Western Springs, IL: Sigourney Press, 2003), 430.

41. Warren Lee Goss, *Recollections of a Private: A Story of the Army of the Potomac* (Scituate, MA: Digital Scanning, 2002), 302.

42. Joseph R. Reinhart, trans. and ed., *Two Germans in the Civil War: The Diary of John Daeuble and the Letters of Gottfried Rentschler, 6th Kentucky Volunteer Infantry* (Knoxville: University of Tennessee Press, 2004), 28–29.

43. Holcomb, *Southern Sons, Northern Soldiers,* 98–99.

44. John William De Forest, *A Volunteer's Adventures: A Union Captain's Record of the Civil War,* ed. James H. Croushore (Baton Rouge: Louisiana State University Press, 1996), 93–94.

45. Stephen W. Sears, *Landscape Turned Red: The Battle of Antietam* (New Haven, CT: Ticknor & Fields, 1983), 70–71, 175–76; Keith S. Bohannon, "Dirty, Ragged, and Ill-Provided For: Confederate Logistical Problems in the 1862 Maryland Campaign and Their Solutions," in *The Antietam Campaign,* ed. Gary W. Gallagher (Chapel Hill: University of North Carolina Press, 1999), 116.

46. Smith and Baker, *"Burning Rails as We Please,"* 75, 98.

47. George W. Fox to brother, June 25, 1864, Civil War Letters of the Fox Brothers, eHistory, Ohio State University, Columbus, http://ehistory.osu.edu/osu/sources/letters/fox/.

48. Thomas E. Pope, *The Weary Boys: Colonel J. Warren Keifer and the 110th Ohio Volunteer Infantry* (Kent, OH: Kent State University Press, 2002), 54–67.

49. Robert G. Tanner, *Retreat to Victory? Confederate Strategy Reconsidered* (Wilmington, DE: SR Books, 2001), 51–59.

50. John O. Casler, *Four Years in the Stonewall Brigade,* 2nd ed. (Columbia: University of South Carolina Press, 2005), 86.

51. Randall Allen and Keith S. Bohannon, eds., *Campaigning with "Old Stonewall": Confederate Captain Ujanirtus Allen's Letters to His Wife* (Baton Rouge: Louisiana State University Press, 1998), 112.

52. John M. Follett to wife, May 5, 1863, Follett Brothers Letters, eHistory, Ohio State University, Columbus, http://ehistory.osu.edu/osu/sources/letters/follett_brothers/.

53. G. Ward Hubbs, ed., *Voices from Company D: Diaries by the Greensboro Guards, Fifth Alabama Infantry Regiment, Army of Northern Virginia* (Athens: University of Georgia Press, 2003), 161.

54. Robert C. Black III, *The Railroads of the Confederacy* (Chapel Hill: University of North Carolina Press, 1952, 1998), 8–11, 148–63; John E. Clark Jr., *Railroads in the Civil War: The Impact of Management on Victory and Defeat* (Baton Rouge: Louisiana State University Press, 2001), 45–48.

55. Roger Pickenpaugh, *Rescue by Rail: Troop Transfer and the Civil War in the West, 1863* (Lincoln: University of Nebraska Press, 1998), 92–93; Clark, *Railroads in the Civil War,* 97–98; DeWitt Boyd Stone Jr., ed., *Wandering to Glory: Confederate Veterans Remember Evans' Brigade* (Columbia: University of South Carolina Press, 2002), 104–5; Jennifer Cain Bohrnstedt, ed., *While Father Is Away: The Civil War Letters of William H. Bradbury* (Lexington: University Press of Kentucky, 2003), 240; Lenette S. Taylor, *"The Supply for Tomorrow Must Not Fail": The Civil War of Captain Simon Perkins Jr., a Union Quartermaster* (Kent, OH: Kent State University Press, 2004), 69.

56. Stephen W. Sears, *On Campaign,* 3, 5, 15.

57. Popchock, *Soldier Boy,* 19–20.

58. Chapman, *Bright and Gloomy Days,* 70.

59. Guy R. Everson and Edward H. Simpson Jr., eds., *Far, Far from Home: The Wartime Letters of Dick and Tally Simpson, 3rd South Carolina Volunteers* (New York: Oxford University Press, 1994), 250–52.

60. Sears, *For Country, Cause and Leader,* 332, 334.

61. Holcomb, *Southern Sons, Northern Soldiers,* 115.

62. Michael B. Ballard, *Vicksburg: The Campaign That Opened the Mississippi* (Chapel Hill: University of North Carolina Press, 2004), 69–70.

63. Goss, *Recollections of a Private,* 303–6.

64. Sellers, *A People at War,* Daniel R. Larned to sister, March 24, 1862, April 29, 1863, Daniel Reed Larned Correspondence, reels 59, 60.

65. Ibid., March 24, 1862, reel 59.

66. Ibid., S. W. Browning to wife, March 11, 1863, Silas W. Browning Papers, reel 6.

67. Rosenblatt and Rosenblatt, *Hard Marching Every Day,* 134–35.

68. Joseph T. Glatthaar, *The March to the Sea and Beyond: Sherman's Troops in the Savannah and Carolinas Campaign* (New York: New York University Press, 1985), 52–65.

69. Sellers, *A People at War,* Joseph Lester to father and sisters, June 21, 1863, Joseph Lester Collection, reel 58.

70. David C. Rankin, ed., *Diary of a Christian Soldier: Rufus Kinsley and the Civil War* (Cambridge: Cambridge University Press, 2004), 103–4.

71. Ibid., 98, 102, 104.

72. Bohrnstedt, *While Father Is Away,* 1–13, 225, 242.

73. Earl B. McElfresh, *Maps and Mapmakers of the Civil War* (New York: Harry N. Abrams, 1999), 17–22.

74. Mary A. Giunta, ed., *A Civil War Soldier of Christ and Country: The Selected Correspondence of John Rodgers Meigs, 1859–1864* (Urbana: University of Illinois Press, 2006), 186–87, 192–93.

75. Jedediah Hotchkiss, *Make Me a Map of the Valley: The Civil War Journal of Stonewall Jackson's Topographer,* ed. Archie P. McDonald (Dallas, TX: Southern Methodist University Press, 1973), xix; George G. Kundahl, *Confederate Engineer: Training and Campaigning with John Morris Wampler* (Knoxville: University of Tennessee Press, 2000), 219.

76. Robert Knox Sneden, *Eye of the Storm: A Civil War Odyssey,* ed. Charles F. Bryan Jr. and Nelson D. Lankford (New York: Free Press, 2000), 10, 12–14, 29, 135–36.

77. Bohrnstedt, *While Father Is Away,* 243.

78. James B. Bartholomees, *Buff Facings and Gilt Buttons: Staff and Headquarters Operations in the Army of Northern Virginia, 1861–1865* (Columbia: University of South Carolina Press, 1998), 108–110; Harry L. Jackson, *First Regiment Engineer Troops P.A.C.S.: Robert E. Lee's Combat Engineers* (Louisa, VA: R.A.E. Design and Publishing, 1998), 51.

79. McElfresh, *Maps and Mapmakers,* 29–30, 69.

80. Bohrnstedt, *While Father Is Away,* 242–43.

81. Eric A. Campbell, ed., *"A Grand Terrible Dramma": From Gettysburg to Petersburg: The Civil War Letters of Charles Wellington Reed* (New York: Fordham University Press, 2000), 287–88, 292–93, 306–7, 309.

82. Bohrnstedt, *While Father Is Away,* 242, 244.

83. Ronald Mosely, ed., *The Stillwell Letters: A Georgian in Longstreet's Corps, Army of Northern Virginia* (Macon, GA: Mercer University Press, 2002), 46, 90, 151.

84. M. Jane Johansson, ed., *Widows by the Thousand: The Civil War Letters of Theophilus and Harriet Perry, 1862–1864* (Fayetteville: University of Arkansas Press, 2000), 33–34.

85. William G. Le Duc, *This Business of War: Recollections of a Civil War Quartermaster* (St. Paul: Minnesota Historical Society Press, 2004), 72–93.

86. Kundahl, *Confederate Engineer,* 146.

87. Sears, *On Campaign,* ix–xvii, 176.

88. William C. Davis and Meredith L. Swentor, eds., *Bluegrass Confederate: The Headquarters Diary of Edward O. Guerrant* (Baton Rouge: Louisiana State University Press, 1999), 90, 92.

89. Sears, *On Campaign,* xvi.

90. Morrison, *A History of the Ninth Regiment Illinois Volunteer Infantry,* 94.

91. Sneden, *Eye of the Storm,* 36–38, 136–37, 148–50.

92. Giunta, *A Civil War Soldier,* 186–87, 200–1, 224, 241–42.

93. Stephen W. Sears, *To the Gates of Richmond: The Peninsula Campaign* (Boston: Houghton Mifflin, 1992), 24; William J. Miller, "I Only Wait for the River: McClellan and His Engineers on the Chickahominy," in *The Richmond Campaign of 1862: The Peninsula and the Seven Days,* ed. Garry W. Gallagher (Chapel Hill: University of North Carolina Press, 2000), 47; Edward Hagerman, *The American Civil War and the Origins of Modern Warfare: Ideas, Organization, and Field Command* (Bloomington: Indiana University Press, 1992), 234–39; Philip Katcher, *American Civil War Armies,* Vol. 3, *Specialist Troops* (Oxford: Osprey, 1987), 8–9, 22–23.

94. Earl J. Hess, *Field Armies and Fortifications in the Civil War Era: The Eastern Campaigns, 1861–1864* (Chapel Hill: University of North Carolina Press, 2005), 11–27; Phillip M. Thienel, *Mr. Lincoln's Bridge Builders: The Right Hand of American Genius* (Shippensburg, PA: White Mane, 2000), viii–xii, 20–22; Kundahl, *Confederate Engineer,* 142–44, 161–62; Jackson, *First Regiment Engineer Troops,* 1–13.

95. Ulysses S. Grant, *Personal Memoirs of U. S. Grant and Select Letters, 1839–1865,* ed. Mary Drake McFeely and William S. McFeely (New York: Library of America, 1990), 314.

96. Hess, *Field Armies and Fortifications,* 11–27; Thienel, *Mr. Lincoln's Bridge Builders,* 20–22, 27, 30; Hagerman, *American Civil War and the Origins of Modern Warfare,* 233–39; Kundahl, *Confederate Engineer,* 161; Ed Malles, ed., *Bridge Building in Wartime: Colonel Wesley Brainerd's Memoir of the 50th New York Volunteer Engineers* (Knoxville: University of Tennessee Press, 1997), 17, 269–70, 278–80; Billings, *Hard Tack and Coffee,* 377–93.

97. John M. Follett to parents and sister, April 5, 1863, Follett Brothers Letters, eHistory, Ohio State University, Columbus, http://ehistory.osu.edu/osu/sources/letters/follett_brothers/; William L. Shea and Terrence J. Winschel, *Vicksburg Is the Key: The Struggle for the Mississippi River* (Lincoln: University of Nebraska Press, 2003), 154–55; Michael B. Ballard, *Vicksburg: The Campaign That Opened the Mississippi* (Chapel Hill: University of North Carolina Press, 2004), 360, 367–69; Noah Andre Trudeau, *The Last Citadel: Petersburg, Virginia, June 1864–April 1865* (Baton Rouge: Louisiana State University Press, 1991), 99–105.

98. Holcomb, *Southern Sons, Northern Soldiers,* 157.

99. Malles, *Bridge Building in Wartime,* 327–31.

100. Palladino, *Diary of a Yankee Engineer,* 4, 7–8, 21, 62, 158 (quotation), 198–99.

101. Ibid., 3.

102. Thienel, *Mr. Lincoln's Bridge Builders,* 20–22, 27, 30; Malles, *Bridge Building in Wartime,* 17, 42, 44, 269–70; Hess, *Field Armies and Fortifications,* 12.

103. Thienel, *Mr. Lincoln's Bridge Builders,* 32–63, 63 (quotation); William J. Miller, "I Only Wait for the River," 44–65.

104. Malles, *Bridge Building in Wartime,* 282–85; George C. Rable, *Fredericksburg! Fredericksburg!* (Chapel Hill: University of North Carolina Press, 2002), 156–73.

105. Edward K. Eckert and Nicholas J. Amato, eds., *Ten Years in the Saddle: The Memoir of William Woods Averell, 1851–1862* (San Rafael, CA: Presidio Press, 1978), 360.

106. Eckert and Amato, *Ten Years in the Saddle,* 328 (quotation), 328–30.

107. Ibid., 327.

108. Stephen Z. Starr, *The Union Cavalry in the Civil War,* Vol. 1, *From Fort Sumter to Gettysburg, 1861–1863* (Baton Rouge: Louisiana State University Press, 1979), 270–73; Stephen W. Sears, *Chancellorsville* (Boston: Houghton Mifflin, 1996), 49, 271; John Randolph Poole, *Cracker Cavaliers: The 2nd Georgia Cavalry under Wheeler and Forrest* (Macon, GA: Mercer University Press, 2000), 162; Eckert and Amato, *Ten Years in the Saddle,* 328; Samuel M. Blackwell Jr., *In the First Line of Battle: The 12th Illinois Cavalry in the Civil War* (DeKalb: Northern Illinois University Press, 2002), 39–40.

109. Oates, *Confederate Cavalry,* 78–81.

110. Blackwell, *In the First Line of Battle,* 80–81.

7 ENGAGING THE ENEMY

THE EDGE OF BATTLE

Often pickets, the trip wire of a defending army, made first contact with an advancing enemy, while attackers often sent out a forward guard. Skirmishers also preceded advancing columns perhaps a half to three-quarters of a mile to the front to " 'feel' the enemy," not knowing "what bush, tuft of grass, or hillock may conceal his deadly foe."[1] These men moved forward as they "played a deadly game of 'Bo-peep,' hiding behind logs, fences, rocks and bushes" as they fired on their counterparts.[2] "But onward they must go," explained New Jerseyan Peter Vrendenburgh, "till routed by a charge of superior numbers, cavalry or checked by artillery."[3]

Meanwhile, men near the field waiting to commence the battle had time to reflect on their present circumstances and what awaited them in the very near future. If they expected to engage the enemy on the following day, soldiers spent time thinking about their families, their lives, and their souls.[4] On the evening before the assault on South Carolina's Fort Wagner, soldiers of the Sixth Connecticut tended to their accoutrements, while some of them sewed their names on their uniforms to allow ready identification of their bodies if they fell in the attack.[5] New recruits might be eager to engage the enemy, as were the men of the 23rd New York Volunteer Infantry, who were waiting to move on to Richmond in the advance that would end at the First Battle of Bull Run.[6] Other novices were perhaps nervous, as were the men of the Eighth New York Heavy Artillery, who were preparing to fight as untested infantry at Cold Harbor.[7] Veterans knew better and prepared to fight resigned to what awaited them.

On the day of the battle, soldiers again had time for reflection, as they waited to join the fight. At Shiloh, both Indianan George Squier and Mississippian Augustus Meckler waited only a short time before engaging the enemy, but it was long enough to wonder about the thousands of men who would die that day.[8] Connecticut soldier Benjamin Hirst had similar thoughts as he stood in formation, prepared to advance on the heights beyond Fredericksburg in December 1862; time passed slowly "while a shell form the Rebels ever and anon, warned us of what would soon be the Fate of a many."[9] In May 1862 Confederate Edmund Patterson felt these very sensations as he waited to join the fight near Williamsburg, Virginia. "It was the first time that I had ever been called upon to face

HW, April 26, 1862. *The Battle of Pittsburg Landing [Shiloh], April 7, 1862—Final and Victorious Charge of the Union Troops under Major-General Grant.* (*Library of Congress*)

death," he reported. "I felt that in a few moments some of us standing here, vainly trying to jest and appear careless, would be in eternity....I did not feel afraid...but it was a painful nervous anxiety, a longing for action, anything to occupy my attention—nerves relaxed and a dull feeling about the chest that made breathing painful. All the energies of my soul seemed concentrated in the one desire for action."[10]

While waiting in reserve, other men fought with their strained nerves. On May 31 and June 1, 1862, during the battle at Fair Oaks, Virginia, young Vermont soldiers became uneasy as they waited in reserve for two days, listening to the fighting, "watching the smoke of battle, and every moment expecting to be called in."[11] Earlier, Maine soldiers at the First Battle of Bull Run had to stand in reserve for some time, adding to the tense wait for combat. Abner Small reported that his brigade "stayed in that woods road for four mortal hours, longer hours than I had ever known....The long suspense fretted us. Our nerves jumped." As they waited, they prayed.[12] Mississippian Augustus Meckler, probably one of thousands who did so at Shiloh, "made a sincere, honest surrender" of himself "to God," prayed to live, and promised to "honor his name & benefit my fellow creatures" if granted his request.[13]

It was at this moment before joining the fray, not during the fight, when so much was beyond the control of the individual soldier, that men revealed their true nature. "All the demands of active service call for courage," Abner Small explained, "but the real test comes before the battle—in the rear line...waiting." There the men at "the edge of battle" could witness the danger that awaited them and be "near enough to feel its fierce pulsations and get an occasional shock of its power."[14]

For Confederate Edmund Patterson, standing in reserve bred an impatience to do something to help the dying soldiers in the fight. In June 1862, on the Virginia peninsula, he and his comrades marched to battle, then "spent the whole evening listening to the most terrific fire." He had feelings that "cannot be described" as he waited, hearing the battle play out around him. It was, he later noted, the same "restless, feverish feeling" that accompanied going into battle. He knew fellow soldiers were dying, and he had the urge "no matter what the danger...to rush to their assistance." "While you watch the progress of the conflict you become weary," he explained, "and great drops of perspiration will stand upon your forehead."[15] At Shiloh, Sam Watkins and his fellow Tennesseans listened to the battle unfold beyond their sight; they were in the dark about the fight, curious about the meaning of all the noise and eager to hear news of the Confederate progress.[16]

It was on the "edge of battle" that soldiers might witness the consequences of fighting and start to worry about their own fate. Marching toward battle at Shiloh, Mississippi, soldiers approaching the fight saw men "torn to mince meat by cannon balls. Some still writhing in the agonies of death."[17] At an artillery skirmish in Maryland on the day before Antietam, Connecticut soldier Samuel Fiske found the situation to be "not...a pleasant one." He and the rest of his regiment watched the balls seek out targets, crouched, swore, prayed, but did not run, even after seeing the projectiles do some damage. He admitted that he could calculate the improbable chance of him being hit by one of the "murderous messengers of destruction"; nevertheless, "somehow the one chance looms up rather disproportionately in your view."[18]

The fighting that these men heard or witnessed could unnerve less steady men. So could the mayhem they glimpsed before they also became embroiled in the fight. Indianan George Squier moved on toward the enemy at Shiloh accompanied by the noise of battle and similar scenes of destruction. "We soon met some with the loss of fingers, some without a hand, some with a broken leg or arm; in fact [they were] wounded in every conceivable place," he later recalled. He also admitted, "I mention this because at *that* time it rather daunted my fervor and for the first time I doubted my courage."[19]

THE FIGHT

Once soldiers came to the point of grappling with the enemy, they often felt a release of the tension as they entered into a world of confusion, noise, and excitement that helped them forget about any notion of parade ground order. Confederate Sam Watkins experienced a dreamlike state as he stood ready to engage the enemy at Shiloh. "I seemed to be in sort of a haze" until shaken from his stupor by the "siz, siz, siz" of Yankee rifle balls. The call to charge, accompanied by rebel yells and Yankee hurrahs, released the building tension, at least for Watkins. "I had been feeling mean all morning as if I had stolen sheep," he later reported, "but when the order to charge was given, I got happy." Watkins, in fact, "felt happier than a fellow does when he professes religion at a big Methodist camp-meeting." Indeed, he recalled that the charge "was fun" and that "everybody looked happy." They were ready to enjoy their victory, halted only when word came of their commanding general's death.[20] Other soldiers initially faced fire with weak knees, feeling faint as the enemy shot at them, especially if men nearby were falling, until they steeled themselves for the action. As New Yorker Frank Wilkeson recalled, "One has to string up nerves and take a firm grip on himself morally, and hold himself in the battle flames for a few moments until warmed to passion."[21]

Confusion in Battle

Once engaged, there was little chance to operate neatly under fire, despite all of the campground training. Fighting in the wilderness of Virginia in the spring of 1864, for example, was particularly troublesome given that the battlefield was covered with its "dense growth of pine or of oak," barring some clearings. In one area, Theodore Lyman, an officer on Meade's staff, reported that there was a "low, continuous, thick growth of small saplings, fifteen to thirty feet high and seldom larger than one's arm." At some points, troops could not see more than 50 yards. "This was the *terrain*," Lyman complained, "on which we were to manœuvre a great army."[22]

Men charged over uneven terrain, undergrowth, and muddy fields to reach the enemy, all of which mixed with the usual confusion of misunderstood orders or miscalculated distances. Once the firing commenced, soldiers were more likely than not to see confusion reign. At Antietam, Connecticut soldiers experienced an "indescribable confusion" made worse, according to Samuel Fiske, by their lack of direction as they engaged and disengaged the enemy "promiscuously, according to our own ideas through the whole day."[23] At Chancellorsville, one Alabaman reported that he "never saw such confusion in my life—men scattered & mixed up every way," as the men engaged in a "running fight."[24] South Carolinian Berry Benson, who had once expected battle to unfold as if it were an orderly drill routine, noticed that once the shooting started, "every man goes on fighting on his own hook; firing as, and when, he likes," sometimes with lowly private soldiers, who had an eye for the main chance and a disregard for the chain of command, ordering their comrades to charge the enemy.[25]

All of this confusion could result in poor fire discipline and unintended casualties. At Antietam, Connecticut soldiers "didn't know what they were expected to do, and sometimes in the excitement, fired on their own men."[26] At Chancellorsville, some Confederates fired without taking proper aim, aiming high or discharging their weapons into the dirt directly in front of themselves. One Alabaman feared being killed by fellow Confederates. Despite his efforts, he and other soldiers could not prevent the wounding of some of their own comrades by friendly fire.[27]

Earlier in the war, Abner Small's Maine boys grappled with the enemy at the First Bull Run in a smoke-shrouded atmosphere that obscured the enemy. "I can only recall that we stood there and blazed away," Small reported. "There was a wild uproar of shouting and firing. The faces near me were inhuman."[28] Confusion was all the more apparent when the enemy attacked unsuspecting soldiers, as the Confederates did the Yankees at Shiloh and Chancellorsville. In October 1864 Confederate troops surprised Yankee troops near Middletown, Virginia, who "were thrown into confusion before they had time to rally for effective resistance." The result was a field "covered with stragglers, panic stricken and running for dear life." Men fled their positions in the face of the "rebel hordes" in reckless confusion, totally disorganized in "disgraceful flight."[29] In the end, what order came to a battle was the result of disciplined men who, according to rebel Berry Benson, had confidence in their comrades and who kept "dressed upon the colors in some rough fashion."[30]

Such battlefield confusion provided Irishman Peter Welsh, color sergeant of the 28th Massachusetts, with the optimistic reassurances he needed to convince his anxious wife that carrying the regimental flag was not dangerous. He told her not to worry for his safety because "the smoke of powder the noise of firearms and cannon and the excittement of the battle field makes it impossible" for the enemy to hit him. In fact, if they aimed at him, in all likelihood, he assured her, "those on either side of the colors for the lenght of the company are more likely to get struck then the color bearer." He was only partly correct. While he survived serious fighting as color sergeant, he could not escape the fate suffered by so many color-bearers; he died in May 1864 from a wound received while carrying his regimental flag at Spotsylvania Court House.[31] Welsh and all color-bearers, in fact, were prime targets and suffered for it. At one engagement, a group of rapid-loading Kentucky Unionists fired several coordinated volleys at the Confederate colors, "and at every volley the flag would fall."[32] But heroic men quickly snatched up the flags and continued to carry them in battle, despite the danger. As Maine soldier Charles Mattocks remarked in May 1863, no one could help but notice that almost all of his division's color sergeants received special honors.[33]

The confusion of battle limited the soldiers' perception of the drama in which they were engaged and forced men to concentrate on the actions immediate for their survival. Edmund Patterson reported that while he was fighting on the Virginia peninsula at Gaines Mill, "by the time we had gone half a mile we were as much confused as the Yankees, for no one paid attention to company or regiment, but each devoted his entire attention to loading and firing as fast as possible."[34] Abner Small recalled that "after the first volley of musketry, he is a rare man who theorizes, or speculates on the action of his comrade, or of his regiment, much more on that of the commanding general three miles distant."[35] Warren Lee Goss concurred, admitting that men were too caught up with their own immediate experiences to notice much more. Goss, after Antietam, explained that the fighting soldier concentrated "his energies and attention to the small focus of individual action."[36] Such battlefield experience led Illinois soldier John King to agree with the saying that "no man ever saw all of a battle."[37]

Aside from concentrating on their own tasks, soldiers found the natural landscape to be an obstruction to their view of the larger event. Port Gibson, for example, was a decidedly rugged battlefield. John Follett and men from his regiment had been in reserve until ordered to move out, whence they commenced marching "over hills, through ravines, over gullies, and through can breaks" before they came on the Confederates. They then "drove them from one hill into a hollow, up another hill and into another hollow," at which point they exchanged fire with the enemy for several hours, before another regiment "drove...[the] rebs out of their hole."[38] Abner Small understood the impact of terrain on the perceptions of soldiers. "The inequalities of the ground, the wooded slopes and deep ravines, the fog, the dense smoke, and the apparent and often real confusion of troops moving in different directions under different orders," Small explained, "utterly preclude the possibility of a correct detailed observation of a battle of any magnitude."[39]

The artificial landscape of rifle pits, trenches, and siege lines also limited soldiers' perspectives of battle. Soldiers might have accepted such limitations as fair trade-off for the safety fortifications apparently offered them, but for the wearing effect that such fighting had on their nerves. Digging into the earth provided soldiers with unpleasant surroundings, but if those ditches became home for long sieges, men became convinced that anything was better than living like moles. Jasper Barritt of the 76th Illinois, a veteran of Grant's Mississippi campaign, concluded, "I don't care about seigeing an other place as we did Vicksburg...for Id rather plow corn any day than to lay in a rifle pit in the hot sun there is but little fun in it."[40] But Confederates within the Vicksburg works suffered the greatest psychological and physical strain. From mid-May until early July, defenders at the Mississippi River bastion, worn down by hunger and exposed to the elements in their trenches, "endured as much as mortals ever endured in an army—every day from daylight until late in the night—sometimes all night, we were in the midst of hissing shells and balls of every character that were ever manufactured."[41]

Later in the war, soldiers in the works around Petersburg also suffered and complained. In October 1864 Confederate Charles Trueheart admitted that such warfare "is more wearing out—in mind and patience certainly, than the open field campaign." A regular battle on open ground in the past ended with the survivors enjoying "a period of comparative quiet, and absence from the presence of the hated Yankees." But at Petersburg, "the Stars and Stripes flaunt in our faces, only a few hundred yards distant (indeed, in some places their lines are only 75 or 100 yards apart)." The sound of rifle fire and artillery shells was unending and the casualties they produced regular. "Some poor fellow of our Brigade of 600," Trueheart reported, "is almost daily borne to the rear, killed or wounded."[42] In January 1865 William C. Leak of the 17th South Carolina Infantry found the trenches at Petersburg to be especially miserable. "It is just like living in a hog pen," he reported.[43]

Sounds and Sights of the Battlefield

Whether in fields, forests, or fortifications, the sounds that these men endured added to the chaotic state of affairs. The shouting and yelling of the enemy and the screaming of the wounded and dying combined with the explosions of the weapons they fired to create an aural hell. Confederate clerk Edward Guerrant admitted that battles sounded much better at a distance. "Imagination's ear conveys to the mind no vulgar idea of broken legs & necks & bleeding sides & heads," he allowed.[44]

Indeed, many combatants considered the sounds of battle to be incredible and tried to describe what they heard in letters, journals, and memoirs. Guerrant wrote that "the bullets whistled thicker and [faster until] it seemed I could catch a—singular, keen, savage, [yel]l as they whirled past." And yet those bullets seemed to "whisper unwelcome [words]" in his ears even as they made that incredible sound.[45] For Oliver Wendell Holmes Jr., bullets made "a most villainous greasy slide through the air."[46] But Marcus Woodcock's description of the movement of the enemy's grape and canister as "*hurting sounds*" was most appropriate.[47] It was the "peculiar sound" made by those "Death messengers" whizzing past his head that New York Lieutenant Henry C. Lyon "would never forget in this world."[48]

Bullets rattled or whizzed and whistled, hissing and zipping through the air, or sang as they flew by with an unmelodious tune, but artillery bombardments and explosions were deafening, and shells roared by like tornadoes. Benjamin Hirst, caught between the path of Union and Confederate artillery shells on July 3, 1863, at Gettysburg, recalled the roar of the bombardment to sound as if "all the Demons of Hell were set loose, and were Howling through the Air."[49] Abner Small advised that "the shock from a bursting shell will scatter a man's thoughts as the iron fragments will scatter the leaves over head."[50] All of this noise made men long for quiet, as did staff officer Daniel Reed Larned, who complained after Cold Harbor that "there is not five consecutive minutes when the boom of cannon & firing of muskets is not heard."[51]

If sounds of flying ordnance were frightening, the screams and moans of the unfortunate men who caught the metal that whizzed around the field could be unnerving reminders of what awaited those men who had to continue to fight. The sights of battle that accompanied such noise added to the harrowing experience. Battle scenes provided a surreal landscape for some soldiers. Edward Guerrant seemed to find all possible cover from enemy fire to have shrunken to a size too small to shield him. But he also noted that the world around him appeared grim. "The sky looked [gray] and pall; the Earth gloomy," he reported. "Everything wore the aspect of *death earnestness.* It was a trial, the agony of the Soul."[52]

Battlefield scenes also reminded men of what they could become if it were not for their good fortune. Men fought with dead friends and enemies witnessing their bravery and their cowardice. They stumbled over bodies in various states of dismemberment, some with missing limbs, others with brains oozing out of their heads, some without heads. Not only did men witness the consequences of shot and ball, but they also saw the projectiles perform their work at close range. At the First Bull Run, Elisha Hunt Rhodes "emerged from the woods" and "saw a bomb shell strike a man in the breast and literally tear him to pieces."[53] Sam Watkins recalled watching at the battle of Franklin, Tennessee, how "the blood spurts in a perfect jet from the dead and wounded."[54] At New Madrid, in March 1862, Illinois lieutenant Charles W. Wills saw cannon balls take both legs off one soldier and pass through the torso of another, "a pretty hard sight."[55]

There were soldiers who allowed such things to weaken their resolve. In May 1863, after some hard fighting at Port Gibson, Mississippi, some Yankees "were taken suddenly sick, and . . . left the field" when ordered to fix bayonets and charge the enemy.[56] A few days later, in the Virginia theater, there were also Yankees who balked as the battle crashed around them. New Yorker Robert Cruikshank reported that "some of the boys that were behind the largest trees in the woods . . . began to move back to look for larger." Their regimental major threatened to run them through with his sword, which apparently steadied them.[57] At Cold Harbor, on June 1, 1864, some Union soldiers, including men of the Third Vermont, halted their advance, fell to the ground, and did their best to dig up the ground for protection with bayonet or whatever metal utensils were at hand.[58]

What was astonishing was not that men hesitated, panicked, or "skedaddled" in battle but that so many of them rallied and stayed in the firing line in spite of the hellish noise and sights. One Yankee recounted his experience at the fight near Williamsburg, Virginia, in 1862. "The constant hissing of the bullets, with their sharp ping or bizz whispering around and sometimes into us, gave me a sickening feeling and a cold perspiration," he told an acquaintance; "I felt weak around my knees—a sort of faintness and lack of strength in the joints of my legs, as if they would sink from under me." The feelings continued as he watched comrades fall from the "murderous" "snap, snap, crack, crack." However, he regained his composure and assumed a calmer demeanor, sensing he would do fine. "Seeing I was not killed at once, in spite of the noise, my knees recovered from their unpleasant limpness, and my mind gradually regained its balance and composure." Furthermore, the experience acted as an inoculation against future uneasiness and, he admitted, "I never afterwards felt these disturbing influences to the same degree."[59] Later, writing about his experiences at Port Hudson, John W. De Forest explained that fighting was not "delightful," but "just tolerable; you can put up with it; but you can't honestly praise it." The men who continued to fight did so in spite of all that made them hesitate. "The man who does not dread to die or to be mutilated is a lunatic," he wrote. "The man who, dreading these things still faces them for the sake of duty and honor is a hero."[60]

Men remained in the fight because they overcame their fear or because they simply forgot to be concerned about their lives. Some soldiers lost any sense of being in peril by ignoring the danger, perhaps assuming that it simply did not matter because their fates were in God's hands anyway, or perhaps because they were too young to know any better. Indianan George Squier recalled that despite his unnerving approach to his fight at Shiloh, he settled down to shooting away at the enemy "as cool and composed as if sitting down for a chat or shooting squirrels."[61] When Lieutenant John Q. A. Campbell fought at Iuka, Mississippi, in September 1862, he "was utterly unconscious of danger" and "felt no emotion nor sorrow" even as men dropped all around him. He later admitted, "There was a strange lack of *feeling* with me that followed me through the entire action. Out of battle and in a battle, I find myself two different beings."[62]

Battle Madness and Humor

While these men fought coolly, others were noticeably excited by the fighting. In one engagement, Kentucky Unionist Marcus Woodcock listened to men cheering "each other with their voices, whooping and hollering, laughing and talking, and some *cursing* and *swearing,* but shooting all the time." The men showed no fear; "some were looking as calm as death" just firing and loading as quickly as they could, but others "seemed to be wrought up to the highest pitch of anger, and every yell of pain they heard from our ranks caused them to utter curses and imprecations against the enemy, and to renew their exertions."[63] There were soldiers who fought in states that could only have been described as a kind of battle-induced sickness, blood lust, or even temporary insanity. At the First Bull Run, Elisha Hunt Rhodes believed that some of the men "became crazy from the excitement."[64] Confederate John Wickersham also recalled soldiers, full of blasphemies and "delirious" with excitement, who "become mad in the frenzy and excitement of combat."[65]

On May 12 and into the next day's early hours, the hand-to-hand fighting at Spotsylvania that resulted in some 12,000 casualties at what became known as the Bloody Angle surpassed and distorted anything that could be judged heroic. Yankee Wilbur Fisk attributed the fighting to "determined bravery," but such fierce and very personal face-to-face slaughter, with men shooting the enemy in the head or bayoneting them at close range while they climbed up on the bodies of dead and wounded comrades, could only have been the result of a kind of collective battle madness. When Fisk returned to the site after the fight had ended, he saw bodies piled one on top of the other, upward to five deep, on the Confederate side.[66]

Soldiers admitted to having wild sensations that some civilians might not consider reasonable in a sane person. In July 1864, after fighting near Atlanta, Confederate B. S. King confessed that in all of his battle experiences, when he saw a blue uniform, "a feeling more like a fiend than human takes possession of me and I only feel an intense desire to kill, to strike to the earth all that come in my reach."[67] And in September of that year, a New York engineer had indescribable feelings while enduring a Confederate attack, but he did admit that he "felt like rushing in among the rebs and slaying them."[68] "With what eagerness do we thirst for the blood of our enemy and tear down the fabric made in God's own image," Illinois colonel Frank Sherman wondered in June 1863. "I confess that there is something terribly intoxicating in battle when our sympathy for the mangled and torn of its destructive work is passed by without a thought or a feeling for the poor wretches writhing in mortal agony beneath our feet."[69]

In the midst of all the carnage of battle, some soldiers released tension by laughing at gruesome scenarios that most likely would have sobered them in civilian life. In 1862, during a battle in Louisiana, Captain John W. De Forest joked with his men.[70]

Night after battle: Hospital attendants—collecting the wounded after the engagement—within our lines near Hatchers run. (*Library of Congress*)

At Gettysburg, a lieutenant in Abner Small's regiment picked up a rifle with the ramrod still in the muzzle and blasted away, sending it out with a "crazy wiz that set the boys of his company to laughing." "It was strange to hear laughter there," Small admitted, "with dead men by."[71] Loyalist Kentuckian Marcus Woodcock recalled that some of his Unionist comrades "were pleased apparently, and seemed to laugh heartily at the occasional *tumble* of a rebel as if it were the gambols of a circus clown."[72]

Sometimes the humor in battle came more from the absurd situations in which some soldiers found themselves. On September 14, 1862, at the Battle of Crampton's Gap, a Vermont soldier climbing over a ledge fell some 20 feet into a crevice, where a Confederate soldier had accidentally preceded him. After an initial exchange of angry looks, the rebel "burst out laughing," noting that both soldiers were "in a fix." They agreed to wait out the fight, with the soldier of the victorious side taking the other man prisoner.[73]

WOUNDED IN BATTLE

There was also the surprise that men experienced in the middle of a battle when they discovered that "fatal" wounds were much less serious than they first had assumed. At Shiloh, Arkansan Henry Stanley fell over after feeling the impact of a bullet at his midriff. Stomach wounds generally were fatal, so he expected to die, only to realize that the ball had done its work on his mangled belt buckle.[74] When Confederate Johnny Green, also fighting at Shiloh, felt a bullet strike him in the chest, he was certain that he would be dead in seconds. Nevertheless, he survived. "The ball had passed through the stock of my gun, split on the iron ramrod of my gun," he reported, "and the other piece had passed through my jacket & buried itself in a little testament in my jacket pocket."[75]

Still, all men could not be so fortunate. The wounded, too, tried to describe the experience they had had on the battlefield. In August 1862 Yankee William Ray was hit in the back of the head by a ball and "spun around on my heels like a boys top and fell with my heels in the air and spun around for a few seconds" before he was able to make his way to the rear.[76] Oliver Wendell Holmes Jr. probably spoke for many of those men who survived their woundings when he reported that he felt "as if a horse had kicked me." He toppled and began to think of his death. Holmes was fortunate; he soon made it to a hospital for treatment.[77]

As with Holmes, other men lying wounded on the field thought of their immediate futures. At Frayser's Farm in June 1862, a Confederate soldier lay wounded, thinking he would die and end up in an unmarked grave, until a Yankee heeded his call for water.[78] Texan Robert Campbell received two leg wounds at the Second Bull Run and immediately began to think about "home—loved ones—Yankee prisons and a lingering death." His throat became parched while he lay on the ground, reminded of his thirst by the cries for water of the wounded and dying who were all around him. At nightfall, Georgians finally rescued him and transported him to a hospital.[79] Men such as Campbell suffered their wounds and would have to deal with their consequences in hospitals and perhaps later as invalids back home. As the war took a more cynical turn for some men, such wounds—serious but not deadly—became in their minds tickets home for a period of recovery away from the front.[80]

Men who survived battle joyfully wondered how they had come through the carnage unscathed. Some thanked God, as Pennsylvanian Milton McJunkin did after Fair Oaks. For McJunkin, "it was a miracle" that he had survived such bloody work, while for private John C. Arnold, another soldier from the Keystone State who survived fierce Virginia fighting in May 1864, "it was gods will that I should not be killed."[81] Abner Small was simply pleased with his own good fortune: "I felt a strange exaltation," he remarked of his survival of the battle at Fredericksburg. "I was horribly glad to be alive and unhurt." He could not help but be selfish in his satisfaction. "What mattered it if men around me had fallen, and shrieked in agony, pleaded for succor, cried and prayed and cursed! I was safe; dead at the moment to all human sympathy."[82]

AFRICAN AMERICANS IN COMBAT

African Americans, both slave and free, fought bravely in several battles, despite the initial lack of faith that many whites had in their abilities as soldiers. Black troops, however, experienced an added horror on the battlefield when they encountered Confederate soldiers who refused to accept their surrender. The official policy of the Confederacy labeled black men under arms as slave insurrectionists, to be returned to their masters, if captured. Government policy, however, turned out to be only one concern for black troops, formerly slaves or freemen. Confederate soldiers became particularly outraged when they encountered African Americans in blue uniforms during battle. Their cold-hearted hatred of armed black men meant that even when the heat of battle passed, they could not stop themselves from continuing to eliminate the dangerous threat. Black men carrying weapons struck fear into the hearts of white Southerners. Armed blacks challenged the very meaning of Southern society, made a mockery of the Confederate cause, humiliated all whites, and raised concerns of rape and destruction in white communities. Before the Battle of Olustee, Florida, in February 1864, Confederates hoped to show black troops that they had made a fatal error in raising their arms to the master race. An officer of Florida cavalry warned his men that slaves in Union ranks "have come to steal, pillage, run over the state and murder, kill and rape our wives, daughters and sweethearts."[83]

Consequently it was not unusual for Confederates to deal with black soldiers on the battlefield in the harshest manner as well as the white men who encouraged them and fought along side of them, even if they surrendered. At Fort Pillow, Tennessee, on April 12, 1864, Confederate troopers under Nathan Bedford Forrest massacred both black and white soldiers after they had surrendered. "They called them out and shot them down," reported Ransome Anderson, a former slave turned soldier, who served with the heavy artillery at the fort.[84] Both Confederates and white Union officers confirmed such treatment at Fort Pillow and elsewhere. One Confederate who had been at Fort Pillow reported that "the poor deluded negroes would run up to our men fall upon their knees and with uplifted hands scream for mercy but they were ordered to their feet and then shot down." He also noted that "the whitte men fared little better."[85]

Confederates could not miss noticing black troops arrayed against them and paid particular attention to them at the Petersburg crater debacle. There, according to Lieutenant Colonel Delevan Bates, commanding the 30th U.S. Colored Infantry, "many a dusky warrior had his brains knocked out with the butt of a musket, or was run thru with a bayonet while vainly imploring for mercy."[86] Another officer of the 30th, Captain David Proctor, reported that he "saw bayonets plunged into colored men who had surrendered," while a Confederate later reported witnessing a rebel soldier fire point blank into a wounded black soldier's stomach. It was only one of many "bloody tragedies" of which he later learned Confederates, who "seemed infuriated at the idea of having to fight negroes," perpetrated at the Crater.[87] Despite these outrages and government threats to return them to slavery, members of the U.S. Colored Troops ended up in prison pens, such as the infamous Andersonville, Georgia, stockade, along with their captured white counterparts.

VETERANS AND COMBAT

Soldiers who survived the horrors of combat evolved into veterans, who became accustomed to the danger of battle and the unpleasant duties it involved, understanding that it was their job to risk death while they did their best to kill the enemy even as they approached their work in a more matter-of-fact manner. Men who once had been overly concerned about what the generals had in store for them became unconcerned about the strategies of their superiors. Chaplain Twichell believed that over two years in the army had "bred an indifference concerning destination and prospect, to which in my first campaign I was an utter stranger." As a new soldier, he had "fretted and wondered and worried, anxious to find out what was brewing—time, place, why and wherefore, as if, forsooth, it was at all necessary or expedient that I should be in the counsels of our chiefs." As an old soldier, he realized that most of the things over which he had worried were well beyond his control. He had lost his curiosity about his military future. "I have lain down under my blanket and slept without knowing or asking the geographical locality of the bivouac," he admitted, leaving everything to Providence.[88]

Novice soldiers who once endured the nerve-racking moments before a fight came to approach battle with a similar degree of indifference. In 1862 New Jersey officer Peter Vredenburg assured his father that he could withstand the tension while awaiting battle because he had already "experienced the hour before the battle several times."[89]

Some men, such as Alabaman James Williams, who confessed so to his wife, actually enjoyed this "strange exciting life." The danger commensurate with it did not bother Williams. "I sleep well at night *as* I used to do," he probably unwisely admitted to her, "and am happy too."[90] Others believed that battle experience had made them not only better soldiers, but also "wiser and better" men, as Pennsylvanian Milton McJunkin informed his mother.[91]

Men who learned that they had little control over the enemy's bullets came to accept the consequences of battle with less emotion than when they had been recruits. After the bloodbath at Spotsylvania, in which so many of his friends and acquaintances had died, Vredenburgh confessed to his father that the prospects of renewed fighting failed to disturb him. "All I can say," he informed his father, "is that we have lived in the most intense state of excitement for so long now if we were certain the enemy would charge us in five minutes I would go on to finish this letter without giving them a second thought." A few days later, he told his mother that with death all around him, "it makes it seem but a short step from this to the next world." The men, consequently, became fatalistic. "You have no idea with what perfect indifference everyone seems to regard life out here," he admitted.[92]

One New Yorker recognized a hardening in his comrades as they faced Lee's army at Petersburg. "They do not care but little for bullets than they would for snow balls," he claimed.[93] In August 1864 Arkansan veteran Captain Alex Spence identified a similar condition in his regiment, which, over the past three months, had been under fire some 50 days. "We are used to getting shot at," even if the men did not consider it a pleasant experience. Some soldiers, including Spence, also became indifferent to killing the hated enemy. In September 1864 Spence reported to his mother and father that he "had the pleasure the other day of making two Yankees 'bite the dust' & got me a fine hat."[94]

Dead Federal soldiers on battlefield at Gettysburg, Pennsylvania. (*Library of Congress*)

Not only did experienced soldiers harbor little sentiment for dead enemies, they also could become indifferent to the comrades and friends falling next to them, or at least ignore them until they had time to reflect on the battle. They accepted the carnage of battle with less emotion than they had in the past because it had become an unavoidable consequence of their efforts to get the job done. It might have been a sensibility that was especially necessary for those men who worked with the dying. As Union surgeon Daniel M. Holt explained, "Had anyone told me a year ago that I could look upon such horrors and feel no mental disturbances, I should not have believed them." "Yet so it is," he admitted. "I pass over putrefying bodies of the dead...and feel as little unconcerned as though they were two hundred pigs."[95] Confederate hospital steward John Apperson would have understood the Yankee doctor's feelings. Men continued to be jolly, he noticed, while other workers carried bodies to the "dead house" because "no lifeless frame can touch upon the feelings of the hardened soldier."[96] Even a caring individual like Chaplain Twichell admitted after Gettysburg to being able to stomach things that "would have driven me crazy a year ago."[97] But when some veterans believed they had seen enough to turn their souls cold, they could find themselves shaken out of their indifference by the next scene of carnage that they witnessed. Looking over the "swollen, black and hideously unnatural" remains at Gettysburg, Union soldier Wilbur Fisk concluded that the sight was "ghastly beyond description." "I thought I had become hardened to almost anything," he reported, "but I cannot say I ever wish to see another sight like I saw on the battlefield of Gettysburg."[98]

No matter how sensitive or insensitive to bloodshed and gore, many a soldier accepted such scenes, carrying on with the same grim fatalism that infected Vrendenburgh's New Jersey comrades. Victories on the battlefield did not bring an end to the conflict, so some soldiers failed to give much thought to what might come in the future if the war ever did end. New York veteran Frank Wilkeson, who presented a very bleak picture of his wartime experiences, recalled that men were "depressed in spirits" as they prepared to fight at Cold Harbor in June 1864. Veterans who had fought with McClellan were now "sad" and "indifferent." Some of these men, Wilkeson later reported, were "so tired of the strain on their nerves that they wished they were dead and their troubles over."[99]

Men like Wilkeson and his despondent comrades could turn up in any regiment at any given time, but there were plenty of veterans who wished to survive the war. They continued to fight, but with more prudence than they had known as recruits. Caution, to these soldiers, was not cowardice. At the outset of the war, men viewed soldiers who were overly concerned about their personal safety as cowards, but experience made them all the wiser. By 1864, soldiers who failed to take precautions, such as hiding behind trees or removing markings of rank to discourage enemy snipers, were the fools. Indeed, veterans with some battle experience became cautious as the war dragged on, especially if they were Yankees whose terms of enlistment were nearly completed.

Experienced soldiers also came to believe that they knew as well as any general how to judge the prospects of successfully attacking fortified lines or when to call an end to a fight. There were a few occasions when troops simply refused to charge daunting fortifications, as did some Union soldiers during an attack on Vicksburg, who disobeyed their officers' orders to charge while they did their best to avoid Confederate fire.[100] And a Confederate veteran recalled that it was only normal for sensible, experienced men to seek "any shelter within reach." He also noted that such men knew that it was best not to risk themselves when "satisfied that they could not accomplish their purpose."[101]

By some standards, such men were cowards; other observers were less harsh in their judgment. In May 1864, during the Battle of the Wilderness in Virginia, Union

Wounded soldiers escaping from the burning woods of the Wilderness, May 6, 1864 by Alfred R. Waud. (*Library of Congress*)

veterans decided to retreat and did so in good order. "They were not running, nor pale, nor scared, nor had they thrown away their guns," reported Union staff officer Theodore Lyman. "They had fought all they meant to fight for the present, and there was an end of it!"[102] As a Union surgeon explained, the citizen volunteer approaches risk with an appropriate degree of thoughtfulness: "he knows just as well as his commander, and sometimes better, when he can advance, and when he can fall back; in other words, when he can win, or when he must lose."[103]

NOTES

1. Bernard A. Olsen, ed., Upon the Tented Field (Red Bank, NJ: Historic Projects, 1993), 183.

2. Rufus R. Dawes, A Full Blown Yankee of the Iron Brigade: Service with the Sixth Wisconsin Volunteers, ed. Alan T. Nolan (Lincoln: University of Nebraska Press, 1999), 81.

3. Olsen, Upon the Tented Field, 183.

4. William L. Shea and Terrance J. Winschel, Vicksburg Is the Key: The Struggle for the Mississippi River (Lincoln: University of Nebraska Press, 2003), 143.

5. Stewart J. Petrie, MD, ed., *Letters and Journal of a Civil War Surgeon* (Raleigh, NC: Pentland Press, 1998), 59–60.

6. Edmund J. Raus Jr., *Banners South: A Northern Community at War* (Kent, OH: Kent State University Press, 2005), 36.

7. Gordon C. Rhea, *Cold Harbor: Grant and Lee, May 26–June 3, 1864* (Baton Rouge: Louisiana State University Press, 2002), 331–32.

8. Julie Doyle, John David Smith, and Richard M. McMurry, eds., *This Wilderness of War: The Civil War Letters of George W. Squier, Hoosier Volunteer* (Knoxville: University of Tennessee Press, 1998), 10–11; document 7 in John F. Marszalek and Clay Williams, "Mississippi Soldiers in the Civil War," *Mississippi History Now,* http://mshistory.k12.ms.us/index.php?s=extra&id=183.

9. Robert L. Bee, ed., *The Boys from Rockville: Civil War Narratives of Sgt. Benjamin Hirst, Company D, 14th Connecticut Volunteers* (Knoxville: University of Tennessee Press, 1998), 73–75.

10. John G. Barrett, ed., *Yankee Rebel: The Civil War Journal of Edmund DeWitt Patterson* (Knoxville: University of Tennessee Press, 2004), 19.

11. Ted Tunnell, ed., *Carpetbagger from Vermont: The Autobiography of Marshall Harvey Twitchell* (Baton Rouge: Louisiana State University Press, 1989), 37.

12. Harold Adams Small, ed., *The Road to Richmond: The Civil War Memoirs of Major Abner R. Small of the Sixteenth Maine Volunteers: Together with the Diary That He Kept When He Was a Prisoner of War* (New York: Fordham University Press, 2000), 21.

13. Document 7 in Marszalek and Williams, "Mississippi Soldiers in the Civil War."

14. Small, *Road to Richmond,* 185.

15. Barrett, *Yankee Rebel,* 29.

16. Watkins, *"Company Aytch,"* 26.

17. Document 7 in Marszalek and Williams, "Mississippi Soldiers in the Civil War."

18. Stephen W. Sears, ed., *Mr. Dunn Browne's Experiences in the Army: The Civil War Letters of Samuel W. Fiske* (New York: Fordham University Press, 1998), 7.

19. Doyle et al., *This Wilderness of War,* 10–11.

20. Watkins, *"Company Aytch,"* 27.

21. Frank Wilkeson, *Turned Inside Out: Recollections of a Private Soldier in the Army of the Potomac* (Lincoln: University of Nebraska Press, 1997), 190.

22. George R. Agassiz, ed., *Meade's Headquarters, 1863–1865: Letters of Colonel Theodore Lyman from the Wilderness to Appomattox* (Boston: Massachusetts Historical Society, 1922), 89.

23. Sears, *Mr. Dunn Browne's Experiences,* 9.

24. G. Ward Hubbs, ed., *Voices from Company D: Diaries by the Greensboro Guards, Fifth Alabama Infantry Regiment, Army of Northern Virginia* (Athens: University of Georgia Press, 2003), 161.

25. Susan Williams Benson, ed., *Berry Benson's Civil War Book: Memoirs of a Confederate Scout and Sharpshooter* (Athens: University of Georgia Press, 1992), 22–23.

26. Sears, *Mr. Dunn Browne's Experiences,* 9.

27. Hubbs, *Voices from Company D,* 161–62.

28. Small, *Road to Richmond,* 22.

29. Emil Rosenblatt and Ruth Rosenblatt, eds., *Hard Marching Every Day: The Civil War Letters of Private Wilbur Fisk, 1861–1865* (Lawrence: University Press of Kansas, 1992), 267–68.

30. Benson, *Berry Benson's Civil War Book,* 22.

31. Lawrence Frederick Kohl, with Margaret Cossè Richard, eds., *Irish Green and Union Blue: The Civil War Letters of Peter Welsh* (New York: Fordham University Press, 1986), 11, 81–82 (quotation), 156–58.

32. Kenneth W. Noe, ed., *A Southern Boy in Blue: The Memoir of Marcus Woodcock, 9th Kentucky Infantry (U.S.A.)* (Knoxville: University of Tennessee Press, 1996), 132–33.

33. Philip N. Racine, ed., *"Unspoiled Heart": The Journal of Charles Mattocks of the 17th Maine* (Knoxville: University of Tennessee Press, 1994), 36.

34. Barrett, *Yankee Rebel,* 33.

35. Small, *Road to Richmond,* 184.

36. Warren Lee Goss, *Recollections of a Private: A Story of the Army of the Potomac* (Scituate, MA: Digital Scanning, 2002), 115.

37. Claire E. Swedberg, ed., *Three Years with the 92d Illinois: The Civil War Diary of John M. King* (Mechanicsburg, PA: Stackpole Books, 1999), 117.

38. John M. Follett to wife, May 5, 1863, Follett Brothers Letters, eHistory, Ohio State University, Columbus, http://ehistory.osu.edu/osu/sources/letters/follett_brothers/.

39. Small, *Road to Richmond,* 22, 184.

40. John R. Sellers, ed., *A People at War: Civil War Manuscripts from the Holdings of the Library of Congress* (Alexandria, VA: Chadwyck-Heakey, 1989–1990), Jasper N. Barritt to brother, April 2, 1864, reel 3.

41. Charles Swift Northen III, ed., *All Right Let Them Come: The Civil War Diary of an East Tennessee Confederate* (Knoxville: University of Tennessee Press, 2003), 93–95.

42. Edward B. Williams, ed., *Rebel Brothers: The Civil War Letter of the Truehearts* (College Station: Texas A&M University Press), 126.

43. DeWitt Boyd Stone Jr., ed., *Wandering to Glory: Confederate Veterans Remember Evans' Brigade* (Columbia: University of South Carolina Press, 2002), 212.

44. William C. Davis and Meredith Swentor, eds., *Bluegrass Confederate: The Headquarters Diary of Edward O. Guerrant* (Baton Rouge: Louisiana State University Press, 1999), 90.

45. Ibid., 92.

46. Mark De Wolfe Howe, ed., *Touched with Fire: Civil War Letters and Diary of Oliver Wendell Holmes, Jr., 1861–1864* (New York: Fordham University Press, 2000), 50.

47. Noe, *A Southern Boy in Blue,* 198–99.

48. Emily N. Radigan, ed., *"Desolating This Fair Country": The Civil War Diary and Letters of Lt. Henry C. Lyon, 34th New York* (Jefferson, NC: McFarland, 1999), 121.

49. Bee, *Boys from Rockville,* 148–52.

50. Small, *Road to Richmond,* 185.

51. Sellers, *A People at War,* D. R. Larned to sister, June 4, 1864, Daniel Reed Larned Correspondence, reel 60.

52. Davis and Swentor, *Bluegrass Confederate,* 92.

53. Robert Hunt Rhodes, ed., *All for the Union: The Civil War Diary and Letters of Elisha Hunt Rhodes* (New York: Vintage Books, 1992), 26.

54. Watkins, *"Company Aytch,"* 202.

55. Mary E. Kellog, comp., *Army Life of an Illinois Soldier, Including a Day-by-Day Record of Sherman's March to the Sea: The Letters and Diary of Charles W. Wills* (Carbondale: Southern Illinois University Press, 1996), 68.

56. John M. Follett to wife, May 5, 1863, Follett Brothers Letters, History, Ohio State University, Columbus, http://ehistory.osu.edu/osu/sources/letters/follet_brothers/.

57. Robert Cruikshank to wife, May 8, 1863, Robert Cruikshank Letters, eHistory, Ohio State University, Columbus, http://ehistory.osu.edu/osu/sources/letters/cruikshank/.

58. Gordon C. Rhea, *Cold Harbor: Grant and Lee, May 26–June 3, 1864* (Baton Rouge: Louisiana State University Press, 2002), 233.

59. Goss, *Recollections of a Private,* 39.

60. John William De Forest, *A Volunteer's Adventures: A Union Captain's Record of the Civil War,* ed. James H. Croushore (Baton Rouge: Louisiana State University Press, 1996), 123–24.

61. Doyle et al., *This Wilderness of War,* 11–12.

62. Mark Grimsley and Todd D. Miller, eds., *The Union Must Stand: The Civil War Diary of John Quincy Adams Campbell, Fifth Iowa Volunteer Infantry* (Knoxville: University of Tennessee Press, 2000), 60.

63. Noe, *A Southern Boy in Blue,* 132–33.

64. Rhodes, *All for the Union,* 33.

65. Kathleen Gorman, ed., *Boy Soldier of the Confederacy: The Memoir of Johnnie Wickersham* (Carbondale: Southern Illinois University Press, 2006), 98.

66. J. Tracy Powers, *Lee's Miserables: Life in the Army of Northern Virginia from the Wilderness to Appomattox* (Chapel Hill: University of North Carolina Press, 1998), 26–27; Rosenblatt and Rosenblatt, *Hard Marching Every Day,* 221.

67. Tammy Harden Galloway, ed., *Dear Old Roswell: The Civil War Letters of the King Family of Roswell, Georgia* (Macon, GA: Mercer University Press, 2003), 81.

68. Anita Palladino, ed., *Diary of a Yankee Engineer: The Civil War Story of John H. Westervelt, Engineer, 1st New York Volunteer Engineer Corps* (New York: Fordham University Press, 1997), 173.

69. C. Knight Aldrich, ed., *Quest for a Star: The Civil War Letters and Diaries of Colonel Francis T. Sherman of the 88th Illinois* (Knoxville: University of Tennessee Press, 1999), 46.

70. De Forest, *A Volunteer's Adventures,* 61.

71. Small, *Road to Richmond,* 100.

72. Noe, *A Southern Boy in Blue,* 132–33.

73. Goss, *Recollections of a Private,* 99–100.

74. Joseph Allen Frank and George Reeves, *"Seeing the Elephant": Raw Recruits at the Battle of Shiloh* (Westport, CT: Greenwood Press, 1989), 115.

75. A. D. Kirwin, ed., *Johnny Green of the Orphan Brigade: The Journal of a Confederate Soldier,* new ed. (Lexington: University Press of Kentucky, 2002), 31–32.

76. Lance Herdegen and Sherry Murphy, eds., *Four Years with the Iron Brigade: The Civil War Journal of William Ray, Company F, Seventh Wisconsin Volunteers* (Cambridge, MA: Da Capo Press, 2002), 139–41.

77. Howe, *Touched with Fire,* 23.

78. Barrett, *Yankee Rebel,* 52–54.

79. George Skoch and Mark W. Perkins, eds., *Lone Star Confederate: A Gallant and Good Soldier of the Fifth Texas Infantry* (College Station: Texas A&M University Press, 2003), 79.

80. Larry J. Daniel, *Soldiering in the Army of Tennessee: A Portrait of Life in a Confederate Army* (Chapel Hill: University of North Carolina Press, 1991), 163.

81. Richard Sauers, ed., *The Bloody 85th: The Letters of Milton McJunkin, a Western Pennsylvania Soldier in the Civil War* (Daleville, VA: Schroeder, 2000), 39; Sellers, *A People at War,* John C. Arnold to wife and family, May 28, 1864, John Carvel Arnold Letters, reel 1.

82. Small, *Road to Richmond,* 68.

83. Quoted in George S. Burkhardt, *Confederate Rage, Yankee Wrath: No Quarter in the Civil War* (Carbondale: Southern Illinois University Press, 2007), 88.

84. Donald Yacovone, ed., *Freedom's Journey: African American Voices of the Civil War* (Chicago: Lawrence Hill Books, 2004), 147.

85. Quoted in Noah Andre Trudeau, *Like Men of War: Black Troops in the Civil War, 1862–1865* (Boston: Little, Brown, 1998), 166.

86. Quoted in ibid., 246.

87. Keith Wilson, ed., *Honor in Command: Lt. Freeman S. Bowley's Civil War Service in the 30th United States Colored Infantry* (Gainesville: University Press of Florida, 2006), 153–54.

88. Peter Messent and Steve Courtney, eds., *The Civil War Letters of Joseph Hopkins Twichell* (Athens: University of Georgia Press, 2006), 269.

89. Olsen, *Upon the Tented Field,* 29.

90. John Kent Folmar, ed., *From That Terrible Field: Civil War Letters of James M. Williams, Twenty-first Alabama Infantry Volunteers* (Tuscaloosa: University of Alabama Press, 1981), 56–57.

91. Richard Sauers, *Bloody 85th,* 88–90.

92. Olsen, *Upon the Tented Field,* 236, 237.

93. Robert F. Harris and John Niflot, comps., *Dear Sister: The Civil War Letters of the Brothers Gould* (Westport, CT: Praeger, 1998), 130.

94. Mark K. Christ, ed., *Getting Used to Being Shot At: The Spence Family Civil War Letters* (Fayetteville: University of Arkansas Press, 2002), 97, 103.

95. James M. Greiner, Janet L. Coryell, and James R. Smither, eds., *A Surgeon's Civil War: The Letters and Diary of Daniel M. Holt, M.D.* (Kent, OH: Kent State University Press, 1994), 21.

96. John Herbert Roper, ed., *Repairing the "March of Mars": The Civil War Diaries of John Samuel Apperson, Hospital Steward in the Stonewall Brigade, 1861–1865* (Macon, GA: Mercer University Press, 2001), 333.

97. Messent and Courtney, *Civil War Letters of Joseph Hopkins Twichell,* 255.

98. Rosenblatt and Rosenblatt, *Hard Marching Every Day,* 116.

99. Frank Wilkeson, *Turned Inside Out,* 127.

100. Michael B. Ballard, *Vicksburg: The Campaign that Opened the Mississippi* (Chapel Hill: University of North Carolina Press, 2004), 347.

101. Carlton McCarthy, *Detailed Minutiae of Soldier Life in the Army of Northern Virginia, 1861–1865* (Lincoln: University of Nebraska Press, 1993), 115.

102. Agassiz, *Meade's Headquarters,* 95.

103. John H. Brinton, *Personal Memoirs of John H. Brinton, Civil War Surgeon, 1861–1865* (Carbondale: Southern Illinois University Press, 1996), 219.

8 THE AFTERMATH OF BATTLE

DEFEAT

Soldiers who had survived battle unscathed could not spend too much time dwelling on their good luck in the immediate aftermath of the fight. Hungry, thirsty, and tired, they had to answer to their basic needs. They also had to deal with the consequences of their work, which meant coping with defeat and retreat or accepting victory and whatever that meant for the moment. Defeated men, exhausted by their activities, drew on the last reservoirs of their strength to remove themselves from harm's way. After some battles, men, motivated by fear of capture or the possibility of becoming one of the dead or wounded, turned the retreat into a route, as the Union forces did at the First Battle of Bull Run "without order or discipline."[1] On other occasions, commanders orchestrated orderly and skillful retrograde movements that saved their armies from further harm and for future fighting. Lee's retreat from Gettysburg was a significant success, for example, and one Confederate veteran remembered with some pride Joseph Johnston's retreats in the Atlanta campaign, conducted with "sagacity" that "met and foiled every effort to cut us off."[2] Then there were the "organized skedaddle[s]" that were somewhere between the two. Charles Mattocks of the 17th Maine noted that in the aftermath of Chancellorsville, the men from the Army of the Potomac withdrew across the Rappahannock without "the least sign of panic or demoralization, nothing but a tired look." Nevertheless, Mattocks could only have used *organized* in the most charitable sense. "Regiments returned to their old camps by the mere handfuls," Mattocks observed, and "men were allowed to please their own fancy as to speed."[3]

Defeated soldiers often harbored feelings of embarrassment and humiliation. For Mattocks, the retreat across the Rappahannock was "a fact which ought to be draped in mourning."[4] After the first Bull Run, Abner Small witnessed retreating soldiers "plodding heavily and panting," who were clearly frustrated by their failure to defeat the rebels. The men were angry. "Every now and then," Small noted, "some man would take his gun by the barrel and mash the stock against a tree."[5]

The hardships of traveling away from a victorious enemy in bad weather and over rough ground added to the defeated army's misery, but even as they retreated, the beaten soldiers began to ask why things turned out they way they did. In June 1862

Massachusetts lieutenant Charles Brewster complained about the "pitiable plight" of the defeated Yankees after Seven Pines, but also tried to make sense of it all. Despondent, wet, and muddy, he bemoaned the human loss in the battle, but he also suggested that the Northern defeat was not entirely due to the soldiers' lack of courage or competence. "Oh if we could only fight these Rebels once, where we could have sight of them, we would avenge the dead of Saturday," he lamented, "but I don't but we have always fight them in woods and swamps."[6]

Other soldiers tried to understand their defeat by looking for external factors that would absolve themselves from appearing as if they had been the cause of the loss, and bad officers frequently bore the brunt of their criticisms. After Shiloh, Confederates blamed their lack of experience and training for their defeat or found that their officers had been lacking in some way.[7] Captain A. C. Hills scoffed at the notion that McClellan's strategic brilliance saved his army on the Virginia peninsula, pronouncing that "the unsurpassed bravery of our troops saved the army from utter annihilation."[8] Yankees who had fought at Fredericksburg correctly blamed their commander, considering it "madness and murder to continue in command one who had demonstrated his lack of ability so plainly as had General Burnside."[9]

Confederates, when admitting to "reverses," salved their bruised morale by blaming defeat not on any weakness in their ranks but on the enemy's overwhelming resources. Arkansan Alex Spence reported to the home folks that at one point in the Atlanta campaign, in September 1864, the Yankees overpowered his brigade because of their superior numbers. "We fought about ten to our one," he explained, and "of course were driven from our trenches."[10] Nevertheless, real defeat was not possible, at least for the soldiers from Arkansas and Texas with whom Spence fought. "*They* will be Killed or captured," he confidently predicted, "but not whipped."[11]

And then there were Confederates who avoided dealing with the emotional consequences of battlefield failure simply by turning defeat into victory. Shiloh, for one Georgian, was a victory.[12] Augustus Mecklin, a Mississippian who had fought at Shiloh, tallied up a descriptive balance sheet of the battle and agreed. Although the Yankees retained possession of the field, "All things compared we have gain[ed] a dearly fought victory."[13] Later, in July 1863, Edgeworth Bird explained to his wife, Sallie, that Gettysburg was an "*unfortunate victory.*" "We did whip them at Gettysburg," he assured Sallie, "but at an awful loss, and the heavy ordnance was all exhausted."[14]

Defeat could indeed be disheartening, and losses depleted morale for both Southern and Northern soldiers. After Fredericksburg, Yankee veteran Warren Lee Goss recalled, "Gloom pervaded every rank."[15] And after Vicksburg, Confederates in the western theater became "very low spirited." Robert Patrick, a Louisianan clerk, noted that he "never saw such depression." In early August, he reported that "desertions are more frequent than ever, and they leave by whole companies, officers and all."[16] But some men overcame the initial problems of defeat by looking forward to having another go at the enemy, wishing for revenge and assuming that they would eventually triumph at some point in the future. In March 1862 Arkansan T. F. Spence expressed sentiments shared by many men at one point or another during the war when he concluded that "the tide will turn in the next *Battle*."[17]

VICTORY

It was only later in the war that Union commanders inaugurated the relentless campaign, paying little attention to old practices of regrouping and resupplying the army after a hard battle. Otherwise, victors found it difficult to pursue the enemy, let alone capture a defeated army. Victorious armies rarely had the energy or resources to continue the attack after a hard fight or, early in the war, the discipline to do so. Also, the confusing nature of battle disrupted military organization; even victorious soldiers became separated from their companies and regiments during the fight and had to spend time searching for their comrades.

The need for fresh intelligence or the problems caused by uncooperative weather hindered advances, but winning soldiers also suffered from exhaustion, hunger, and thirst. Northern-born Confederate Edmund DeWitt Patterson was pleased with his army's victory at Gaines's Mill in June 1862 but was spent for his effort. "I did not know how tired I was until the excitement of the battle was over," he wrote in his diary. "I was almost too weak to stand, and my cheeks as hollow as though emaciated by a long spell of sickness. I dropped down under a bush and slept such a sleep as comes only to a tired soldier after a battle." A drink of whiskey and breakfast the next morning helped set him to rights.[18]

Successful armies that did not rush after the enemy remained near the sight of their triumph for at least a little while. While there, soldiers looked for wounded comrades, buried the dead, and hunted for souvenirs for themselves and the folks back home. For victorious Confederates, battlefields in fact yielded more than trophies; there they found much needed supplies. Aside from gathering up spoils, soldiers had the opportunity to view the human cost of victory, while pondering the meaning of their awful work after the excitement of the fight had passed. As Connecticut's Samuel Fiske reported after Antietam, "The excitement of battle comes in the day of it, but the horrors of it two or three days later."[19] William Child, assistant surgeon of the Fifth New Hampshire, felt the same way after Antietam, concluding that the country's sins must have been significant to deserve such punishment. "The days after the battle are a thousand times worse than the day of the battle," he advised, "and the physical pain is not the greatest pain suffered."[20]

THE DEAD

Iowan Cyrus Boyd observed the field at Iuka, with its dead bodies and ground covered with "*creeping worms,*" and pronounced it "one of the most *horrible* places I was ever in."[21] Confederate diarist Edmund DeWitt Patterson pronounced the consequences of slaughter at Fredericksburg "indescribable." His words, he realized, were simply "too barren" and "powerless to convey to the mind a picture that can in any way compare with the reality."[22] But for some, victory eased the horrors of the battlefield. After comforting his "most intimate friend" in his death throes, Marcus Woodcock latter recalled that he was filled with conflicting emotions. Nevertheless, he admitted, "I felt *good;* and despite the many suffering companions that were lying around I could not avoid occasional remarks of rejoicing at our success." Despite his attempts to focus on the human cost, he still realized that he "felt satisfied because we had whipped the rebels."[23]

Soldiers in control of the battlefield had to cope with the physically and emotionally difficult task of disposing of dead animals and burying those men who had perished in the fight, a task that reminded them of their own tenuous existence. Soldiers identified bodies of their friends and buried them in individual graves when circumstances allowed, but mass graves were common resting places for the battle dead. After the fighting had ended at Shiloh, Iowan Cyrus Boyd witnessed union soldiers tossing dead Confederates into a gully for burial. "Men are in on top of the *dead* straightening out their legs and arms and tramping down so as to make the hole contain as many as possible," he

Burying the dead at Fredericksburg, Virginia, after the Wilderness Campaign, May 1864. (*Library of Congress*)

reported. "Other men on the hillside had ropes with a noose on one end and they would attach this to a mans foot or his head and haul him down to the hollow and roll him in."[24] After the Battle of the Crater at Petersburg, Confederates simply shoveled dirt onto the dead.[25] Such impersonal treatment of deceased friend and foe could upset some men. At Shiloh, Union soldiers found it distressing to watch the dead roughly handled, as burial details piled the bodies into mass graves.[26]

After the fight, the victors often camped near or, in some cases, on the field, not necessarily the best location for respite and the rebuilding of worn spirits, but certainly a location that promoted reflection. In September 1862 Benjamin Hirst and the rest of the raw 14th Connecticut camped on the South Mountain battlefield and had a rude introduction to the consequences of war. "Awoke on the Battle field of yesterday, and getting some Coffee, began to look around," Hirst recorded in his diary, continuing that he "soon saw War without romance." All around him were the broken bodies of soldiers, "their heads shattered to Pieces, others with their bowels protruding while others had lost legs and Arms." He concluded, "What my feelings were, I cannot describe, but I hoped to God never to see such another sight." Hirst soon did, and the Sunday after Antietam, he attended religious services, where "every one wore a More Sober Face than I had observed before."[27]

THE WOUNDED

Men who suffered wounds in battle endured further discomfort and pain as they made their way from the field to nearby regimental hospitals, and then perhaps to general hospitals farther in the rear. Some soldiers earned furloughs, allowing them to travel home to recover and become fit to fight again. Along the way, these men encountered the inadequacies of nineteenth-century medical practice, army bureaucracy, and incompetent surgeons and attendants as well as helpful friends, heroic doctors, careful women nurses, and good Samaritans who helped them survive their ordeals.

The problems concerning the recovery of soldiers wounded in combat began as soon as shot and shell struck down the men. Wounded combatants dragged themselves to the rear or had help from comrades, musicians, stretcher bearers, or infirmary and ambulance corpsmen. Sometimes men were rescued by soldiers who risked their lives to retrieve the wounded, but frequently, hurt soldiers did not receive immediate assistance because of battlefield circumstances. Often the battle continued around them, or their comrades retreated and left them behind, or a lull in the fighting only proved to be temporary.

Thus many a soldier had to endure lying between "two fires," which, according to New Yorker Theodore Ayrault Dodge, who was wounded on the first day of Gettysburg, "was not a pleasant position."[28] After Gettysburg, for example, Union chaplain Joseph Twichell located five wounded men "who had lain two nights on the ground—three of them with broken legs—suffering God alone knows how much."[29] At Spotsylvania, soldiers were pinned down under dead comrades and enemies; "they would raise 2 arms only or turn their bodies showing they were still alive."[30] Later, in 1864, Michigander Joseph McConnell spent all day on the field before Petersburg, with both legs broken. Neither his friends nor his enemies were willing to expose themselves to fire to attempt to rescue him. It was only when darkness came that his comrades located him.[31]

After the fighting ended, other men in McConnell's position waited on the field in pain, hungry and thirsty, hoping someone would at last come to their assistance and help to relieve their suffering. After a fight in Louisiana in April 1864, for example, wounded soldiers "had fallen in lonely and secluded spots, had not as yet been found or given any help, and were suffering a veritable martyrdom."[32] Even the visible wounded had to await assistance as order came to the confusion of the battlefield. New Yorker Newton Colby, who rode through the Antietam field two days after the battle, could do little but feel pity for the mass of wounded rebels still lying about begging for his assistance. He could not escape, however, witnessing the human cost of victory. Colby told his father of a poor Confederate "with one side of his face including one eye and ear—blown off—trying to eat a hard cracker with the well side of his mouth!"[33]

Under better circumstances, trained Union ambulance corpsmen and Confederate infirmary corpsmen helped the disabled soldiers to nearby field hospitals as best they could, using stretchers, ambulances, and mule litters. As the war progressed, there were improvements made in removing men from the battlefield, but circumstances throughout the war often required improvisation. Joseph McConnell's friends put him on some tent cloth and dragged him to safety.[34] Men also used blankets as stretchers when nothing else was available.[35] After the battle of Ball's Bluff, two soldiers had nothing available that resembled a stretcher but still were able to help the severely wounded Oliver Wendell Holmes Jr. to the rear. They made an "armchair" for Holmes by crossing "their hands in such a way that" he "could sit on 'em & put" his "arms around their necks."[36]

Retreat after a defeat was especially hard on the wounded. In the case of McClellan's withdraw on the Virginia peninsula, wounded Yankees "grasped their muskets and hobbled off" away from the enemy. These distressed men found help from comrades and teamsters, but many men were left to their own devices. "Some of the younger and helplessly wounded soldiers cried like children, deploring their fate, after having fought so hard," while they cursed "McClellan and the doctors for not taking them away in ambulances." Men "limped on sticks or improvised crutches," while more men "staggered

Zouave ambulance crew demonstrating removal of wounded soldiers from the field. (*Library of Congress*)

forward, resting every few steps to adjust their bloody bandages." "Stimulated by fear of the enemy," the men "pressed on," but many of them finally could go no farther, falling out to become captives of the pursuing Confederates.[37]

During a battle, or shortly thereafter, wounded soldiers under the best of circumstances received treatment on the field or close behind their lines. Soldiers made their way to a regimental field hospital, which could have been nothing more than a sheltered open area just removed from the fighting, or to a hospital structure that was somewhat more removed from the fighting, at locations usually selected by regimental surgeons. There the men continued to suffer as they waited for the attention of a surgeon. After the first Bull Run, hospital steward John S. Apperson of Virginia saw men "filed like so many precious brutes in porches, tents, houses & wherever they could be lain."[38] After South Mountain, wounded Wisconsin soldier James P. Sullivan found himself lying in a barnyard with hundreds of friends and enemies, "some of them enduring fearful misery."[39]

Doctors and Hospitals

Armies, however, did their best to find the wounded some immediate shelter when possible, so that in the wake of Gettysburg, "the whole country for 10 miles is one vast Hospital. Every Barn & almost every house has been appropriated fo[r] hospitall purposes."[40] All things considered, hospitals near the battlefields were unpleasant places that entailed medical and military risk for the patients. Chaplains did what they could to help alleviate some of the suffering. New York chaplain Joseph Hopkins Twichell assisted wounded men off the battlefield and to nearby hospitals after Chancellorsville but continued to tend to them through the night. "We passed nearly the whole night in arranging them on their stretchers in circles about such fires as we could make in the storm," he reported. He could do very little more, admitting that "warm drinks and fires were all the means we had for combating the evils of the situation." He repeated his efforts at Gettysburg, where he exhausted himself even before the end of the battle. And these experiences were turning him into something more than a chaplain. "Once I could hardly bear the sight of a surgeon's knife," he wrote to his mother after Gettysburg. "Now I can keep my finger calmly on a man's pulse while the keen blade is plunged into his quivering flesh."[41]

At Savage's Station, Virginia, in June 1862, men crowded the rooms and hallways of a house waiting for aid. They listened to the sounds of suffering, disturbed in the night by the identifiable and discouraging noises made by coffins being loaded onto wagons. Surgeons worked in every room, all of which were fairly painted floor to ceiling in blood. Wounded men had lain on the ground nearby for days, leaving the "grass...saturated with blood" that baked under the sun, creating a "stench [that] was like that of a slaughter house!"[42] In the western theater, during the Atlanta campaign, Confederate Sam Watkins visited a similar place. He later recalled that there was no glory there for the suffering common soldiers, who were "being eaten up with the deadly gangrene, and being imperfectly waited on." "I get sick to-day when I think of the agony, and suffering, and sickening stench and odor of dead and dying...of the groaning and wailing," he remembered. "I cannot describe it."[43] To make matters worse, hospitals near the front could come under fire, and a retreating army, such as McClellan's, left the patients to the mercies of the enemy.

Undoubtedly, those who still had their wits in these situations contemplated their own mortality, as they watched men lying near them suffer and die. Holmes understood that "the majority vote of the civilized world declared that with my opinions I was en route for Hell." That realization troubled him for a moment, but he rationalized away any thoughts of recanting his more free-thinking philosophical beliefs; opiates seemed to encourage him to punctuate the process with liberal amounts of profanity.[44] Other men of a more Christian nature made their peace with the world and their God. In September 1862

Field hospital after battle of June 27, 1862, Savage Station, Virginia. (*Library of Congress*)

Chaplain Twichell attended to a dying soldier who remembered his beloved family, who he would leave "with the Lord," and then forgave those men—"if God forgives them"—who had committed the "great wickedness" of starting the war.[45]

At these hospitals, surgeons practiced a form of triage, bandaging and sending back to their units the least hurt, working on the men they believed they could save, and setting those soldiers beyond help out of the way to allow them to die. After the Battle of Williamsburg, a surgeon ordered Vermonter Marshall Harvey Twichell to bury the dead and bring in the wounded but leave behind those men who were near death.[46] In July 1863 South Carolinian Silas Ewell, wounded at Jackson, Mississippi, insisted on having his arm amputated, but the attending surgeon refused because he did not wish to waste his time on a man who would soon die. Ewell had his way and survived, but other dying men, deemed hopeless cases, did not.[47] During the fighting at Atlanta, Sam Watkins came on one of his comrades who had been severely wounded, his torso nearly severed, and set aside to die on his own.[48] Kentuckian Marcus Woodcock, also wounded in the Atlanta campaign, discovered that federal surgeons treated the severely wounded the same way. When he arrived at the hospital, he saw that "many horribly mangled fellows were apparently in the last agonies of death, and some of these were receiving no attention, for in the present emergency all hands of the hospital were engaged with those whom they could *hope* to save, and they could not receive a tithe of the necessary attention."[49]

Under the best of circumstances, surgeons used alcohol to "stimulate" patients and had on hand ether and chloroform to anesthetize soldiers about to experience the bone saw. They also had numbing opiates, such as laudanum and morphine, painkillers much appreciated by surgeon and soldier alike. Chaplain Twichell, left in charge of some wounded Confederates, reported that his bottle of morphine "has been a good angel— blessed be its memory!" Twichell considered it a miracle drug. "Many a restless pillow has been smoothed by it," he noted, "many a tired body has drawn sleep out of it."[50] Indeed, Michigander Charles Hayden admitted that his wound produced the "most terrible pain I ever suffered"; it was only morphine that kept him from "jumping overboard" while traveling to a Cincinnati hospital by ship.[51]

Many a soldier bitterly complained about inadequate medical assistance near the front. One Maine soldier witnessed a young woman risking her own safety to dress the wounds of fallen men and wondered why the cowardly surgeons who claimed they needed to work in the rear could not do the same.[52] And after Chancellorsville, Chaplain Twichell proved he was steadier than the three timid surgeons who abandoned him and the wounded when the army retreated. "The desertion of these Surgeons was an outrage," Twichell angrily wrote. "Cowardice and laziness were the chief causes of it."[53]

Among the complainers were men who believed that surgeons were no better than butchers. Others believed the surgeons were too quick to amputate "on the ground that they could do it more quickly than they could dress the wound; that it made a neater job, thus gratifying professional pride." Thus, according to one Union veteran, "many a poor fellow…came to consciousness only to miss an arm or leg which he perhaps had begged in his last conscious moments to have spared."[54] Indeed, numerous soldiers remarked on the pieces of human detritus surrounding the surgeons' tents, commenting on arms and legs tossed about on the ground, carried away in buckets, or stacked high in piles.

There was indeed no shortage of cowardly, drunken, and incompetent surgeons, but the soldiers' criticism of the doctors and the medical treatment they received was not entirely fair. For example, as Charles B. Johnson, hospital steward for the 130th Illinois, later recalled, rifle balls "almost never failed to fracture and shatter" the bone when they struck, rarely making a neat "round perforation."[55] In such circumstances, there was not much that a doctor could do to treat a shattered arm or leg but to amputate it before gangrene set in. And soldiers who refused amputations for fear of what their wives or sweethearts would think in such circumstances died because they kept their damaged limbs.

Also, many of surgeons performed their duty well near the battlefields, risking safety and freedom. New York surgeon William M. Smith came under fire at a fight in North Carolina in late 1862, for example, but became "busily engaged...in dressing the wounded."[56] And in April 1862 Dr. William M. McPheeters, a Confederate surgeon, treated wounded men at the Battle of Pleasant Hill, Louisiana, until the very last moment, as the Federal forces advanced on his position; while retreating, "minie balls were whistling around me," he reported, "and one or two nearly struck."[57]

Surgeons and attendants also risked their own safety by staying with wounded men, even if it meant that they would become prisoners of war. On the first day of Shiloh, Samuel Eells, assistant surgeon in the 12th Michigan, was too busy to be frightened, as bullets fell "unpleasantly near and thick"; he continued to work on the wounded even after he was captured.[58] Dr. Daniel Holt became a prisoner of the Confederates in Virginia at the battle of Salem Church in 1863 because he refused to retreat when ordered. The unfortunate doctor remained working on the wounded as they came to him, after going without food and with very little sleep for several days, only to walk into the rebel army as he was trying to make his way to the rear. As a captive, he continued, to the point of exhaustion, to tend to the wounded men from his regiment, who also had become prisoners.[59]

Even within their own lines, doctors worked hard under rough conditions. In July 1862, at Harrison's Landing, Virginia, Massachusetts surgeon J. Franklin Dyer "performed amputations on the ground by the light of a single candle stuck in a bayonet."[60] After Antietam, William Child, assistant surgeon of the Fifth New Hampshire, treated 64 men in one day, some with multiple wounds. The next day, he continued his efforts, working from dawn until the end of the day.[61] And in April 1864, after spending the day tending to the wounded, Confederate Dr. McPheeters "took a snack and spread my blanket on the ground without tent and slept soundly." He continued his work the next day until the late afternoon, "busy all the time in amputating limbs, adjusting fractures, elevating depressed skulls, and etc., etc."[62]

Seriously wounded soldiers who survived treatment near the front were transported to the rear, ending up in military hospitals located in their regions' cities. Medical officials did not always have an easy time securing these facilities. Quartermasters, themselves pressed for supplies, especially in the South during latter days of the Confederacy, could prove to be obstreperous in the face of requests from surgeons trying to build hospitals, while citizens could be reluctant to turn over their property for hospital purposes. But both the Confederate and U.S. governments accomplished an extraordinary feat in providing hospital beds for their men.

Chimborazo in Richmond and other newly constructed Northern and Southern government hospitals were well planned and purpose-built; depending on the personnel, they could provide the best treatment available at the time to wounded and sick soldiers. Other hospitals were improvised affairs under canvas or located in tobacco warehouses and other private property, quickly put into service to deal with the numbers of wounded that neither government had expected at the outset of the war. The federal government pressed into service many buildings in the capital, including a large block of townhomes, known as Douglas Hospital, named for having been the residence of the famous Democratic senator and presidential candidate.[63] The hospital at Keokuk, Iowa, was a hotel building, the Estes House, with a roof consisting of canvas stretched between the men and the sky.[64] Moore Hospital in Richmond had been a warehouse.[65] In the wake of major engagements, the sudden increase in wounded men taxed the resources of even the best of these hospitals and certainly strained the efficiency of lesser establishments.

The journey to one of these hospitals could be trying for the wounded men. Wagon transportation frequently lacked springs, and even ambulances were not much better, as men "suffer[ed] yet more from jolting over horrid roads."[66] River transportation and railroads were somewhat better but not without their own problems. Initially, ordinary vessels carried wounded to their destinations. After Shiloh, the number of wounded was so great that Union casualties found makeshift berths on converted cargo ships. But the war also witnessed the development of specialized hospital ships, including converted vessels that adequately served their purpose.[67]

Railroads eventually developed special ambulance cars with bunk bed arrangements for multiple levels of stretchers. However, there were medical men who believed regular boxcars with floors covered with straw were better because their passengers would not be thrown from their resting places when the trains encountered a bad stretch of track. No matter the inherent problems of the various modes of moving men to hospitals, heavy casualties strained resources, forcing medical men to use whatever uncomfortable transportation was available.

Life in the Hospital

Once safely arrived at a general hospital, the soldiers' experiences varied, depending on how well the surgeons in charge executed their duties, on the dispositions and personalities of the various attendants, and on the attitude of the men themselves. Charles Hayden became despondent while in the hospital at Cincinnati, where a surgeon "with a professional fondness of probes" and his associates "all keep feeling around after pieces of bone in the wound as if all the bones in my body were broken & the pieces crammed into this bullet hole." He admitted that physically, he was doing well, but emotionally, he was "lonesome, gloomy, [and] impatient." "I wish I were home," he complained, "or with my Regt."[68] He eventually would go home, which helped his disposition, and then return to his regiment.

Sergeant Henry McAllister of the Fourth Vermont lost a leg after Fredericksburg but possessed the spirit of an individual eager to move on with his life. He assured a friend, "All my aspirations are just as high as ever." "I have sustained a great loss but it might have been worse," he explained, but "I can so shape my course of life that it will be of but little inconvenience. I can get a wooden leg on which I can get around nearly as well as on my old one."[69]

Such a good attitude could flourish in a well-managed hospital with caring and competent staff. Efficient stewards made for well-run hospitals and added to the comfort of the men. Kind matrons became mother figures for the wounded boys, helping them adjust to their circumstances, while keeping up their spirits. Chaplains provided spiritual comfort and wrote letters to the patients' home folks. Female nurses, who often became advocates for their patients, comforted the men, wrote letters to families, fought for better food, and battled incompetent or cold surgeons and stingy stewards, all of which the residents greatly appreciated.

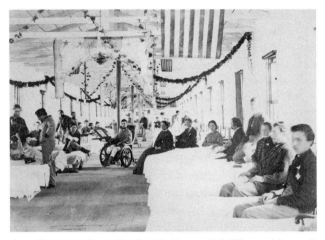

A ward in Armory Square Hospital, Washington, D.C. (*Library of Congress*)

Confederate Kate Cumming went beyond simple nursing to cheer one young soldier by encouraging young ladies to visit him because "nothing pleases him better." In
October 1863 Cumming, "annoyed at something which happened," had decided to leave
her position, until she entered the wards. The soldiers forced her to change her mind.
"When I saw the smile with which I was greeted on every side, and the poor sufferers
so glad to see me," she admitted, "I made up my mind...that happen what may, nothing
will ever make me leave the hospital as long as I can be of any service to the suffering."[70]

Union nurse Jane Stuart Woolsey recalled that "all classes of men were pleased with
a little kindness, grateful for the smallest attention."[71] Along with the female nurses,
women volunteers provided such service in hospitals, where they sponsored special dinners for the patients and performed other kindnesses.[72] New Jersey private Walter G.
Dunn, for example, was at Jarvis General Hospital in Baltimore after being wounded at
Chancellorsville, where he encountered women volunteers who tended to the invalids
and provided meals for them on Thanksgiving and Christmas.[73] Women volunteers also
cheered the spirits of Texan Robert Campbell. Campbell had been wounded twice in the
left leg at the Second Battle of Bull Run and suffered from complications, as he recovered in a Richmond hospital. His stay was made more comfortable by "a bevy of fair
Virginia Ladies...doing all that woman could to alleviate our sufferings."[74]

Private Dunn eventually had an operation to remove a bullet from his shoulder and
was transferred to Haddington General Hospital near Philadelphia, where his experience
was not nearly as pleasant as it had been in Baltimore. In November 1864 he complained
to his future wife, "I left a Hospital where I lacked nothing for comfort, while here everything comfortable is lacking." He was blunt about his situation, describing Haddington
in most unflattering terms. "I never before saw such a comtemptible, ill begotten, long
forsaken chance of a place, as this is," he wrote. "I cannot describe it, nor will I say anything more about it, as I cannot say anything good." The treatment was so poor that his
wound failed to improve, and in December, he returned to Jarvis Hospital.[75]

Other soldiers would have understood Dunn's complaints. Wisconsin soldier Van
Willard, after being wounded at Antietam, was sent to a hospital at Frederick, Maryland.
There he recuperated until November, when he moved on to a hospital in Philadelphia,
where he spent another two months. "Of all the horrible and lonely places, I think a

military hospital the worst—shut up in a narrow, sombre ward, with narrow beds and curtained windows, bare walls, and in fact, everything wearing a cheerless, gloomy aspect of a sick room," he reported. He painted a bleak picture of suffering men, bored during the day and sleepless during the night. There those men who were aware of their surroundings had to deal with "the groans, the screams, the death struggle, and the ravings of the delirious." His experience led him to conclude that "the horrors of the battle field are indeed dark and appalling, but not darker are they or more appalling than are those of the hospital, where life blood trickles slowly away, where strong men waste away day by day and droop and die." Anything was better than a hospital, Willard judged, including camp life and battle.[76] Indeed, in February 1862, Confederate Edward O. Guerrant concluded that the patients of military hospitals were at a disadvantage because their attendants witnessed so much suffering that they became "insensible to grief—or compassion." He believed that "suffering is disregarded where all are compelled to undergo a share." Thus he concluded that he "would rather *die* in a decent—comfortable house than to *live* in one of those miserable abodes of the sick."[77]

Despite the testimonies of the men who found hospitals miserable places to be, there were others who, returning to health, experienced some pleasant time away from the front. At Chimborazo in Richmond, chaplains, dentists, and barbers tended to the spiritual and physical comfort of the inmates. Patients at the Virginia hospital had access to libraries, newspapers, and letters from home to lift their spirits as well as visitors. They also amused themselves playing cards, making toys, and carving chessmen. After Gettysburg, wounded men at the Germantown, Pennsylvania, hospital played cards and checkers to pass the time, even though a self-righteous ward master threatened to confiscate and burn the deck of cards. They could secure passes to visit Philadelphia, just as their ambulatory counterparts at Chimborazo could visit Richmond, where they might get into the usual mischief that appealed to soldiers on the town, including drunken revelries and the smuggling of alcoholic beverages back to the wards. Consequently, many patients who were tired of fighting did not wish to leave the hospital to return to their units. At Chimborazo and other institutions, so-called hospital rats did their best to stay on even after they had recovered by developing new health problems. Sometimes they received the assistance of surgeons who wished to keep them in place to perform the miscellaneous hospital duties to which the men were becoming accustomed.

Legitimate patients adjusted to the institutions' routines and made the best of their circumstances even as they longed to return to their units or go home. They followed daily schedules that reflected military discipline, while they performed useful tasks and entertained themselves as best they could. At Chimborazo, there were set times for breakfast, meeting with doctors, taking medications, and supping. Those patients sufficiently strong performed light duty airing bedding and cleaning and maintaining the wards. Amputees were expected to take on clerical duties and stand guard. Recovering soldiers also served as nurses. At Germantown, men on the mend did similar work. Other recovering soldiers served as guards, although fit soldiers were also detailed to that light duty when necessary.[78]

The Invalid Corps

Some comparatively fit patients did good service in the hospital wards making worthwhile contributions to the well-being of the less able men. At Jarvis Hospital in Baltimore, New Jersey soldier Walter G. Dunn actually enjoyed the work for a while.

Helping out after the admission of Gettysburg wounded, he admitted, "Nothing suits me better than to relieve sufferers." At least on one occasion, he assisted crippled soldiers who had recently received crutches on a walk in a Baltimore park. In the fall of 1863, Dunn was transferred to the Invalid Corps, and for the remainder of the war, he and many other former patients continued to work around the hospitals.[79]

With the establishment of the Invalid Corps in the spring of 1863, Yankee wounded found themselves transferred into the new organization, despite what complaints and excuses the less willing soldiers might muster. Surgeons who had been reluctant to part with the extra help that the hospital rats provided on the wards now transferred men to the Invalid Corps, expecting to continue to receive their assistance. At Chestnut Hill Hospital in Pennsylvania, for example, surgeons examined the men every week, sending the fit back to their regiments and transferring "all those who were fit to do duty round the hospitals, but not fit for a march" into the Invalid Corps.[80]

Many enlisted men were not entirely pleased to find themselves in the new Union organization. They believed that once wounded, they had done their part and should be released from the service. The War Department thought otherwise. If they could hold a pistol and were mobile, they were expected to serve out their enlistments, continuing to contribute to the war effort, including guarding hospitals and tending to the wounded therein. Still, most of the men transferred to the Invalid Corps, later known as the Veteran Reserve Corps, accepted their duties and fulfilled their obligations, although they tended to find hospital duty boring. Dunn, for example, considered a move to clerical duty an improvement over hospital work. "I am really tired of Hospital life, it is so dull," he complained, "the same thing over and over all of the time and no excitement to keep a person alive." When he moved to his new duties with the Eighth Army Corps headquarters, he happily reported, "I can assure you that it is quite an agreeable change from the monotonous life of the Hospital."[81]

Dunn and other wounded men could receive furloughs, which provided them with time away from the army to speed along their recovery. In June 1862 Yankee rebel Edmund Patterson was seriously wounded at Frayser's Farm and, by August, was well enough to have an audience with an examining board of doctors "who say just how long a fellow must be in getting well." He assumed that these men had "looked upon so many mutilated forms that I suppose they can tell about how long it will be before a man can be made of some use." In Patterson's case, the board decided that 45 days would do the trick, "at the end of which time I am expected to be well and ready to undergo more shooting."[82]

The armies expected furloughed men to make their way back to their units once they had recovered, which was problematic. Yankee Samuel Fiske also found men taking advantage of their leave, extending their stays at home with the assistance of family physicians or simply ignoring the deadlines for returning to their units.[83] Braxton Bragg believed that hospital furloughs gave men the opportunity to desert and ordered a stop to them within his jurisdiction. During the Atlanta campaign, Confederate officers in Joe Johnston's army also feared that wounded men on furlough would not make the effort to return to duty. Their fears were well founded, and before the end of the war, the hospital became the starting point for many a deserter's trip home. Despite the fraudulent use of furloughs, the majority of capable men returned to duty. They rejoined their regiments bringing the experience of the veteran, which for good or naught would shape their attitudes and actions, while influencing any new recruits, during their remaining days in the army.[84]

But even after good soldiers returned to active duty, they still could find themselves distressed by wounds that never healed well. Such conditions made them susceptible to additional medical problems. Yankee Charles Hayden, for example, never fully recovered from his wound. He returned to his regiment and active duty but took ill; returned to the Cincinnati hospital; and in March 1864, died of pneumonia, an event probably made more likely by the impact of his wound on his overall health.[85]

Psychological Wounds

Then there were the battlefield wounds that were not visible to soldiers' comrades and beyond the treatment of surgeons, whose kits prominently displayed hacksaws. Combat experience deeply disturbed some men to the point of incapacitating them, preventing them from carrying on their usual army routines. In November 1862 Henry L. Abbott of the 20th Massachusetts described to his father the erratic behavior of his regimental commander, which could only have been the consequence of battle stress. "Col Lee (strictly confidential) is undoubtedly very much shaken in his intellects, at any rate at times," he reported. Some of his fellow officers agreed with Abbott's assessment: "It seems the horrors of Antietam, his previous fatigues & his drinking, completely upset him," although it is possible that his drinking took on a different therapeutic purpose after that bloody affair.

The description Abbott forwarded home strikingly detailed the behavior of a man psychologically undone. "After the battle he was completely distraught. He didn't give any orders. He wouldn't do any thing," Abbott reported. "The next morning he mounted his horse, & without any leave of absences, without letting any body [know] where he was going, he set out alone." Eventually, a fellow officer of the regiment came on the colonel some distance from their camp "without a cent in his pocket, without any thing to eat or drink, without having changed his clothes for 4 weeks, during all which time he had this horrible diarrhea—just getting ready to turn into a stable for the night." The officer tended to him and made him comfortable, but "when the poor old man came back to the regt. they thought he had been on an awful spree, he was so livid & shaky." The officer who had rescued him "says he was just like a little child wandering away from home." In the end, Abbott could only conclude that the man was insane. "Why there is no doubt about it, papa," he wrote, "his wits are unsettled & will be as long as he stays in the army."[86]

PRISONERS OF WAR

Over the course of the war, Confederate forces captured over 211,000 Yankees, while Union troops captured over 462,000 rebels. Many of these men were paroled or exchanged, but almost 410,000 soldiers remained in enemy hands, with 194,743 federals and 214,865 Confederates spending time in a prisoner of war facility.[87] At the outset of the war, neither Confederates nor federals expected the need to house such large numbers of prisoners. Even when there were surges in captives during the first two years of war, officials did not anticipate the need to maintain larger, more sophisticated quarters for the prisoners because they expected to be rid of them by the traditional practices of paroling and exchanging the men. Exchanging prisoners was a practice which allowed both sides to avoid having to guard and provide for large numbers of men over long periods of time. Paroling captives freed armies and officials from the obligation of tending to prisoners by allowing them to go free if they pledged that they would not participate in their government's war effort until they were exchanged. Consequently, during 1861 and into 1862, although their governments did not officially sanction the practices, armies regularly exchanged and paroled prisoners. On July 22, 1862, officials formalized the practice with an agreement, or cartel, that provided for sanctioned paroles and exchanges.

Parolees and Exchanges

Early in the war, paroles were often done informally at the point of capture. In September 1862, for example, Confederate Robert Watson and some comrades fell behind their column's march. They were captured by a Yankee patrol, which paroled them "on the same day for we were too weak to go with them."[88] On a larger scale, in July 1863, U.S. Grant paroled the Confederate troops at Vicksburg, an act that would allow him to continue his campaign without the burden of dealing with his prisoners.[89]

The system of paroles and exchanges had the desired effect of relieving armies of the burden of handling excessive numbers of prisoners. Paroles, however, presented both governments with another set of problems, not the least being the need to keep track of parolees. After initially allowing some parolees significant freedom to return home or remain in convenient cities such as Richmond, governments acknowledged the need to keep these men close at hand, preferably in a military camp. Union soldiers, for example, had to make their way to a camp of instruction to wait for their exchange.[90] Once in such a camp, thousands of Yankees discovered that their situation was much like being in a Confederate prison. Union parolees reporting to the Benton Barracks in St. Louis found themselves underfed and isolated in an inadequate facility.[91] And in 1862 Albert Irwin ended up in a parole camp in Annapolis, Maryland, where, he complained, "I have to sleep on the bare ground every night as there is no tents on hand at present."[92]

Confederate General Braxton Bragg, perceptive in judging the nature of the common soldier, at least in this case, kept western army parolees in such camps before other generals regularly followed his example.[93] Such places were not appealing to paroled soldiers, who believed that their situation was special and freed them of the usual military discipline. Shortly after making their way to a Confederate camp, some friends of Confederate Robert Watson went "home without permission" because of the limbo in which they found themselves and the poor food they had to consume there.[94]

After Vicksburg, Confederate Johnnie Wickersham and other parolees were ordered to regroup at a camp at Demopolis, Alabama, where Wickerhsam recalled they had plenty to eat and, in general, a fine time.[95] Other Confederate parolees at Vicksburg, however, ignored instructions and left for their homes, sometimes with the encouragement of Union troops. One general assumed that these men were not abandoning the cause but had a "determination not to go into a 'parole camp' and a belief they can now be absent from their commands without injury to the service." Confederate officials worried that their armies would lose the service of these men and of other parolees from recent western defeats. That concern led them to order the soldiers to abandon their pledges and return to duty, a practice that did not sit well with the parolees.[96]

Parolees also suffered what usual hardships came with overcrowding in their camps. By the beginning of October 1862, upward to 9,000 Union parolees were packed into Chicago's Camp Douglas. No wonder the dispirited men became discipline problems. Paroled officers enjoyed the luxury of seeking out better quarters in the city, which deprived their subordinates of their supervision. The enlisted men left camp to drink, harass Chicagoans, thieve, and beg on the streets, until troops and police were able to reassert control over them. Even then, discipline remained a problem, as exhibited by the number of barracks set afire by the inmates. Most of the parolees were exchanged before the end of 1862, but those who remained through the winter endured the boredom and disease common to prisoner of war camps.[97]

Because of the initial acceptance of paroles and exchanges, both sides expected an ad hoc system of prisons to suffice. Confederate officials assumed Richmond warehouses and similar facilities elsewhere would serve well enough their temporary prison needs. Union officials likewise made due with what was available in Northern cities located near rail and water transportation. In the spring of 1862, in the Mississippi River town of Keokuk, Iowa, for example, Union officials used abandoned buildings to house prisoners, a practice that suggested problems to come; structural and sanitation problems quickly rendered these places dangerous.[98]

These improvised prisons proved inadequate as the numbers of captives grew because of the policies of both governments. By the middle of 1863, the realization that the war would be one in which resources and endurance would contribute to victory convinced Union authorities that it was unwise to send men back to the ranks of rebel armies. Also, the Confederacy's policy toward black troops and their officers contributed to the change in policy. It outraged Northerners when they learned that black soldiers were to be returned to their masters and white officers treated as instigators of slave insurrection; officials demanded that Confederate authorities treat blacks as prisoners of war.

In April 1864 Ulysses S. Grant, well aware of the manpower problems of the Confederacy, used the issue concerning treatment of black prisoners as a rationale for ending all exchanges. Since regular exchanges did not resume until February 1865, the camps at Andersonville, Georgia, Elmira, New York, Point Lookout, Maryland, and elsewhere became increasingly crowded. The camp at Point Lookout, for example, was built to hold up to 10,000 men but at one point housed 20,000, while officials first planned to house 5,000 men at Elmira, New York, but at one point imprisoned 9,441 Confederates there.[99] The infamous stockade at Andersonville, a camp without barracks, was built to hold some 10,000 prisoners, but eventually, those inadequate facilities held a high Union population of some 33,000 men.[100]

Life as a Prisoner of War

Soldiers who were shipped off to a prison instead of exchanged or paroled had to endure additional humiliations along the way to their destination. Their transportation, the citizens they encountered, and the very conditions in which they eventually found themselves housed contributed to their shame, anger, and depressed morale. Edmund Patterson, the Ohio native turned Alabama Confederate, was captured at Gettysburg and shipped to Fort Delaware in Maryland in what he considered to be very unpleasant circumstances. "This is a day that will be long remembered by all who were in our party," he wrote. The "filthy" boxcars the Confederates boarded were packed so tightly that men could neither sit nor lie down. They also lacked any ventilation once locked up, and the men spent the night in the immobile cars because their captors feared Confederate cavalry would raid the train.[101] Union prisoners experienced comparable treatment at the hands of their captors. By the time Bernhard Domschcke ended up in Charleston,

South Carolina, arriving from Savannah in September 1864, he recalled that he and his comrades "were used to being herded like cattle rather than treated like men."[102]

In their travels to and on their arrival at their destinations, captives became sport for the local residents, who viewed them as curiosities, scapegoats for their own soldiers' sacrifices, or dangerous enemies deserving the harshest possible treatment. Indianapolis women came out of their houses to harass dirty, hungry, tired Confederate prisoners from Fort Donelson as they marched to their destination at Camp Morton.[103] In July 1863, black soldiers captured at Fort Wagner "were greeted by the jeers and taunts" of residents of Charleston, South Carolina.[104] In 1864, civilians watched black prisoners and their officers marched through Petersburg "much after the style of a circus." Residents, including women and children, showered abuse on the Yankees that, according to Freeman S. Bowley, a white officer in the 30th U.S. Colored Infantry, "exceeded anything of the kind that I ever heard."[105] But Southerners were more than curious when they witnessed captured black troops and their white officers on their journey to prison. At Danville, Virginia, civilians, livid at the sight of the black soldiers and their white officers captured at the Crater, demanded they be killed and almost successfully took matters into their own hands, at the expense of two white officers they attempted to hang.[106]

Prisoners, once behind stockade walls, also became sideshow curiosities for citizens eager to see real rebels or Yankees. At Camp Douglas the prisoners were quite an attraction to Chicagoans, who could take advantage of an observation tower to peer into the camp.[107] New Yorkers at Elmira also could observe the enemy by using an observation tower overlooking the compound.[108] In July 1864 the Andersonville Yankees provided additional spectacle for a crowd of Georgians, who gathered to watch the execution of Union camp criminals known as raiders, men who had preyed on vulnerable fellow inmates.[109]

Confinement and its surroundings further humiliated the men, who found themselves in situations that worked away at their self-respect, empathy, and morale. Black soldiers confined at Andersonville after being captured at the Battle of Olustee in Florida suffered the indignity of being stripped of their uniforms, just one act on the part of their captors to deprive them of their identity as soldiers.[110] Confederates heaped other indignities on black troops that ignored their role as soldiers. In 1863, in Louisiana, Confederates captured black soldiers of the First Arkansas, followed the stated policy of their government, and considered them slaves fit to be used as laborers on fortifications, in kitchens, or wherever else they might be needed.[111] After the Battle of the Crater, Confederate authorities allowed masters to reclaim captured runaway slaves serving in the Union army.[112] They also employed contrabands and free blacks alike on fortifications side by side with slaves. That treatment prompted General Benjamin Butler to use Confederates to dig a canal under the supervision of black troops, which must have been an extremely humiliating experience for them.[113] Confederates captured a number of soldiers of the Fifth U.S. Colored Troops, originally organized in Ohio during 1863, and turned over at least two of them to slave masters, but the other captives endured the usual indignities of prisoners of war in spite of the threats of the Richmond government.[114]

The shock of seeing their prison home and the frustration of having little control over their futures also challenged the dignity of prisoners. Rebel Edmund Patterson reported that on the arrival of the Confederates at Fort Delaware, their prison guards brought them to a "barracks situated in a vast mud hole." In his assessment, "a respectable hog would have turned up his nose in disgust at it." The conditions were such that the camp became a "second class hell," in which filthy, lice-infested men with no chance of tidying themselves lost their self-respect. Despair was so common that even he understood why some of the prisoners shamed themselves further by renouncing the Confederacy and taking the oath of allegiance to the United States. In June 1864, after a year at Johnson's Island in Lake Erie, his next prison home, Patterson still found his situation frustrating. "It is so hard to be shut up here when our country needs us so much," he lamented. "It would be better, it seems to me, to be killed at once on the battlefield."[115]

In the best of situations, soldiers accepted the inevitable and passed the time in ways comparable to what they had known in their old army camps. According to George Washington Hall, a Georgian imprisoned at Fort Delaware, "the ingenious human mind naturally seeks employment when cut off & isolated from the remainder of the world." Prisoners, therefore, tried to keep busy in more or less productive ways.[116]

Men in the various camps exchanged news and rumors about the war. They read newspapers when they could get their hands on them, and the fortunate ones received letters from friends and family members. Others engaged in intellectually and spiritually uplifting pursuits. They attended prayer meetings, wrote letters, attended Bible classes, learned German, taught French, sang, read books donated by generous civilians, listened to speeches at Masonic gatherings and on special occasions, and attended gatherings of the Young Men's Christian Association.[117] Virginian John Preston Sheffey, a prisoner at Camp Chase, Ohio, and a lawyer before the war, not only participated in a debate society, but also passed the time with other inmates who had obtained law books, "reviewing that grand science."[118] Charles Mattocks kept his diary up to date "as much for my own amusement as for any better purpose," but he allowed that many prisoners spent a good bit of their time gambling, even on Sundays.[119] Indeed, in one camp, Confederate prisoners started a weekly paper called the *Dixie Discourses,* which published "a scientific article on Poker...much to our amusement and edification."[120]

Energetic prisoners played quoits and other games that had occupied their time in their old army camps.[121] In the Northern camps, Confederates had large-scale snowball fights, which, in one case, lasted half the day, producing "a large number of sore heads and black eyes."[122] And, of course, there was baseball.

Yankees played the game at a camp at Salisbury, North Carolina, and became the subjects of a famous baseball print produced by New York artist-turned-soldier Otto Boetticher after his exchange in 1863. At Rock Island, Confederates still nurtured the competitive spirit and formed teams that matched westerners against easterners. During the summer of 1864, at Johnson's Island, rebel prisoners formed the "Confederate Base Ball Club" and the "Southern Base Ball Club," regularly playing games that attracted the attention of the "sporting characters," who gambled what money they had on the outcomes.[123]

The Horrors of Prison Camp

Such games, however, could not erase the sameness and harshness of prison life, which wore heavily on many a captive, nor could they tempt worn-out men whose only concern had become survival. Confederate Hiram Smith Williams, a native of New Jersey who had settled in Alabama before the war and was captured at Bentonville in March 1865, found prison life "unendurable" after only a short time at Point Lookout prison in Maryland. "The weary monotony of day after day, it is awful," he complained. "I dread the coming of each day."[124] Late in the war, Lieutenant James Campbell, a South Carolina resident confined to Fort Delaware, also found "the monoteny of Prison Life…getting burdensom and still there is no prospects of exchange."[125]

In April 1865 Alabaman Samuel Pickens considered captivity at Point Lookout to be "miserable," lacking any degree of comfort but providing endless annoyance from "lice as big as grains of wheat and as thick as blackberries."[126] Confederate Edmund Patterson, captured at Gettysburg, however, found prison life, in March 1864, to be a "living death." What made it particularly hard for him was the utter lack of privacy. "Perhaps one of the worst features of prison life at this place at present," he recorded in June 1864, "is that it is so public, that is, it is impossible for one to get away from the crowd, the bustle, and confusion….There is not a spot within the walls of this prison to which one can go for quiet reflection and meditation."[127]

Patterson's complaint could have been the consensus of prisoners throughout the two systems. Crowded camps also brought other problems for the prisoners, ranging from lack of proper shelter and sanitation facilities to insufficient rations and medical care, all made worse by the governments' poor planning and policies designed either to extract retribution or to economize. Hunger and the subsequent health problems that accompanied malnutrition loomed large not only at Andersonville, but generally in Northern and Southern camps. Men did what they could to supplement their rations, and some of them, to make up for the lack of meat, trapped vermin. At Johnson Island, Confederates killed and ate rats, "of which there are thousands in the prison," reported Patterson in September 1864. Patterson refrained from joining them, until he could stand no more of his own gnawing hunger. "I cannot say that I am particularly fond of them, but rather than go hungry I will eat them when I can get them," he admitted. "They taste very much like a young squirrel and would be good enough if called by any other name."[128] These hardships resulted in the deaths of over 30,000 federals and almost 26,000 Confederates.[129]

If the initial experiences of captivity did not wear away at dignity and empathy, then these experiences in the stockade had that effect on all but the strongest men. "Steal an individual's freedom and you take his natural joy, you plunder a legitimate buoyancy of spirit, and you pile upon him a load to twist him emotionally and cripple him physically, if not crush him," recalled Union officer and prisoner of war Bernhard Domschcke of the 26th Wisconsin. "Deprived of personal liberty, the victim at once directs each thought and all feelings to his miserable condition."[130] As the war dragged on, as prisons became increasingly crowded, and as men struggled to survive, the loss of self-respect and of concern for fellow humans became all the more apparent. In June 1864, prisoner of war Robert Sneden saw men become hardened to suffering at Andersonville as "nearly all of us had given up all hopes of being exchanged or seeing our homes again." The situation brought out "all the bad qualities in a man," thus allowing the "brutal natures of the ignorant and uneducated men" to "vent in inhuman conduct to their comrades in misery."[131]

Sneden saw all sorts of horrors that robbed men of their humanity. Andersonville was among the worst of the worst camps, but other places shared the same circumstances to one degree or another. At Andersonville, Sneden witnessed brutal thieves, inmates bereft of empathy, prey on weaker men. He watched men waiting for other prisoners to die to be the first "to grab his blanket, tin cup or canteen and clothes before life was out of him." At times, the men did not wait for end to come to their comrades, but "clubbed to death or kicked in the stomach" the dying prisoner "with the exclamation of d__n you why don't you die!" Free of military discipline and personal restraint, prisoners on one occasion fought like animals for a piece of ground when a new stockade opened, leaving comrades with "black eyes and bloody faces." Hospital facilities were inadequate, leaving the sick prisoners to "lie or wallow like hogs in the sand which is teeming with lice and maggots by the million!" Corpses "festering in the hot sun all day" decomposed to the point where they had "to be shoveled into the dead wagon!" Flies, fleas, maggots, and moths pestered the men. Men endured all of these things, while living on starvation rations of cornmeal and "rusty bacon" or some corn bread and "black goober bean or cowpease." Hungry inmates caused "pandemonium" when they heard "the cries of vendors of corn beer or bones with no meat on them."[132]

Under such emotional and physical strain, men abandoned the last of their self-respect. Some gave up and either passively wasted away or attempted suicide. At Andersonville, sick men dragged themselves to the so-called dead line, the point at which they supposedly challenged camp security and became fair target for the guards.[133] Some men tried to ease their circumstances by toadying to their guards.[134] Others took an oath to the enemy's flag, as Confederate Patterson had witnessed. Still other inmates, as Sneden documented, became "cruel, selfish, unscrupulous to do anything to gain their ends."[135]

Despite the chronic despair in prison camps, there remained desperate or brave inmates who willingly risked their lives to escape their emotional and physical torment. Relatively few were successful, their plots foiled by spies, informants, geography, or other circumstances. The saddest cases short of those men who died trying to escape were those men who tasted success, only to be run down by hounds or turned in by civilians. Charles Mattocks of Maine was one of the almost successful escapees. He spent most of November 1864 running from a South Carolina prison and wandering in the North Carolina mountains, until he was caught by Confederate loyalists.[136]

Given the horrible conditions under which these men made decisions about how to live, it was no wonder that prisoners of war found joy in their exchange or final release. In February 1865 Freeman Bowley left a Columbia, South Carolina, prison as an exchanged prisoner; when he and his comrades made it to Union lines, he recalled, they were filled with emotion "and every eye was streaming with tears." In Bowley's case, he was "feeling so happy as to be utterly oblivious to the fact that the soldiers were making irreverent remarks concerning" his comically patched trousers.[137] Iowan Samuel Calvin Jones also recalled the emotions he felt on his release from Libby Prison in February 1865 to be "a transition from want and cruelty, starvation and neglect, misery and pain to freedom and plenty, sunshine and home, under the old flag."[138]

WHY DID EXPERIENCED SOLDIERS KEEP FIGHTING?

Combat experience produced many fatalistic veterans who continued to fight because they were hardened to war, had lost faith in the goodness of man, or had lost hope in the future. Nevertheless, there were veterans who had rational reasons for staying in the ranks, despite their increasing familiarity with the dangers they would face with each new encounter with the enemy. Their motives were not necessarily the same ones that prompted them to enlist in the first place, but they probably did not worry about being consistent in their beliefs. Their ideas and degree of commitment to their causes might have followed the vicissitudes of army life, but they still fought for reasons ranging from their desire for personal advancement to their commitment to their regiments and their causes. In the end, soldiers probably held to several motives at once, ranging from the mercenary to the patriotic, none of which were mutually exclusive. Most of them probably had places in their hearts for various blends of commitment to honor, duty, and country. Soldiers rooted all of these ideas in the assumption that they were involved in a critical fight to protect their way of life, which would guarantee the happiness and security of their families and communities well into the future. Southerners, of course, fought to defend their land from invaders, just as Yankees fought to preserve their precious union. Even if men had not enlisted to protect or to destroy slavery, they understood that they had to fight on, either to defend their peculiar institution or to bring about its abolition to make sure that the future for which they fought would come to pass.

The desire to keep fighting was rooted in the veterans' belief in the righteousness of their cause. Soldiers assumed that God was on their side. Such assumptions sustained men even in defeat, helping them look forward to better results in future battles. Alabaman Joshua Callaway, after reviewing Confederate difficulties through mid-July 1863, admitted to being "very much depressed," but continued to take heart in knowing that "our trust is in God and our cause is just."[139] So, too, Georgian George Washington Hall believed that the Confederacy would succeed because God would support its righteous cause.[140] At the same time, Northern soldiers believed that they had to fight on because theirs was "a good and holy cause," as Colonel Frank Sherman of Illinois explained to his mother.[141] Pennsylvanian African American soldier Jacob E. Christy in fact believed that the Union cause would prevail because it was "God will that this ware Shall not end till the Colord people get their rights."[142]

The pull of the regiment had an important role in how men felt about continuing to serve. They had gone to war with relatives and friends and came to identify their companies as their new families and their regiments as their new communities. They learned teamwork and practiced it in battle, which further solidified regimental bonds. The camaraderie of a tested regiment made it easier for soldiers to stay with their military families through good times and bad, but fear of appearing to be a coward probably added some resolve to soldiers' commitment to their comrades. For many soldiers like Michigander Charles Hayden, only the home folks provided greater comfort than the regiment. Returning to his regiment after recovering from a wound, he "was very cordially received even by those from whom I least expected it."[143]

Good and honest men could not abandon their country or their regiment after they and their comrades had already sacrificed so much without appearing to be cowards, perhaps a particular concern for Southerners steeped in the culture of honor. Alabama volunteer James M. Williams, for example, understood that a man who faltered did not deserve to "be a freeman." Furthermore, the Confederate who abandoned the cause would not be forgotten or forgiven because "there is a record in the hearts of his comrades and another one I believe *above,* that brands him as a slave and cowardly traitor." Indeed, Williams reminded his wife that she had told him that she would rather see him dead "than clasp me to your bosom a living coward."[144]

There was a grim determination exhibited by many veteran soldiers to see the job through to an end. Even in the dark last months of the eastern campaign, Georgian John A. Everett, who had been fighting since the summer of 1861, expected to remain true to his duty, his regiment, and his cause until either death or peace ended his participation in the war.[145] Everett was not alone. Other men exhibited a steely resolve to finish the task to which they had committed themselves in 1861 or 1862. Midwesterner and combat veteran James M. Randall was clear about his mixed emotions concerning his military experience. "I have seen quite enough of war," he told his wife. "I have been exposed to its dangers and hardships plenty long enough to satisfy all my longings for adventure." Nevertheless, he assured her that he had "the utmost confidence in the righteousness of our cause, and feel that before long peace will be restored to our land." That was why he was committed to fighting on. "If it takes another year, and I am needed until the end, I shall always [feel] a just pride, because of the fact that I was able to contribute so much."[146] John H. Ferguson of the 10th Illinois Infantry reenlisted in January 1864 to "share with others in these trials and have the honor of going through the whole campaign from first to last should I live."[147] And Elisha Hunt Rhodes decided to stay on to serve his country and "if God wills, to see the end of this wicked rebellion."[148] Ohioan Sam Evans believed it best to continue the fight regardless of the cost, save the Union, and settle the sectional question once and for all. If Northerners lost their will, they would not be worthy of the legacy left to them by the founders.[149]

For Confederates, failure to continue the fight for the freedom that their Revolutionary fathers had won for them would lead to their own enslavement at the hands of rapacious Yankees. In April 1862 Texan James C. Bates believed that only "if the people of the south have not lost the energy & determination of their sires we *will* gain our independence & be freed from the yoke of tyranny."[150] Also in early 1862, Confederate officer James B. Griffin assured his wife that the men in the ranks would resist subjugation "until we grow old and worn out in service, and that then, our Sons will take the arms from our hands, and spend their lives, if necessary, in battling for Liberty and independence." Better his own son fight and die "rather than, be a Slave, *Yea,* worse than a Slave to Yankee Masters." Defeat would mean disgrace, and Southerners would be undeserving of "the respect of any body, and have no respect for ourselves"; rather, Southerners would become "the most wretched and abject people on the face of the Earth."[151] After one year of war, George Washington Hall of the 14th Georgia Infantry concluded that death was preferable to suffering "slavery and degradation below the beast of the forest" at the hands of Yankees.[152]

Knowledge of the real consequences of invasion reinforced this feeling. In the summer of 1864, Georgian B. S. King wanted vengeance for what the Yankees were doing to his home state. He assured his mother that Sherman's tactics would not work. The invaders would "never subdue us by such fighting, in fact it will have the contrary effect upon us, & will make us more bitter, more determined than ever to never again countenance a Yankee or their nation."[153]

Slavery and the Continued Motivation to Fight

This fear of disgrace, combined with the horror of allowing their wives, families, and communities to fall victim to Yankee tyranny, was a powerful force, clearly linking the white freedom and black slavery that defined the Confederacy. Slavery indeed mattered to Southerners—slaveholders and nonslaveholders alike—as it was the foundation of their society. Without it, there would be economic chaos and white debasement. In June 1862 Texan James C. Bates assured his sister that defeat meant enslaving the white South. Well aware of the actions of the Republican government in Washington, he explained that with a confiscation law already on the books, emancipation would not be far behind. Subjugation of whites and emancipation of blacks were Yankee goals that went hand in hand with the South's destiny of defeat. Bates had earlier become convinced that despite protestations to the contrary, "it is evident to my mind that the real purpose of the war is to 'wipe out slavery.'" Not only did he read captured letters to come to this conclusion, but he observed that the Northern army had "forced" slaves to leave their masters wherever it marched.[154]

African American soldiers in the Union ranks would provide additional evidence of the nefarious Yankee plot to destroy racial equilibrium. They certainly had a vested interest in ending slavery from the outset of the war, and their continued service in the face of prejudice and discrimination steeled their commitment to gaining their fair share of republican rights. James H. Hall, who had served with the 54th Massachusetts for over a year, including at Fort Wagner, argued that African Americans fought for the "proper enjoyment of the rights of citizenship, and a free title and acknowledged share in our noble birthplace."[155] His comrade in the 54th Massachusetts, Jacob E. Christy, pledged that he would "die a trying for our rights so that other that are born hereaffter may live and enjoy a happy life."[156] For Sergeant John C. Brock of the 43rd U.S. Colored Troops, continuing the fight to the end was also a matter of pride. When the war came to an end, he explained, not only will black soldiers have had a hand in bringing peace and liberty to the land, but they will be able to "look back on the days of our trials and tribulations, and behold the record of our deeds on the pages of our national history, bright and unsullied."[157]

Indianan Douglas Risley might have believed that the firing on Fort Sumter was the beginning of the end for slavery, but most Northern soldiers did not start out fighting the abolitionist war that African Americans envisioned.[158] Nevertheless, many of them, as early as the end of the first year of the war, understood the need for slavery to be abolished, especially if they witnessed the institution firsthand. As one enlisted man admitted, "Previous to this war, I hated the name of an abolitionist." Now, after less than a year, "I have seen enough of the beauties of slavery to turn me right around." Furthermore, he now concluded that "the salvation of the country depends on the adoption by the government of a sweeping emancipation policy."[159] Something like that policy took the form of Lincoln's Emancipation Proclamation, and not all soldiers were pleased with it. But the overwhelming majority stood by the president, and veterans in the ranks helped reelect him in 1864 when they had a chance to reverse his policies.

There remained white Union soldiers who held racist views or felt no kindness toward blacks, but more and more of them understood that the institution of slavery polluted republican government. For a reunited nation to prosper and regain its virtue, it had to move into the future unhindered by the shackles of slavery. Joseph Lester, a Wisconsin volunteer who believed the war to be a punishment for slavery, campaigned hard in the western theater and around Atlanta. His experience led him to conclude that "slavery dies hard, very hard." However, that death must be a result of the Union war effort. "The *Restored Union* without that 'nether millstone' to retard its 'Onward March' will *vault* into its acknowledged position of being a First class power and the asylum of the oppressed of all Nations."[160]

NOTES

1. Harold Adams Small, ed., *The Road to Richmond: The Civil War Memoirs of Major Abner R. Small of the Sixteenth Maine Volunteers: Together with the Diary That He Kept When He Was a Prisoner of War* (New York: Fordham University Press, 2000), 22–23.

2. Sumner A. Cunningham, *Reminiscences of the 41st Tennessee: The Civil War in the West,* ed. John A. Simpson (Shippensburg, PA: White Mane, 2001), 76.

3. Philip N. Racine, ed., *"Unspoiled Heart": The Journal of Charles Mattocks of the 17th Maine* (Knoxville: University of Tennessee Press, 1994), 23–24.

4. Ibid., 23.

5. Small, *Road to Richmond,* 22–23.

6. David W. Blight, ed., *When This Cruel War Is Over: The Civil War Letters of Charles Harvey Brewster* (Amherst: University of Massachusetts Press, 1992), 147.

7. Joseph Allen Frank and George A. Reaves, *"Seeing the Elephant": Raw Recruits at the Battle of Shiloh* (Urbana: University of Illinois Press, 2003), 129–47.

8. John R. Sellers, ed., *A People at War: Civil War Manuscripts from the Holdings of the Library of Congress* (Alexandria, VA: Chadwyck-Heakey, 1989–1990), A. C. Hills to Doctor Stedman, July 21, 1862, reel 49.

9. Warren Lee Goss, *Recollections of a Private: A Story of the Army of the Potomac* (Scituate, MA: Digital Scanning, 2002), 135.

10. Mark K. Christ, ed., *Getting Used to Being Shot At: The Spence Family Civil War Letters* (Fayetteville: University of Arkansas Press, 2002), 103.

11. Ibid.

12. Mauriel Phillips Joslyn, ed., *Charlotte's Boys: Civil War Letters of the Branch Family of Savannah* (Berryville, VA: Rockbridge, 1996), 119.

13. Document 7 in Marszalek and Williams, "Mississippi Soldiers in the Civil War," *Mississippi History Now,* http://mshistory.k12.ms.us/index.php?s=extra&id=183.

14. John Rozier, ed., *The Granite Farm Letters: The Civil War Correspondence of Edgeworth and Sallie Bird* (Athens: University of Georgia Press, 1988), 125.

15. Goss, *Recollections of a Private,* 134.

16. F. Jay Taylor, ed., *Reluctant Rebel: The Secret Diary of Robert Patrick, 1861–1865* (Baton Rouge: Louisiana State University Press, 1959), 122.

17. Christ, *Getting Used to Being Shot At,* 31.

18. John G. Barrett, ed., *Yankee Rebel: The Civil War Journal of Edmund DeWitt Patterson* (Knoxville: University of Tennessee Press, 2004), 34–35.

19. Stephen W. Sears, ed., *Mr. Dunn Browne's Experiences in the Army: The Civil War Letters of Samuel W. Fiske* (New York: Fordham University Press, 1998), 11.

20. Merrill C. (Tom) Sawyer, Betty Sawyer, and Timothy C. Sawyer, trans., *Letters from a Civil War Surgeon: The Letters of Dr. William Child of the Fifth New Hampshire Volunteers* (Solon, ME: Polar Bear, 1995), 34.

21. Mildred Throne, ed., *The Civil War Diary of Cyrus F. Boyd, Fifteenth Iowa Infantry, 1861–1863* (Millwood, NY: Kraus Reprint, 1977), 70–71.

22. Barrett, *Yankee Rebel,* 88.

23. Kenneth W. Noe, ed., *A Southern Boy in Blue: The Memoir of Marcus Woodcock, 9th Kentucky Infantry (U.S.A.)* (Knoxville: University of Tennessee Press, 1996), 136–37.

24. Throne, *Civil War Diary of Cyrus F. Boyd,* 41–42.

25. Thomas D. Cockrell and Michael B. Ballard, eds., *A Mississippi Rebel in the Army of Northern Virginia: The Civil War Memoirs of Private David Holt* (Baton Rouge: Louisiana State University Press, 1995), 289.

26. Frank and Reaves, *"Seeing the Elephant,"* 122.

27. Robert L. Bee, ed., *The Boys from Rockville: Civil War Narratives of Sgt. Benjamin Hirst, Company D, 14th Connecticut Volunteers* (Knoxville: University of Tennessee Press, 1998), 18, 23.

28. Stephen W. Sears, ed., *On Campaign with the Army of the Potomac: The Civil War Journal of Theodore Ayrault Dodge* (New York: Cooper Square Press, 2001), 305.

29. Peter Messent and Steve Courtney, eds., *The Civil War Letters of Joseph Hopkins Twichell* (Athens: University of Georgia Press, 2006), 249.

30. Bernard A. Olsen, ed., *Upon the Tented Field: An Historical Account of the Civil War as Told by the Men Who Fought and Gave Their Lives* (Red Bank, NJ: Historic Projects, 1993), 236.

31. Lois Bryan Adams, *Letters from Washington, 1863–1865,* ed. Evelyn Leasher (Detroit, MI: Wayne State University Press, 1999), 188.

32. Edwin C. Bears, ed., *A Louisiana Confederate: Diary of Felix Pierre Poché,* trans. Eugenie Watson Somdal (Natchitoches: Louisiana Studies Institute, Northwestern State University, 1972), 111.

33. Newton T. Colby, *The Civil War Papers of Lt. Colonel Newton T. Colby, New York Infantry,* ed. William E. Hughes (Jefferson, NC: McFarland, 2003), 154–55.

34. Adams, *Letters from Washington,* 188.

35. John D. Billings, *Hardtack and Coffee: The Unwritten Story of Army Life* (Lincoln: University of Nebraska Press, 1993), 314–15.

36. Mark De Wolfe Howe, ed., *Touched with Fire: Civil War Letters and Diary of Oliver Wendell Holmes, Jr., 1861–1864* (New York: Fordham University Press, 2000), 25.

37. Robert Knox Sneden, *Eye of the Storm: A Civil War Odyssey,* ed. Charles F. Bryan Jr. and Nelson D. Lankford (New York: Free Press, 2000), 68–92.

38. John Herbert Roper, ed., *Repairing the "March of Mars": The Civil War Diaries of John Samuel Apperson, Hospital Steward in the Stonewall Brigade, 1861–1865* (Macon, GA: Mercer University Press, 2001), 117.

39. William J. K. Beaudot and Lance J. Herdegen, eds., *An Irishman in the Iron Brigade: The Civil War Memoirs of James P. Sullivan, Sergt., Company K, 6th Wisconsin Volunteers* (New York: Fordham University Press, 1993), 63–64.

40. Jeffrey D. Marshall, ed., *A War of the People: Vermont Civil War Letters* (Hanover, NH: University Press of New England, 1999), 171.

41. Messent and Courtney, *Civil War Letters of Joseph Hopkins Twichell,* 232–34, 249, 255 (quotation).

42. Sneden, *Eye of the Storm,* 68–73.

43. Sam Watkins, *"Company Aytch," or a Side Show of the Big Show and Other Sketches,* ed. M. Thomas Inge (New York: Penguin Putnam, 1999), 171.

44. Howe, *Touched with Fire,* 27–30.

45. Messent and Courtney, *Civil War Letters of Joseph Hopkins Twichell,* 175.

46. Ted Tunnell, ed., *Carpetbagger from Vermont: The Autobiography of Marshall Harvey Twitchell* (Baton Rouge: Louisiana State University Press, 1989), 36–37.

47. DeWitt Boyd Stone Jr., ed., *Wandering to Glory: Confederate Veterans Remember Evans' Brigade* (Columbia: University of South Carolina Press, 2002), 124–25.

48. Watkins, *"Company Aytch,"* 172.

49. Noe, *A Southern Boy in Blue,* 294–95.

50. Messent and Courtney, *Civil War Letters of Joseph Hopkins Twichell,* 234.

51. Stephen W. Sears, ed., *For Country, Cause and Leader: The Civil War Journal of Charles B. Hayden* (New York: Ticknor & Fields, 1993), 340.

52. Racine, *"Unspoiled Heart,"* 30.

53. Messent and Courtney, *The Civil War Letters of Joseph Hopkins Twichell,* 233.

54. John D. Billings, *Hardtack and Coffee,* 309.

55. Charles Beneulyn Johnson, MD, *Muskets and Medicine or Army Life in the Sixties* (Philadelphia: F. A. Davis, 1917), 132.

56. Thomas P. Lowrey, MD, ed., *Swamp Doctor: The Diary of a Union Surgeon in the Virginia and North Carolina Marshes* (Mechanicsburg, PA: Stackpole Books, 2001), 94.

57. Cynthia DeHaven Pitcock and Bill J. Gurley, eds., *I Acted from Principle: The Civil War Diary of Dr. William M. McPheeters, Confederate Surgeon in the Trans-Mississippi* (Fayetteville: University of Arkansas Press, 2002), 138–39.

58. Sellers, *A People at War,* Henry Eells to dear friends, April 13, 1862, Samuel Henry Eells Papers, reel 24.

59. James M. Greiner, Janet L. Coryell, and James R. Smither, eds., *A Surgeon's Civil War: The Letters and Diary of Damniel M. Holt, M.D.* (Kent, OH: Kent State University Press, 1994), 92–96.

60. J. Franklin Dyer, *The Journal of a Civil War Surgeon,* ed. Michael B. Chesson (Lincoln: University of Nebraska Press, 2003), 28.

61. Sawyer et al., *Letters from a Civil War Surgeon,* 33.

62. Pitcock and Gurley, *I Acted from Principle,* 141.

63. Frank. R. Freemon, *Gangrene and Glory: Medical Care during the Civil War* (Urbana: University of Illinois Press, 2001), 48.

64. Michael A. Ross, *Justice of Shattered Dreams: Samuel Freeman Miller and the Supreme Court during the Civil War Era* (Baton Rouge: Louisiana State University Press, 2003), 63.

65. Donald B. Koonce, ed., *Doctor to the Front: The Recollections of Confederate Surgeon Thomas Fanning Wood, 1861–1865* (Knoxville: University of Tennessee Press, 2000), 31; Freemon, *Gangrene and Glory,* 34.

66. Messent and Courtney, *Civil War Letters of Joseph Hopkins Twichell,* 233.

67. Alfred Jay Bollett, *Civil War Medicine: Challenges and Triumphs* (Tucson, AZ: Galen Press, 2002), 112–15; Laura L. Behling, ed., *Hospital Transports: A Memoir of the Embarkation of the Sick and Wounded from the Peninsula of Virginia in the Summer of 1862* (Albany: State University of New York Press, 2005), 7–14, passim; Theodore J. Karamanski, *Rally 'Round the Flag: Chicago and the Civil War* (Chicago: Nelson-Hall, 1993), 94–95; Peter Josyph, ed., *The Wounded River: The Civil War Letters of John Vance Lauderdale, M.D.* (East Lansing: Michigan State University Press, 1993), 30–31.

68. Sears, *For Country, Cause and Leader,* 341.

69. Marshall, *A War of the People,* 130–31.

70. Kate Coming, *Kate: The Journal of a Confederate Nurse,* ed. Richard Barksdale Harwell (Baton Rouge: Louisiana State University Press, 1987), 164.

71. Jane Stuart Woolsey, *Hospital Days: Reminiscences of a Civil War Nurse* (Roseville, MN: Edinborough Press, 2001), 95.

72. Ella Jane Bruen and Brian M. Fitzgibbons, eds., *Through Ordinary Eyes: The Civil War Correspondence of Rufus Robbins, Private, 7th Regiment, Massachusetts Volunteers* (Westport, CT: Praeger, 2000), 186.

73. Judith A. Bailey and Robert I. Cotton, eds., *After Chancellorsville: Letters from the Heart, the Civil War Letters of Private Walter G. Dunn and Emma Randolph* (Baltimore: Maryland Historical Society, 1998), 21, 23.

74. George Skoch and Mark W. Perkins, eds., *Lone Star Confederate: A Gallant and Good Soldier of the Fifth Texas Infantry* (College Station: Texas A&M University Press, 2003), 82–83.

75. Bailey and Cotton, *After Chancellorsville,* 142, 150.

76. Steven S. Raab, ed., *With the 3rd Wisconsin Badgers: The Living Experience of the Civil War through the Journals of Van R. Willard* (Mechanicsburg, PA: Stackpole Books, 1999), 96–97.

77. William C. Davis and Meredith L. Swentor, eds., *Bluegrass Confederate: The Headquarters Diary of Edward O. Guerrant* (Baton Rouge: Louisiana State University Press, 1999), 40.

78. Carol Cranmer Green, *Chimborazo: The Confederacy's Largest Hospital* (Knoxville: University of Tennessee Press, 2004), 46, 69–70, 73, 76–77; Lance Herdegen and Sherry Murphy, eds., *Four Years with the Iron Brigade: The Civil War Journal of William Ray, Company F, Seventh Wisconsin Volunteers* (Cambridge, MA: Da Capo Press, 2002), 197–213; Sears, *Mr. Dunn Browne's Experiences,* 172; Emil Rosenblatt and Ruth Rosenblatt, eds., *Hard Marching Every Day: The Civil War Letters of Private Wilbur Fiske, 1861–1865* (Lawrence: University Press of Kansas, 1992), 300.

79. Bailey and Cotton, *After Chancellorsville,* 5, 11, 16.

80. David Herbert Donald, ed., *Gone for a Soldier: The Civil War Memoirs of Private Alfred Bellard* (Boston: Little, Brown, 1975), 231–232.

81. Bailey and Cotton, *After Chancellorsville,* 28, 36.

82. Barrett, *Yankee Rebel,* 40–44.

83. Sears, *Mr. Dunn Browne's Experiences,* 172.

84. Mark A. Weitz, *More Damning Than Slaughter: Desertion in the Confederate Army* (Lincoln: University of Nebraska Press, 2005), 80–81, 103, 167–69; Glenna R. Schroeder-Lein, *Confederate Hospitals on the Move: Samuel H. Stout and the Army of Tennessee* (Columbia: University of South Carolina Press, 1994), 137; Freemon, *Gangrene and Glory,* 156–57.

85. Sears, *For Country, Cause and Leader,* 343, 362.

86. Robert Garth Scott, ed., *Fallen Leaves: The Civil War Letters of Major Henry Livermore Abbott* (Kent, OH: Kent State University Press, 1991), 143, 146.

87. Charles W. Sanders Jr., *While in the Hands of the Enemy: Military Prisons of the Civil War* (Baton Rouge: Louisiana State University Press, 2005), 1; Margaret E. Wagner, Gary W. Gallagher, and Paul Finkelman, eds., *The Library of Congress Civil War Desk Reference* (New York: Simon & Schuster, 2002), 583–96.

88. R. Thomas Campbell, ed., *Southern Service on Land and Sea: The Wartime Journal of Robert Watson CSA/CSN* (Knoxville: University of Tennessee Press, 2002), 47–48.

89. Michael B. Ballard, *Vicksburg: The Campaign That Opened the Mississippi* (Chapel Hill: University of North Carolina Press, 2004), 399.

90. Sanders, *While in the Hands of the Enemy,* 133–34.

91. Ibid.

92. Sellers, *A People at War,* Albert Irwin to Bernard J. D. Irwin, September 21, 1862, Bernard John Dowling Irwin Papers, reel 57.

93. Weitz, *More Damning Than Slaughter,* 291.

94. Campbell, *Southern Service on Land and Sea,* 50.

95. Kathleen Gorman, ed., *Boy Soldier of the Confederacy: The Memoir of Johnnie Wickersham* (Carbondale: Southern Illinois University Press, 2006), 69–70.

96. Armstead L. Robinson, *Bitter Fruits of Bondage: The Demise of Slavery and the Collapse of the Confederacy, 1861–1865* (Charlottesville: University of Virginia Press, 2005), 220–225, 221 (quotation).

97. Karamanski, *Rally 'Round the Flag,* 142–44.

98. Ross, *Justice of Shattered Dreams,* 63–64.

99. Wagner et al., *Library of Congress Civil War Desk Reference,* 589, 590.

100. William Marvel, *Andersonville: The Last Depot* (Chapel Hill: University of North Carolina Press, 1994), 180, 284 n. 39.

101. John G. Barrett, *Yankee Rebel,* 119–20.

102. Bernhard Domschcke, *Twenty Months in Captivity: Memoirs of a Union Officer in Confederate Prisons,* ed. and trans. Frederic Trautmann (Rutherford, NJ: Fairleigh Dickinson University Press, 1987), 99.

103. Cunningham, *Reminiscences of the 41st Tennessee,* 17.

104. Luis F. Emilio, *A Brave Black Regiment: The History of the 54th Massachusetts, 1863–1865,* 2nd enlarged ed. (New York: Da Capo Press, 1995), 400.

105. Noah Andre Trudeau, *Like Men of War: Black Troops in the Civil War, 1862–1865* (Boston: Little, Brown, 1998), 247–48, 248 (quotation).

106. Keith Wilson, *Honor in Command: Lt. Freeman S. Bowley's Civil War Service in the 30th United States Colored Infantry* (Gainesville: University Press of Florida, 2006), 160.

107. Karamanski, *Rally 'Round the Flag,* 141; Cunningham, *Reminiscences of the 41st Tennessee,* 22.

108. Michael P. Gray, *The Business of Captivity: Elmira and Its Civil War Prison* (Kent, OH: Kent State University Press, 2001), 23–25.

109. Sneden, *Eye of the Storm,* 244.

110. Ibid., 225.

111. Trudeau, *Like Men of War,* 102.

112. Edward A. Miller Jr., *The Black Civil War Soldiers of Illinois: The Story of the Twenty-ninth U.S. Colored Infantry* (Columbia: University of South Carolina Press, 1998), 79.

113. Trudeau, *Like Men of War,* 310–11.

114. Versalle F. Washington, *Eagles on Their Buttons: A Black Infantry Regiment in the Civil War* (Columbia: University of Missouri Press, 1999), 89–90.

115. Barrett, *Yankee Rebel,* 120–22, 181–82.

116. Sellers, *A People at War,* entry for May 26, 1864, George Washington Hall Memoir and Diary, reel 43.

117. Barrett, *Yankee Rebel,* 141, 157–58, 160, 161, 167, 174; Racine, *"Unspoiled Heart,"* 157, 203; James I. Robertson Jr., ed., *Soldier of Southwestern Virginia: The Civil War Letters of Captain John Preston Sheffey* (Baton Rouge: Louisiana State University Press, 2004), 222; Sneden, *Eye of the Storm,* 253; see document 7 in Marszalek and Williams, "Mississippi Soldiers in the Civil War."

118. Robertson, *Soldier of Southwestern Virginia,* 223.

119. Racine, *"Unspoiled Heart,"* 144.

120. Roger S. Durham, ed., *A Confederate Yankee: The Journal of Edward William Drummond, a Confederate Soldier from Maine* (Knoxville: University of Tennessee Press, 2004), 58.

121. Barrett, *Yankee Rebel,* 126–27; Durham, *A Confederate Yankee,* 54.

122. Barrett, *Yankee Rebel,* 157.

123. Durham, *A Confederate Yankee,* 54, 56; George B. Kirsch, *Baseball in Blue and Gray: The National Pastime during the Civil War* (Princeton, NJ: Princeton University Press, 2003), 42–47; Barrett, *Yankee Rebel,* 190.

124. Lewis N. Wynne and Robert A. Taylor, eds., *This War So Horrible: The Civil War Diary of Hiram Smith Williams* (Tuscaloosa: University of Alabama Press, 1993), 131.

125. Terry A. Johnston Jr., ed., *"Him on the One Side and Me on the Other": The Civil War Letters of Alexander Campbell, 79th New York Infantry Regiment and James Campbell, 1st South Carolina Battalion* (Columbia: University of South Carolina Press, 1999), 149.

126. G. Ward Hubbs, ed., *Voices from Company D: Diaries by the Greensboro Guards, Fifth Alabama Infantry Regiment, Army of Northern Virginia* (Athens: University of Georgia Press, 2003), 370.

127. Barrett, *Yankee Rebel,* 159, 171–72.

128. Ibid., 194–95.

129. Sanders, *While in the Hands of the Enemy,* 1. For statistics of individual camps, see Wagner et al., *Library of Congress Civil War Desk Reference,* 583–96.

130. Domschcke, *Twenty Months in Captivity,* 49.

131. Sneden, *Eye of the Storm,* 229.

132. Ibid., 202–88.

133. Marvel, *Andersonville,* 157; Sneden, *Eye of the Storm,* 231.

134. Domschcke, *Twenty Months in Captivity,* 50–51.

135. Sneden, *Eye of the Storm,* 214.

136. Racine, *"Unspoiled Heart,"* 228–47.

137. Wilson, *Honor in Command,* 208–9.

138. Samuel C. Jones, *Reminiscences of the 22nd Iowa Infantry: Giving Its Organization, Marches, Skirmishes, Battles, and Sieges, as Taken from the Diary of Lieutenant S. C. Jones of Company A* (Iowa City: Press of the Camp Pope Bookshop, 1993), 92.

139. Judith Lee Hallock, ed., *The Civil War Letters of Joshua K. Callaway* (Athens: University of Georgia Press, 1997), 114.

140. Sellers, *A People at War,* entry for June 17, 1862, George Washington Hall Memoir and Diary, reel 43.

141. C. Knight Aldrich, ed., *Quest for a Star: The Civil War Letters and Diaries of Colonel Francis T. Sherman of the 88th Illinois* (Knoxville: University of Tennessee Press, 1999), 46.

142. Andrew J. Torget and Edward L. Ayers, *Two Communities in the Civil War* (New York: W. W. Norton, 2007), 138.

143. Sears, *For Country, Cause and Leader,* 349.

144. John Kent Folman, ed., *From That Terrible Field: Civil War Letters of James M. Williams, Twenty-first Alabama Infantry Volunteers* (Tuscaloosa: University of Alabama Press, 1981), 92–93.

145. J. Tracy Powers, *Lee's Miserables: Life in the Army of Northern Virginia from the Wilderness to Appomattox* (Chapel Hill: University of North Carolina Press, 1998), 313–14.

146. J. M. Randall to wife, November 3, 1864, James M. Randall Diary, eHistory, Ohio State University, Columbus, http://ehistory.osu.edu/osu/sources/letters/randall/.

147. Janet Correll Ellison, ed., with assistance from Mark A. Weitz, *On to Atlanta: The Civil War Diaries of John Hill Ferguson, Illinois Tenth Regiment of Volunteers* (Lincoln: University of Nebraska Press, 2001), 5.

148. Robert Hunt Rhodes, ed., *All for the Union: The Civil War Diary and Letters of Elisha Hunt Rhodes* (New York: Vintage Books, 1992), 127–28.

149. Christine Dee, ed., *Ohio's Civil War: The Civil War in Documents* (Athens: Ohio University Press, 2006), 124.

150. Richard Lowe, ed., *A Texas Cavalry Officer's Civil War: The Diary and Letters of James C. Bates* (Baton Rouge: Louisiana University Press, 1999), 111.

151. Judith N. McArthur and Orville Vernon Burton, eds., *A Gentleman and an Officer: A Military and Social History of James B. Griffin's Civil War* (New York: Oxford University Press, 1996), 163.

152. Sellers, *A People at War,* entry for June 17, 1862, George Washington Hall Memoir and Diary, reel 43.

153. Tammy Harden Galloway, ed., *Dear Old Roswell: The Civil War Letters of the King Family of Roswell, Georgia* (Macon, GA: Mercer University Press, 2003), 81, 92 (quotation).

154. Lowe, *A Texas Cavalry Officer's Civil War,* 123, 133–34.

155. Edwin S. Redkey, ed., *A Grand Army of Black Men: Letters from African-American Soldiers in the Union Army, 1861–1865* (Cambridge: Cambridge University Press, 1992), 205–8, 229–68.

156. Torget and Ayers, *Two Communities,* 138.

157. Eric Ledell Smith, ed., "The Civil War Letters of Quartermaster Sergeant John C. Brock, 43rd Regiment, United States Colored Troops," in *Making and Remaking Pennsylvania's Civil War,* ed. William Blair and William Pencak (University Park: Pennsylvania State University, 2001), 161.

158. Douglas G. Risley to parents, March 15, 1862, Civil War Pension File, Record Group 15, National Archives Building, Washington, DC.

159. Quoted in Howard N. Meyer, *The Amendment That Refused to Die: Equality and Justice Deferred, the History of the Fourteenth Amendment,* updated ed. (Lanham, MD: Madison Books, 2000), 41.

160. Sellers, *A People at War,* Joseph Lester to sister Charlotte, October 1, 1864, Joseph Lester Collection, reel 58.

9   THE TRANSITION TO PEACE

APPOMATTOX AND THE END OF THE CONFEDERACY

Lee's surrender at Appomattox Court House sent waves of delirium through the ranks of the Army of the Potomac. Charles Mattocks had rejoined the army after being exchanged as a prisoner of war shortly before Lee's surrender, but he now made clear that he did not regret that decision. "I am thankful that [I] got back in time for the funeral!" he informed his mother, who had objected to his return. Now, he, his fellows in the 17th Maine, and the rest of the Army of the Potomac were "wild with excitement." "It appeared as if the Army was crazy," reported New Jersey soldier George Fox. "Every one was so glad and such hurrahing I never heard before." Men made speeches and cheered.[1] Bands played in celebration, and cannon fired salutes to victory, while soldiers discharged their rifles into the air and "howled like mad."[2] On the following evening, some soldiers celebrated with "improvised fireworks" by "shooting rebel fuses from their muskets with small charges of powder," giving the appearance of "hundreds of Roman candles" creating a "beautiful" display against a backdrop of flickering campfires.[3] When word spread to other Union armies, men reacted with comparable enthusiasm. Down in Florida, Justus Silliman and his comrades "were so overwhelmed with joy" that they "shook hands together, hugged each other and cut up all sorts of antics in our ecstacy."[4]

The surrender of the Army of Northern Virginia did not remove all opposition to Union forces from the field. Nevertheless, Northern soldiers believed it was the decisive moment. Lee's army had been the "main strength" of the Confederacy, and now it had laid down its arms.[5] Union soldiers, including skeptics in Sherman's forces, well understood the significance of Lee's surrender. With Lee finished and Johnston "hemmed in," Taylor Peirce expected to "be at home soon." "Our country is safe the war over and my life spared to once more partake of the joys of home," he happily wrote to his wife. He and other Iowans now discussed their own imminent "emancipation" from the army and "the pleasures of our meeting with the home circle." For Peirce and his comrades, the future looked bright. The flag still flew, slavery was gone, and the nation was "about to enter a career of greatness and prosperity never equaled by any known on earth." Now, with "Victory won," he was "impatient to wend [his] way for the old home and little ones," never again "to be disturbed by the hoarse clarion of the Canons Roar."[6] When the end finally came, Iowan Charles Musser placed these thoughts in a larger perspective. By defeating the rebellion, he explained, the United States had proven to other nations that "man is capable of Self-Government."[7]

THE ASSASSINATION OF PRESIDENT LINCOLN

Union soldiers, unfortunately, had their celebratory moods dashed in the days after Lee's capitulation by Abraham Lincoln's assassination. Justus Silliman witnessed the quick shifting in the mood of the soldiers on duty with him in Florida. "It seemed as though from the sunshine of our joy," he explained, "we had become suddenly enveloped in a dark and gloomy cloud that was horrible to contemplate."[8] After recovering from the numbing blow of the sad news, many soldiers reacted with visceral thoughts of revenge. Men filled with hate promised to show no mercy to any rebel if there were any more battles and advocated "a complete *annihilation* of the whole cursed race" of Southerners.[9] But Taylor Peirce thought of a vengeance that would have a long, humiliating effect on the erstwhile Confederacy. He prescribed turning over the rebel states to their former slaves to "go in now and make a clean shucking of the South." "I am in favor of having the South Settled with a better breed of dogs," he explained, "and therefore let the negroes take it."[10]

Men of the 33rd Iowa Infantry, in Alabama at the time, also contemplated the revenge they would take on any rebels who confronted them in battle, but they and probably most other Union soldiers soon moved past the point of rage to immerse themselves in "that deep grief which the whole loyal nation felt."[11] Soldiers now turned from ebullient celebrations to somber ceremonies. Commands flew flags at half staff, draped in black, while cannon punctuated the daylong mourning. Regimental bands played solemn tunes during religious services. Soldiers held meetings to honor the late president. All the while, the thoughtful men among them tried to make sense of Lincoln's death. Perhaps they had held him in too high esteem, some men worried, revering him in a way that they should reserve for God; or perhaps they had been too proud of him, and the assassination was to humble them. Taylor Peirce pondered the assassination's meaning and could not disconnect it from the central cause of the war. He wondered why all of the bloodshed had not sufficiently cleansed the nation of "the sin of slavery," which now also required the martyrdom of the president. He could only imagine that the "magnitude of the national Sin must necessarily require proportionate attonement."[12]

CONFEDERATE DESPAIR AND DEFIANCE

Confederate soldiers expressed mixed feelings about the death of their enemy president, but they were preoccupied with their own troubles as they came to grips with the surrender of their armies. The news of Lee's surrender elicited disbelief, anger, and sorrow from those remaining soldiers still committed to the cause. It also brought forth frustration, despair, and defiance from some men who were trying to decide how to cope with their own national disaster. When Virginian William Thomas Poague learned of Lee's surrender, he later recalled, "All at once my heart got to my throat and everything around me became dim and obscure." He witnessed men crying "like children." Some soldiers "sat on the ground with faces buried in their hands, quietly sobbing." Men grabbed hold of one another, "their bodies trembling and shaking," while "others, struck dumb and with blanched faces, seemed to strain their eyes to catch the form of some awful horror that suddenly loomed before them."[13] The men of the Fourth Alabama were also shamed by their circumstances. "The mortification of having to march up and stack arms in front of a host of men," one member recalled, "whom we had every right to consider, man for man, that we were their superiors, from past experience on many battlefields, was most galling to our proud spirits."[14]

At Appomattox, men accepted Grant's generous terms of surrender and rations from their erstwhile enemies, pledged their parole, and began to think about home. Many were happy that it was all over, having grown "tired of being handled like cattle by officers and civilians," and were just as eager as their enemy to return to their families.[15] Other men drew on reservoirs of pride to exercise at least one final act of defiance. Color-bearers hid their flags or cut them into small pieces to distribute among their comrades to prevent the symbol of their regiment and their cause from falling into enemy hands.[16] Some men thought of joining other armies without official sanction or traveling to the trans-Mississippi Confederacy, indicating that they were not as sure as their Yankee counterparts that the end of Lee was the end of the Confederacy. Members of Terry's Texas Rangers, for example, were determined to continue to wage war. They decided to try to reach Johnston's army from Virginia but then shifted their destination to the Confederate army in Alabama. When they learned of its surrender, they kept moving westward, expecting to fight on beyond the Mississippi River.[17]

Soldiers in Confederate armies in Virginia and across the South did not initially accept the finality of Lee's surrender, but as the reality of defeat spread westward, men despaired for the future. For some men, including Samuel A. Burney, who was on commissary duty in southwestern Georgia, giving up meant giving in to a world controlled by hated Northerners and freed slaves. "Our condition will be truly deplorable and the exulting & tyrannical Yankee and with the negroes freed around us," he lamented. "Oh, what a wretched society we will have." He found a "peace of submission" worse than war and committed himself to fight on, if only his leaders would ask.[18] Louisiana soldier Felix Pierre Poché also feared the new order and became depressed. He found no comfort in returning to his family after learning of the surrenders of Lee and Johnston because it would not be "compensation for the humiliation and despair" he felt; rather, instead of submitting to the "yoke of our implacable enemy, and to live under the domination of a people whom we hold justly so in horror," he was "inclined to ask God to take me from this world before the realization of our enemy's scheme."[19]

Despite this uneasiness, soldiers had little choice but to face reality. When the generals in Virginia finished their parley, most of Lee's men agreed that they had to accept defeat of their army and, perhaps, their cause. In Louisiana, David Pierson observed that even if Jefferson Davis made his way to the western Confederacy, it would be of no use. "The soldiers are disheartened & disgusted," he confessed, "and determined not to sacrifice their lives to gratify anybody's ambition."[20]

In Texas, despite political talk of creating a trans-Mississippi bastion of resistance, when men learned of the surrender of Lee and Johnston, discipline and the will to fight deteriorated to the point where they were ready to give up. Soldiers at Brownsville, for example, began to disband when they heard the news, and hundreds of men walked away from their post at Galveston. One of the men stationed at Galveston professed that even though the army had stopped the mutiny there, the men were "not going into any more fights for fear that we might get Kild" because they knew "how things stands East of the Missipi."[21]

As time passed, veterans would try to fathom why they had failed to win. Whether God had abandoned them because of the sin of slavery, or the economic might of the North had overwhelmed them, or the home front had grown weary of the contest would provide starting points for contemplation into the next century. Soldiers across the South accepted defeat probably thinking of these explanations, but they also were weary and fatalistic about the end of their crusade. They might have wondered why they had sacrificed so much for such an outcome but knew that they must look to dealing with their immediate needs and, perhaps, the future.

Most Confederates knew that they were lucky to be alive and that they indeed had a future to construct. Texan William Fletcher, stunned by the outcome of events and worried that he and his comrades might end up in a Northern prison, came to see there was not much he could do about the Confederacy's demise. "I awoke, as it were," he later recalled, "to realize that there was a future," and "day by day the sunshine of my being grew brighter."[22] Rudolph Coreth, another Texan, worried about the "terrible events" that would follow the end of slavery, but once he realized that further resistance would not stop emancipation, "the prospect of [his own] personal freedom" became "really very nice."[23] Georgian Charles Olmstead explained that despite the difficulty of accepting its outcome, he was "weary of war and of the long separation from my wife and children." Now he was pleased to be going home to begin a new life "while I was still young, and blessed with a vigorous and unmutilated body."[24]

The willingness to lay down their arms, however, did not mean that soldiers renounced the validity of their old cause. Louisianan Douglas Cater, who had campaigned with the Army of Tennessee, accepted that they would "make the best of it" but refused to acknowledge the error of their cause. "I still believe that I have been engaged in a just cause and shall not despair of living in a free and independent Confederacy," Cater wrote, "but the time for more fighting is *not now*." Cater believed he would "make a good citizen" and professed a willingness "to share the fate of my friends in the seceded states."[25]

Surrender lapped over the Confederacy from Appomattox westward, but soldiers experienced it in many different ways. Men in the Army of Northern Virginia submitted to a formal ceremony on April 12, stacking their arms and turning over their furled flags to their former enemies. Soldiers elsewhere were spared the humiliation of ceremonial submission and participated in surrenders that were more bureaucratic procedure than anything else. Sherman did not require a formal surrender of Johnston's army, allowing it, as one midwesterner observed, "to furl its ill-starred banners and lay down its arms in the seclusion of its own camp." The federal camp exhibited some sensitivity to their enemy's ill fortune by avoiding an official army-wide victory celebration marked by "blare of band" and the "peel of cannon," but the generals failed to prevent individual groups of Yankees from having their own noisy festivities.[26]

The subdued end of the Army of Tennessee, rather than the formal surrender of the Army of Northern Virginia, was the norm across the old Confederacy, as rebels turned over their rifles, signed their paroles, and walked away from the war. There were many Confederate soldiers throughout the South, like those Texas Rangers, who simply refused to participate in any act of submission, subdued or otherwise. A defiant Berry G. Benson absented himself from the formal surrender ceremonies of the Army of Northern Virginia, shouldered his rifle one more time, and began to march down to North Carolina to continue fighting with Johnston's army. He was able to catch a train and arrived at Greensboro, only to learn that Johnston was planning to surrender. He still could not give up at that point, so he decided to make his way home without ever bow-ing to the enemy.[27]

Like Berry Benson, Confederates from Virginia to Texas simply walked away from their armies, not wishing or waiting to sign paroles. Others realized that it was only prac-tical to go through the formalities and obtain a piece of paper that would allow them to begin new lives. In the border state of Tennessee, former Confederates gathered in Nashville to sign oaths and obtain their paroles, apparently eager to put the war behind them. One rebel remarked that he did not care what kind of oath was required of him, as long as "they give me no more fight." Another veteran remarked that he had seen his home place and that he would now "take a hundred oaths if they want me to." Yankee William Bradbury also encountered a group of 300 former rebels in Tennessee, of whom only 4 preferred to remain prisoners of war, rather than take the oath; in another group of 200 men, only 2 chose not to pledge their allegiance to the Union.[28] At least these men appeared to be ready to accept defeat, if they could finally have peace.

CONFEDERATES MAKE THEIR WAY HOME

Once soldiers accepted defeat, they began to make their way home, taking advan-tage of rail transportation, steamboats, mules, and horses. Some men made use of shoe leather, others walked barefoot, driven by their desire to get home. Some men trudging along to their destination were fortunate to be able to hitch rides on wagons for part of the journey. The defeated moved out alone or traveled with what was left of their regi-ments, companies, or clusters of wartime companions for the camaraderie of the group or for their own protection. These men arrived home in days or weeks, depending on how far afield they had campaigned. Along the way, white civilians shook their hands, thanked them, and cried over them.[29]

There was no guarantee that modern conveyances provided the speediest and safest way home for these travelers. Trains and steamboats were neither comfortable nor safe when crowded with veterans. Missourian Johnny Wickersham recalled an unpleasant journey up the Mississippi River to his home state. Confederates "were loaded on every passing steamboat in much the same manner that cattle are loaded in a box car."[30] Trains also proved to be "slow and risky," and the veterans rode in overcrowded passenger cars and cattle cars with improvised seating.[31] Cars and roadbeds were in disrepair after four years of war, adding to the likelihood of derailments and other accidents. After one seri-ous accident, Gordon Bradwell decided to walk for a while, as he made his way from Virginia to Georgia, but boarded a train in Augusta, Georgia, which then derailed en route to Atlanta. Finally, he was able to travel in comfort in passenger cars on a stretch of rail between Atlanta and Macon, bidding farewell to comrades who arrived at their destinations along the way. He completed the last part of his journey, from Albany in southwest Georgia to Bainbridge, by stage.[32]

Travel of any sort could be "uncomfortable & disagreeable in the extreme" for men who lacked money for normal expenses, which would have been the case for most Con-federate veterans.[33] Union soldiers shared rations with surrendered Confederates, which helped, but travel remained a struggle for many of the former rebels. Kentuckian Johnnie Green, paroled after Johnston surrendered, began his journey back to civilian life with only "$2.50 in silver, a pocketful of confederate money, a horse & one days ration."[34] At least some South Carolinians, ever the unbending rebels, accepted Confederate money from Johnston's men as they moved through the state, but other white and black civilians aided impoverished veterans, generously refusing to take payment for food, shelter, or services rendered, even when they were near the limits of their own resources.[35] Johnnie Wickersham, who had lost his place on a Mississippi River steamer and lacked the funds to secure passage on another, walked home to Missouri, helped along the way by African Americans who shared their meager stores with him.[36]

There were Confederate soldiers who did not wait for charity as they made their way through the war-wrecked South. They stole from civilians and government warehouses and generally contributed to the chaotic postwar climate. Perhaps they were hardened by the war, desperate to survive, or eager to extract revenge on civilians for not having given them greater support. They also justified their actions by their own tatterdemalion appearance, hunger, or the fact that their now defunct civil government had long forgotten about their pay or had given them so little of it. Regardless of the reason, they seemed to have lost all respect for the property of others. Men from the Army of Northern Virginia who traveled into North Carolina after their surrender disrupted the discipline of Johnston's still organized army as they made their way home, taking what they needed as they passed through the camps.[37] Even Johnston's men believed that since they had received little pay from the government for their years of fighting, they would be justified in stealing "any Confederate property they could lay their hands on."[38]

Veterans making their way through Georgia rioted and broke into Confederate commissary stores at Augusta in the northeastern part of the state and at Thomasville in the southwestern corner. Georgia private Gordon Bradwell admitted securing new clothing "and much other plunder" from the warehouses at Augusta, which allowed him to toss his vermin-infested uniform into the Savannah River.[39] Bradwell might have felt doubly justified for his actions after seeing warehouses in southwest Georgia along the rail

Chattanooga, Tennessee: Confederate prisoners at railroad depot. (*Library of Congress*)

line filled to "capacity with Confederate corn and army supplies," enough, he believed, "to supply all the armies we had in the field, while we were starving in Virginia."[40]

Across the old Confederacy, in Texas, former soldiers initiated a lawlessness that was a prelude to the state's desperado culture of the Reconstruction era. Most veterans stole to feed themselves as they traveled home, but the violence in Texas also went beyond that necessity. Like their counterparts back east, men broke into government warehouses, considering the supplies therein compensation for their years of sacrifice. Some of these men formed into "predatory bands, utterly irresponsible, recognizing no rights of property" that "utterly sacked" Hempstead, Texas, including the town's stores and Confederate property there. The men seemed to be taking out their anger on their old government because they demolished Confederate stores they were unable to carry away.[41]

On their journey home, Confederate soldiers encountered Yankees who were reasserting their government's authority in the region, something that the veterans had to endure even after they arrived at their destinations. The Union soldiers had the legitimate task of reminding white Southerners what the war's conclusion meant. Usually, checking a Confederate parolee's papers was enough, but sometimes the victors' actions grated on the pride of their former adversaries. Some men returning to Tennessee, for example, were guarded by black troops. The African American troops made matters worse for the returning rebels by ridiculing them, which was a sure and maddening reminder of the changed circumstances.[42]

As the former rebels arrived home during the spring and summer and settled in to their new routines, they submitted to the same sort of minor annoyances or humiliations that they had endured during their travels. Elisha Hunt Rhodes thought it amusing to ask "all sorts of questions" of former rebels, who worried about whether they would be subjected to arrest and trial for their wartime actions.[43] In Danville, Virginia, federal authorities ordered paroled Confederate officers to report to the provost marshal if they refused to remove their uniforms; at one point, Union soldiers actually "stood at street corners with shears, to cut off brass buttons &c." to remove the last symbols of rebellion from worn gray coats.[44] More humiliating, in Charleston, South Carolina, ex-Confederates were harassed by members of the 54th Massachusetts. The former rebels found it "verry hard…to give a way" to the black soldiers who crowded them on the streets, but as one member of the 54th Massachusetts confessed, if the Confederates refused, "We knock them out of our way And if they don't like that we take them up and put them in the Guard house."[45] Such actions were annoying, but so, too, was the very presence of Yankees in the southland. As one Confederate officer recalled, on his arrival in Richmond, Virginia, he saw that "officers in blue were lounging about *our* usual haunts." Perhaps it was deeply upsetting to him that "soldiers in blue had usurped the places of our boys in gray."[46]

Civilians honored and received their returning soldiers in subdued ways that lacked the fanfare with which they had sent the boys off to war. There were no grand reviews, but small acknowledgments of the boys' return. On their way home, soldiers might have encountered civilians who shook their hands, thanked them, and cried over them. A small group of citizens meeting men at the depot or station or a warm greeting from an old acquaintance encountered on the street or at church services were the likely scenarios on their return to their communities. In Richmond, Virginia, women discretely honored soldiers by waving "little white handkerchiefs" from their windows, while a notice in the Savannah, Georgia, newspaper alerted the community to the return of one of the city's officers.[47]

The men did not expect extravagant displays when they arrived home, but it was the family welcome that brought some joy back into their lives. Even so, there were men who surprised families who had no idea about when they might see their boys again. Some veterans returned so changed by the war—boys grown into men or sons gaunt with hunger—that their families at first did not recognize them, especially if the home folk had assumed that they had perished in the war. For these veterans the home-coming was the point from which their lives might at least appear to start to return to their normal routines. When Philip Stephenson and his brother finally arrived at their family home in St. Louis, Missouri, they had an emotional reunion with their parents, ate breakfast, and then attended Sunday services, as they had probably done on untold occasions before the war had separated them.[48]

The situations that soldiers confronted when they arrived home, however, were hardly normal. Men were still uncertain as to how the Yankees would deal with them; indeed, Gordon Bradwell's veteran brother even feared that Yankees would hang him for his part in the rebellion.[49] Their homes and farms might have been equally unrec-ognizable, having suffered greatly from the war, leaving their families in pressing cir-cumstances, perhaps brooding over the end of their dream for independence as well as their economic future. Soldiers' slaves, if they had owned slaves, were now free, with their own expectations for the future, a troubling concern even for their nonslaveholding neighbors, who had enjoyed the benefits of white supremacy. Friends were dead, buried on far-flung battlefields. Some veterans discovered that their wives had taken up with other men, while others learned that relatives had passed away.

UNION SOLDIERS RETURN HOME

After the surrender of the armies of Lee and Johnston, the victors gathered in the Washington, D.C., area "and soon on every slope and ridge ... lay the camps of Sherman and the Army of the Potomac, musical by day, smoky and twinkling by night, picturesque always."[50] To reach those campsites, soldiers marched over Virginia terrain that had seen many bloody battles, stopping along the way at old Confederate works and old Yankee campgrounds. The veterans passed through the wilderness of Virginia, where they saw skeletons of men who had fallen there, sometimes piled up in stacks of bones.[51]

Soldiers converged on the capital for two days of parading in front of an audience filled with grateful civilians. The VI Corps of the Army of the Potomac arrived too late to participate in this Grand Review, but its uneventful journey through Virginia must have been common to the other units that had gone before it. Moving north from Danville toward Richmond, the men traveled on a slow-moving train. Thomas W. Hyde, commander of the corps, later recalled that "no incident, beyond running into a cow or two occurred" along the way. Leaving the rail line, the men walked on toward the capi-tal. Hyde remembered that this "peaceful march to Washington over familiar war-worn ground seemed very queer." It was now odd, so Hyde reported, to be traveling "with no firing or the picket line at night."[52]

What was not odd, however, was the toll taken on men by the march. One member of the VI Corps reported men dropping out of the ranks, dying because of the heat and their officers' relentless push to the capital.[53] Sherman's soldiers marched northward at a brisk pace, which wore on the weaker men. John Hill Ferguson noted that the 10th Illinois marched 33 miles toward Washington on one day and another 25 the next; he concluded that "these last two day's marching will be layed down as amongst the

Victorious Soldiers Return by Alfred R. Waud depicts African American troops after their mustering out being welcomed by the black community at Little Rock, Arkansas on April 20, 1865. *Harper's Weekly,* May 19, 1866. (*Library of Congress*)

hardest and most trying of our experience." Indeed, Ferguson noted that in his division alone, "some 14 within the last two days fell dead on the road and many others were sun struck that will not recover soon."[54] Other men in Sherman's ranks reported 25-mile-a-day stretches, and William B. Miller of the 75th Indiana figured at one point that he had marched 195 miles in eight days, "a foolish piece of business." Exhausted men dropped to the ground with sunstroke, but the boys kept pushing on as a matter of pride, not wishing to show any vulnerability that might make them appear to belong to a lesser army than its Potomac counterpart.[55]

As regiments from both armies reached Washington, they produced a steady stream of sick soldiers for the area hospitals, weakened by "measles, chronic diarrhea, typhomalarial fever" and worn down by their ordeal. Sadly, some men marched their last victorious steps into those hospitals. The various camp illnesses had always been the most deadly enemies of the troops, and they paid no heed to the war's end or to the eastern or western origins of the rival Union armies.[56]

Some soldiers complained about having to march for the review, but when the time came on May 23, the men who had finally defeated Lee paraded down Pennsylvania Avenue.[57] Sherman's boys followed the next day. When the two armies finally finished the military display, over 150,000 men marched from the capitol area past the reviewing stand by the White House.[58]

Both armies enjoyed enthusiastic receptions from the crowds. The general consensus was that the Army of the Potomac was a much more polished concern, but that Sherman's army had its own unique qualities, which, according to some observers, gave them a superior "military appearance."[59] One of Sherman's generals reported, "People doubtless thought us a military mob, but I believe it is generally conceded that we were in marching and military appearance at least equal to the Potomacs."[60] Indeed, Lois Bryan Adams, who was present at both parades, concluded that the westerners marched with a purpose that suggested they meant business. "No one can look at troops like these," she reported, "without feeling sure that an enemy's country, through which they have once marched, must be pretty thoroughly conquered."[61] Colonel Charles Wainwright, an officer in Meade's army, even conceded that the people preferred Sherman's army to the eyes-front Army of the Potomac because Americans "are not a military people." But he also was impressed with Sherman's men, their marching, and their "magnificent physique." He wondered whether "such a body of men of the same number can be found together in the world."[62]

There were other parades as men began their reentry into civilian life. General George Thomas's men, who, as their commander described them, bore "on their bronzed and furrowed brows the ennobling marks of years of hardship, suffering and privation, undergone in defense of freedom and the integrity of the Union," paraded in Nashville on May 9.[63] Communities across the North honored their returning soldiers in like manner on a smaller scale throughout the remainder of 1865. In June, local troops led by George G. Meade marched in review in Philadelphia.[64] And in September, the famous African American 54th Massachusetts arrived at Boston greeted by black militiamen, citizens, a band, and a collation. One of its companies returned to New Bedford, where it enjoyed a comparable welcome that included a meeting at city hall, speeches, and another feast presented by the town's black residents.[65]

Disbanding the Army

But the impressive Grand Review in the reunited nation's capital was a fitting collective symbol of victory and the war's end. The monumental gathering of the two great Union armies was also the beginning of the complicated process of disbanding an army of over a million men who were in the field in April 1865. Unlike the soldiers in its Confederate counterpart, the volunteers in the U.S. Army could not just drift away. Their organizations had to maintain themselves until they returned to their states. Soldiers would need to sign payroll forms, turn in their gear, purchase their rifles if they wished, and make sure all their records were in order before they received their final pay. The last pieces of red tape had to be tied around the trifolded bundles of official documents before the citizen-soldiers could go home.

The government essentially relied on the well-practiced procedures it had used during the war to muster men into the military, only altering them now to move men back into civilian life, with the longest-serving regiments being at the top of the list for discharge. Armies gathered at central locations to begin the process, with the Army of the Potomac remaining near Washington, while Sherman's men traveled by rail to Louisville and regiments across the South assembled in Nashville, New Orleans, and other cities. Once the regiments completed the necessary paperwork and were dismissed from the federal service, they traveled to their states of origin, converging on the rendezvous camps set aside for them. At their final destination, the government made sure the veterans' paperwork was in order and the money due to them paid out.[66]

At any point in the demobilization process, the soldiers could find themselves waiting—waiting for orders to depart for home, waiting for transportation, waiting for paperwork. After the Grand Review, men dallied around Washington waiting for orders to send them on their way. Soldiers therefore had time to take "the city by storm... making the most of Washington while the opportunity lasts."[67] In early June Thomas J. Davis of the 18th Wisconsin Volunteers described a full tourist's schedule to his wife, explaining that he had "been nearly all over the City and have seen a great [many] things that I have wished to see for a long time." He had "visited the Capitol, the Patent Office, the Treasury Department, the Washington Monument, General Taylor's residence, and the White House... and also Ford's Theatre where President Lincoln was assassinated."[68]

The amusements of the capital, however, did not completely diminish the veterans' eagerness to be on their way. Many a soldier who had withstood long separation from his family now became homesick and very impatient with the army bureaucracy. At the VI Corps hospital in Alexandria, Virginia, over a week after the Washington review, Vermonter Wilbur Fisk, then on detached service there, complained to his hometown newspaper that the men were "getting dreadfully out of patience at the delay that keeps us here doing nothing." Only the clerks were busy, but they did not work fast enough to suit the men. "We want our papers," Fisk wrote, "that we may be discharged and sent home." When he heard rumors that the government might keep them in service for garrison duty, he allowed that some veterans might like the assignment, but, he added, "I haven't seen one of them." No, he assured his hometown folk, "all are anxious to be discharged at the earliest possible moment."[69] Even Thomas J. Davis, who seemed to have enjoyed his site seeing, wanted to return home to his "gentle-spirited, kind, and loving wife."[70]

Entire regiments became quite emphatic about their desire to leave. On June 23, 1865, New Jersey soldiers in the Washington area marched with banners and torches aloft, demanding their rights.[71] On the first of July 1865, soldiers of the 105th Pennsylvania and the 7th New Jersey, stationed near Washington, assembled on a parade ground, stacked their guns, and refused to do any more soldiering. New Jerseyan George Fox witnessed the event and explained that the mutinous soldiers believed that their "time was out now the War is over and they want to be discharged." The men complained that "they have fought to free the Niggar and have got themselves in bondage." Fox predicted that if something was not done soon, the men would leave for home without permission because "they are determined to have their Rights." Apparently, so, too, was Fox. Since the government owed him six months' pay, he planned to stick around until he had his money in hand. "Then," he promised his younger brother, "I am coming Home whether discharged or not for I am not a going to be used like an infernal niggar [any] longer."[72]

In camp near the capital city, Michigan soldiers listened to politicians make speeches. Bored men put up with inspections designed to keep them out of trouble, but soldiers still found ways to pilfer civilian property. The men strained under military discipline, but most of them probably remained stoical about their time in military limbo. "Beans and hard-tack are about played out," one soldier told a visitor. "We shall be home soon, and thinking of that is both sauce and seasoning—we can eat anything between now and then."[73]

Military Duties after the Civil War

During the summer of 1865, some volunteers discovered that their discharges were not forthcoming because the nation still required them to perform military duties in the South. Foreign involvement in Mexico kept some regiments under arms. It was a duty that many soldiers resented because it was beyond what they had volunteered to do, and it would further delay their return to their families for some time. Along with various white and black regiments, for example, the 7th Vermont and the 29th Iowa went to Texas. The disgruntled Iowans left Texas in July 1865; the Vermonter men finally came home in April 1866.[74]

Once the threat from south of the border passed, numerous other duties kept volunteer soldiers in the ranks through 1865 into the next year. The 12th Illinois Cavalry had been sent to Texas after the war because of the government's concern with Mexico, but for almost a year, it performed Reconstruction duties there, policing a swath of the eastern part of the state.[75] Back east, Taylor Peirce reported that soldiers from his regiment had scattered across Georgia to "gather up government property and protect the citizens from their own returned soldiers."[76] The 54th Massachusetts continued to perform guard duty in Charleston, South Carolina, through the summer of 1865.[77] Units were stationed across the South for similar duties as the country embarked on Reconstruction, but by August 1865, the volunteers were becoming tired of it all. According to General Carl Schurz, who traveled across the South during the summer of 1865, the men still on duty "say that the war is over, that they were enlisted for the war, and that they want to go home."[78]

Understandably, Schurz also discovered that the discipline of these troops was "rather lax," with the men performing "their duties with less spirit than the exigencies of their situation require."[79] Brigadier General William Francis Bartlett, for example, noted that the troops under his command were "restless and dissatisfied about getting mustered out, it is almost impossible to get men and officers to do their duty properly." Bartlett tried to enforce discipline, admitting that he had "roughed more officers, and reduced more noncoms. to the ranks, these last two or three weeks, than in any other *year* of service."[80]

Other soldiers were simply "spoiling with inactivity and Idleness" and spent their energy in creating mayhem and mutiny.[81] In early July, some soldiers—"the worst demoralized and dissatisfied soldiers" that William Vermilion had "ever seen"—went on a binge in DeValls Bluff, Arkansas, where they drank, broke into stores, and threatened to tear up the town before other soldiers brought them under control.[82] During the summer, in Texas, discipline deteriorated among African American troops, who were unhappy with the monotonous work, disease, and conflicts with white residents, while racial tensions between black and white troops stationed in Charleston, South Carolina, led to fighting in the streets, which on July 8 turned into a race riot.[83]

Discipline was indeed a problem, as soldiers found themselves in the new, relaxed atmosphere of their peaceful camps. The conditions simply encouraged unsoldierly behavior. Members of the 57th Massachusetts stationed not far from Washington had light duties and time for recreation but began to consider orders to be more akin to suggestions.[84] During May, Elisha Hunt Rhodes and his Rhode Islanders patrolled a section of railroad in Virginia, which he did not consider difficult duty. Their camp was pleasant and relatively safe; they had fresh food; they wore straw hats. As far as Rhodes was concerned, the work "beats all the soldiering that I have ever performed," and he and his men deserved the light duty "making up for years of hardship."[85]

To the south, Iowan Taylor Peirce could "hardly realize the quiet and relaxation of Military discipline" in his North Carolina encampment.[86] In May, some men of the 22nd Iowa had "what the boys call a 'Soft Snap'" guarding a boat running between Augusta and Savannah, Georgia.[87] The camps of African American soldiers also became "a point of attraction for colored women," whose visits no doubt broke their monotonous camp routines.[88] And from the end of the war until mid-July, members of the 10th Ohio Cavalry occupied Salem, North Carolina, where they had an "influence on the community [that] was evil, and only evil, and that continually."[89]

Peace and quiet combined with a little rowdiness might have suited some soldiers, but others just found the postwar duty boring. Taylor Peirce found the quiet duty to be dull after his 22nd Iowa Infantry moved to Hamburg, South Carolina. In June he was engaged in writing a history of the regiment, but ennui seemed to have enveloped all of the men. "All is quiet in the Camp," he informed his wife. "Not a sound or an incident occurs to disturb the peaceful monotony of our daily lives." The men performed their duty and the "workings of the Government progress." They enforced the laws and collected government property, but "without having any influence on our lives or actions." "We arise at revellie in the morning if we feel like it," he informed his wife. "Eat our meals and lay down at Tattoo in the evening if we are sleepy." The officers dispensed with drill; the men ignored military etiquette; "and in fact we are laying inactive and passive like a great living body which after having undergone the extreme of physical Exertion and the object accomplished lays exhausted and quiet to recover its wanted vigor."[90]

As some soldiers became accustomed to a quieter South, they came to believe that there were opportunities in the region that good Yankees could exploit. James G. Gallagher, a soldier with the Fourth Vermont who remained on duty at Danville for a while in May, came to see the region as a fine place for Northerners to live. The climate Gallagher pronounced "truly delightful," while he judged the young local women "very fair looking." It was a land of opportunity, where "by a little application of energy and industry which they have bee accustomed to, they could in a few years become independent."[91] Indeed, some Connecticut soldiers stationed in Florida expected to stay in the state "because of the lucrative employment they can obtain in Jacksonville."[92]

At the same time, other men witnessed the early signs of the complications of the Reconstruction era for which they had no preparation. Soldiers began to deal with disputes between ex-masters and their former slaves in an increasingly hostile environment for men in blue uniforms. Taylor Peirce, for example, came on former South Carolina slaveholders who did not wish to abandon the system and "are trying to hold them still."[93] In Arkansas William Vermilion became aware of whites violently abusing ex-slaves.[94] In Virginia, shortly after the war, Elisha Rhodes settled disputes between blacks and whites but also noticed that with so many ex-Confederates "loafing about," there was some danger for Yankees who wandered too far from camp.[95] Indeed, during the summer, Union soldiers in the Atlanta, Georgia, area had their hands filled trying to stop atrocities against ex-slaves; a "small detachment . . . sent out to serve an order upon a planter, had been driven back by an armed band of over twenty men headed by an officer in rebel uniform." Soldiers elsewhere in Georgia experienced similar dangers; men guarding cotton at Madison, Georgia, for example, "had several times been attacked by armed bands." Already, by August, officers in the state were too shorthanded to make certain that they could secure the fruits of victory, or at least the safety of the ex-slaves there.[96]

The veterans stayed on doing their duty and resenting the delay in their own discharges, but government policy dictated that they did so in increasingly smaller numbers. It might have taken longer than the men had expected, but mustering out of volunteers was the inevitable end. Thus, when soldiers learned that finally, they were to go home, they were overjoyed and full of excitement. In July, men in the Eighth New Jersey "cheered untill they were so hoarse they could not speak loud," and Rhode Islanders in Virginia became "wild with joy" when they learned of their impending discharges.[97] Patriots, to be sure, but the men believed it was now time to tend to their own lives. Illinois soldier George F. Cram explained it well when he told his mother that "everybody is expecting the most perfect happiness, the day home again meets their eye."[98]

For most soldiers, it was only a matter of time before they tested Cram's notion as their government relentlessly pursued military economy. By mid-October 1865, the War Department had sent home over 785,000 men from the over 1-million-man force. By the end of 1866, Congress had reorganized the regular army, and most white volunteers had gone home. At that time, of the over 11,000 volunteer soldiers still in the ranks, 10,000 were the later enlisted U.S. Colored Troops.[99]

The Journey Northward

The journey home for these men was usually uneventful, if not particularly comfortable. Many regiments encountered generous civilians along their routes home, who cheered and fêted them. But the actual traveling could be wearisome. Wisconsin boys, for example, traveled on flatcars exposed to the elements.[100] At Cairo, Illinois, William Wiley and his comrades in the 77th Illinois "were loaded into some dirty boxcars without any kind of seats." Furthermore, he recorded, the railroad "didn't even give us any straw as they do with hogs when they ship them." When the men became tired of standing or sitting, they swaddled themselves in their blankets, stretching out on the dirty floor, where they "bumped and bounced around until morning," at which time they discovered they had involuntarily moved from one end of the car to the next. It was "one of the roughest roads that mortal man ever road over," concluded Wiley.[101]

Travel by water also had its challenges for the war-weary soldiers. When regiments of midwesterners stationed in Alabama boarded a steamer for New Orleans on the first leg of their journey home, members of the 19th Iowa discovered that the officers in charge expected them to share their deck with a number of mules. The Iowans objected, feeling that "they did out rank a mule," but could not dissuade the officers from loading the animals. The men locked on their bayonets and drove off the mules. The quartermaster officers countered the attack by calling for another regiment to enforce their will and load the animals. Finally, to avoid violence, the colonel of the 19th Iowa removed his men to wait for a different transport, rather than suffer the indignity of berthing with mules. William Wiley was on that transport and noticed that the contest between mule and man had damaged the vessel. Illinois soldiers worried that the vessel was not seaworthy, but it set off on its journey, with the men in charge unconcerned about the ship's condition. Wiley surmised, "Soldiers were cheap when the war was over and they had no farther use for us so they seen us adrift in our crippled boat."[102]

Wiley and his fellow Illinoisans made it home, despite their worries, but soldiers on one Mississippi River boat were not as fortunate. In late April 1865, 2,222 crewman and passengers, most of whom had been Union prisoners of war, crowded onto the *Sultana,* which would take them up the river, at Vicksburg, Mississippi. The overcrowding would have been bad enough—the vessel was built to hold a total 376 people—but on April 27, 1865, the steamboat exploded and sank. It was a disaster that resulted in the deaths of some 1,700 people, again, almost all of them being the former prisoners of war.[103]

Soldiers put up with discomfort in their travel arrangements because they knew they were on their way home. Charles Musser, who endured a terrible sea sickness on the first leg of his journey home, dismissed the difficulties. "We was on our way home," he wrote to his father, "and did not think so much about it as we would had we been going the other way."[104] The soldiers' relief and joy in being alive and about to leave behind the rigors of military life, along with their frustration with the delays that kept them in uniform, sometimes bubbled over in an exuberant disregard for discipline and an enthusiastic consumption of alcohol. Urban crossroads, train depots, and rendezvous camps became scenes of disorderly behavior that might have prompted some citizens to wonder if these men would ever adjust to the peaceful life of civilians. Soldiers throughout New England, according to one officer, who was in charge of keeping the peace there, "did not readily endure restraint." When confined to their rendezvous camps, where "money was plentiful," the men used bribes to influence the guards, and "riots were sometimes organized involving the entire camp." In Burlington, Vermont, for example, returning soldiers rioted in the town; members of the Veteran Reserve Corps finally quelled the two days of disturbances in late June 1865. The local command of invalids arrested some of the rioters, placed others in irons, shot two, and mounted an armed guard of 70 men in the town, after which "perfect order was restored."[105]

New Englanders were not alone in their bad behavior. At Davenport, Iowa, discharged regiments "had made great disturbances and 'played smash' generally."[106] In Chicago, the 105th Illinois did not receive the welcome they had expected, finding on their arrival neither collation nor quarters prepared for them. They took their revenge one evening by staging a bayonet charge in a Chicago beer garden.[107] Trenton, New Jersey, avoided such trouble when politicians realized they had not prepared welcomes for disappointed returning soldiers and corrected the error.[108]

Men at the rendezvous camps found that they were once again waiting, stuck in the military routine in uncomfortable surroundings, held hostage by the clerks who completed their final paperwork. In late June, at Readville, men from the 34th Massachusetts complained about delays; they would have to wait a week in the "old lousy camp ground" for the paymaster to pay them off. It was, according to Charles Moulton, "a burning shame to keep men lying around here and especially oblige them to dispense their happy 4th of July festivities after all their glorious anticipation."[109]

In June, Thomas Davis left Washington and went with other members of Sherman's army to Louisville. At Louisville, the men waited as the army slowly sent home the regiments over the course of the summer. Davis became increasingly disgruntled with military life and the way his officers dealt with his perceived grievances. He and other Wisconsin troops were bored and restive, "getting quite impatient," according to Davis, because they were "being kept in such total ignorance and claim that we have at least the right to know whether we are to be discharged soon or kept in the service." Indeed, Davis himself decided to go absent without leave to take his complaints directly to President Andrew Johnson. He later admitted to his wife that he "did a rash act but I am too sensitive to bear abuse for nothing." He proclaimed that he would "never be a military dog in time of peace to come at the whistleing of a few bigoted despots." He never did clear his paperwork or receive his discharge.[110] Clearly a citizens' army was not to be kept waiting once the nation's crisis had passed.

Soldiers stuck in such unhappy circumstances frequently looked for novel ways to break their routines. Some of Davis's Wisconsin comrades, for example, dispelled camp monotony by going into a nearby wheat field "through curiosity" to bind the harvest "as fast as the reaper cuts it."[111] Other men simply took advantage of the social amenities and vices offered by nearby towns and cities to ease their boredom. Discipline could suffer as a result. By early June, Camp Curtin, in Pennsylvania, rapidly expanded into a larger version called Camp Return, and thousands of men crowded into the place. While the Pennsylvanians had no real welcome home when they arrived at the camp, they did stage a ceremonial returning of their battle flags to the governor, who visited them. Glad handing with the governor, however, was not sufficient amusement for most of them. They visited nearby drinking establishments, all of which the authorities temporarily shuttered. As time dragged on, the soldiers became irritable, fought among themselves, and showed disrespect to their officers. By late summer, even their guards were carousing in Harrisburg.[112] The Pennsylvanians surely misbehaved, but it was apparently enough to keep the men of the 33rd Iowa on good behavior while they waited for their discharges to allow them the opportunity to walk the streets of Davenport. There they happily observed the pleasant, good-looking women of the town, who far surpassed in beauty their "sallow, listless and puny-looking" Southern counterparts.[113]

When things went smoothly and men finally moved on to their hometowns, the veterans enjoyed a warm welcome by their old friends, their families, and sympathetic citizens. The soldiers enjoyed—even expected—the fuss and were upset when timing or indifference deprived them of it. But, as with their Confederate counterparts, it was meeting the home folk again that brought the ultimate satisfaction for most of them. When William Ray of the Seventh Wisconsin saw his mother waiting for him at the doorway of the family home, he opened the gate to the yard, at which point, he recalled, "I felt a thrill of joy run through my whole frame."[114]

The Disbanding of Regiments

Men discharged from regiments across the North might listen to one more speech, enjoy one more feast at the expense of civilians, collect their pay, joke with one another, shake hands, settle debts, offer a parting word to friends, and then set out for home. Western men, according to one veteran, "are made of too stern stuff to show much emotion at such parting."[115] However, as men looked around at their thinned ranks, they could not help but recall comrades left behind on the field of battle or already at home convalescing. When Freeman S. Bowley bade good-bye to his company of African American soldiers of the 30th U.S. Colored Infantry, he noticed that of the 160 men listed on the muster roll, only 60 were there to accept his handshake. "The others," he recalled, "had died or been disabled." Those men still present crisply saluted and then marched into "the crowded streets of Baltimore." There "the ranks dissolved in the moving tide of civil life, never more to be reunited, and the glorious old 30th was only a memory."[116]

The disbanding of a regiment could indeed be an emotional affair for the soldiers who had come to consider their units to be families. William Wiley of the 77th Illinois explained the sentiment when his regiment was finally mustered out in July 1865. The men were happy to be going home, content in the knowledge that they had accomplished what they had enlisted to do. "But yet we could not keep a feeling of sadness at the thought of breaking up our organization and seperating perhaps many of us never to meet again," he wrote in his diary. "As there is a strong bond of friendship ataches between soldiers after three years of campaigning together cemented by mutual; experiences hardships and deprivations which no one could fully apreciate but those that had experienced it."[117]

Elisha Hunt Rhodes had similar feelings. Rhodes had matured in the army, advancing from a raw enlisted man to the commander of the Second Rhode Island Infantry.

When he and his men returned to Providence in mid-July, they were met with a nice welcome by the local folks, paid off, and discharged. It was an emotional moment for Rhodes and the men. Before going their separate ways, the soldiers lined up, and their colonel shook hands with each one. "It was sad, yet joyful, for the war was over and we are at home. No more suffering, no more scenes of carnage and death." Now, Rhodes realized, "at last I am a simple citizen."[118]

Rhodes's comment about returning to the role of "simple citizen" was a thought shared by veterans across the North as they pocketed their discharge papers and embraced their families. The idea played on a sore theme that had been one of the troubling aspects of their wartime lives. During his service, many a soldier had complained about how officers treated him as an "unfree" man, even though he was a citizen volunteer. Now the soldiers emphasized their return to freedom and full citizenship. Pennsylvanian Joel Molyneux's last comments in his diary made this clear: "Are home at last, safe and sound, and my own man again!"[119] Wisconsin Captain John Henry Otto also noted that discharge documents, "black on white," "restored us to citizenship and liberty."[120]

ADJUSTMENT TO CIVILIAN LIFE

Returning veterans were aware that their wartime experiences had changed them, and many wondered if that change was for the better. Army life had provided them with experiences that they never would have had in peacetime. Young men who had never been far from home for any amount of time before the war had marched across distant states, with some of them enjoying "a wild, reckless freedom in soldiering" and a "delight in the fierce excitement of a campaign."[121] They had lived in camps of men and did things that had left them rough and hard, or as Illinois cavalryman Charles Wills judged, "awfully depraved." They had killed men, had watched friends die, and had come close to death themselves. Men like Wills and Confederate Philip Stephenson lost faith in the innate goodness of humankind.[122] Unsurprisingly, there were older veterans who wondered if they could take up their lives where they had left off and younger ones, mere schoolboys in 1861, who worried if they could even start new civilian lives. Some resentful Northern veterans came home to see neighbors who had profited from the war and worried if they would ever have their chance at economic success. Defeated Confederates not only worried about restoring their fortunes, but also their manly pride, their place in society, and white supremacy. Indeed, before the end of the summer, former Confederates not only began to settle scores with Unionist neighbors, but they also began a simmering guerrilla war that would not end until they had regained control of their state governments.

Making the transition from the excitement of army life to the routine of civilian life energized some soldiers and troubled others. Problems of readjustment could be as minor as being unable to sleep in soft beds after spending years lying on hard ground to more serious consequences. Some men felt they were now without a purpose and considered a return "to routine daily employment in slow shop and store...not favorable to our habits of life."[123] As early as April 1864, New Jersey private Walter G. Dunn, who had been wounded at Chancellorsville, caused his future wife some concern when he informed her that "I think that an adventurous life in some wild Country would suit me exactly as I like to be in the midst of excitement." He worried that he would be unable to "content" himself back home in New Jersey once he left the army.[124] For

A romanticized scene of a Civil War soldier being welcomed home by family. (*Library of Congress*)

Taylor Peirce, "the army with its scenes of excitement, its dangers its dificulties and exertion I fear has awakened feeling in me that are incompatible with a live of Ease and qui[e]t." These were feelings he hoped would pass when he returned to his family. He also worried that his service had left him financially in an awkward place as well as physically too old to regain lost ground. "After 3 years of Soldiering," he complained, "a man of my age will be so much worn out that I do not see what I can do that will make me a living."[125]

Reentering the economy was a major concern for returning veterans. Taylor Peirce recalled the financial difficulties of 1857 and wondered if there would be work enough for him to support his wife.[126] After four years of military service and with the war all but over, Charles Wills considered his service "a terrible waste of time for me" since it had kept him from making "a start in life yet." More important, he worried that his army service left him unfit for civilian life. "I have almost a dread of being a citizen, of trying to be sharp, and trying to make money," he wrote. "I don't dread the work...but I am sure that civil life will go sorely against the grain for a time. Citizens are not like soldiers, and I like soldiers ways much the best."[127]

Confederate Philip D. Stephenson was a good example of the youngster gone off to war to return not quite a man, but certainly different from the boy of 1861, now filled with worries about readjusting to civilian life. The initial meeting with his parents appeared to mark a return to normal, but he understood that it would not be as simple as taking up an old Sunday routine. Stephenson calculated that he had been in more than 17 fights, while his brother had been party to 30. The two of them had "matured to men, not only by the flight of time but by the experiences packed into those four years." Yet, his parents wished him to pick up where he had left off and return to his studies. The thought of becoming a schoolboy again struck him as being "absurd" after "playing the man for four bloody years." Nevertheless, Stephenson and his brother, like all Confederate veterans, had to come to grips with making their way in a new world. The young men had thought of starting new lives in Mexico but, after a week with their family, realized that "it would have killed our parents." The war had deprived him, now just approaching his 20th birthday, of the usual experiences of a boy about to become a man. He was world weary and skeptical thanks to a war that seemed to have "crushed out of sight" all that had been good. He later recalled that "life's prospects stretched before me, a dreary sterile flat, and I looked on it with loathing." For Stephenson, the temporary answer was to find a position to "learn business ways," yet the former soldier boy still remained restless in his new civilian life. He continued to have a "desire to roam" and was "disgust[ed] with the tame sordid life" he was now living.[128]

The Effects of Physical and Psychological Wounds on Civilian Life

Such disenchantment could be particularly hard on soldiers who came home with physical or psychological wounds. In 1862 the federal government established a pension system that provided modest monthly stipends for disabled veterans to help such individuals.[129] After the war the federal government attempted to help thousands of amputees readjust to civilian life by providing them with prosthetic devises. Southern states also had their own programs for Confederate veterans, hoping such devices would assist the men to return to economically productive lives.[130] But such well-intentioned programs only addressed the more apparent consequences of war wounds. Men still had to come to grips with the long-term effects of their disfigurement, including how wives and sweethearts might react to them. They might turn their disfigurement into a badge of honor, but many of them still had to deal with lingering pain long after they resumed their civilian lives. Poorly fitted prosthetic arms and legs added to the discomfort men endured from imagined pain in their missing limbs.[131] Even those veterans who did not wear the devises could experience lingering discomfort.

Veterans returned home with wounds ranging from gunshot scars, chronic intestinal problems, and respiratory illnesses to debilitating psychological damage. Some former soldiers dealt with their postwar physical and psychological discomforts by relying on the opiates their regimental surgeons had used to treat everything from pain to diarrhea. Some veterans medicated themselves with readily available alcohol. Those who struggled on with the pain and mental distress never had an easy time of it. Mental illness or chronic diarrhea were harder to translate into a heroic badge of honor than the visible display of courage shown by an empty sleeve, but they nonetheless altered veterans' lives in ways that might have even exceeded the troubles caused by amputations. Soldiers suffered from these physical problems long after the war had ended and endured conditions that weakened their constitutions when faced with new physical problems. Marvin Maloney of the First Michigan Sharpshooters died in 1892, laid low by lingering camp disease. John Randolph Lewis, who lost his left arm at the Battle of the Wilderness, suffered for decades from the abscessing wound of the amputation. Joshua Lawrence Chamberlain, most famous for his exploits with the 20th Maine at Gettysburg, had been seriously wounded at Petersburg, which left him with a lifelong legacy of pain that caused him and his marriage to suffer. Chamberlain and his wife did not divorce, but other veterans did. Again, it was not clear if the parties could directly place the blame on wartime experiences, but white officers in black regiments, for example, divorced at a rate that exceeded national norms.[132]

The restlessness that Philip Stephenson and so many other veterans experienced on their reentry to civilian life was probably a sign of the mental stress that they brought home with them from the war. One of Walter Dunn's friends, another New Jersey soldier, appeared to be depressed after his return home or, as one observer commented, "laboring under some heavy grief"; his minister believed the soldier, who would not talk about his troubles, was "broken hearted."[133] Such melancholy could plague veterans the remainder of their lives and sometimes with very unhappy results. One veteran who had served as a lieutenant in a black regiment ended up institutionalized. A veteran of the First Michigan Sharpshooters complained of being unwell ever since an artillery shell exploded near him; he never adjusted to civilian life and committed suicide. Another former officer in a black regiment, who was involved with reburying Union soldiers after the war, committed suicide.[134]

As one Union officer later explained, stressful events would trigger episodes of battle flashbacks. He noted that his mental distress had become a part of his existence; he had "borne it all with a might small amount of sympathy from those about me." "Soldiers have lost a leg or an arm," he continued, "and never suffered as much as I have done from the breaking down of my nervous system there at Fort Harrison" in Virginia.[135]

Some men never overcame their depression, irritability, and restlessness. Some of those individuals violently abused their families or simply abandoned them to become vagabonds.[136] Veterans with amputated limbs, mental illnesses, and opiate addictions, disconnected from their old communities, squatted in dilapidated buildings on Bowery Street in New York City. Residents referred to these men as "bummers," borrowing the name used by Southerners to describe the undisciplined foragers from Sherman's army and introducing the shortened form *bum* into the vernacular.[137] Indeed, New York City experienced an increase in arrests immediately after the war, and other cities probably had comparable problems because of unemployed and antisocial veterans.[138] In Massachusetts, Pennsylvania, and Illinois, during the earliest years after the war, veterans also made up a significant majority of prison inmates.[139]

Damaged, sad men were part of the legacy of the war, but many more veterans, despite their injuries, eventually reentered civilian society as productive individuals. Sooner or later, they had to make peace with themselves, pick up the pieces of their lives, and at least make a living for themselves and their families. The unsettled Stephenson found God, the adventure-craving Dunn married his New Jersey sweetheart, and untold numbers of men rebuilt their lives with varying degrees of success.

Veterans Working Their Way Back to Civilian Life

Most men did not have the luxury to dwell on their anxieties about the future. They had to jump into the task of making a living simply to survive, especially in the war-ravaged South. Dave Carey Nance, a Texan who was 18 years old when the war began, went into the fields to work his family's crop the day after he arrived home.[140] Confederate Kentuckian Johnny Green made his way home to Kentucky and immediately went to work cutting, hauling, and selling wood.[141] And the unrepentant William Fletcher of Terry's Texas Rangers returned home from North Carolina, collected his father's carpentry tools, and "went on a job at $1.50 per day" not far from where he had been working before he went off to war.[142]

Landed Confederate veterans began to bring their farms back to life. They signed contracts with their former slaves, began working their fields, and, as Captain John Coleman noted in his diary, hoped "the arrangement may prove beneficial to all."[143] In 1865 Samuel Hildebrand, with the help of only one ex-slave, raised a fair corn crop; during 1866 he rented a larger, better place, and by the end of the 1867 season, he "succeeded in rendering myself and family as comfortable as could be expected."[144] Veterans, such as the unyielding Georgia Confederate Berry Benson, also developed prosaic middle-class careers as teachers and accountants, while other former soldiers picked up their professional education where they had left off.[145]

All the while, the veterans worked to find places for themselves, they tended to their families, or, if they had yet to start their own, they settled down, married their sweethearts, and prepared for the future. John S. Apperson, hospital steward in the Stonewall Brigade, for example, resumed his medical education at the University of Virginia, became a physician, and eventually fathered 11 children.[146] John Preston Sheffey, a Virginia cavalryman who had been a prisoner of war at Camp Chase, had married his sweetheart during the war. During the summer of 1865, he worked hard at making a comfortable place for his wife, hiring help and buying furniture for their new home. Despite his wartime experiences and postwar difficulties, he assured his wife that "our lot will not be so hard a one as that of most other people, and if we only pull together heartily, ever strengthening each other's hands, we will soon have every comfort around us." Sheffey could look to a better future "with resolution and hope," as long as his wife was by his side. "We may have sunshine in our house and hearts," he assured his wife, "whatever circumstance may surround us." He, too, sired a large family and built a successful legal career.[147]

A number of Northern officers sought positions in the regular army and the Freedmen's Bureau, but most Yankees were eager to get back to civilian employment and resume normal lives. Even before the 34th Massachusetts mustered out, Charles Moulton reported that "some of our boys have already found positions on farms and railroads and gone to work," while the regiment languished in the Readville camp waiting for discharges.[148] As with their Southern counterparts, married men became reacquainted with their families, while unmarried veterans wed and started families. To provide for themselves and their families, they returned to their farms, trades, businesses, and law practices or looked for new jobs.

Some Northern soldiers received assistance in their reentry to the workplace. Sometimes relatives helped find them a place, as did George Cram's uncle, who took the veteran into his publishing business. Other veterans had help from individuals who made a special effort to find places for the former warriors, as was the case in New Jersey. In New York City, William Oland Bourne sponsored left-handed writing contests to prove to businesses that the penmanship of veteran amputees was equal to the task of any available clerical position. New York City veterans also could register with employment agencies, which were especially concerned with finding work for disabled soldiers. And the federal government gave preferential treatment to Northern veterans, both disabled and honorably discharged, when hiring for government positions.[149]

Northern men returned to school or took chances on new ventures, abandoning their old professions for new ones. Veterans in Chicago unwilling to resume their old jobs, for example, attended commercial colleges to improve their prospects, while the insurance industry that was coming into prominence in that city provided former soldiers there with new business opportunities.[150] William Vermilion, who had been a physician before he joined the 36th Iowa, studied law after he returned home, perhaps because he had become disenchanted with medicine's failure to keep soldiers healthy.[151] Benjamin Baker discovered that farming troubled his wounded arm, so he went back to school, becoming an educator and a minister.[152]

The desire to improve one's economic condition, along with the restlessness common to nineteenth-century Americans, a restlessness perhaps exaggerated by the veterans' wartime experiences, encouraged or compelled men to look for better lives beyond their old antebellum homes. Confederate veterans joined the postwar pattern of westward migration to new territories and California. Thousands even migrated to Northern states to farm, practice law, or conduct business. Charles C. Jones Jr., a Georgia veteran, for example, moved to New York to practice law. He might have been disenchanted with planting because it was clear that the workings of free labor on his family lands troubled him, but he was clearly searching for economic opportunity.[153] The more unreconstructed among Jones's comrades, however, determined that they could not live among Yankees, or even in their own states, as long as they were ruled by their former enemies. They left the country for Europe, Canada, and Latin America, especially Mexico and Brazil, although many of them only sojourned abroad and eventually returned to the United States.[154]

Southern veterans unhappy with the prospects offered in their old communities were joined in their migrations by Yankees who moved on to different states or parts of the country to seek out new opportunities. By one estimate, almost one-third of the veteran population of Wisconsin emigrated, while veterans from other states filled the void they left behind.[155] Veteran Henry Matrau returned to Michigan, married in 1867, and moved on to Nebraska, where he worked for the railroad and then for his own coal and lumber concerns.[156] Other veterans saw the South as a land of opportunity and sought their fortunes there. Some of these men, who would quickly and unfairly earn the derogatory name of "carpetbagger," had mixed motives that included a noble commitment to securing the fruits of victory by remaking the social framework of the South. The southern climate appealed to Ohio veteran and lawyer Albion Tourgée, for example, but he also wished to continue to work for progressive wartime ideals, including helping the freedmen, while finding his fortune along the way.[157]

Black Veterans' Adjustment to Civilian Life

The economic and social adjustment to civilian life of black veterans was even more complex than that of white veterans. Throughout the postwar South, black veterans rarely could expect more than to work as sharecroppers and tenant farmers, while in the North, they continued to perform hard manual labor and farmwork. Still, there were examples of success that provided some substance to the old free-labor promise of advancement coming from hard work. The postwar careers of members of the 29th U.S. Colored Infantry, an organization rooted in Illinois, illustrated the problems and pitfalls awaiting black veterans. Most men who had served in the 29th returned to the communities from which they had enlisted, although former slaves from the border states and the upper South remained in the Midwest. There and elsewhere, they engaged in the hard manual labor they had known before the war, with some men trying to work their way up the economic ladder, with varying degrees of success. As with white veterans, some of them ended up on the wrong side of the law, although it was not clear if their misfortunes were directly caused by their wartime misfortunes.[158]

Race, slavery, and antebellum poverty complicated the lives of black veterans, but black soldiers had the wartime experience to improve their peacetime lives. Noncommissioned officers had gained supervisory experience, enlisted men had gained confidence, and many black soldiers had learned to read during the war.[159] Afterward, some took advantage of new educational opportunities, becoming teachers, doctors, lawyers, and businessmen. Ohioan Milton Holland of the Fifth U.S. Colored Infantry, for example, became a lawyer, obtained a position with the post office, and then engaged in finance.[160]

With victory came the promise that black veterans and their families would have a future that would leave behind their inferior antebellum status. Black veterans understood that it was up to them to lay claim to their new rights. Soldiers from Missouri, well aware of the promise that education held for advancing the future of their community, collected funds to establish a school back home; their efforts planted the seed for what grew into Lincoln University.[161] Beginning in 1867, across the South, they engaged in the politics of Reconstruction, while from the end of the war, throughout the North, they continued to push for their civil and political rights. In Chicago, for example, veterans joined a black militia company, the Hannibal Guards, which provided a starting point for their political activities.[162]

But black veterans also attracted special scorn from white Southerners that at times turned violent. In Maryland, a former soldier reported that Confederate veterans attacked returning black veterans. And in May 1866, during a riot in Memphis, Tennessee, the mob singled out black veterans, tracked down men still in uniform, and looked for the residences of their families.[163] African Americans quickly discovered that their fight to claim their place in a reunited nation would take much longer than they had expected when they began enlisting in significant numbers in 1863.

NOTES

1. Philip N. Racine, ed., *"Unspoiled Heart": The Journal of Charles Mattocks of the 17th Maine* (Knoxville: University of Tennessee Press, 1994), 268; George W. Fox to Charles H. Fox, April 16, 1865, Civil War Letters of the Fox Brothers, eHistory, Ohio State University, Columbus, http://ehistory.osu.edu/osu/sources/letters/fox/.

2. Robert Hunt Rhodes, ed., *All for the Union: The Civil War Diary and Letters of Elisha Hunt Rhodes* (New York: Vintage Books, 1992), 222; George W. Fox to Charles H. Fox, April 9, 1865, Civil War Letters of the Fox Brothers, eHistory, Ohio State University, Columbus, http://ehistory.osu.edu/osu/sources/letters/fox/.

3. Allan Nevins, ed., *A Diary of Battle: The Personal Journals of Colonel Charles S. Wainwright, 1861–1865* (New York: Da Capo Press, 1998), 523.

4. Edward Marcus, ed., *A New Canaan Private in the Civil War: Letters of Justus M. Silliman, 17th Connecticut Volunteers* (New Canaan, CT: New Canaan Historical Society, 1984), 99.

5. Nevins, *A Diary of Battle,* 521.

6. Richard L. Kiper, ed., *Dear Catherine, Dear Taylor: The Civil War Letters of a Union Soldier and His Wife* (Lawrence: University Press of Kansas, 2002), 382.

7. Barry Popchock, ed., *Soldier Boy: The Civil War Letters of Charles O. Musser, 29th Iowa* (Iowa City: University of Iowa Press, 1995), 206.

8. Marcus, *A New Canaan Private,* 100.

9. Bernard A. Olsen, ed., *Upon the Tented Field: An Historical Account of the Civil War as Told by the Men Who Fought and Gave Their Lives* (Red Bank, NJ: Historic Projects, 1993), 310; Jeffrey D. Marshall, ed., *A War of the People: Vermont Civil War Letters* (Hanover, NH: University Press of New England, 1999), 302–3 (quotation).

10. Kiper, *Dear Catharine, Dear Taylor,* 385.

11. A. F. Sperry, *History of the 33d Iowa Infantry Volunteer Regiment, 1863–6,* ed. Gregory J. W. Urwin and Cathy Kunzinger Urwin (Fayetteville: University of Arkansas Press, 1999), 166.

12. Kiper, *Dear Catharine, Dear Taylor,* 384.

13. William Thomas Pogue, *Gunner with Stonewall: Reminiscences of William Thomas Pogue, Lieutenant, Captain, Major and Lieutenant Colonel of Artillery, Army of Northern Virginia, CSA, 1861–65: A Memoir Written for His Children in 1903,* ed. Monroe F. Cockrell (Lincoln: University of Nebraska Press, 1998), 124.

14. Jeffrey D. Stocker, ed., *From Huntsville to Appomattox: R. T. Coles's History of the 4th Regiment, Alabama Volunteer Infantry, C.S.A., Army of Northern Virginia* (Knoxville: University of Tennessee Press, 1996), 193.

15. Minetta Altgelt Goyne, ed., *Lone Star and Double Eagle: Civil War Letters of a German-Texas Family* (Fort Worth: Texas Christian University Press, 1982), 169.

16. Pogue, *Gunner with Stonewall,* 125–26; DeWitt Boyd Stone Jr., ed., *Wandering to Glory: Confederate Veterans Remember Evans' Brigade* (Columbia: University of South Carolina Press, 2002), 245; Stocker, *From Huntsville to Appomattox,* 193.

17. J.K.P. Blackburn, *Reminiscences of the Terry Rangers,* reprinted in *Terry Texas Ranger Trilogy,* ed. Thomas W. Cutrer (Austin, TX: State House Press, 1996), 173–77.

18. Nat Turner, ed., *A Southern Soldier's Letters Home: The Civil War Letters of Samuel Burney, Army of Northern Virginia* (Macon, GA: Macon University Press, 2002), 293–94.

19. Edwin C. Bears, ed., *A Louisiana Confederate: Diary of Felix Pierre Poché,* trans. Eugenie Watson Somdal (Natchitoches: Louisiana Studies Institute, Northwestern State University, 1972), 237.

20. Thomas W. Cutrer and T. Michael Parrish, eds., *Brothers in Gray: The Civil War Letters of the Pierson Family* (Baton Rouge: Louisiana State University Press, 1997), 256–57, 259–60.

21. Robert L. Kerby, *Kirby Smith's Confederacy: The Trans-Mississippi South, 1863–1865* (New York: Columbia University Press, 1972), 419–23, 421 (quotation).

22. William A. Fletcher, *Rebel Private: Front and Rear, Memoirs of a Confederate Soldier* (New York: Dutton, 1995), 194–96.

23. Goyne, *Lone Star and Double Eagle,* 169.

24. Quoted in Scott Walker, *Hell's Broke Loose in Georgia: Survival in a Civil War Regiment* (Athens: University of Georgia Press, 2005), 243.

25. John R. Sellers, ed., *A People at War: Civil War Manuscripts from the Holdings of the Library of Congress* (Alexandria, VA: Chadwyck-Heakey, 1989–1990), Doug Cater to cousin Laurence, May 16, 1865, Douglas J. and Rufus W. Cater Papers, reel 11.

26. Quoted in Noah Andre Trudeau, *Out of the Storm: The End of the Civil War, April–June 1865* (Baton Rouge: Louisiana State University Press, 1995), 242.

27. Susan Williams Benson, ed., *Berry Benson's Civil War Book: Memoirs of a Confederate Scout and Sharpshooter* (Athens: University of Georgia Press, 1992), 202–3.

28. Jennifer Cain Bohrnstedt, ed., *While Father Is Away: The Civil War Letters of William H. Bradbury* (Lexington: University Press of Kentucky, 2003), 274.

29. Marilyn Mayer Culpepper, *Trials and Triumphs: The Women of the American Civil War* (East Lansing: Michigan State University Press, 1991), 374–75.

30. Kathleen Gorman, ed., *Boy Soldier of the Confederacy: The Memoir of Johnnie Wickersham* (Carbondale: Southern Illinois University Press, 2006), 132.

31. Nathaniel Cheairs Hughes Jr., ed., *The Civil War Memoir of Philip Daingerfield Stephenson, D.D.: Private, Company K, 13th Arkansas Volunteer Infantry, Loader, Piece No. 4, 5th Company, Washington Artillery, Army of the Tennessee, CSA* (Baton Rouge: Louisiana State University Press, 1998), 372; Walker, *Hell's Broke Loose,* 244; G. Ward Hubbs, ed., *Voices from Company D: Diaries by the Greensboro Guards, Fifth Alabama Infantry Regiment, Army of Northern Virginia* (Athens: University of Georgia Press, 2003), 389.

32. Pharris Deloach Johnson, ed., *Under the Southern Cross: Soldier Life with Gordon Bradwell and the Army of Northern Virginia* (Macon, GA: Mercer University Press, 1999), 241–45.

33. Hubbs, *Voices from Company D,* 390.

34. A. D. Kirwin, ed., *Johnny Green of the Orphan Brigade: The Journal of a Confederate Soldier* (Lexington: University Press of Kentucky, 2002), 197–201.

35. Walker, *Hell's Broke Loose,* 244; Fletcher, *Rebel Private,* 194–211; Carlton McCarthy, *Detailed Minutiae of Soldier Life in the Army of Northern Virginia, 1861–1865* (Lincoln: University of Nebraska Press, 1993), 157–76; Kirwin, *Johnny Green,* 197–207; Richard Lowe, *Walker's Texas Division, C.S.A.: Greyhounds of the Trans-Mississippi* (Baton Rouge: Louisiana State University Press, 2004), 254; Hubbs, *Voices from Company D,* 390; William Miller Owen, *In Camp and Battle with the Washington Artillery of New Orleans* (Baton Rouge: Louisiana State University Press, 1999), 393.

36. Gorman, *Boy Soldier,* 132–33.

37. Dan T. Carter, *When the War Was Over: The Failure of Self-Reconstruction in the South, 1865–1867* (Baton Rouge: Louisiana State University Press, 1985), 12–13.

38. Sumner A. Cunningham, *Reminiscences of the 41st Tennessee: The Civil War in the West,* ed. John A. Simpson (Shippensburg, PA: White Mane, 2001), 134.

39. Johnson, *Under the Southern Cross,* 241–45; Carter, *When the War Was Over,* 12–13; Virginia Ingraham Burr, ed., *The Secret Eye: The Journal of Ella Gertrude Clanton Thomas, 1848–1889* (Chapel Hill: University of North Carolina Press, 1990), 260.

40. Johnson, *Under the Southern Cross,* 241–45.

41. Lowe, *Walker's Texas Division,* 254–55.

42. Fred Arthur Bailey, *Class and Tennessee's Confederate Generation* (Chapel Hill: University of North Carolina Press, 1987), 108–10.

43. Rhodes, *All for the Union,* 227, 231.

44. Thomas W. Hyde, *Following the Greek Cross, or Memories of the Sixth Army Corps* (Columbia: University of South Carolina Press, 2005), 267; Torget and Ayers, *Two Communities,* 209.

45. Torget and Ayers, *Two Communities,* 208.

46. Owen, *In Camp and Battle,* 395.

47. Earl Schenck Miers, ed., *When the World Ended: The Diary of Emma LeConte* (Lincoln: University of Nebraska Press, 1987), 98; Russell K. Brown, *Our Connection with Savannah: A History of the 1st Battalion Georgia Sharpshooters* (Macon, GA: Mercer University Press, 2004), 155; Owen, *In Camp and Battle,* 395.

48. Hughes, *Civil War Memoir of Philip Daingerfield Stephenson,* 382–83.

49. Johnson, *Under the Southern Cross,* 245.

50. Jane Stuart Woolsey, *Hospital Days: Reminiscence of a Civil War Nurse,* ed. Daniel John Hoisington (Roseville, MN: Edinborough Press, 2001), 128.

51. Jeffrey L. Patrick and Robert J. Willey, eds., *Fighting for Liberty and Right: The Civil War Diary of William Bluffton Miller, First Sergeant, Company K, Seventy-fifth Indiana Volunteer Infantry* (Knoxville: University of Tennessee Press, 2005), 346–48; Robert Cruikshank Narrative, May 15, 1865, Robert Cruikshank Letters, eHistory, Ohio State University, Columbus, http://ehistory.osu.edu/osu/sources/letters/cruikshank/.

52. Hyde, *Following the Greek Cross,* 268.

53. Thomas E. Pope, *The Weary Boys: Colonel J. Warren Keifer and the 110th Ohio Volunteer Infantry* (Kent, OH: Kent State University Press, 2002), 110.

54. Janet Correll Ellison, ed., with assistance from Mark W. Weitz. *On to Atlanta: The Civil War Diaries of John Hill Ferguson, Illinois Tenth Regiment of Volunteers* (Lincoln: University of Nebraska Press, 2001), 123–24.

55. Patrick and Willey, *Fighting for Liberty,* 343–44.

56. Woolsey, *Hospital Days,* 128.

57. Ibid., 130.

58. Trudeau, *Out of the Storm,* 317–23.

59. Charles F. Larimer, ed., *Love and Valor: The Intimate Civil War Letters Between Captain Jacob and Emeline Ritner* (Western Springs, IL: Sigourney Press, 2000), 445.

60. Milo M. Quaife, ed., *From the Cannon's Mouth: The Civil War Letters of General Alpheus S. Williams* (Lincoln: University of Nebraska Press, 1995), 390.

61. Lois Bryan Adams, *Letter from Washington, 1863–1865,* ed. Evelyn Leasher (Detroit, MI: Wayne State University Press, 1999), 265.

62. Nevins, *A Diary of Battle,* 529–30.

63. Freeman Cleaves, *Rock of Chickamauga: The Life of General George H. Thomas* (Norman: University of Oklahoma Press, 1948), 283, 284 (quotation).

64. Edward J. Hagerty, *Collis' Zouaves: The 114th Pennsylvania Volunteers in the Civil War* (Baton Rouge: Louisiana State University Press, 1997), 314.

65. Luis F. Emilio, *A Brave Black Regiment: The History of the 54th Massachusetts, 1863–1865,* 2nd enlarged ed. (New York: Da Capo Press, 1995), 320–21.

66. Trudeau, *Out of the Storm,* 378; William B. Holberton, *Homeward Bound: The Demobilization of the Union and Confederate Armies, 1865–1866* (Mechanicsburg, PA: Stackpole Books, 2001), 154; Richard N. Current, *The History of Wisconsin,* Vol. 3, *The Civil War Era, 1848–1873* (Madison: State Historical Society of Wisconsin, 1976), 371; Edward A. Miller Jr., *The Black Civil War Soldiers of Illinois: The Story of the Twenty-ninth U.S. Colored Infantry* (Columbia: University of South Carolina Press, 1998), 166; Warren Wilkinson, *Mother, May You Never See the Sights I Have Seen: The Fifty-seventh Massachusetts Veteran Volunteers in the Army of the Potomac* (New York: Harper & Row, 1990), 359.

67. Adams, *Letter from Washington,* 268.

68. Thomas P. Nanzig, ed., *The Badax Tigers: From Shiloh to the Surrender with the 18th Wisconsin Volunteers* (Lanham, MD: Rowman & Littlefield, 2002), 326.

69. Emil Rosenblatt and Ruth Rosenblatt, eds., *Hard Marching Every Day: The Civil War Letters of Private Wilbur Fisk, 1861–1865* (Lawrence: University Press of Kansas, 1992), 330.

70. Nanzig, *Badax Tigers,* 326.

71. Bradley M. Gottfried, *Kearny's Own: The History of the First New Jersey Brigade in the Civil War* (New Brunswick, NJ: Rutgers University Press, 2005), 247–48.

72. George W. Fox to [Charles H. Fox], July 1, 1865, Civil War Letters of the Fox Brothers, eHistory, Ohio State University, Columbus, http://ehistory.osu.edu/osu/sources/letters/fox/.

73. Adams, *Letter from Washington,* 267, 270 (quotation).

74. Wilkinson, *Mother, May You Never See,* 359; Noah Andre Trudeau, *Like Men of War: Black Troops in the Civil War, 1862–1865* (Boston: Little, Brown, 1998), 458; Popcock, *Soldier Boy,* 216; Marshall, *A War of the People,* 314; Holberton, *Homeward Bound,* 81–85.

75. Samuel M. Blackwell Jr., *In the First Line of Battle: The 12th Illinois Cavalry in the Civil War* (DeKalb: Northern Illinois University Press, 2002), 157–72.

76. Kiper, *Dear Catherine, Dear Taylor,* 404.

77. Emilio, *A Brave Black Regiment,* 312.

78. Brooks D. Simpson, LeRoy P. Graf, and John Muldowny, eds., *Advice after Appomattox: Letters to Andrew Johnson, 1865–1866* (Knoxville: University of Tennessee Press, 1987), 113.

79. Ibid.

80. Wilkinson, *Mother, May You Never See,* 360.

81. Kiper, *Dear Taylor, Dear Catherine,* 419.

82. Donald C. Elder III, ed., *Love amid the Turmoil: The Civil War Letters of William and Mary Vermilion* (Iowa City: University of Iowa Press, 2003), 322–23.

83. Trudeau, *Like Men of War,* 460; Robert J. Zalimas Jr., "A Disturbance in the City: Black and White Soldiers in Postwar Charleston," in *Black Soldiers in Blue: African American Troops in the Civil War Era,* ed. John David Smith (Chapel Hill: University of North Carolina Press, 2002), 374–76.

84. Wilkinson, *Mother, May You Never See,* 361.

85. Rhodes, *All for the Union,* 229–30.

86. Kiper, *Dear Catherine, Dear Taylor,* 390.

87. Samuel C. Jones, *Reminiscences of the 22nd Iowa Infantry: Giving Its Organization, Marches, Skirmishes, Battles, and Sieges, as Taken from the Diary of Lieutenant S. C. Jones of Company A* (Iowa City: Press of the Camp Pope Bookshop, 1993), 103–4.

88. Simpson et al., *Advice after Appomattox,* 113.

89. Sarah Bahnson Chapman, ed., *Bright and Gloomy Days: The Civil War Correspondence of Captain Charles Frederic Bahson, a Moravian Confederate* (Knoxville: University of Tennessee Press, 2003), lvi–lviii.

90. Kiper, *Dear Catherine, Dear Taylor,* 406.

91. Marshall, *A War of the People,* 309–10.

92. Marcus, *A New Canaan Private,* 109.

93. Kiper, *Dear Catherine, Dear Taylor,* 404.

94. Elder, *Love amid the Turmoil,* 325–26.

95. Rhodes, *All for the Union,* 229–30.

96. Simpson et al., *Advice after Appomattox,* 90–91.

97. George W. Fox to [Charles H. Fox], July 8, 1865, Civil War Letters of the Fox Brothers, eHistory, Ohio State University, Columbus, http://ehistory.osu.edu/osu/sources/letters/fox/; Rhodes, *All for the Union,* 238.

98. Jennifer Cain Bohrnstedt, ed., *Soldiering with Sherman: Civil War Letters of George F. Cram* (DeKalb: Northern Illinois University Press, 2000), 169–70.

99. Trudeau, *Out of the Storm,* 378; Russell F. Weigley, *History of the United States Army* (New York: Macmillan, 1967), 262.

100. Current, *Civil War Era,* 372.

101. Terrence J. Winschel, ed., *The Civil War Diary of a Common Soldier: William Wiley of the 77th Illinois Infantry* (Baton Rouge: Louisiana State University Press, 2001), 180.

102. Ibid., 175–77.

103. Chester D. Berry, ed., *Loss of the Sultana and Reminiscences of Survivors* (Knoxville: University of Tennessee Press, 2005), vii.

104. Popchock, *Soldier Boy,* 217.

105. Paul A. Cimbala, "The Veteran Reserve Corps and the Northern People," in *Union Soldiers and the Northern Home Front: Wartime Experiences, Postwar Adjustments,* ed. Paul A. Cimbala and Randall M. Miller (New York: Fordham University Press, 2002), 202; Paul A. Cimbala, "Union Corps of Honor," *Columbiad* 3 (Winter 2000): 80; Lt. Col. Garrick Mallery to Brig. Gen. James B. Fry, October 20, 1865, box 36, Letters Rec'd, Veteran Reserve Corps, Records of the Provost Marshal General's Office, Record Group 110, National Archives Building, Washington, DC (quotations).

106. Sperry, *History of the 33d Iowa Infantry Volunteer Regiment,* 190.

107. Theodore J. Karamanski, *Rally 'Round the Flag: Chicago and the Civil War* (Chicago: Nelson-Hall, 1993), 239–40.

108. William Gillette, *Jersey Blue: Civil War Politics in New Jersey, 1854–1865* (New Brunswick, NJ: Rutgers University Press, 1995), 311.

109. Lee C. Drickamer and Karen D. Drickamer, eds., *Fort Lyons to Harper's Ferry: On the Border of North and South with "Rambling Jour," the Civil War Letters and Newspaper Dispatches of Charles H. Moulton (34th Mass. Vol. Inf.)* (Shippensburg, PA: White Mane, 1987), 242.

110. Nanzig, *Badax Tigers,* 329–30.

111. Ibid., 328.

112. William J. Miller, *Civil War City: Harrisburg, Pennsylvania, 1861–1865* (Shippensburg, PA: White Mane, 1990), 215–20.

113. Sperry, *History of the 33d Iowa Infantry Volunteer Regiment,* 190–91.

114. Lance Herdegen and Sherry Murphy, eds., *Four Years with the Iron Brigade: The Civil War Journal of William Ray, Company F, Seventh Wisconsin Volunteers* (Cambridge, MA: Da Capo Press, 2002), 388.

115. Sperry, *History of the 33d Iowa Infantry Volunteer Regiment,* 192.

116. Keith Wilson, ed., *Honor in Command: Lt. Freeman S. Bowley's Civil War Service in the 30th United States Colored Infantry* (Gainesville: University Press of Florida, 2006), 236.

117. Winschel, *Civil War Diary,* 175.

118. Rhodes, *All for the Union,* 239–40.

119. Kermit Moyneux Bird, ed., *Quill of the Wild Goose: Civil War Letters and Diaries of Private Joel Molyneux, 141st P.V.* (Shippensburg, PA: Burd Street Press, 1996), 294.

120. David Gould and James B. Kennedy, eds., *Memoirs of a Dutch Mudsill: The "War Memories" of John Henry Otto, Captain, Company D, 21st Regiment Wisconsin Volunteer Infantry* (Kent, OH: Kent State University Press, 2004), 377.

121. Kenneth W. Noe, ed., *A Southern Boy in Blue: The Memoir of Marcus Woodcock, 9th Kentucky Infantry (U.S.A.)* (Knoxville: University of Tennessee Press, 1996), 50; Rosenblatt and Rosenblatt, *Hard Marching Every Day,* 343.

122. Mary E. Kellog, comp., *Army Life of an Illinois Soldier, Including a Day-by-Day Record of Sherman's March to the Sea: Letters and Diary of Charles W. Wills* (Carbondale: Southern Illinois University Press, 1996), 135–36; Hughes, *Civil War Memoir of Philip Daingerfield Stephenson,* 386.

123. Miller, *Civil War City,* 220.

124. Judith A. Bailey and Robert I. Cottom, eds., *After Chancellorsville: Letters from the Heart, the Civil War Letters of Private Walter G. Dunn and Emma Randolph* (Baltimore: Maryland Historical Society, 1998), 51.

125. Kiper, *Dear Catherine, Dear Taylor,* 406–7.

126. Ibid., 390.

127. Mary E. Kellogg, comp., *Army Life of an Illinois Soldier, Including a Day-by-Day Record of Sherman's March to the Sea: Letters and Diary of Charles W. Wills* (Carbondale: Southern Illinois University Press, 1996), 370.

128. Hughes, *Civil War Memoir of Philip Daingerfield Stephenson,* 383–87.

129. Theda Skocpol, *Protecting Soldiers and Mothers: The Political Origins of Social Policy in the United States* (Cambridge, MA: Belknap Press of Harvard University Press, 1992), 106–7.

130. Alfred Jay Bollett, MD, *Civil War Medicine: Challenges and Triumphs* (Tucson, AZ: Galen Press, 2002), 144, 160; Ansley Herring Wegner, *Phantom Pain: North Carolina's Artificial-Limb Program for Confederate Veterans* (Raleigh: Office of Archives and History, North Carolina Department of Cultural Resources, 2004), 18, 20–35.

131. Wegner, *Phantom Pain,* 18–19; Frances Clarke, "'Honorable Scars': Northern Amputees and the Meaning of Civil War Injuries," in Cimbala and Miller, eds., *Union Soldiers,* 361–94.

132. Raymond J. Herek, *These Men Have Seen Hard Service: The First Michigan Sharpshooters in the Civil War* (Detroit, MI: Wayne State University Press, 1998), 367; Paul A. Cimbala, *Under the Guardianship of the Nation: The Freedmen's Bureau and the Reconstruction of Georgia, 1865–1870* (Athens: University of Georgia Press, 1997), 10; Jeremiah E. Goulka, ed., *The Grand Old Man of Maine: Selected Letters of Joshua Lawrence Chamberlain, 1865–1914* (Chapel Hill: University of North Carolina Press, 2004), x–xi; Joseph T. Glatthaar, *Forged in Battle: The Civil War Alliance of Black Soldiers and White Officers* (New York: Macmillan, 1990), 238.

133. Bailey and Cottom, *After Chancellorsville,* 241–42.

134. Glatthaar, *Forged in Battle,* 238–39; Herek, *These Men Have Seen Hard Service,* 366–67.

135. Quoted in Glatthaar, *Forged in Battle,* 241–42.

136. Eric T. Dean Jr., *Shook Over Hell: Post-traumatic Stress, Vietnam, and the Civil War* (Cambridge, MA: Harvard University Press, 1997), 161–79.

137. Scott Nelson and Carol Sheriff, *A People at War: Civilians and Soldiers in America's Civil War* (New York: Oxford University Press, 2007), 228; Kenneth L. Kusmer, *Down and Out, on the Road: The Homeless in American History* (New York: Oxford University Press, 2002), 37.

138. Edward K. Spann, *Gotham at War: New York City, 1860–1865* (Wilmington, DE: Scholarly Resources, 2002), 191.

139. Kusmer, *Down and Out,* 37.

140. B. P. Gallaway, *The Ragged Rebel: A Common Soldier in W. H. Parsons' Texas Cavalry, 1861–1865* (Austin: University of Texas Press, 1988), 131.

141. Kirwin, *Johnny Green,* 207.

142. Fletcher, *Rebel Private,* 213.

143. Stone, *Wandering to Glory,* 246.

144. Kirby Ross, ed., *Autobiography of Samuel S. Hildebrand: The Renowned Missouri Bushwacker* (Fayetteville: University of Arkansas Press, 2005), 157.

145. Benson, *Berry Benson's Civil War Book,* xvi–xvii.

146. John Herbert Roper, ed., *Repairing the "March of Mars": The Civil War Diaries of John Samuel Apperson, Hospital Steward in the Stonewall Brigade, 1861–1865* (Macon, GA: Mercer University Press, 2001), 619–20.

147. James I. Robertson Jr., ed., *Soldier of Southwestern Virginia: The Civil War Letters of Captain John Preston Sheffey* (Baton Rouge: Louisiana State University Press, 2004), 228–31.

148. Drickamer and Drickamer, *Fort Lyon to Harpers Ferry,* 242.

149. Bohrnstedt, *Soldiering with Sherman,* 173; Gillette, *Jersey Blue,* 311; Clarke, "Honorable Scars," 370; Spann, *Gotham at War,* 191; Patrick J. Kelley, *Creating a National Home: Building the Veterans' Welfare State, 1860–1900* (Cambridge, MA: Harvard University Press, 1997), 56–57.

150. Karamanski, *Rally 'Round the Flag,* 242.

151. Elder, *Love amid the Turmoil,* 331.

152. Benson Bobrick, *Testament: A Soldier's Story of the Civil War* (New York: Simon & Schuster, 2003), 182–85.

153. Robert Manson Myers, ed., *The Children of Pride: A True Story of Georgia and the Civil War* (New Haven, CT: Yale University Press, 1972), 1307–11.

154. James L. Roark, *Masters without Slaves: Southern Planters in the Civil War and Reconstruction* (New York: W. W. Norton, 1977), 120–31; Daniel E. Sutherland, *The Confederate Carpetbaggers* (Baton Rouge: Louisiana State University Press, 1988), 1–7.

155. Current, *Civil War Era,* 372–73.

156. Marcia Reid-Green, ed., *Letters Home: Henry Matrau of the Iron Brigade* (Lincoln: University of Nebraska Press, 1993), 127.

157. Mark Elliot, *Color-Blind Justice: Albion Tourgée and the Quest for Racial Equality from the Civil War to Plessy v. Ferguson* (New York: Oxford University Press, 2006), 103–14.

158. Miller, *Black Civil War Soldiers,* 175, 177–78, 196–97, 200–2.

159. Donald R. Shaffer, *After the Glory: The Struggles of Black Civil War Veterans* (Lawrence: University Press of Kansas, 2004), 16–21.

160. Versalle F. Washington, *Eagle on Their Buttons: A Black Regiment in the Civil War* (Columbia: University of Missouri Press, 1999), 79.

161. Trudeau, *Like Men of War,* 463.

162. Karamanski, *Rally 'Round the Flag,* 244.

163. Trudeau, *Like Men of War,* 463–64; Shaffer, *After the Glory,* 37.

EPILOGUE: VETERANS' CONNECTIONS WITH THEIR PAST

Almost from the surrender of Confederate forces, veterans talked, argued, and wrote about the events of the war even as they set their sights on new endeavors. Southern veterans in particular were quick to defend their honor when challenged by insensitive Northerners.[1] These former Confederates remained unrepentant as they embarked on what they came to consider the evil days of Reconstruction. But the rebel veterans directed the main of their energy to rebuilding their lives, restoring the racial hierarchy, and redeeming their states from the Yankee occupiers, not memorializing their war. The past could wait, as they grappled with the present. After the veterans' return "to their devastated homes, and throughout the entire Reconstruction period, thoughts, time and energies were directed in an entirely different channel from that in which they had so long been engaged," veteran Robert T. Coles recalled, as he explained why he had waited so long to write his history of his regiment, the Fourth Alabama. "The war was a closed book, there being no leisure moments for writing history." Indeed, Coles could finally begin his regimental history of the Fourth Alabama Infantry in 1909 because, as he put it, whites had "subdued" black political activity and had "banished" carpetbaggers from the land; only then "the time was right" to become a scholar of the war.[2]

During the Reconstruction era, Northern veterans also had much to do besides think of the past. However, for those Yankee veterans who understood the connection between the war, its aftermath, and the importance of Reconstruction for preserving Union victory, the present was intimately connected to their earlier experiences. For these men, the memory of the war could not be trivialized or forgotten because the meaning of the war still had a very active role in their lives.

As late as 1875, Maine veteran, former Freedmen's Bureau agent, and Georgia politician John Emory Bryant refused to give up on the goals of racial justice and economic opportunity for African Americans that the war had unleashed. Reconstruction was a continuation of the fight between the two labor systems that had been at the heart of the war, and that fight required the North's continued commitment.[3] Earlier, at the end of 1867, Massachusetts veteran and South Carolina Freedmen's Bureau officer Erastus

Everson also saw the war's connection with his work in the heart of the old Confederacy. He offered to stay on with the Reconstruction agency as a civilian if "I might as far as possible be an instrument of perpetuating the principles which caused me to leave home in 1861 & which in part have been my guide and support under the trials & hardships since endured."[4]

African American veterans understood that their future was inextricably linked to the past. Henry McNeil Turner and other black veterans who became active in Southern politics believed the promise of equality made during the war still required their attention during the Reconstruction era. So, too, did their comrades in the North, who understood that the freedom and equality promised in the war required tending in the loyal states that still discriminated against African Americans on a number of levels. On occasion, they made public demonstrations of their commitment to the Union cause. In the former Confederacy, during Reconstruction, they celebrated emancipation and Union victory, even in the face of white resentment, by parading in their uniforms. And during the 1860s and 1870s, black veterans in New Bedford, Massachusetts, celebrated the civic holidays in uniform.[5]

In the Northern states, there were also thoughtful white veterans who understood the connection between the war, its goals, the problems of Reconstruction, and the sacrifices they had already made. Maine veteran Joshua Lawrence Chamberlain, writing a year after Lee's surrender, was adamant on the issue of Reconstruction and its connection to the legacy of Union veterans. "We fought for liberty, in its widest and best sense," he explained. "If we fail to attain these ends then was the blood of our heroes poured out in vain, and our treasure worse than wasted." Furthermore, "It seems little else than absolute madness to hasten to reinvest with political power the very men who precipitated upon us the horrors of civil war," meaning his former enemies, "and a little less than cowardly wickedness to turn our backs upon the millions whose humble and despised condition did not prevent them from befriending the county when it was most in need of friends," meaning the former slaves of the South. For Chamberlain, white Southerners did not appear sufficiently contrite, and the federal government was letting the former rebels get away with it.[6]

If these developments continued, it would only be a matter of time before former Confederates were reshaping the outcome of the war to suit their needs. Indeed, that became the case, as white Southerners regained control of their communities at the same time that Northerners abandoned Reconstruction, redefined their economic ideas, and accepted the racism that the war had previously challenged. Confederate veterans had not been able to win the war, but they certainly contributed to winning the peace for the white South.

White Union veterans such as Everson, Chamberlain, and Bryant, along with their black comrades, saw a successful Reconstruction as the ratification of their wartime work and therefore worthy of their attention. Confederate veterans, on the other hand, considered resistance to federal postwar policies, which included protecting black rights, as a way to honor their past, while, with the rebirth of white racial and economic dominance, exerting control over their future. Beyond the fight over Reconstruction, however, few veterans made serious conscious and systematic efforts immediately after the war to connect the present with the past. They reentered civilian life, never quite shaking the influence of the war, but not yet ready or able to revisit it in detail. Most Northern and Southern veterans concerned themselves with their efforts to rescue their fortunes. Northern and Southern politicians might use the conflict to their electoral

Grand review of the great veteran armies of Grant and Sherman at Washington, on the 23rd and 24th of May, 1865. Sherman's grand army. Looking up Pennsylvania Ave. from the Treasury Buildings, during the passage of the "Red Star" Division. (*Library of Congress*)

benefit during the 1870s, and service in either army became an important electoral qualification. However, Americans appeared to have lost all but a superficial interest in the war as they rebuilt their nation. During the 1870s, Northern veterans, for example, could not even sustain the few news journals aimed at them.[7]

Eventually, veterans reveled in their past, but it took some time for them to arrive at that place in their lives. Those men who began to participate in veterans' activities immediately after the war, however, prepared the way for their comrades who would eventually embrace their examples in significant numbers once Reconstruction had ended. During the 1860s and 1870s, former Confederate soldiers joined local veterans' organizations or army associations that catered to their interests and needs.[8] As early as the 1860s, veterans organized themselves to help comrades and their families by providing financial aid and burial funds. Frequently, during the 1860s, Southern women, concerned with memorializing Confederate dead, asked veterans to join them in their cause, which in some cases led to the development of veterans' organizations such as the Northeast Mississippi Confederate Veterans Association. Veterans also formed organizations around their old military units, such as the Washington Light Infantry Charitable Association, founded in 1865.[9] In late 1870, veterans in Virginia organized the Association of the Army of Northern Virginia; in 1877, western veterans established the Association of the Army of Tennessee.[10]

During Reconstruction, Northern veterans organized associations based on their places of residence or past unit affiliations, just as their Confederate counterparts were doing. Massachusetts Civil War soldier-artist Charles W. Reed, for example, became involved in the Ninth Battery Associates, which was formed sometime before 1870.[11] National organizations, such as the Military Order of the Loyal Legion (MOLLUS) and the Grand Army of the Republic (GAR), also provided opportunities for veterans to remain connected to their wartime experiences. Founded in 1865, MOLLUS limited its membership to officers, which allowed the men to maintain the status they had gained during the war; its goals were to memorialize the war and promote patriotism. In 1866, all Union veterans, including African Americans, could join the GAR, although black veterans could not count on eager acceptance in every post across the land.[12]

In addition to establishing organizations and memorializing their dead comrades, there were some veterans who began to write about the war. Tennessee Confederate Sumner A. Cunningham wrote his reminiscences of the 41st Tennessee Infantry before the end of the Reconstruction era but intended it for a limited audience. When he printed it in 1872, he distributed 300 copies to his friends. Still, he had the foresight to deposit a copy with the state library, which would ensure that he had some say in the telling of Tennessee's contribution to the Confederacy.[13]

Texan Robert Campbell also quickly wrote down his experiences lest people forget the Confederate cause. Soon after he returned from the war, he began composing his memoirs for his family, again preserving memories for a limited audience but nonetheless still making sure he had his say. The recollections were unpleasant, the cause noble, the future "gloomy," but he felt compelled to take up the task: "Tis but a natural conclusion, that since the Yankees look upon us as a conquered and vile race that they will veto the publication of a history of this war by Southern Talent and especially where that history wears the garb of truth." Consequently, the "best history of the past bloody days will be found in the memories" of the men "who figured in the scenes." If Campbell had not been able to save the Confederacy, he would save its history from mendacious Northerners.[14]

During the late 1860s and early 1870s, other men joined Campbell and Cunningham in their efforts to preserve history. Many of them first looked to gathering documents about and writing the history of their particular military units. In 1865, for example, Joshua Lawrence Chamberlain and a committee of former Union officers were gathering materials for an "authentic, impartial, and thorough" history of the Fifth Corps of the Army of the Potomac.[15] And A. F. Sperry, enlisted man and musician, published a history of his 33rd Iowa Infantry in 1866, with the intention of eliciting "warm and pleasant" memories of their "noble" regiment among his former comrades.[16]

On the Confederate side, in 1866, Edward Porter Alexander began to write an unfinished history of the First Corps of the Army of Northern Virginia.[17] Not much later, in 1869, however, Confederate veterans took on a larger task, when, concerned that the federal government would define history through its planned collection of wartime documents, they became involved in forming the Southern Historical Society. That organization's goal was to gather its own collection of documents to provide the country with a correct, honorable history of their lost cause. In 1876 the society began publishing the *Southern Historical Society Papers,* which would provide rebel veterans ample opportunity not only to present the so-called real history of the war, but to attack one another as they argued about whose version of past events was correct.[18]

During the 1870s, army veteran scribblers began to write their memoirs, but the great popularity of such publications would come in the next decade. So, too, the veterans' national organizations would have to wait for some time before they attracted the attention of the men they called to their ranks. These organizations remained stunted and almost perished before gaining a stronger foothold among veterans. From the outset, MOLLUS suffered from bureaucratic inefficiency and, more important, a lack of interest on the part of potential members that hindered its growth.[19] The GAR also seemed to suffer from the veterans' inability or lack of desire to join. After the war in Chicago, for example, former soldiers founded two chapters of the GAR, both of which failed to sustain themselves. Indeed, throughout the country, the GAR was in serious difficulty. By 1871 the organization was also hobbled by substantial debt.[20]

With the passing of time, it was almost inevitable that older, settled men who wished to recall their youth or who were in positions to help less fortunate comrades joined organizations and used the printed word and memorial orations to convince the public to acknowledge their contributions to their causes. During the 1880s, veterans, secure in their families and livelihoods, began to revisit their youthful wartime experiences with a much greater commitment than ever before. As nostalgia set in, they saw veterans' organizations as a way to reconnect with old comrades and their youth. In 1889 Confederate veterans established a national alternative to local organizations with the founding of the United Confederate Veterans (UCV). Émigré Confederates even established chapters in six Northern cities. By the early 1890s the UCV had taken up the challenge to promulgate a "correct" history of the war through publications and exhibitions.[21]

Confederate veterans also directed their efforts to preserving the memory of their war by honoring their dead comrades and caring for their cemeteries. They also provided charity for their less fortunate comrades, including burial assistance and funding for soldiers' homes. Better off veterans, for example, were central to the fundraising campaign for a soldiers' home in Richmond, Virginia, while former soldiers-turned-politicians led campaigns for establishing such homes in other states. The Louisiana Division of the Army of Tennessee Association also helped to establish a soldiers' home, along with spending an extraordinary amount of money for a cemetery monument in New Orleans.[22]

During the latter decades of the nineteenth century, Northerners witnessed a revival of their veterans' organizations and a concern with memorializing their wartime experiences. By the end of the century, MOLLUS, by its nature an exclusive organization, had 20 chapters and a membership of some 8,000 veterans.[23] The GAR, because of its inclusiveness, attracted many more veterans. During the early 1880s, for example, Chicago, a city that could not support 2 chapters in the 1860s, supported 10 GAR chapters. During the late 1870s, the GAR had only attracted 30,000 veterans to its chapters; by 1890 it had 428,000 veterans in its ranks.[24] It even followed Union veterans into the old Confederacy. Vermont native John Randolph Lewis and other transplanted Yankees came together under the GAR banner in Atlanta, Georgia, to celebrate their wartime experience, while Vicksburg, Mississippi, had segregated GAR posts for black and white veterans.[25]

During the 1880s and 1890s, Northern veterans turned to their national and local organizations to express their patriotic sentiments, honor fallen comrades, and engage in eleemosynary activities, just as they had attempted to do immediately after the war, but now in strengthened numbers. The organizations also provided opportunities for their members to give speeches at Memorial Day, Independence Day, and other patriotic functions, by which they could remind citizens of their wartime sacrifices.[26] Additionally, a revived MOLLUS and a growing GAR lobbied Congress for support of veterans' issues, from patriotism to veterans' welfare. The GAR, for example, pushed for an expanded pension system for veterans.[27]

Old soldiers from the North and the South also came to grips with their past by visiting the battlefields of their youth. Joshua Lawrence Chamberlain attended the 25th Anniversary of Gettysburg, 1888, when "25,000 pilgrims returned to their old fields."[28] For the 50th anniversary in 1913, over 50,000 veterans from both Union and Confederate armies gathered in Pennsylvania, many of them living under canvas, as they had done in the old days.[29] While Gettysburg remained a favorite reunion site for veterans, other battlefields attracted visitors and provided settings for new monuments to those who had fought there. In November 1897, for example, veterans of the 75th Pennsylvania, an ethnically German regiment and participants in the battle of Chattanooga, gathered in Tennessee to dedicate a monument to their service in that state.[30] In 1890, veterans from Northern and Southern regiments gathered at Vicksburg for a joint reunion. Not to be outdone by their eastern counterparts, Vicksburg veterans pushed for their own 50th anniversary reunion, which finally came to pass in 1917.[31]

Veterans' organizations and reunions allowed for former soldiers to socialize with other men of like mind and experience. As Iron Brigade veteran James Sullivan noted, "It is very gratifying for comrades in the army to meet one another and talk of the times when they tramped through mud knee deep, or sweetly slept on three fence rails, or when they fiercely charged and drove the enemy, or how they bravely fell back when overpowered and defeated."[32] Veterans' reunions and veterans' organizations meetings also provided opportunities for men to present historical research about their units, which in some cases proved to be the seed for larger regimental histories, or to begin raising funds for monuments to make certain their accomplishments and sacrifices were not forgotten by younger generations.

During the 1880s, memoirs and regimental histories poured from the pens of veterans. Sam Watkins claimed to have taken up his pen as "a pastime and pleasure, as there is nothing that so much delights the old soldiers as to revisit the scenes and battlefields with which he was once so familiar."[33] But Watkins and other veterans also had more serious matters in mind as they told their stories. Confederates such as Watkins took the opportunity to justify their actions to their children and grandchildren, while explaining why they suffered defeat, all of which might have allowed them to exorcise the demons of past battles. Virginian John O. Casler, an enlisted man in the Stonewall Brigade, ended his 1893 memoir praising the steel of Southern women and his army comrades and blaming defeat on the remainder of the Confederate nation's lack of will.[34] Of course, Tennessean Sam Watkins was not shy about absolving the dedicated enlisted man from blame while laying the cause for defeat on blundering officers.[35] Unsurprisingly, more than one rebel memoirist mentioned that the overwhelming material resources of their enemies accounted for their surrender.

The wartime leaders among the veteran authors took advantage of a renewed interest in the war to debate various aspects of the conflict, engaging in lively print battles in various magazines to protect reputations as much as to preserve history. Advocacy was never far below the surface of any essay concerning the war. Former Confederate general and postwar Republican politician James Longstreet, for example, was much maligned by Virginians concerned with finding a scapegoat for Gettysburg and with preserving the reputation of their beloved Robert E. Lee; he defended himself and in turn criticized his critics in print.[36] Likewise, former Union general Carl Schurz defended himself and his German troops' performance at Chancellorsville, where they had broken in the face of Jackson's surprise attack, in his early twentieth-century memoirs and other writings.[37]

Enlisted men, however, did not assume that only their officers had the exclusive right to shape the nation's memories. They admitted that Ulysses S. Grant and the other big men had something to say about the war and that they could claim their fame for the parts they played. However, they refused to yield to them as the sole authoritative historical source. As far as they were concerned, they, too, had a unique—and perhaps superior—perspective to present to the public. Union veteran John D. Billings, for example, did not believe that battle pieces told the whole story of the war and offered in his 1887 volume *Hardtack and Coffee* a look at the common, everyday experiences of the soldier's life.[38] Frank Wilkeson, another Union veteran, made it clear with some pride in his 1886 book that the common soldier was the critical element of the Civil War army. "I was a private soldier in the war to suppress the rebellion," he opened his memoir. "The enlisted men, of whom I was one, composed the army," he declared. "We won or lost the battles."[39] In his 1890 memoir *Recollections of a Private,* Union veteran Warren Lee Goss proclaimed the Army of the Potomac to have been "the people in arms," and it was that particular strength that allowed it to endure to victory. "In our great army," he wrote, "the private soldier who carried forty rounds of cartridges and a brave heart, who fought without expectation of reward or promotion, was its truest hero and the fittest representative of its conquering spirit." It was the sacrifices of these men that "saved the nation and preserved the union of states."[40]

Confederate enlisted men felt the same way about their wartime efforts. Southern women had been memorializing Confederate enlisted dead for some time, but Carlton McCarthy used his 1882 book to present the common soldier's experiences, assuming that the men who fought and died for the Lost Cause deserved more than being remembered by nothing more than their unit designations in the larger histories of the war. The fame of men such as Lee and Jackson, McCarthy argued, "is an everlasting monument to the mighty deeds of the nameless host who followed them through so much toil and blood to glorious victories."[41]

Veterans, be they officers or enlisted men, probably more than anything else desired to leave behind a favorable record of their sacrifices and accomplishments for their descendents. By the 1880s, Union veterans realized that future generations might be at risk of forgetting the heroism of the Civil War generation. W. G. Putney, a veteran who had a hand in producing the history of an Illinois artillery battery, believed that every former soldier wished for "his relatives, children and friends" to know how he and his comrades "had helped to restore order to what was once a slave-ridden, war-distracted country."[42] Philadelphia doctor John H. Brinton completed his memoir in 1891, aware that his children would consider the war—a war that "was *everything*" to those men who had fought in it—some unfamiliar historical event that shared the distant past with the American Revolution. He wished his descendents to remember his generation's accomplishments as well as to come to know him.[43]

Midwesterner James P. Sullivan worried about his and his comrades' legacy as he became more involved with researching his own past. After the war, his life followed the common trajectory of so many Civil War veterans. He returned to his family, left Wisconsin for Dakota Territory, and eventually returned sometime before 1880. Obviously, he had a life to live, but he began to think about his army days and read what others wrote about the war. Perhaps bored with his farm life, he began to put down his own stories two decades after he had experienced some exciting times. He discovered how likely it was that the memory of his great contribution to American history would fade when, in 1883, he went to the State Historical Society in Madison, Wisconsin. There he found that all the society had on his old brigade was a general history; there were no other records of the brigade or its constituent regiments. "The only such evidence I discovered showing that there ever existed such a body of men as the Iron Brigade, was a case containing a photograph of the Rebel Battle Flag captured by our regiment at Gettysburg, and a short extract from the official report of General Doubleday, in regard to the part taken by the regiment in that battle," he explained somewhat indignantly. "I think that a state that annually appropriates thousands of dollars wrung from poor and often needy farmers to support Professors of agriculture, state fairs, and to educate lawyers, might spare a few dollars to prepare a record of the patriotism of those who gave health, wealth, life and limb, for the honor of our state." Furthermore, the state would do well, he argued, to spend some of its budget on "encouraging reunions and meetings of the late soldiers" because "it would have more effect in promoting patriotism and love of country than all the buncombe speeches ever delivered."[44]

As time passed, the veterans who attended these reunions enjoyed memories of a virtuous, patriotic past that helped to diminish and soften recollections of the horrors of war and of the ideological differences, particularly involving race and slavery, that had provoked secession and bloodshed. It all seemed to have been a terrible misunderstanding that now had little meaning. As Sam Watkins had suggested in 1882, the "argument" was long over. "America has no north, no south, no east, no west . . . and we can laugh at the absurd notion of there being a north and a south."[45]

Importantly, as old soldiers gathered with old comrades and former enemies at battlefield reunions, they and the events they sponsored became engines of sectional reconciliation. The veterans, who might assume that civilians, somehow less virtuous than they were, would never understand their experiences, now found common ground with their former enemies. Confederate veterans came to accept that there were Yankees who were true national heroes. Many white Northern veterans looked at Reconstruction, acknowledged its failure, and agreed with their Southern counterparts that black freedom might not have been a good thing; better to emphasize the "War for the Union," rather than an emancipationist policy that came forward after so many of them had rallied to the flag.

Let bygones be bygones and look to the future, so the rationale went. Americans in general, and veterans in particular, could now discuss the events of the war without paying attention to the causes and the consequences. The veterans themselves became symbols of national reconciliation and their heroic deeds the focus of an admiring country. As William Hodges Mann, the governor of Virginia, admonished the old veterans who gathered at Gettysburg on the 50th anniversary of the battle, the men who fought the war should hold the nation's attention, not the old debates that might have led to the bloodshed.[46] Thus the war became not a fight for freedom or slavery, but an exhibition of valor, honor, and heroism, traits shared equally by both sides. It was an idea that veterans basking in the glory could accept, if they happened to be white. And those Northern white veterans among them who still could remember that the victory should have meant an expansion of liberty that included their black comrades were no longer heard.

But even as the nation and veterans moved toward a compatible reunion, there remained an undercurrent of thinking that would not ignore past ideals. There were former rebels who questioned the enthusiasm that some of their number had for making men such as Ulysses S. Grant into national heroes worthy of their veneration, as it might diminish the validity of their own cause.[47] Even if some men could accept the

Confederate Veteran Memorial. Veterans in uniform leaving the memorial, Arlington, Virginia 1914. (*Library of Congress*)

nationalization of sectional war heroes, they refused to waver from their beliefs that secession had been constitutional and that their cause had been righteous. These men would eventually convince many of their former enemies of the honorable nature of their cause and raise their own sectional heroes to national status. In the end, these Confederates had less to retract about their wartime ideals than did their Northern counterparts who went along with the process of reconciliation.

There were white Southern veterans who understood the role that slavery played in bringing about secession and war, but it had been Northerners who had pressed the issue, forcing the hand of the South. Soon after the war, Texan J.K.P. Blackburn, who, in his memoirs, offered no apologies for his actions, accused "Abolitionist fanatics" and their Republican representatives who wished to stir up a slave rebellion for bringing on the war. Secession and war in fact were acts of "self- preservation...the first law of nature," he argued, because "what could the South expect but humiliation and destruction of her institutions from such a set?" The seceded states had simply claimed their constitutional rights to leave an unhappy union and fought for "the cause of human liberty as did our forefathers in other years."[48]

An unapologetic, unabashed John Singleton Mosby also made it clear that the section's peculiar institution was at the heart of the war. In June 1907 he did not equivocate when he wrote that "the South went to war on account of Slavery." Since slavery was legal, he argued, there was good reason to fight to protect it, but Southerners could not ignore the old institution's connection with the war. "South Carolina went to war—as she said in her Secession Proclamation—because slavery wd. not be secure under Lincoln," Mosby explained, and "South Carolina ought to know what was the cause for her seceding."[49]

Confederate veterans for the most part, however, built an honorable memory of the crisis that stressed they had made an honest stand for states' rights and the true Constitution. In 1878 Georgia veteran Charles Colcock Jones Jr. delivered an oration that forcefully absolved the Confederate cause of any wrong; the heroic dead soldiers he praised had in fact sacrificed their lives for liberty and the true Constitution.[50] Even decades after the war, Sam Watkins remained "as firm in my convictions to-day of the right of secession as I was in 1861." Confederates, Watkins explained, fought for their Constitutional rights, while Yankees fought "for Union and power," he explained.[51] Men such as Watkins provided literary ammunition for the growing cult of the Lost Cause. By the end of the century, however, Confederate veterans had constructed a story of their experience that explained the war and their defeat in terms that suited the post-Reconstruction needs of their section.[52]

Former rebels were strong in their convictions, but there were Union veterans who remained equally committed to their past ideals. Certainly many of them, as they grew older, enjoyed the warm feelings of shaking hands with enemies who shared their experiences, even admitting there was honor inherent in the Confederate cause. Nevertheless, from the end of the war, through Reconstruction, and to the end of the century, there were Union veterans, including members of the GAR, who were disturbed by a growing tendency to welcome home their old enemies, while forgetting some key ideals that had propelled them to and then kept them in the ranks.[53] Alvin C. Voris, a former Union general and GAR member, challenged the idea of a Confederate Lost Cause that shared an equal moral standing with Northern wartime goals. For Voris, sectional reconciliation was commendable, but it could not erase the past. Northern soldiers had fought not only to preserve the Union, but to rid the nation of slavery and to protect the institutions that made their land great. The fruits of Northern victory included the guaranteeing of the rights of black Americans, who had helped to win that victory.[54]

Other veterans shared Voris's views. For example, Albion Tourgée, involved in Reconstruction politics in North Carolina, claimed that his Civil War service had changed the way he viewed African Americans; he remained a supporter of black rights for the rest of his life, writing novels about their plight and serving as their advocate before the Supreme Court in *Plessy v. Ferguson.*[55] Vermont veteran Marshall Harvey Twitchell paid significant attention to his Reconstruction activities, his role as a Republican politician in Louisiana, and his near-assassination in his autobiography completed at the end of the nineteenth century. Although he never published the volume, he seemed to have wished people to remember more than the fact that he had fought for the Union and that he extended his service to the cause through Reconstruction.[56] And as late as 1911, Joshua Lawrence Chamberlain was not ready to water down the reasons why Northerners fought the war. When presented with the plan to establish an "Order of the Blue and Gray," he praised it as a "noble" thing to do, but he was clear that he would not accept any diminution of the importance of the Union cause. "We were fighting for our Country, with all that this involves," he explained, "not only for the defence of its institutions, but for the realization of its vital principles and declared ideas." "The fight to preserve it from destruction has a historical, if not moral, value which should not be lost sight of," he continued. Furthermore, Chamberlain made it clear that he was "not in sympathy with any movement or proposition which would deny, obscure or ignore that fact."[57]

Four decades after the war, Robert Beecham, who had been an officer with the 23rd U.S. Colored Infantry, declared, "The American Civil War…grew directly out of the question of slavery." Furthermore, the "most remarkable fact connected with the great war" was "that the Afro-American came forward cheerfully and volunteered his strength, his brawn, his heart's blood to save the honor of the flag that to him and his race had been the symbol of every dishonor."[58] Black veteran George Washington Williams, in his 1888 book *A History of Negro Troops in the War of the Rebellion, 1861–1865,* provided the evidence.[59] The course of American history into the twentieth century, however, illustrated that in spite of the views of men such as Beecham and Tourgée, reconciliation proceeded at a pace and in a fashion that allowed white veterans to enjoy their memories at the expense of an honest history of the war.

NOTES

1. Gaines M. Foster, *Ghosts of the Confederacy: Defeat, the Lost Cause, and the Emergence of the New South* (New York: Oxford University Press, 1987), 34–35; David W. Blight, *Race and Reunion: The Civil War in American Memory* (Cambridge, MA: Belknap Press of Harvard University Press, 2001).

2. Jeffrey D. Stocker, ed., *From Huntsville to Appomattox: R. T. Coles's History of the 4th Regiment, Alabama Volunteer Infantry, C.S.A., Army of Northern Virginia* (Knoxville: University of Tennessee Press, 1999), 9–10.

3. Eric Foner, *Politics and Ideology in the Age of Civil War* (New York: Oxford University Press, 1980), 124–27.

4. Quoted in Paul A. Cimbala, "Lining Up to Serve: Wounded and Sick Union Officers Join Veteran Reserve Corps during Civil War," *Reconstruction Prologue* 35 (Spring 2003): 47.

5. Donald R. Shaffer, *After the Glory: The Struggles of Black Civil War Veterans* (Lawrence: University Press of Kansas, 2004), 68–95; William Blair, *Cities of the Dead: Contesting the Memory of the Civil War in the South, 1865–1914* (Chapel Hill: University of North Carolina Press, 2004), 23, 27, 36; Earl F. Mulderink III, "A Different Civil War: African American Veterans in New Bedford, Massachusetts," in *Union Soldiers and the Northern Home Front Wartime Experiences, Postwar Adjustments,* ed. Paul A. Cimbala and Randall M. Miller (New York: Fordham University Press, 2002), 426

6. Jeremiah E. Goulka, ed., *The Grand Old Man of Maine: Selected Letters of Joshua Lawrence Chamberlain, 1865–1914* (Chapel Hill: University of North Carolina Press, 2004), 16–17.

7. Stuart McConnell, *Glorious Contentment: The Grand Army of the Republic, 1865–1900* (Chapel Hill: University of North Carolina Press, 1992), 20–22.

8. Charles Reagan Wilson, *Baptized in Blood: The Religion of the Lost Cause, 1865–1920* (Athens: University of Georgia Press, 1980), 30; Blight, *Race and Reunion,* 140–70.

9. William W. White, *The Confederate Veteran* (Tuscaloosa, AL: Confederate, 1962), 9–25.

10. Foster, *Ghosts of the Confederacy,* 53, 91.

11. Eric A. Campbell, ed., *"A Grand Terrible Dramma": From Gettysburg to Petersburg: The Civil War Letters of Charles Wellington Reed* (New York: Fordham University Press, 2000), 332–33.

12. Dana B. Shoaf, "'For Every Man Who Wore the Blue': The Military Order of the Loyal Legion of the United States and the Charges of Elitism after the Civil War," in Cimbala and Miller, *Union Soldiers,* 463–88; Mulderink, "A Different Civil War," 430; Donald R. Shaffer, "'I Would Rather Shake Hands with the Blackest Nigger in the Land': Northern Black Civil War Veterans and the Grand Army of the Republic," in Cimbala and Miller, *Union Soldiers,* 442–62; McConnell, *Glorious Contentment;* Mary R. Dearing, *Veterans in Politics: The Story of the G.A.R.* (Baton Rouge: Louisiana State University Press, 1952).

13. Sumner A. Cunningham, *Reminiscences of the 41st Tennessee: The Civil War in the West,* ed. John A. Simpson (Shippensburg, PA: White Mane, 2001), xiv.

14. George Skoch and Mark W. Perkins, ed., *Lone Star Confederate: A Gallant and Good Soldier of the Fifth Texas Infantry* (College Station: Texas A&M University Press, 2003), xi, 3–4 (quotation).

15. Goulka, *Grand Old Man of Maine,* 10.

16. A. F. Sperry, *History of the 33d Iowa Infantry Volunteer Regiment, 1863–6,* ed. Gregory J. W. Urwin and Cathy Kunzinger Urwin (Fayetteville: University of Arkansas Press, 1999), 3.

17. Thomas W. Cutrer, ed., *Longstreet's Aide: The Civil War Letters of Major Thomas J. Goree* (Charlottesville: University Press of Virginia, 1995), 156–57; Gary W. Gallagher, ed., *Fighting for the Confederacy: The Personal Recollections of General Edward Porter Alexander* (Chapel Hill: University of North Carolina Press, 1989), xv; Blight, *Race and Reunion,* 158–64.

18. Thomas J. Pressly, *Americans Interpret Their Civil War* (New York: Free Press, 1965), 104–6; Foster, *Ghosts of the Confederacy,* 50; William Garrett Piston, *Lee's Tarnished Lieutenant: James Longstreet and His Place in Southern History* (Athens: University of Georgia Press, 1987), 133–36; Wilson, *Baptized in Blood,* 123–24.

19. Shoaf, "'For Every Man Who Wore the Blue,'" 465–66.

20. McConnell, *Glorious Contentment,* 20; Theodore J. Karamanski, *Rally 'Round the Flag: Chicago and the Civil War* (Chicago: Nelson-Hall, 1993), 243; Dearing, *Veterans in Politics,* 189.

21. Wilson, *Baptized in Blood,* 30; Foster, *Ghosts of the Confederacy,* 104–26; Daniel E. Sutherland, *The Confederate Carpetbaggers* (Baton Rouge: Louisiana State University Press, 1988), 136–38.

22. R. B. Rosenburg, *Living Monuments: Confederate Soldiers' Homes in the New South* (Chapel Hill: University of North Carolina Press, 1993), 9, 30, 34; White, *Confederate Veteran,* 98–114.

23. Shoaf, "'For Every Man Who Wore the Blue,'" 466–67.

24. Gerald F. Linderman, *Embattled Courage: The Experience of Combat in the American Civil War* (New York: Free Press, 1987), 275; Karamanski, *Rally 'Round the Flag,* 243.

25. Paul A. Cimbala, *Under the Guardianship of the Nation: The Freedmen's Bureau and the Reconstruction of Georgia, 1865–1870* (Athens: University of Georgia Press, 1997), 226; Christopher Waldrop, *Vicksburg's Long Shadow: The Civil War Legacy of Race and Remembrance* (Lanham, MD: Rowman & Littlefield, 2005), 195.

26. Emil Rosenblatt and Ruth Rosenblatt, eds., *Hard Marching Every Day: The Civil War Letters of Private Wilbur Fisk, 1861–1865* (Lawrence: University of Kansas Press, 1992), 347–368; Karamanski, *Rally 'Round the Flag,* 243.

27. Dearing, *Veterans in Politics,* 274, 284–86.

28. Goulka, *Grand Old Man of Maine,* 136.

29. Blight, *Race and Reunion,* 6–9, 383–85.

30. Christian B. Keller, *Chancellorsville and the Germans: Nativism, Ethnicity, and Civil War Memory* (New York: Fordham University Press, 2007), 156.

31. Waldrop, *Vicksburg's Long Shadow,* 194–228.

32. William J. K. Beaudot and Lance J. Herdegen, eds., *An Irishman in the Iron Brigade: The Civil War Memoirs of James P. Sullivan, Sergt., Company K, 6th Wisconsin Volunteers* (New York: Fordham University Press, 1993), 80–81.

33. Sam Watkins, *"Company Aytch," or a Side Show of the Big Show and Other Sketches,* ed. M. Thomas Inge (New York: Penguin Putnam, 1999), 5.

34. John O. Casler, *Four Years in the Stonewall Brigade,* 2nd ed. (Columbia: University of South Carolina Press, 2005), 306.

35. Watkins, *"Company Aytch,"* 31, 33, 40, 64, 67, 83, 89, passim.

36. Piston, *Lee's Tarnished Lieutenant,* 125–36, 141–50, passim.

37. Keller, *Chancellorsville and the Germans,* 151–53.

38. John D. Billings, *Hardtack and Coffee: The Unwritten Story of Army Life* (Lincoln: University of Nebraska Press, 1993).

39. Frank Wilkeson, *Turned Inside Out: Recollections of a Private Soldier in the Army of the Potomac* (Lincoln: University of Nebraska Press, 1997), 1.

40. Warren Lee Goss, *Recollections of a Private: A Story of the Army of the Potomac* (Scituate, MA: Digital Scanning, 2002), iv.

41. Carlton McCarthy, *Detailed Minutiae of Soldier Life in the Army of Northern Virginia, 1861–1865* (Lincoln: University of Nebraska Press, 1993), 1–2.

42. Thaddeus C. S. Brown, Samuel J. Murphy, and William G. Putney, *Behind the Guns: The History of Battery I, 2nd Regiment, Illinois Light Artillery,* ed. Clyde C. Walton (Carbondale: Southern Illinois University Press, 1965, 2000), xxv.

43. John H. Brinton, *Personal Memoirs of John H. Brinton, Civil War Surgeon, 1861–1865* (Carbondale: Southern Illinois University Press, 1996), 11–13.

44. Beaudot and Herdegen, *An Irishman in the Iron Brigade,* 2–3, 80, 88 n. 17.

45. Watkins, *"Company Aytch,"* 4.

46. David W. Blight, *Beyond the Battlefield: Race, Memory, and the American Civil War* (Amherst: University of Massachusetts Press, 2002), 138.

47. Peter S. Carmichael, *The Last Generation: Young Virginians in Peace, War, and Reunion* (Chapel Hill: University of North Carolina Press, 2005), 233.

48. J.K.P. Blackburn, *Reminiscences of the Terry Rangers,* reprinted in *Terry Texas Ranger Trilogy,* ed. Thomas W. Cutrer (Austin, TX: State House Press, 1996), 179–81.

49. Peter A. Brown, ed., *Take Sides with the Truth: The Postwar Letters of John Singleton Mosby to Samuel F. Chapman* (Lexington: University Press of Kentucky, 2007), 74.

50. John R. Neff, *Honoring the Civil War Dead: Commemoration and the Problem of Reconciliation* (Lawrence: University Press of Kansas, 2005), 165–66.

51. Watkins, *"Company Aytch,"* 7.

52. Carmichael, *Last Generation,* 235.

53. Nina Silber, *The Romance of Reunion: Northerners and the South, 1865–1900* (Chapel Hill: University of North Carolina Press, 1993), 97; M. Keith Harris, "Slavery, Emancipation, and Veterans of the Union Cause: Commemorating Freedom in the Era of Reconciliation, 1885–1915," *Civil War History* 53 (September 2007): 264–90.

54. Jerome Mushkat, ed., *A Citizen-Soldier's Civil War: The Letters of Brevet Major General Alvin C. Voris* (DeKalb: Northern Illinois University Press, 2002), 15–16.

55. Mark Elliott, *Color-Blind Justice: Albion Tourgée and the Quest for Racial Equality from the Civil War to Plessy v. Ferguson* (New York: Oxford University Press, 2006).

56. Ted Tunnell, ed., *Carpetbagger from Vermont: The Autobiography of Marshall Harvey Twitchell* (Baton Rouge: Louisiana State University Press, 1989).

57. Goulka, *Grand Old Man of Maine,* 253.

58. Michael E. Stevens, ed., *As If It Were Glory: Robert Beecham's Civil War from the Iron Brigade to the Black Regiments* (Madison, WI: Madison House, 1998), 165.

59. George Washington Williams, *A History of the Negro Troops in the War of the Rebellion, 1861–1865* (New York: Negro Universities Press, 1969).

SELECTED BIBLIOGRAPHY

PRIMARY SOURCES

Online Material and Microfilm

Primary Source Collection, eHistory, Ohio State University, Columbus, Ohio, http://ehistory.osu.edu/osu/sources/.

Sellers, John R., ed. *A People at War: Civil War Manuscripts from the Holdings of the Library of Congress.* 60 reels. Alexandria, VA: Chadwyck-Healey, 1989–1990.

Published Correspondence, Diaries, and Memoirs

Adams, Lois Bryan. *Letter from Washington, 1863–1865.* Edited by Evelyn Leasher. Detroit, MI: Wayne State University Press, 1999.

Agassiz, George R., ed. *Meade's Headquarters, 1863–1865: Letters of Colonel Theodore Lyman from the Wilderness to Appomattox.* Boston: Massachusetts Historical Society, 1922.

Allen, Randall, and Keith S. Bohannon, eds. *Campaigning with "Old Stonewall": Confederate Captain Ujanirtus Allen's Letters to His Wife.* Baton Rouge: Louisiana State University Press, 1998.

Armstrong, Gordon, ed. *Illinois Artillery Officer's Civil War.* College Station, TX: Virtualbookworm.com Publishing, 2005.

Bailey, Judith A., and Robert I. Cottom, eds. *After Chancellorsville: Letters from the Heart, the Civil War Letters of Private Walter G. Dunn and Emma Randolph.* Baltimore: Maryland Historical Society, 1998.

Baker, T. Lindsay, ed. *Confederate Guerrilla: The Civil War Memoir of Joseph Bailey.* Fayetteville: University of Arkansas Press, 2007.

Barrett, John G., ed. *Yankee Rebel: The Civil War Journal of Edmund DeWitt Patterson.* Knoxville: University of Tennessee Press, 2004. First published 1966 by University of North Carolina Press.

Bears, Edwin C., ed. *A Louisiana Confederate: Diary of Felix Pierre Poché.* Translated by Eugenie Watson Somdal. Natchitoches: Louisiana Studies Institute, Northwestern State University, 1972.

Beasecker, Robert, ed. *"I Hope to Do My Country Service": The Civil War Letters of John Bennitt, M.D., Surgeon, 19th Michigan Infantry.* Detroit, MI: Wayne State University Press, 2005.

Beaudot, William J. K., and Lance J. Herdegen, eds. *An Irishman in the Iron Brigade: The Civil War Memoirs of James P. Sullivan, Sergt., Company K, 6th Wisconsin Volunteers.* New York: Fordham University Press, 1993.

Bee, Robert L., ed. *The Boys from Rockville: Civil War Narratives of Sgt. Benjamin Hirst, Company D, 14th Connecticut Volunteers.* Knoxville: University of Tennessee Press, 1998.

Bennett, Stewart, and Barbara Tillery, eds. *The Struggle for the Life of the Republic: A Civil War Narrative by Brevet Major Charles Dana Miller, 76th Ohio Volunteer Infantry.* Kent, OH: Kent State University Press, 2004.

Benson, Susan Williams, ed. *Berry Benson's Civil War Book: Memoirs of a Confederate Scout and Sharpshooter.* Athens: University of Georgia Press, 1992. First published 1962.

Bergeron, Arthur W., Jr., ed. *The Civil War Reminiscences of Major Silas T. Grisamore, C.S.A.* Baton Rouge: Louisiana State University Press, 1993.

Berry, Chester D., ed. *Loss of the Sultana and Reminiscences of Survivors.* Knoxville: University of Tennessee Press, 2005.

Billings, John D. *Hardtack and Coffee: The Unwritten Story of Army Life.* Lincoln: University of Nebraska Press, 1993. First published 1887 by George M. Smith.

Blackburn, J.K.P. *Reminiscences of the Terry Rangers.* Reprinted in *Terry Texas Ranger Trilogy,* ed. Thomas W. Cutrer. Austin, TX: State House Press, 1996.

Blight, David W., ed. *When This Cruel War Is Over: The Civil War Letters of Charles Harvey Brewster.* Amherst: University of Massachusetts Press, 1992.

Blomquist, Ann K., and Robert A. Taylor, eds. *This Cruel War: The Civil War Letters of Grant and Malinda Taylor, 1862–1865.* Macon, GA: Mercer University Press, 2000.

Bohrnstedt, Jennifer Cain, ed. *Soldiering with Sherman: Civil War Letters of George F. Cram.* DeKalb: Northern Illinois University Press, 2000.

———. *While Father Is Away: The Civil War Letters of William H. Bradbury.* Lexington: University Press of Kentucky, 2003.

Brinton, John H. *Personal Memoirs of John H. Brinton, Civil War Surgeon, 1861–1865.* Carbondale: Southern Illinois University Press, 1996. First published 1914 by Neale.

Brown, Peter A., ed. *Take Sides with the Truth: The Postwar Letters of John Singleton Mosby to Samuel F. Chapman.* Lexington: University Press of Kentucky, 2007.

Bruen, Ella Jane, and Brian M. Fitzgibbons, eds. *Through Ordinary Eyes: The Civil War Correspondence of Rufus Robbins, Private, 7th Regiment, Massachusetts Volunteers.* Westport, CT: Praeger, 2000.

Brumgardt, John R. *Civil War Nurse: The Diary and Letters of Hannah Ropes.* Knoxville: University of Tennessee Press, 1980.

Buckingham, Peter H., ed. *All's for the Best: The Civil War Reminiscences and Letters of Daniel W. Sawtelle, Eight Maine Volunteer Infantry.* Knoxville: University of Tennessee Press, 2001.

Byrne, Frank L., and Jean Powers Soman, eds. *Your True Marcus: The Civil War Letters of a Jewish Colonel.* Kent, OH: Kent State University Press, 1985.

Campbell, Eric A., ed. *"A Grand Terrible Dramma": From Gettysburg to Petersburg: The Civil War Letters of Charles Wellington Reed.* New York: Fordham University Press, 2000.

Chadwick, Bruce, ed. *Brother against Brother: The Lost Civil War Diary of Lt. Edmund Halsey.* Secaucus, NJ: Birch Lane Press Book, Carol Publishing Group, 1997.

Chapman, Sarah Bahnson, ed. *Bright and Gloomy Days: The Civil War Correspondence of Captain Charles Frederic Bahnson, a Moravian Confederate.* Knoxville: University of Tennessee Press, 2003.

Christ, Mark K., ed. *Getting Used to Being Shot At: The Spence Family Civil War Letters.* Fayetteville: University of Arkansas Press, 2002.

Clark, Willene B., ed. *Valleys of the Shadow: The Memoir of Confederate Captain Reuben G. Clark.* Knoxville: University of Tennessee Press, 1994.

Cockrell, Monroe F., ed. *Gunner with Stonewall: Reminiscences of William Thomas Poague, Lieutenant, Captain, Major and Lieutenant Colonel of Artillery, Army of Northern Virginia, CSA, 1861–65: A Memoir Written for His Children in 1903.* Lincoln: University of Nebraska Press, 1998. First published 1957 by McCowat-Mercer Press.

Cockrell, Thomas D., and Michael B. Ballard, eds. *A Mississippi Rebel in the Army of Northern Virginia: The Civil War Memoirs of Private David Holt.* Baton Rouge: Louisiana State University Press, 1995.

Colby, Newton T. *The Civil War Papers of Lt. Colonel Newton T. Colby, New York Infantry.* Edited by William E. Hughes. Jefferson, NC: McFarland, 2003.

Collier, John S., and Bonnie B. Collier, eds. *Yours for the Union: The Civil War Letters of John W. Chase, First Massachusetts Light Artillery.* New York: Fordham University Press, 2004.

Cumming, Kate. *Kate: The Journal of a Confederate Nurse.* Edited by Richard Barksdale Harwell. Baton Rouge: Louisiana State University Press, 1987. First published 1959.

Cunningham, Sumner A. *Reminiscences of the 41st Tennessee: The Civil War in the West.* Edited by John A. Simpson. Shippensburg, PA: White Mane, 2001.

Currie, Ruth Douglas, ed. *Emma Spaulding Bryant: Civil War Bride, Carpetbagger's Wife, Ardent Feminist, Letters and Diaries, 1860–1900.* New York: Fordham University Press, 2004.

Cutrer, Thomas W., ed. *Longstreet's Aide: The Civil War Letters of Major Thomas J. Goree.* Charlottesville: University Press of Virginia, 1995.

———, ed. *Oh, What a Loansome Time I Had: The Civil War Letters of Major William Morel Moxley, Eighteenth Alabama Infantry, and Emily Beck Moxley.* Tuscaloosa: University of Alabama Press, 2002.

———, ed. *Our Trust Is in the God of Battles: The Civil War Letters of Robert Franklin Bunting, Chaplain, Terry's Texas Rangers, C.S.A.* Knoxville: University of Tennessee Press, 2006.

Cutrer, Thomas W., and T. Michael Parrish, eds. *Brothers in Gray: The Civil War Letters of the Pierson Family.* Baton Rouge: Louisiana State University Press, 1997.

Davis, William C., and Meredith L. Swentor, eds. *Bluegrass Confederate: The Headquarters Diary of Edward O. Guerrant.* Baton Rouge: Louisiana State University Press, 1999.

Dawes, Rufus R. *A Full Blown Yankee of the Iron Brigade: Service with the Sixth Wisconsin Volunteers.* Edited by Alan T. Nolan. Lincoln: University of Nebraska Press, 1999. First published 1937 by E. R. Alderman.

Dee, Christine, ed. *Ohio's Civil War: The Civil War in Documents.* Athens: Ohio University Press, 2006.

Dodd, E. S. *The Diary of Ephraim Shelby Dodd.* Reprinted in *Terry Texas Ranger Trilogy,* ed. Thomas W. Cutrer. Austin, TX: State House Press, 1996.

Domschcke, Bernhard. *Twenty Months in Captivity: Memoirs of a Union Officers in Confederate Prisons.* Edited and translated by Frederic Trautman. Rutherford, NJ: Fairleigh Dickinson University Press, 1987.

Donald, David Herbert, ed. *Gone for a Soldier: The Civil War Memoirs of Private Alfred Bellard.* Boston: Little, Brown, 1975.

Doyle, Julie A., John David Smith, and Richard M. McMurry, eds. *This Wilderness of War: The Civil War Letters of George W. Squier, Hoosier Volunteer.* Knoxville: University of Tennessee Press, 1998.

Drickamer, Lee C., and Karen D. Drickamer, eds. *Fort Lyons to Harper's Ferry: On the Border of North and South with "Rambling Jour," the Civil War Letters and Newspaper Dispatches of Charles H. Moulton (34th Mass. Vol. Inf.).* Shippensburg, PA: White Mane, 1987.

Duncan, Russell, ed. *Blue-Eyed Child of Fortune: The Civil War Letters of Colonel Robert Gould Shaw.* Athens: University of Georgia Press, 1992.

Durham, Roger S., ed. *The Blues in Gray: The Civil War Journal of William Daniel Dixon and the Republican Blues Daybook.* Knoxville: University of Tennessee Press, 2000.

Dyer, J. Franklin. *The Journal of a Civil War Surgeon.* Edited by Michael B. Chesson. Lincoln: University of Nebraska Press, 2003.

Elder, Donald C., III, ed. *Love amid the Turmoil: The Civil War Letters of William and Mary Vermilion.* Iowa City: University of Iowa Press, 2003.

Elliott, Sam Davis, ed. *Doctor Quintard, Chaplain C.S.A. and Second Bishop of Tennessee: The Memoir and Civil War Diary of Charles Todd Quintard.* Baton Rouge: Louisiana State University Press, 2003.

Ellison, Janet Correll, ed., with assistance from Mark W. Weitz. *On to Atlanta: The Civil War Diaries of John Hill Ferguson, Illinois Tenth Regiment of Volunteers.* Lincoln: University of Nebraska Press, 2001.

Engs, Robert F., and Corey M. Brooks, eds. *Their Patriotic Duty: The Civil War Letters of the Evans Family of Brown County, Ohio.* New York: Fordham University Press, 2007.

Everson, Guy R., and Edward H. Simpson Jr. *Far, Far from Home: The Wartime Letters of Dick and Tally Simpson, 3rd South Carolina Volunteers.* New York: Oxford University Press, 1994.

Favill, Josiah Marshall. *The Diary of a Young Officer: Serving with the Armies of the United States during the War of the Rebellion.* Baltimore: Butternut & Blue, 2000.

Fletcher, William A. *Rebel Private: Front and Rear, Memoirs of a Confederate Soldier.* New York: Dutton, 1995. First published 1908 by Press of the Greer Print.

Folmar, John Kent, ed. *From That Terrible Field: Civil War Letters of James M. Williams, Twenty-first Alabama Infantry Volunteers.* Tuscaloosa: University of Alabama Press, 1981.

Franklin, John Hope, ed. *The Diary of James T. Ayers: Civil War Recruiter.* Baton Rouge: Louisiana State University Press, 1999. First published 1947 by Illinois State Historical Society.

Gallagher, Gary W., ed. *Fighting for the Confederacy: The Personal Recollections of General Edward Porter Alexander.* Chapel Hill: University of North Carolina Press, 1989.

Galloway, Tammy Harden, ed. *Dear Old Roswell: The Civil War Letters of the King Family of Roswell, Georgia.* Macon, GA: Mercer University Press, 2003.

Giunta, Mary A., ed. *A Civil War Soldier of Christ and Country: The Selected Correspondence of John Rodgers Meigs, 1859–1864.* Urbana: University of Illinois Press, 2006.

Gooding, James Henry. *On the Altar of Freedom: A Black Soldier's Civil War Letters from the Front,* ed. Virginia M. Adams (Amherst: University of Massachusetts Press, 1991), 54.

Gorman, Kathleen, ed. *Boy Soldier of the Confederacy: The Memoir of Johnnie Wickersham.* Carbondale: Southern Illinois University Press, 2006.

Goss, Warren Lee. *Recollections of a Private: A Story of the Army of the Potomac.* Scituate, MA: Digital Scanning, 2002. First published 1890 by Thomas Y. Crowell.

Gould, David, and James B. Kennedy, eds. *Memoirs of a Dutch Mudeill: The "War Memories" of John Henry Otto, Captain, Company D, 21st Regiment Wisconsin Volunteer Infantry.* Kent, OH: Kent State University Press, 2004.

Goulka, Jeremiah E., ed. *The Grand Old Man of Maine: Selected Letters of Joshua Lawrence Chamberlain, 1865–1914.* Chapel Hill: University of North Carolina Press, 2004.

Goyne, Minetta Altgelt, ed. *Lone Star and Double Eagle: Civil War Letters of a German-Texas Family.* Fort Worth: Texas Christian University Press, 1982.

Grant, Ulysses S. *Personal Memoirs of U. S. Grant and Select Letters, 1839–1865.* Edited by Mary Drake McFeely and William S. McFeely. New York: Library of America, 1990.

Greiner, James M., Janet L. Coryell, and James R. Smither, eds. *A Surgeon's Civil War: The Letters and Diary of Daniel M. Holt, M.D.* Kent, OH: Kent State University Press, 1995.

Griffin, Richard N., ed. *Three Years a Soldier: The Diary and Newspaper Correspondence of Private George Perkins, Sixth New York Independent Battery, 1861–1864.* Knoxville: University of Tennessee Press, 2006.

Grimsley, Mark, and Todd D. Miller, eds. *The Union Must Stand: The Civil War Diary of John Quincy Adams Campbell, Fifth Iowa Volunteer Infantry.* Knoxville: University of Tennessee Press, 2000.

Hallock, Judith Lee, ed. *The Civil War Letters of Joshua K. Callaway.* Athens: University of Georgia Press, 1997.

Harris, Robert F., and John Niflot, comps. *Dear Sister: The Civil War Letters of the Brothers Gould.* Westport, CT: Praeger, 1998.

Harris, William C., ed. *"In the Country of the Enemy": The Civil War Reports of a Massachusetts Corporal.* Gainesville: University Press of Florida, 1999.

Herberger, Charles F., ed. *A Yankee at Arms: The Diary of Lieutenant Augustus D. Ayling, 29th Massachusetts Volunteers.* Knoxville: University of Tennessee Press, 1999.

Herdegen, Lance, and Sherry Murphy, eds. *Four Years with the Iron Brigade: The Civil War Journal of William Ray, Company F, Seventh Wisconsin Volunteers.* Cambridge, MA: Da Capo Press, 2002.

Hess, Earl J., ed. *A German in the Yankee Fatherland: The Civil War Letters of Henry A. Kircher.* Kent, OH: Kent State University Press, 1983.

Holcomb, Julie, ed. *Southern Sons, Northern Soldiers: The Civil War Letters of the Remley Brothers, 22nd Iowa Infantry.* DeKalb: Northern Illinois University Press, 2004.

Holland, Katherine S., ed. *Keep All My Letters: The Civil War Letters of Richard Henry Brooks, 51st Georgia Infantry.* Macon, GA: Mercer University Press, 2003.

Hotchkiss, Jedediah. *Make Me a Map of the Valley: The Civil War Journal of Stonewall Jackson's Topographer.* Edited by Archie P. McDonald. Dallas, TX: Southern Methodist University Press, 1973.

Howard, Oliver Otis. *Autobiography of Oliver Otis Howard, Major General United States Army.* 2 vols. New York: Baker & Taylor, 1906.

Howe, Mark De Wolfe, ed. *Touched with Fire: Civil War Letters and Diary of Oliver Wendell Holmes, Jr., 1861–1864.* New York: Fordham University Press, 2000. First published 1946 by Harvard University Press.

[Hoyt, Noah Webster]. *The Civil War Diaries of Noah Webster Hoyt: 28th Regiment Connecticut Volunteers.* Special ed. Stamford, CT: Stamford Historical Society, 1996.

Hubbs, G. Ward, ed. *Voices from Company D: Diaries by the Greensboro Guards, Fifth Alabama Infantry Regiment, Army of Northern Virginia.* Athens: University of Georgia Press, 2003.

Hughes, Nathaniel Cheairs, Jr.. *The Civil War Memoir of Philip Daingerfield Stephenson, D.D.: Private, Company K, 13th Arkansas Volunteer Infantry, Loader, Piece No. 4, 5th Company, Washington Artillery, Army of the Tennessee, CSA.* Baton Rouge: Louisiana State University Press, 1998. First published 1995 by UCA Press.

———. *I'll Sting If I Can: The Life and Prison Letters of Major N. F. Cheairs, C.S.A.* Signal Mountain, TN: Mountain Press, 1998.

Hughes, William E., ed. *The Civil War Papers of Lt. Colonel Newton T. Colby, New York Infantry.* Jefferson, NC: McFarland, 2003.

Hyde, Thomas W. *Following the Greek Cross, or Memories of the Sixth Army Corps.* Columbia: University of South Carolina Press, 2005.

Jaquette, Henrietta Stratton, ed. *South after Gettysburg: Letters of Cornelia Hancock, 1863–1868.* New York: Thomas Y. Crowell, 1956. First published 1937.

Johansson, M. Jane, ed. *Widows by the Thousand: The Civil War Letters of Theophilus and Harriet Perry, 1862–1864.* Fayetteville: University of Arkansas Press, 2000.

Johnson, Charles Beneulyn, MD. *Muskets and Medicine or Army Life in the Sixties.* Philadelphia: F. A. Davis, 1917.

Johnson, Pharris Deloach, ed. *Under the Southern Cross: Soldier Life with Gordon Bradwell and the Army of Northern Virginia.* Macon, GA: Mercer University Press, 1999.

Johnston, Terry A., Jr., ed. *"Him on the One Side and Me on the Other": The Civil War Letters of Alexander Campbell, 79th New York Infantry Regiment and James Campbell, 1st South Carolina Battalion.* Columbia: University of South Carolina Press, 1999.

Joiner, Gary D., Marilyn S. Joiner, and Clifton D. Cardin, eds. *No Pardons to Ask, nor Apologies to Make: The Journal of William Henry King, Gray's 28th Louisiana Infantry Regiment.* Knoxville: University of Tennessee Press, 2006.

Jones, Samuel C. *Reminiscences of the 22nd Iowa Infantry: Giving Its Organization, Marches, Skirmishes, Battles, and Sieges, as Taken from the Diary of Lieutenant S. C. Jones of Company A.* Iowa City: Press of the Camp Pope Bookshop, 1993. First published 1907 by S. C. Jones.

Joslyn, Mauriel Phillips, ed. *Charlotte's Boys: Civil War Letters of the Branch Family of Savannah.* Berryville, VA: Rockbridge, 1996.

Kallgren, Beverly Hayes, and James L. Crouthamel, eds. *"Dear Friend Anna": The Civil War Letters of a Common Soldier from Maine.* Orono: University of Maine Press, 1992.

Kellogg, Mary E., comp. *Army Life of an Illinois Soldier, Including a Day-by-Day Record of Sherman's March to the Sea: Letters and Diary of Charles W. Wills.* Carbondale: Southern Illinois University Press, 1996. First published 1906 by Globe Printing.

Kiper, Richard L., ed. *Dear Catherine, Dear Taylor: The Civil War Letters of a Union Soldier and His Wife.* Lawrence: University Press of Kansas, 2002.

Kirwin, A. D., ed. *Johnny Green of the Orphan Brigade: The Journal of a Confederate Soldier.* Lexington: University of Kentucky Press, 2002. First published 1956.

Kohl, Lawrence Frederick, ed., with Margaret Cossé Richard. *Irish Green and Union Blue: The Civil War Letters of Peter Welsh, Color Sergeant, 28th Regiment Massachusetts Volunteers.* New York: Fordham University Press, 1986.

Koonce, Donald B., ed. *Doctor to the Front: The Recollections of Confederate Surgeon Thomas Fanning Wood, 1861–1865.* Knoxville: University of Tennessee Press, 2000.

Larimer, Charles F., ed. *Love and Valor: The Intimate Civil War Letters between Captain Jacob and Emeline Ritner.* Western Springs, IL: Sigourney Press, 2000.

Lassen, Coralou Peel, ed. *Dear Sarah: Letters Home from a Soldier of the Iron Brigade.* Bloomington: Indiana University Press, 1999.

Looby, Christopher, ed. *The Complete Civil War Journal and Selected Letters of Thomas Wentworth Higginson.* Chicago: University of Chicago Press, 2000.

Lowe, David W., ed. *Meade's Army: The Private Notebooks of Lt. Col. Theodore Lyman.* Kent, OH: Kent State University Press, 2007.

Lowe, Jeffrey C., and Sam Hodges, eds. *Letters to Amanda: The Civil War Letters of Marion Hill Fitzpatrick, Army of Northern Virginia.* Macon, GA: Mercer University Press, 1998.

Lowe, Richard, ed. *A Texas Cavalry Officer's Civil War: The Diary and Letters of James C. Bates.* Baton Rouge: Louisiana State University Press, 1999.

Lowry, Thomas P., ed. *Swamp Doctor: The Diary of a Union Surgeon in the Virginia and North Carolina Marshes.* Mechanicsburg, PA: Stackpole Books, 2001.

Lu Doc, William G., ed. *This Business of War: Recollections of a Civil War Quartermaster.* St. Paul: Minnesota Historical Society Press, 2004. First published 1963 by North Central.

Malles, Ed, ed. *Bridge Building in Wartime: Colonel Wesley Brainerd's Memoir of the 50th New York Volunteer Engineers.* Knoxville: University of Tennessee Press, 1997.

Mannis, Jedediah, and Galen R. Wilson, eds. *Bound to Be a Soldier: The Letters of Private James T. Miller, 111th Pennsylvania Infantry, 1861–1864.* Knoxville: University of Tennessee Press, 2001.

Marcus, Edward, ed. *A New Canaan Private in the Civil War: Letters of Justus M. Silliman, 17th Connecticut Volunteers.* New Canaan, CT: New Canaan Historical Society, 1984.

Marshall, Jeffrey D., ed. *A War of the People: Vermont Civil War Letters.* Hanover, NH: University Press of New England, 1999.

McArthur, Judith N., and Orville Vernon Burton, eds. *A Gentleman and an Officer: A Military and Social History of James B. Griffin's Civil War.* New York: Oxford University Press, 1996.

McCarthy, Carlton. *Detailed Minutiae of Soldier Life in the Army of Northern Virginia, 1861–1865.* Lincoln: University of Nebraska Press, 1993. First published 1882 by Carlton McCarthy.

McMurray, Richard M., ed. *An Uncompromising Secessionist: The Civil War of George Knox Miller, Eight (Wade's) Confederate Cavalry.* Tuscaloosa: University of Alabama Press, 2007.

Messent, Peter, and Steve Courtney, eds. *The Civil War Letters of Joseph Hopkins Twichell.* Athens: University of Georgia Press, 2006.

Montgomery, George, Jr., ed. *Georgia Sharpshooter: The Civil War Diary and Letters of William Rhadamanthus Montgomery, 1839–1906.* Macon, GA: Mercer University Press, 1997.

Mosely, Ronald, ed. *The Stillwell Letters: A Georgian in Longstreet's Corps, Army of Northern Virginia.* Macon, GA: Mercer University Press, 2002.

Mulligan, William H., Jr., ed. *A Badger Boy in Blue: The Civil War Letters of Chauncey H. Cooke.* Detroit, MI: Wayne State University Press, 2007.

Murr, Erika L., ed. *A Rebel Wife in Texas: The Diary and Letters of Elizabeth Scott Neblett, 1852–1864.* Baton Rouge: Louisiana State University Press, 2001.

Mushkat, Jerome, ed. *A Citizen-Soldier's Civil War: The Letters of Brevet Major General Alvin C. Voris.* DeKalb: Northern Illinois University Press, 2002.

Myers, Robert Manson, ed. *The Children of Pride: A True Story of Georgia and the Civil War.* New Haven, CT: Yale University Press, 1972.

Nanzig, Thomas P., ed. *The Badax Tigers: From Shiloh to the Surrender with the 18th Wisconsin Volunteers.* Lanham, MD: Rowman & Littlefield, 2002.

Nevins, Allan, ed. *A Diary of Battle: The Personal Journals of Colonel Charles S. Wainwright, 1861–1865.* New York: Da Capo Press, 1998. First published 1962 by Harcourt.

Noe, Kenneth W., ed. *A Southern Boy in Blue: The Memoir of Marcus Woodcock, 9th Kentucky Infantry (U.S.A.).* Knoxville: University of Tennessee Press, 1996.

Northen, Charles Swift, III, ed. *All Right Let Them Come: The Civil War Diary of an East Tennessee Confederate.* Knoxville: University of Tennessee Press, 2003.

Olsen, Bernard A., ed. *Upon the Tented Field: An Historical Account of the Civil War as Told by the Men Who Fought and Gave Their Lives.* Red Bank, NJ: Historic Projects, 1993.

Palladino, Anita, ed. *Diary of a Yankee Engineer: The Civil War Story of John H. Westervelt, Engineer, 1st New York Volunteer Engineer Corps.* New York: Fordham University Press, 1997.

Pate, James P., ed. *When This Evil War Is Over: The Civil War Correspondence of the Francis Family.* Tuscaloosa: University of Alabama Press, 2006.

Patrick, Jeffrey L., and Robert J. Willey, eds. *Fighting for Liberty and Right: The Civil War Diary of William Bluffton Miller, First Sergeant, Company K, Seventy-fifth Indiana Volunteer Infantry.* Knoxville: University of Tennessee Press, 2005.

Pitcock, Cynthia DeHaven, and Bill J. Gurley, eds. *I Acted from Principle: The Civil War Diary of Dr. William M. McPheeters, Confederate Surgeon in the Trans-Mississippi.* Fayetteville: University of Arkansas Press, 2002.

Popchock, Barry, ed. *Soldier Boy: The Civil War Letters of Charles O. Musser, 29th Iowa.* Iowa City: University of Iowa Press, 1995.

Porter, Horace. *Campaigning with Grant.* New York: Da Capo Press, 1986. First published 1897 by Century.

Quaife, Milo M., ed. *From the Cannon's Mouth: The Civil War Letters of General Alpheus S. Williams.* Lincoln: University of Nebraska Press, 1995. First published 1959 by Wayne State University Press / Detroit Historical Society.

Rabb, Steven S., ed. *With the 3rd Wisconsin Badgers: The Living Experience of the Civil War through the Journals of Van R. Willard.* Mechanicsburg, PA: Stackpole Books, 1999.

Racine, Philip N., ed. *"Unspoiled Heart": The Journal of Charles Mattocks of the 17th Maine.* Knoxville: University of Tennessee Press, 1994.

Radigan, Emily N., ed. *"Desolating This Fair Country": The Civil War Diary and Letters of Lt. Henry C. Lyon, 34th New York.* Jefferson, NC: McFarland, 1999.

Rankin, David C., ed. *Diary of a Christian Soldier: Rufus Kinsley and the Civil War.* Cambridge: Cambridge University Press, 2004.

Redkey, Edwin S., ed. *A Grand Army of Black Men: Letters from African-American Soldiers in the Union Army, 1861–1865.* Cambridge: Cambridge University Press, 1992.

Reid-Green, Marcia, ed. *Letters Home: Henry Matrau of the Iron Brigade.* Lincoln: University of Nebraska Press, 1993.

Reinhart, Joseph R., trans. and ed. *Two Germans in the Civil War: The Diary of John Daeuble and the Letters of Gottfried Rentschler, 6th Kentucky Volunteer Infantry.* Knoxville: University of Tennessee Press, 2004.

Reyburn, Philip J., and Terry L. Wilson, eds. *"Jottings from Dixie": The Civil War Dispatches of Sergeant Major Stephen F. Fleharty, U.S.A.* Baton Rouge: Louisiana State University Press, 1999.

Rhodes, Robert Hunt, ed. *All for the Union: The Civil War Diary and Letters of Elisha Hunt Rhodes.* New York: Vintage Books, 1992.

Robertson, James I., Jr., ed. *Soldier of Southwestern Virginia: The Civil War Letters of Captain John Preston Sheffey.* Baton Rouge: Louisiana State University Press, 2004.

Roe, David D., ed. *A Civil War Soldier's Diary: Valentine C. Randolph, 39th Illinois Regiment.* With commentary and annotations by Stephen R. Wise. DeKalb: Northern Illinois University Press, 2006.

Roper, John Herbert, ed. *Repairing the "March of Mars": The Civil War Diaries of John Samuel Apperson, Hospital Steward in the Stonewall Brigade, 1861–1865.* Macon, GA: Mercer University Press, 2001.

Rosenblatt, Emil, and Ruth Rosenblatt, eds. *Hard Marching Every Day: The Civil War Letters of Private Wilbur Fisk, 1861–1865.* Lawrence: University Press of Kansas, 1992. First published 1983 by Rosenblatt.

Rozier, John, ed. *The Granite Farm Letters: The Civil War Correspondence of Edgeworth and Sallie Bird.* Athens: University of Georgia Press, 1988.

Samito, Christian G., ed. *Commanding Boston's Irish Ninth: The Civil War Letters of Colonel Patrick R. Guiney, Ninth Massachusetts Volunteer Infantry.* New York: Fordham University Press, 1998.

———, ed. *"Fear Was Not in Him": The Civil War Letters of Major General Francis C. Barlow, U.S.A.* New York: Fordham University Press, 2004.

Sauers, Richard, ed. *The Bloody 85th: The Letters of Milton McJunkin, a Western Pennsylvania Soldier in the Civil War.* Daleville, VA: Schroeder, 2000.

Sawyer, Merrill C. (Tom), Betty Sawyer, and Timothy C. Sawyer, eds. *Letters from a Civil War Surgeon: The Letters of Dr. William Child of the Fifth New Hampshire Volunteers.* Solon, ME: Polar Bear, 1995.

Schurz, Carl. *Report on the Condition of the South.* New York: Arno Press / New York Times, 1969.

Scott, Robert Garth, ed. *Fallen Leaves: The Civil War Letters of Major Henry Livermore Abbott.* Kent, OH: Kent State University Press, 1991.

Sears, Stephen W., ed. *Mr. Dunn Browne's Experiences in the Army: The Civil War Letters of Samuel W. Fiske.* New York: Fordham University Press, 1998.

———. *On Campaign with the Army of the Potomac: The Civil War Journal of Theodore Ayrault Dodge.* New York: Cooper Square Press, 2001.

Sherman, William T. *The Memoirs of William T. Sherman.* 2 vols. New York: Da Capo Press, 1984. First published 1875 by Appleton.

Simpson, Brooks D., and Jean V. Berlin, eds. *Sherman's Civil War: Selected Correspondence of William T. Sherman, 1860–1865.* Chapel Hill: University of North Carolina Press, 1999.

Skinner, Arthur N., and James L. Skinner, ed. *The Death of a Confederate: Selections form the Letters of the Archibald Smith Family of Roswell, Georgia, 1864–1956.* Athens: University of Georgia Press, 1996.

Skoch, George, and Mark W. Perkins, eds. *Lone Star Confederate: A Gallant and Good Soldier of the Fifth Texas Infantry.* College Station: Texas A&M University Press, 2003.

Small, Harold Adams, ed. *The Road to Richmond: The Civil War Memoirs of Major Abner R. Small of the Sixteenth Maine Volunteers: Together with the Diary That He Kept When He Was a Prisoner of War.* New York: Fordham University Press, 2000. First published 1956 by University of California Press.

Smith, Barbara Bentley, and Nina Bentley Baker, eds. *"Burning Rails as We Pleased": The Civil War Letters of William Garrigues Bentley, 104th Ohio Volunteer Infantry.* Jefferson, NC: McFarland, 2004.

Smith, John David, and William Cooper Jr., eds. *A Union Woman in Civil War Kentucky: The Diary of Frances Peter.* Lexington: University Press of Kentucky, 2000.

Sneden, Robert Knox. *Eye of the Storm: A Civil War Odyssey.* Edited by Charles F. Bryan and Nelson D. Lankford. New York: Free Press, 2000.

Stevens, Michael E., ed. *As If It Were Glory: Robert Beecham's Civil War from the Iron Brigade to the Black Regiments.* Madison, WI: Madison House, 1998.

Stone, DeWitt Boyd, Jr., ed. *Wandering to Glory: Confederate Veterans Remember Evans' Brigade.* Columbia: University of South Carolina Press, 2002.

Sutherland, Daniel E., ed. *Reminiscences of a Private: William E. Bevens of the First Arkansas Infantry, C.S.A.* Fayetteville: University of Arkansas Press, 1992.

Swedberg, Claire, E., ed. *Three Years with the 92d Illinois: The Civil War Diary of John M. King.* Mechanicsburg, PA: Stackpole Books, 1999.

Taylor, F. Jay, ed. *Reluctant Rebel: The Secret Diary of Robert Patrick, 1861–1865.* Baton Rouge: Louisiana State University Press, 1959.

Throne, Mildred, ed. *The Civil War Diary of Cyrus F. Boyd, Fifteenth Iowa Infantry, 1861–1863.* Millwood, NY: Kraus, 1977. First published 1953 by State Historical Society of Iowa.

Tower, R. Lockwood, ed. *Lee's Adjutant: The Wartime Letters of Colonel Walter Herron Taylor, 1862–1865.* Columbia: University of South Carolina Press, 1995.

Towne, Stephen E., ed. *A Fierce, Wild Joy: The Civil War Letters of Colonel J. Wood, 48th Indiana Volunteer Infantry Regiment.* Knoxville: University of Tennessee Press, 2007.

Trudeau, Noah Andre, ed. *Voices of the 55th: Letters from the 55th Massachusetts Volunteers.* Dayton, OH: Morningside House, 1996.

Tunnell, Ted, ed. *Carpetbagger from Vermont: The Autobiography of Marshall Harvey Twitchell.* Baton Rouge: Louisiana State University Press, 1989.

Turner, Nat, ed. *A Southern Soldier's Letters Home: The Civil War Letters of Samuel Burney, Army of Northern Virginia.* Macon, GA: Mercer University Press, 2002.

Tuttle, Russell M. *The Civil War Journal of Lt. Russell M. Tuttle, New York Volunteer Infantry Tappan.* Edited by George H. Tappan. Jefferson, NC: McFarland, 2006.

Ward, Eric, ed. *Army Life in Virginia: The Civil War Letters of George C. Benedict.* Mechanicsburg, PA: Stackpole Books, 2002.

Watkins, Sam. *"Company Aytch," or a Side Show of the Big Show and Other Sketches.* Edited by M. Thomas Inge. New York: Penguin Putnam, 1999. First published 1882 by Cumberland Presbyterian.

Weaver, C. P., ed. *Thank God My Regiment African an African One: The Civil War Diary of Colonel Nathan W. Daniels.* Baton Rouge: Louisiana State University Press, 1998.

Wilkeson, Frank. *Turned Inside Out: Recollections of a Private Soldier in the Army of the Potomac.* Lincoln: University of Nebraska Press, 1997. First published 1887 by G. P. Putnam's Sons.

Williams, Edward B., ed. *Rebel Brothers: The Civil War Letters of the Truehearts.* College Station: Texas A&M University Press, 1995.

Wilson, Keith, ed. *Honor in Command: Lt. Freeman S. Bowley's Civil War Service in the 30th United States Colored Infantry.* Gainesville: University Press of Florida, 2006.

Winschel, Terrence, ed. *The Civil War Diary of a Common Soldier: William Wiley of the 77th Illinois Infantry.* Baton Rouge: Louisiana State University Press, 2001.

Wittenberg, Eric J., ed. *"We Have It Damn Hard Out Here": The Civil War Letters of Sergeant Thomas W. Smith, 6th Pennsylvania Cavalry.* Kent, OH: Kent State University Press, 1999.

Woodworth, Steven E., ed. *The Musick of the Mocking Birds, the Roar of the Cannon: The Civil War Diary and Letters of William Winters.* Lincoln: University of Nebraska Press, 1998.

Woolsey, Jane Stuart. *Hospital Days: Reminiscence of a Civil War Nurse.* Roseville, MN: Edinborough Press, 2001. First published 1996.

Wynne, Lewis N., and Robert A. Taylor, eds. *This War So Horrible: The Civil War Diary of Hiram Smith Williams.* Tuscaloosa: University of Alabama Press, 1993.

SECONDARY SOURCES

Soldier and Veteran Life

Bailey, Fred Arthur. *Class and Tennessee's Confederate Generation.* Chapel Hill: University of North Carolina Press, 1987.

Bartholomees, James B. *Buff Facings and Gilt Buttons: Staff and Headquarters Operations in the Army of Northern Virginia, 1861–1865.* Columbia: University of South Carolina Press, 1998.

Bobrick, Benson. *Testament: A Soldier's Story of the Civil War.* New York: Simon & Schuster, 2003.

Bollett, Alfred Jay. *Civil War Medicine: Challenges and Triumphs.* Tucson, AZ: Galen Press, 2002.

Burton, William I. *Melting Pot Soldiers: The Union's Ethnic Regiments.* New York: Fordham University Press, 1998.

Bruce, Susannah Ural. *The Harp and the Eagle: Irish-American Volunteers and the Union Army, 1861–1865.* New York: New York University Press, 2006.

Carmichael, Peter S. *The Last Generation: Young Virginians in Peace, War, and Reunion.* Chapel Hill: University of North Carolina Press, 2005.

Cimbala, Paul A. "Lining Up to Serve: Wounded and Sick Union Officers Join Veteran Reserve Corps during Civil War, Reconstruction." *Prologue* 35 (Spring 2003): 38–49.

———. "Soldiering on the Home Front: The Veteran Reserve Corps and the Northern People." In *Union Soldiers and the Northern Home Front: Wartime Experiences, Postwar Adjustments,* eds. Paul A. Cimbala and Randall M. Miller, 182–218. New York: Fordham University Press, 2002.

———. "Union Corps of Honor." *Columbiad* 3 (Winter 2000): 59–91.

Cimbala, Paul A., and Randall M. Miller, eds. *Union Soldiers and the Northern Home Front: Wartime Experiences, Postwar Adjustments.* New York: Fordham University Press, 2002.

Cornish, Dudley T. *The Sable Arm: Negro Troops in the Union Army, 1861–1865.* New York: W. W. Norton, 1956.

Cunliffe, Marcus. *Soldiers and Civilians: The Martial Spirit in America, 1775–1865.* Boston: Little, Brown, 1968.

Cunningham, H. H. *Doctors in Gray: The Confederate Medical Service.* 2nd ed. Baton Rouge: Louisiana State University Press, 1960.

Daniel, Larry J. *Soldiering in the Army of the Tennessee: A Portrait of Life in a Confederate Army.* Chapel Hill: University of North Carolina Press, 1991.

Davis, William C. *Lincoln's Men: How President Lincoln Became Father to an Army and a Nation.* New York: Free Press, 1999.

Dean, Eric T., Jr. *Shook Over Hell: Post-traumatic Stress, Vietnam, and the Civil War.* Cambridge, MA: Harvard University Press, 1997.

Dearing, Mary R. *Veterans in Politics: The Story of the GAR.* Baton Rouge: Louisiana State University Press, 1952.

Flannery, Michael A. *Civil War Pharmacy: A History of Drugs, Drug Supply and Provision, and Therapeutics for the Union and Confederacy.* Binghamton, NY: Pharmaceutical Products Press, 2004.

Frank, Joseph Allen. *With Ballot and Bayonet: The Political Socialization of American Civil War Soldiers.* Athens: University of Georgia Press, 1998.

Frank, Joseph Allen, and George Reeves. *"Seeing the Elephant": Raw Recruits at the Battle of Shiloh.* Westport, CT: Greenwood Press, 1989.

Freemon, Frank. R. *Gangrene and Glory: Medical Care during the Civil War.* Urbana: University of Illinois Press, 2001. First published 1998 by Fairleigh Dickinson University Press.

Glatthaar, Joseph T. *Forged in Battle: The Civil War Alliance of Black Soldiers and White Officers.* New York: Macmillan, 1990.

———. *The March to the Sea and Beyond: Sherman's Troops in the Savannah and Carolinas Campaigns.* New York: New York University Press, 1986.

Green, Carol Cranmer. *Chimborazo: The Confederacy's Largest Hospital.* Knoxville: University of Tennessee Press, 2004.

Harris, M. Keith. "Slavery, Emancipation, and Veterans of the Union Cause: Commemorating Freedom in the Era of Reconciliation, 1885–1915." *Civil War History* 53 (September 2007): 264–90.

Hess, Earl J. *The Union Soldier in Battle: Enduring the Ordeal of Combat.* Lawrence: University Press of Kansas, 1997.

Holberton, William B. *Homeward Bound: The Demobilization of the Union and Confederate Armies, 1865–1866.* Mechanicsburg, PA: Stackpole Books, 2001.

Horigan, Michael. *Elmira: Death Camp of the North.* Mechanicsburg, PA: Stackpole Books, 2002.

Hubbs, G. Ward. *Guarding Greensboro: A Confederate Company in the Making of a Southern Community.* Athens: University of Georgia Press, 2003.

Keller, Christian B. *Chancellorsville and the Germans: Nativism, Ethnicity, and Civil War Memory.* New York: Fordham University Press, 2007.

———. "Keystone Confederates: Pennsylvanians Who Fought for Dixie." In *Making and Remaking Pennsylvania's Civil War,* eds. William Blair and William Pencak, 1–22. University Park: Pennsylvania State University Press, 2001.

Kundahl, George G. *Confederate Engineer: Training and Campaigning with John Morris Wampler.* Knoxville: University of Tennessee Press, 2000.

Linderman, Gerald F. *Embattled Courage: The Experience of Combat in the American Civil War.* New York: Free Press 1987.

Manning, Chandra. *What This Cruel War Was Over: Soldiers, Slavery, and the Civil War.* New York: Alfred A. Knopf, 2007.

Marvel, William. *Andersonville: The Last Depot.* Chapel Hill: University of North Carolina Press, 1994.

McAdams, Benton. *Rebels at Rock Island: The Story of a Civil War Prison.* DeKalb: Northern Illinois University Press, 2000.

McConnell, Stuart. *Glorious Contentment: The Grand Army of the Republic, 1865–1900.* Chapel Hill: University of North Carolina Press, 1992.

McElfresh, Earl B. *Maps and Mapmakers of the Civil War.* New York: Harry N. Abrams, 1999.

McPherson, James M. *For Cause and Comrades: Why Men Fought in the Civil War.* New York: Oxford University Press, 1997.

Miller, Edward A., Jr. *The Black Civil War Soldiers of Illinois.* Columbia: University of South Carolina Press, 1998.

Phillips, Jason. *Diehard Rebels: The Confederate Culture of Invincibility.* Athens: University of Georgia Press, 2007.

Powers, J. Tracy. *Lee's Miserables: Life in the Army of Northern Virginia from the Wilderness to Appomattox.* Chapel Hill: University of North Carolina Press, 1998.

Raus, Edmund J., Jr. *Banners South: A Northern Community at War.* Kent, OH: Kent State University Press, 2005.

Robertson, James I. *Soldiers Blue and Gray.* New York: Warner Books, 1991.

Rosenburg, R. B. *Living Monuments: Confederate Soldiers' Homes in the New South.* Chapel Hill: University of South Carolina Press, 1993.

Sanders, Charles W., Jr. *While in the Hands of the Enemy: Military Prisons of the Civil War.* Baton Rouge: Louisiana State University Press, 2005.

Schroeder-Lein, Glenna R. *Confederate Hospitals on the Move: Samuel H. Stout and the Army of Tennessee.* Columbia: University of South Carolina Press, 1994.

Shaffer, Donald R. *After the Glory: The Struggles of Black Civil War Veterans.* Lawrence: University Press of Kansas, 2004.

Shattuck, Gardiner H., Jr. *A Shield and Hiding Place: The Religious Life of the Civil War Armies.* Macon, GA: Mercer University Press, 1987.

Skocpol, Theda. *Protecting Soldiers and Mothers: The Political Origins of Social Policy in the United States.* Cambridge, MA: Belknap Press of Harvard University Press, 1992.

Sutherland, Daniel E. *The Confederate Carpetbaggers.* Baton Rouge: Louisiana State University Press, 1988.

Taylor, Lenette S. *"The Supply for Tomorrow Must Not Fail": The Civil War of Captain Simon Perkins Jr., a Union Quartermaster.* Kent, OH: Kent State University Press, 2004.

Trudeau, Noah Andre. *Like Men of War: Black Troops in the Civil War, 1862–1865.* Boston: Little, Brown, 1998.

Wegner, Ansley Herring. *Phantom Pain: North Carolina's Artificial-Limbs Program for Confederate Veterans.* Raleigh: Office of Archives and History, North Carolina Department of Cultural Resources, 2004.

Weitz, Mark A. *More Damning Than Slaughter: Desertion in the Confederate Army.* Lincoln: University of Nebraska Press, 2005.

White, William W. *The Confederate Veteran.* Tuscaloosa, AL: Confederate, 1962.

Wiley, Bell I. *The Life of Billy Yank: The Common Soldier of the Union.* Garden City, NY: Doubleday, 1971. First published 1952 by Bobbs-Merrill.

———. *The Life of Johnny Reb: The Common Soldier of the Confederacy.* Garden City, NY: Doubleday, 1971. First published 1943 by Bobbs-Merrill.

Wilson, Keith P. *Campfires of Freedom: The Camp Life of Black Soldiers during the Civil War.* Kent, OH: Kent State University Press, 2002.

Woodworth, Steven E. *While God Is Marching On: The Religious World of Civil War Soldiers.* Lawrence: University Press of Kansas, 2001.

Company, Regimental, Division, Brigade, Branch, and Army Histories

Bailey, Anne J. *Between the Enemy and Texas: Parsons's Texas Cavalry in the Civil War.* Fort Worth: Texas Christian University Press, 1989.

Beatie, Russel H. *The Army of the Potomac.* Vol. 1, *Birth of Command, November 1860–September 1861.* New York: Da Capo Press, 2002.

———. *The Army of the Potomac.* Vol. 2, *McClellan Takes Command, September 1861–February 1862.* New York: Da Capo Press, 2004.

———. *The Army of the Potomac.* Vol. 3, *McClellan's First Command, March–May 1862.* New York: Savas Beatie, 2007.

Bergemann, Kurt D. *Brackett's Battalion: Minnesota Cavalry in the Civil War and Dakota War.* St. Paul: Minnesota Historical Society Press, 2004.

Blackwell, Samuel M., Jr. *In the First Line of Battle: The 12th Illinois Cavalry in the Civil War.* DeKalb: Northern Illinois University Press, 2002.

Brown, Thaddeus C. S., Samuel J. Murphy, and William G. Putney. *Behind the Guns: The History of Battery I, 2nd Regiment, Illinois Light Artillery.* Edited by Clyde C. Walton. Carbondale: Southern Illinois University Press, 1965.

Daniel, Larry J. *Cannoneers in Gray: The Field Artillery of the Army of Tennessee.* Rev. ed. Tuscaloosa: University of Alabama Press, 2005.

———. *Days of Glory: The Army of the Cumberland, 1861 1865.* Baton Rouge: Louisiana State University Press, 2004.

Emilio, Luis F. *A Brave Black Regiment: The History of the 54th Massachusetts, 1863–1865.* 2nd enlarged ed. New York: Da Capo Press, 1995. First published 1894 by unknown publisher, Boston.

Fowler, John D. *Mountaineers in Gray: The Nineteenth Tennessee Volunteer Infantry Regiment, C.S.A.* Knoxville: University of Tennessee Press, 2004.

Giles, L. B. *Terry's Texas Rangers.* Reprinted in *Terry Texas Ranger Trilogy,* ed. Thomas W. Cutrer. Austin, TX: State House Press, 1996.

Gottfried, Bradley M. *Kearny's Own: The History of the First New Jersey Brigade in the Civil War.* New Brunswick, NJ: Rutgers University Press, 2005.

Hagerty, Edward J. *Collis' Zouaves: The 114th Pennsylvania Volunteers in the Civil War.* Baton Rouge: Louisiana State University Press, 1997.

Hess, Earl J. *Lee's Tar Heels: The Pettigrew-Kirkland-MacRae Brigade.* Chapel Hill: University of North Carolina Press, 2002.

Hoffman, Mark. *"My Brave Mechanics": The First Michigan Engineers and Their Civil War.* Detroit, MI: Wayne State University Press, 2007.

Hughes, Nathaniel Cheairs, Jr. *The Pride of the Confederate Artillery: The Washington Artillery in the Army of Tennessee.* Baton Rouge: Louisiana State University Press, 1997.

Jackson, Harry L. *First Regiment Engineer Troops P.A.C.S.: Robert E. Lee's Combat Engineers.* Louisa, VA: R.A.E. Design and Publishing, 1998.

Jenkins, Kirk C. *The Battle Rages Higher: The Union's Fifteenth Kentucky Infantry.* Lexington: University Press of Kentucky, 2003.

Jones, Terry L. *Lee's Tigers: The Louisiana Infantry in the Army of Northern Virginia.* Baton Rouge: Louisiana University Press, 1987.

Krick, Robert K. *Parker's Virginia Battery C.S.A.* 2nd rev. ed. Wilmington, NC: Broadfoot, 1989. First edition published 1975 by Virginia Book Company.

Laboda, Lawrence R. *From Selma to Appomattox: The History of the Jeff Davis Artillery.* New York: Oxford University Press, 1994.

Lowe, Richard. *Walker's Texas Division C.S.A.: Greyhounds of the Trans-Mississippi.* Baton Rouge: Louisiana State University Press, 2004.

McGowen, Stanley S. *Horse Sweat and Powder Smoke: The First Texas Cavalry in the Civil War.* College Station: Texas A&M University Press, 1999.

McMurray, Richard M. *Two Great Rebel Armies: An Essay in Confederate Military History.* Chapel Hill: University of North Carolina Press, 1989.

Miller, Edward A., Jr. *The Black Civil War Soldiers of Illinois: The Story of the Twenty-ninth U.S. Colored Infantry.* Columbia: University of South Carolina Press, 1998.

Moe, Richard. *The Last Full Measure: The Life and Death of the First Minnesota Volunteers.* New York: Avon Books, 1994.

Nolan, Alan T. *The Iron Brigade: A Military History.* Bloomington: Indiana University Press, 1994. First published 1961.

Owen, William Miller. *In Camp and Battle with the Washington Artillery of New Orleans.* Baton Rouge: Louisiana State University Press, 1999. First published 1885 by Ticknor.

Poole, John Randolph. *Cracker Cavaliers: The 2nd Georgia Cavalry under Wheeler and Forrest.* Macon, GA: Mercer University Press, 2000.

Pope, Thomas E. *The Weary Boys: Colonel J. Warren Keifer and the 110th Ohio Volunteer Infantry.* Kent, OH: Kent State University Press, 2002.

Prokopowicz, Gerald J. *All for the Regiment: The Army of the Ohio, 1861–1862.* Chapel Hill: University of North Carolina Press, 2001.

Reid, Thomas. *Spartan Band: Burnett's 13th Texas Cavalry in the Civil War.* Denton: University of North Texas Press, 2005.

Robertson, James I., Jr. *The Stonewall Brigade.* Baton Rouge: Louisiana State University Press, 1978.

Rowell, John W. *Yankee Artillerymen: Through the Civil War with Eli Lilly's Indiana Battery.* Knoxville: University of Tennessee Press, 1975.

———. *Yankee Cavalrymen: Through the Civil War with the Ninth Pennsylvania Cavalry.* Knoxville: University of Tennessee Press, 1971.

Starr, Stephen Z. *The Union Cavalry in the Civil War.* 3 vols. Baton Rouge: Louisiana State University Press, 1979–1985.

Stocker, Jeffrey D., ed. *From Hunstville to Appomattox: R. T. Coles's History of the 4th Regiment, Alabama Volunteer Infantry, C.S.A., Army of Northern Virginia.* Knoxville: University of Tennessee Press, 1996.

Walker, Scott. *Hell's Broke Loose in Georgia: Survival in a Civil War Regiment.* Athens: University of Georgia Press, 2005. Concerns the 57th Georgia Infantry.

Washington, Versalle F. *Eagles on Their Buttons: A Black Regiment in the Civil War.* Columbia: University of Missouri Press, 1999. Concerns the Fifth U.S. Colored Troops.

Wert, Jeffrey D. *Sword of Lincoln: The Army of the Potomac.* New York: Simon & Schuster, 2005.

Wilkenson, Warren. *Mother, May You Never See the Sights I Have Seen: The Fifty-seventh Massachusetts Veteran Volunteers in the Army of the Potomac, 1864–1865.* New York: Harper & Row, 1990.

Wilkenson, Warren, and Steven E. Woodworth. *A Scythe of Fire: Through the Civil War with One of Lee's Most Legendary Regiments.* New York: Perennial, 2003.

Woodworth, Steven E. *Nothing but Victory: The Army of the Tennessee, 1861–1865.* New York: Alfred A. Knopf, 2005.

Battle and Campaign Histories

Bailey, Anne J. *The Chessboard of War: Sherman and Hood in the Autumn Campaign of 1864.* Lincoln: University of Nebraska Press, 2000.

Brown, Kent Masterson. *Retreat from Gettysburg: Lee, Logistics, and the Pennsylvania Campaign.* Chapel Hill: University of North Carolina Press, 2005.

Cooling, Benjamin Franklin. *Forts Henry and Donelson: The Key to the Confederate Heartland.* Knoxville: University of Tennessee Press, 1987.

Cozzens, Peter. *The Darkest Days of the War: The Battles of Iuka and Corinth.* Chapel Hill: University of North Carolina Press, 1997.

———. *The Shipwreck of Their Hopes: The Battles for Chattanooga.* Urbana: University of Illinois Press, 1994.

———. *This Terrible Sound: The Battle of Chickamauga.* Urbana: University of Illinois Press, 1992.

Daniel, Larry J. *Shiloh: The Battle That Changed the Civil War.* New York: Simon & Schuster, 1997.

Davis, William C. *Battle at Bull Run: A History of the First Major Campaign of the Civil War.* Baton Rouge: Louisiana State University Press, 1981. First published 1977 by Doubleday.

Gallager, Gary W., ed. *The Antietam Campaign.* Chapel Hill: University of North Carolina Press, 1999.

———, ed. *Chancellorsville: The Battle and Its Aftermath.* Chapel Hill: University of North Carolina Press, 1996.

———, ed. *The Fredericksburg Campaign: Decision on the Rappahannock.* Chapel Hill: University of North Carolina Press, 1995.

———, ed. *The Richmond Campaign of 1862: The Peninsula and the Seven Days.* Chapel Hill: University of North Carolina Press, 2000.

———, ed. *The Shenandoah Valley Campaign of 1862.* Chapel Hill: University of North Carolina Press, 2003.

————, ed. *The Shenandoah Valley Campaign of 1864*. Chapel Hill: University of North Carolina Press, 2006.

————, ed. *The Spotsylvania Campaign*. Chapel Hill: University of North Carolina Press, 1998.

————, ed. *The Third Day at Gettysburg and Beyond*. Chapel Hill: University of North Carolina Press, 1994.

————, ed. *The Wilderness Campaign*. Chapel Hill: University of North Carolina Press, 1997.

Hess, Earl J. *Banners to the Breeze: The Kentucky Campaign, Corinth, and Stones River*. Lincoln: University of Nebraska Press, 2000.

————. *Field Armies and Fortifications in the Civil War: The Eastern Campaigns, 1861–1864*. Chapel Hill: University of North Carolina Press, 2005.

————. *Trench Warfare under Grant and Lee: Field Fortifications in the Overland Campaign*. Chapel Hill: University of North Carolina Press, 2007.

Hughes, Nathaniel Cheairs. *Bentonville: The Final Battle of Sherman and Johnston*. Chapel Hill: University of North Carolina Press, 1996.

Jones, James Pickett. *Yankee Blitzkreig: Wilson's Raid through Alabama and Georgia*. Lexington: University of Kentucky Press, 1976.

Marvel, William. *Lee's Last Retreat: The Flight to Appomattox*. Chapel Hill: University of North Carolina Press, 2002.

McDonough, James Lee. *Stones River—Bloody Winter in Tennessee*. Knoxville: University of Tennessee Press, 1980.

Piston, William Garrett, and Richard W. Hatcher III. *Wilson's Creek: The Second Battle of the Civil War and the Men Who Fought It*. Chapel Hill: University of North Carolina Press, 2000.

Rable, George C. *Fredericksburg! Fredericksburg!* Chapel Hill: University of North Carolina Press, 2002.

Rafuse, Ethan S. *A Single Grand Victory: The First Campaign and Battle of Manassas*. Wilmington, DE: SR Books, 2002.

Rhea, Gordon C. *The Battle of the Wilderness, May 5–6, 1864*. Baton Rouge: Louisiana State University Press, 1994.

————. *The Battles for Spotsylvania Court House and the Road to Yellow Tavern, May 7–12, 1864*. Baton Rouge: Louisiana State University Press, 1997.

————. *Cold Harbor: Grant and Lee, May 26–June 3, 1864*. Baton Rouge: Louisiana State University Press, 2002.

————. *To the North Anna River*. Baton Rouge: Louisiana State University Press, 2000.

Sears, Stephen W. *Chancellorsville*. Boston: Houghton Mifflin, 1996.

————. *Gettysburg*. Boston: Houghton Mifflin, 2003.

————. *Landscape Turned Red: The Battle of Antietam*. New Haven, CT: Ticknor & Fields, 1983.

————. *To the Gates of Richmond: The Peninsula Campaign*. Boston: Houghton Mifflin, 1992.

Shea, William L., and Earl J. Hess. *Pea Ridge: Civil War Campaign in the West*. Chapel Hill: University of North Carolina Press, 1992.

Shea, William L., and Terrence J. Winschel. *Vicksburg Is the Key: The Struggle for the Mississippi River*. Lincoln: University of Nebraska Press, 2003.

Sutherland, Daniel E. *Fredericksburg and Chancellorsville: The Dare Mark Campaign*. Lincoln: University of Nebraska Press, 1998.

Trudeau, Noah Andre. *Bloody Roads South: The Wilderness to Cold Harbor, May–June 1864*. Boston: Little, Brown, 1989.

————. *Out of the Storm: The End of the Civil War, April–June 1865*. Baton Rouge: Louisiana State University Press, 1995.

Woodworth, Steven E. *Beneath a Northern Sky: A Short History of the Gettysburg Campaign.* Wilmington, DE: SR Books, 2003.

Other Select Secondary Sources

Black, Robert C., III. *The Railroads of the Confederacy.* Chapel Hill: University of North Carolina Press, 1998. First published 1952.

Blair, William. *Cities of the Dead: Contesting the Memory of the Civil War in the South, 1865–1914.* Chapel Hill: University of North Carolina Press, 2004.

Blight, David W. *Race and Reunion: The Civil War in American Memory.* Cambridge, MA: Belknap Press of Harvard University Press, 2001.

Burkhardt, George S. *Confederate Rage, Yankee Wrath: No Quarter in the Civil War.* Carbondale: Southern Illinois University Press, 2007.

Campbell, Jacqueline Glass. *When Sherman Marched North from the Sea: Resistance on the Confederate Home Front.* Chapel Hill: University of North Carolina Press, 2003.

Carter, Dan T. *When the War Was Over: The Failure of Self-Reconstruction in the South, 1865–1867.* Baton Rouge: Louisiana State University Press, 1985.

Cimbala, Paul A., and Randall M. Miller, eds. *An Uncommon Time: The Civil War and the Northern Home Front.* New York: Fordham University Press, 2002.

Clark, John E., Jr. *Railroads in the Civil War: The Impact of Management on Victory and Defeat.* Baton Rouge: Louisiana State University Press, 2001.

Cunliffe, Marcus. *Soldiers and Civilians: The Martial Spirit in America, 1775–1865.* Boston: Little, Brown, 1968.

Flannery, Michael A. *Civil War Pharmacy: A History of Drugs, Drug Supply and Provision, and Therapeutics for the Union and Confederacy.* New York: Pharmaceutical Products Press, 2004.

Gallman, J. Matthew. *Mastering Wartime: A Social History of Philadelphia during the Civil War.* Cambridge: Cambridge University Press, 1990.

Gillette, William. *Jersey Blue: Civil War Politics in New Jersey, 1854–1865.* New Brunswick, NJ: Rutgers University Press, 1995.

Goff, Richard D. *Confederate Supply.* Durham, NC: Duke University Press, 1969.

Gray, Michael P. *The Business of Captivity: Elmira and Its Civil War Prison.* Kent, OH: Kent State University Press, 2001.

Grimsley, Mark. *The Hard Hand of War: Union Military Policy toward Southern Civilians, 1861–1865.* Cambridge: Cambridge University Press, 1995.

Hattaway, Herman. *Shades of Blue and Gray: An Introductory Military History of the Civil War.* Columbia: University of Missouri Press, 1997.

Haughton, Andrew. *Training, Tactics and Leadership in the Confederate Army of Tennessee: Seeds of Failure.* London: Frank Cass, 2000.

Inscoe, John C., and Gordon B. McKinney. *The Heart of Confederate Appalachia: Western North Carolina in the Civil War.* Chapel Hill: University of North Carolina Press, 2000.

Johnson, Russell L. *Warriors into Workers: The Civil War and the Formation of Urban-Industrial Society in a Northern City.* New York: Fordham University Press, 2003.

Jordan, Ervin L., Jr. *Black Confederates and Afro-Yankees in Civil War Virginia.* Charlottesville: University of Virginia Press, 1995.

Karamanski, Theodore J. *Rally 'Round the Flag: Chicago and the Civil War.* Chicago: Nelson-Hall, 1993.

Kusmer, Kenneth L. *Down and Out, on the Road: The Homeless in American History.* New York: Oxford University Press, 2002.

Lowry, Thomas P. *The Story the Soldiers Wouldn't Tell: Sex in the Civil War.* Mechanicsburg, PA: Stackpole Books, 1994.

McPherson, James M. *Battle Cry of Freedom: The Civil War Era.* New York: Oxford University Press, 1988.

Miller, William J. *Civil War City: Harrisburg, Pennsylvania, 1861–1865, the Training of an Army.* Shippensburg, PA: White Mane, 1990.

Mitchell, Robert E. "The Organizational Performance of Michigan's Adjutant General and the Federal Provost Marshal General in Recruiting Michigan's Boys in Blue." *Michigan Historical Review* 28 (Fall 2002): 115–62.

Murdock, Eugene C. *One Million Men: The Civil War Draft in the North.* Madison: State Historical Society of Wisconsin, 1971.

Neff, John R. *Honoring the Civil War Dead: Commemoration and the Problem of Reconciliation.* Lawrence: University Press of Kansas, 2005.

Newton, Steven H. *Joseph E. Johnston and the Defense of Richmond.* Lawrence: University Press of Kansas, 1998.

Niven, John. *Connecticut for the Union: The Role of the State in the Civil War.* New Haven, CT: Yale University Press, 1965.

O'Connor, Thomas H. *Civil War Boston: Home Front and Battlefield.* Boston: Northeastern University Press, 1997.

Perry, James M. *Touched with Fire: Five Presidents and the Civil War Battles That Made Them.* New York: Public Affairs, 2003.

Pickenpaugh, Roger. *Rescue by Rail: Troop Transfer and the Civil War in the West, 1863.* Lincoln: University of Nebraska Press, 1998.

Robinson, Armstead L. *Bitter Fruits of Bondage: The Demise of Slavery and the Collapse of the Confederacy, 1861–1865.* Charlottesville: University of Virginia Press, 2005.

Ross, Michael A. *Justice of Shattered Dreams: Samuel Freeman Miller and the Supreme Court during the Civil War Era.* Baton Rouge: Louisiana State University Press, 2003.

Schroeder-Lein, Glenna R. *Confederate Hospitals on the Move: Samuel H. Stout and the Army of Tennessee.* Columbia: University of South Carolina Press, 1994.

Shannon, Fred Albert. *The Organization and Administration of the Union Army, 1861–1865.* 2 vols. Gloucester, MA: Peter Smith, 1965.

Silber, Nina. *The Romance of Reunion: Northerners and the South, 1865–1900.* Chapel Hill: University of North Carolina Press, 1993.

Smith, John David, ed. *Black Soldiers in Blue: African American Troops in the Civil War Era.* Chapel Hill: University of North Carolina Press, 2002.

Spann, Edward K. *Gotham at War: New York City, 1860–1865.* Wilmington, DE: Scholarly Resources, 2002.

Urwin, Gregory J. W., ed. *Black Flag over Dixie: Racial Atrocities and Reprisals in the Civil War.* Carbondale: Southern Illinois University Press, 2004.

Weigley, Russell F. *A Great Civil War: A Military and Political History, 1861–1865.* Bloomington: Indiana University Press, 2000.

Williams, David. *A People's History of the Civil War: Struggles for the Meaning of Freedom.* New York: New Press, 2005.

Williams, George Washington. *A History of the Negro Troops in the War of the Rebellion, 1861–1865.* New York: Negro Universities Press, 1969. First published 1888 by Harpers & Brothers.

INDEX

ABOUT THE AUTHOR

PAUL A. CIMBALA is Professor of History at Fordham University and author of a number of books including *Under the Guardianship of the Nation: The Freedmen's Bureau and the Reconstruction of Georgia, 1865–1870, An Uncommon Time: The Civil War and the Northern Home Front* (with Randall M. Miller), and *Historians and Race: Autobiography and the Writing of History* (with Robert F. Himmelberg).